MW01487166

To Monica and my Parents

"ALL I WANT TO KNOW IS WHERE I'M GOING TO DIE SO I'LL NEVER GO THERE."

Buffett and Munger – A Study in Simplicity and Uncommon, Common Sense

By Peter Bevelin

Copyright © 2016 by Post Scriptum AB. All rights reserved.
Second Printing 2017
Third Printing 2022
Fourth Printing 2024

For permission to use copyrighted material,
grateful acknowledgment is made to the copyright holders on next pages,
which are hereby made part of this copyright page.
Every reasonable attempt and effort has been made to identify and contact the
owners of any copyrighted materials appearing in this book. The author and
publisher extend their apologies for any unintentional errors or omissions and
encourage any copyright owners inadvertently missed to contact them. Any
errors, oversight or omissions will be corrected in subsequent editions.

PCA Publications L.L.C. Published under license from Post Scriptum AB.

Disclaimer of Warranties and Exclusions of Damages: The author and publisher
make no representations or warranties with respect to the accuracy or
completeness of the contents of this book and specifically disclaim any implied
warranties of merchantability or fitness for a particular purpose. The advice
and strategies contained herein may not be suitable for your situation. You
should consult with a professional advisor before making any financial or life
style decisions. Neither the publisher nor the author shall be liable for any loss
of profit or any other commercial damages, including but not limited to special,
incidental, consequential, or other damages.

Some of the names, characters, places and incidents in this book are products of
the author's imagination or are used fictitiously. Any resemblance to actual
events, locales, or persons, living or dead, is entirely coincidental.

Printed in the United States of America by Walsworth Publishing Company.

ISBN 978-1-68184-048-2

– PERMISSIONS AND ACKNOWLEDGMENTS –

Excerpt from The Great Minds of Investing, by William Green, applicable text written by Dr. Gisela Baur. Text Copyright © 2015 by ACATIS Investment GmbH; all rights reserved.

Excerpt from "Track record is everything." From Across the Board, October 1991. Copyright © 1991 by Across the Board.Reprinted by permission by permission of The Conference Board Review; all rights reserved.

Excerpt(s) from THE SNOWBALL: WARREN BUFFETT AND THE BUSINESS OF LIFE by Alice Schroeder, copyright © 2008, 2009 by Alice Schroeder. Used by permission of Bantam Books, an imprint of Random House, a division of Penguin Random House LLC. All rights reserved. Any third party use of this material, outside of this publication, is prohibited. Interested parties must apply directly to Penguin Random House for permission

Excerpt from Discover Your True North, by Bill George. Copyright © 2015 by Bill George. Reprinted by permission of Bill George; all rights reserved.

Excerpt from Notes from the Meeting Dr. George Athanassakos and Ivey MBA and HBA students had with Mr. Warren Buffett, Omaha March 31, 2008, March 30, 2012, January 31, 2014, February 27, 2015. Copyright © The Ben Graham Center for Value Investing, Ivey Business School, Western University, www.bengrahaminvesting.ca Reprinted by permission of The Ben Graham Center for Value Investing; all rights reserved. These notes may in some cases not accurately reflect Mr. Buffett's direct quotes but may instead be paraphrases of Mr. Buffett's words.

Excerpt from The Snowball: Warren Buffett and the Business of Life, by Alice Schroder. Copyright © 2008 by Alice Schroeder. Reprinted by permission of Bloomsbury Publishing Plc.

Peter Boodell, Boodell & Company Capital Management.

Warren E. Buffett incl. excerpt from Warren Buffett's Letters to Berkshire Hathaway shareholders, by Warren Buffett. Copyright © 1977 – 2014 by Warren E. Buffett. Reprinted by permission of Warren E. Buffett; all rights reserved.

Excerpt from Transcript of Warren Buffett's 'Ask Warren' appearance on CNBC's Squawk Box, March 1, 2010 and March 4, 2013, buffettwatch.cnbc.com; Unofficial transcript of Warren Buffett, Charlie Munger and Bill Gates appearing live with Becky Quick on CNBC's Squawk Box, Monday, May 5, 2014, buffettwatch.cnbc.com; Warren Buffett's 'Ask Warren' appearance on CNBC's Squawk Box, March 2, 2015,cnbc.com and Charles Munger interview by CNBC, May 4, 2012, cnbc.com. Copyright © 2010, 2012, 2013, 2015 by NBC Universal Archives. Used by permission of NBC News Archives LLC; all rights reserved.

Excerpt from Conversations from the Warren Buffett Symposium, Cardozo Law Review (1997), vol. 19. Edited by Lawrence A. Cunningham and reissued by Cunningham in 2016. Used with permission of Warren E. Buffett, Charles T. Munger and Lawrence A. Cunningham. All rights reserved.

Fortune

Steven N. Friedman, Santangel's Review

Sham Gadd, Gad Partners Fund, LP

Guru Focus.com

Handelsblatt Global Edition

Brief quotes from pp. 33, 39, 45, 47-48, 52-53 [277 words] from WORKING TOGETHER by MICHAEL D. EISNER with AARON COHEN. Copyright © 2010 by Michael D. Eisner. Reprinted by permission of HarperCollins Publishers.

Brief quotes from pp. 19, 20, 83 from THE MIDAS TOUCH by JOHN TRAIN. Copyright © 1987 by John Train. Reprinted by permission of HarperCollins Publishers.

Excerpt from "Managing the Crisis You Tried to Prevent" by Norman R. Augustine, Harvard Business Review, November 1995 Issue, Copyright © 1995 by the Harvard Business School Publishing Corporation; all rights reserved.

Excerpt from "In the Money: Alumni financiers take stock of the market and careers spent trying to beat it" by Margie Kelley, Harvard Law Bulletin, Summer 2001, Copyright © 2001 by the Harvard Law Bulletin; all rights reserved.

Excerpt from *Damn Right: Behind the Scenes with Berkshire Hathaway Billionaire Charlie Munger* by Janet Lowe. Copyright © 2000 by Janet Lowe. Reprinted by permission of John Wiley and Sons. All rights reserved.

Excerpt from "Notes from Warren Buffett meeting with University of Maryland MBA Students" by David Kass, November 15, 2013, www.blogs.rhsmith.umd.edu/davidkass

Excerpt from Of Permanent Value: The Story of Warren Buffett, by Andrew Kilpatrick. Copyright © 2004 by Andrew Kilpatrick. Reprinted by permission of Andrew Kilpatrick.

Kiplinger Magazine

Dang Lee, DNL Capital Management

Martin Lee

Levo League

The Motley Fool

Charles T. Munger

Excerpt from *Outstanding Investor Digest (OID)* are reprinted by permission from Outstanding Investor Digest, Inc. Copyright © 1986 – 2010; All rights reserved. Telephone: (212) 925 3885. Website: www.oid.com

The Omaha World-Herald

Shane Parrish, Farnam Street

Excerpt from Poor Charlie's Almanack: The Wit and Wisdom of Charles T. Munger, by Peter D. Kaufman, Copyright © 2005, 2006 by PCA Publication, L.L.C. Reprinted by permission of PCA Publication, L.L.C. All rights reserved.

Excerpt from Warren Buffett's Unconventional Advice to MBAs, by Ethan Baron. Copyright © 2014 by poetsandquants.com. Reprinted by permission of poetsandquants.com; all rights reserved.

Excerpt from "Warren Buffett on What's Next in the Payment Industry", Interview by Business Wire CEO Cathy Baron Tamraz, October 17, 2009. Copyright © 2009 by PYMNTS.com. Reprinted by permission of PYMNTS.com

Excerpt from Buffett: The Making of an American Capitalist, by Roger Lowenstein. Copyright © 1995 by Random House. Reprinted by permission of Penguin Random House. All rights reserved.

Ronald Redfield, Redfield, Blonsky, Starinsky, LLC

Richard M. Rockwood

Excerpt from "Getting There: A Book of Mentors", by Gillian Zoe Segal, Copyright © 2015 by Gillian Zoe Segal. Reprinted by permission of Gillian Zoe Segal; all rights reserved.

Stanford Lawyer magazine

Stanford University Rock Center for Corporate Governance Rockcenter

Whitney Tilson

George Traganidas

Excerpt from "When I Buy a Company, I'm a Journalist", taped interview with Arizona State University Professor Jeff Cunningham, Walter Cronkite School of Journalism, March 5, 2015. Copyright © 2015 by Walter Cronkite School of Journalism and Mass Communication. Reprinted by permission by permission of The Walter Cronkite School of Journalism and Mass Communication. All rights reserved.

Jason Zweig

– INTRODUCTION –

"Outside science, it is amazing how little impact there can be from a powerful idea...Everyone's experience is that you teach only what a reader almost knows, and that seldom."

- Charles T. Munger

On and off during the last five years I have been writing on a memo for myself (I have found this to be an excellent way to learn and pass the time) in the form of a discussion/dialogue between four characters. It's a story about the fictitious Seeker and his visit to the "Library of Wisdom" where he meets another fictitious character—the Librarian—along with Warren Buffett and Charles Munger.

It was a lot of fun and I learned a lot writing this memo. I believe in what the late author Terry Pratchett said, "While a book has got to be worthwhile from the point of view of the reader it's got to be worthwhile from the point of view of the writer as well." And the material in this book mirrors the prescription of Charles Munger's comment after writing his The Psychology of Human Misjudgment talk, "After all, I assembled the material in this Talk to help me succeed in practical thinking and not to gain advantage in making public any would-be-clever notions."

What has been reinforced in writing this memo is the efficiency, simplicity, clarity and common sense or judgment that are the hallmarks of Buffett and Munger. Both have a remarkable ability to eliminate folly, simplify things and boil down issues to their essence and get right to the point—and focus on simple and timeless truths. They are the Einsteins of business and wisdom. I love it! So if there is one goal of this book, it is simplicity and to better understand how they think.

Many thanks to Warren Buffett and Charles Munger for their lessons and their kind permission to quote extensively from their speeches, interviews, and annual meetings and for their compliments of my memorandum—the foundation for this book. The reader should be aware that some of the quotes in this book may not accurately reflect Mr. Buffett's and Mr. Munger's exact but may instead be paraphrases of their words that capture the essence of what was said. The intention has been to be faithful to their wording and intent. Any misconceptions or errors are mine alone.

As with my other books I have been fortunate to work with Peter Kaufman in turning my memo into this book—I am deeply grateful to him. As I have said before and is reinforced at every meeting with Peter— he is one of the smartest businessmen and nicest human beings I know. I am delighted and fortunate to have him as a friend. Many thanks also to Marcus Kaufman, Carl Foote and Mike Borgsdorf. Huge thanks also to Henry Emerson who permitted me to quote extensively from *Outstanding Investor Digest.*

Finally, I wish to thank my beloved and amazing wife, Monica, who drew the silhouettes on the cover page. Monica, you are the best—as Winnie the Pooh may have said, "If you live to be a hundred, I want to live to be a hundred minus one day so I never have to live without you."

Peter Bevelin
February 2016

p.s. I couldn't resist throwing in this quote—a fitting character trait of Warren Buffett and Charles Munger:

"Every man of genius is a stranger and a pilgrim on the earth, unlike other men, seeing everything as it were at a different angle."

— Havelock Ellis

– CONTENTS –

*"If thou wouldst live long, live well; for Folly and Wickedness
shorten Life."*

-Benjamin Franklin

–PART ONE–

ON FATAL MISTAKES, PREVENTION AND SIMPLICITY

"Search men's governing principles, and consider the wise, what they shun and what they cleave to."

— *Marcus Aurelius*[1]

The man is lying on his sofa and feeling miserable.

"I thought everything was great. But in less than 48 hours my life as I knew it would be over. And I never saw it coming."

"Why did I make so many lousy decisions? Marriage, job, investments, education, business, friends—all is a wreck. I thought I was smart but I am broke and broken. Mentally. Physically."

"How did it end up like this? If I only could turn back the clock. Would it have made a difference? Or would I still make the same mistakes? Was there a way I could have had a better life?"

The man soon dozed off and started dreaming.........

He was standing on the stairs on the entrance to a large ancient building. He looked up and noticed the inscription "The Library of Wisdom."

A lady came towards him and introduced herself as the Librarian, "What are you seeking?"

SEEKER   "That is the question."

LIBRARIAN "Yes, it is. You sure know a question when you see it."

SEEKER   "How can I get in?"

LIBRARIAN "Are you to get in at all? That's the key question. So tell me what you want."

SEEKER   "I want a lot of things but I will settle for wisdom."

LIBRARIAN "So far so good."

SEEKER   "I have done so many stupid things in my life. I want to learn how I can make better decisions so I can help my children so they don't do the same dumb things I've done. Can you help me?"

LIBRARIAN "Good answer—if we can make better decisions we avoid a lot of misery. Some people who come here are just interested in a shortcut

1

formula for how they can become rich and successful. We can't help with that. We can only give some guidance for how to improve your chance of becoming wiser."

"Please enter."

The Seeker entered the door and came into a hall with a couple of doors.

On one of the doors hang a sign marked *General Wisdom from Buffett and Munger.*

The Seeker opened the door and looked around and saw two individuals sitting in a sofa. "Hey, I recognize these people. It is the successful and wise duo of Warren Buffett and Charles Munger. On a scale of 1 to 10, these guys rates at least 15. They're so bright, I gotta wear shades."

SEEKER   "Can any of you tell me the secret to becoming a wise person?"

LIBRARIAN "First tell them what you want."

SEEKER   "To paraphrase Groucho Marx, 'Gentlemen, I may talk like an idiot, and look like an idiot. But don't let that fool you. I'm really an idiot.'"[2]

"I have done a lot of stupid things in my life and I probably need to have my head examined but now I want to wise up."

"Can you help a nutty and failed person?"

Mistakes are a fact of life

BUFFETT   "I don't believe in beating yourself over it, you're going to make mistakes."[3]

MUNGER   "Of course, there's going to be some failure in making the correct decisions…I think it's important to review your past stupidities so you are less likely to repeat them, but I'm not gnashing my teeth over it or suffering or enduring it. I regard it as perfectly normal to fail and make bad decisions."[4]

BUFFETT   "You don't want to expect perfection in yourself. You want to strive to do your best. It's too demanding to expect perfection in yourself."[5]

SEEKER   "But I want to be like you guys—I don't want to make any mistakes."

BUFFETT   "Everyone makes mistakes[6]…There is no question that you are going to make mistakes in life. I've made a lot, and I'm going to make more[7]… that's the nature of making a lot of decisions[8]…To try to live your life totally free of mistakes is a life of inaction."[9]

MUNGER   "Stupidity is inevitable. It happens to everyone[10]…I for certain have made a lot of dumb decisions in my life but not as many as most people."[11]

BUFFETT   "Wrong decisions are part of life. Being able to make them work out anyway is one of the abilities of those who are successful."[12]

SEEKER "So what are you saying—what can you help me with?"

LIBRARIAN "To make fewer dumb mistakes than other people. And how to fix them faster if you make them."

MUNGER "It's amazing the number of mistakes you can make in a long life with things still working out."[13]

SEEKER "Good, at least it gives me some comfort."

Don't bother about mistakes that don't actually matter

MUNGER "We have lots of stupidity left in us at Berkshire. But you can live with quite a bit if you avoid the most extreme follies of man[14]...We have avoided a subset of stupidities—the important ones."[15]

BUFFETT "You've got to make sure that the mistakes don't kill you and you hope the big ones work out."[16]

LIBRARIAN "Mistakes don't matter if they are harmless. Or to quote *Dr. House* from the television medical drama, 'Mistakes are as serious as the results they cause!'"[17]

BUFFETT "You only have to be right on a very, very few things in your lifetime as long as you never make any big mistakes[18]...You just have to make sure your blunders are never fatal, and you don't want to make them on the really big decisions."[19]

"I don't want to make any mistakes that jeopardize, in a significant way, anything that's important."[20]

SEEKER "Like what?"

LIBRARIAN "Some decisions are important and some are not. Many of your decisions have only small consequences or costs. But some—and some you can do something about—have far-reaching implications for your life."

"This is where you have to give yourself time and think before you act—on the really big decisions—where mistakes are costly."

SEEKER "Such as?"

LIBRARIAN "Big life issues like choosing the right spouse, education, career, friends, place to live, investment or taking care of your health. A wrong choice in these matters may haunt you a long, long time or may even 'kill' you."

BUFFETT "If you are lucky on health and...on your spouse, you are a long way home."[21]

SEEKER "Ok, tell me now how I can be wiser."

"But don't make it too complicated. I am not that smart."

BUFFETT "The sign above the players' entrance to the field at Notre Dame reads 'Play Like a Champion Today.' I sometimes joke that the sign at Nebraska reads 'Remember Your Helmet.' Charlie and I are 'Remember Your Helmet' kind of guys.' We like to keep it simple."[22]

3

MUNGER "We have a passion for keeping things simple."[23]

SEEKER "Great. So where should we start?"

Avoiding problems is better than being forced to solve them

MUNGER "Wisdom is prevention but very few people do much about it."[24]

SEEKER "Count me in as one of those."

LIBRARIAN "I once read that Einstein said, 'A clever person solves a problem. A wise person avoids it.' I don't know if Einstein really said this but it is a good advice. And how can you avoid problems if you don't first try to prevent them from happening by preparing yourself?"

BUFFETT "It wasn't raining when Noah built the ark...and he didn't even look that smart for 39 days. But there are some things you have to think ahead on, and prevention...is enormously important."[25]

MUNGER "I particularly recommend attention to the idea that an ounce of prevention is worth a pound of cure—except it really isn't often a mere pound. An ounce of prevention is often worth a ton of cure."[26]

"Many things are easier to prevent than fix...You get in a dumb enough situation, like trying to cross a train track when there's a train coming, and you end up with a problem that's extremely hard to fix."[27]

LIBRARIAN "As Montaigne said, 'How much easier it is not to get into it than to get out of it!'"[28]

SEEKER "You tell me! There are so many times I have felt like the mouse in the old saying—'I don't want the cheese. I just want to get out of the trap.'"

MUNGER "Most people approaching problems get fatuous ideas that they can fix them easily. And, of course, it can't be fixed easily....And that's why a lot of the correct thinking should be preventive...There are all kinds of things that are unfixable once they've occurred."[29]

"What is working poorly is usually either uncorrectable or 10 times harder to correct than you may think."[30]

BUFFETT "Sometimes no amount of cure will overcome the mistakes of the past."[31]

"I think it's way better if the solutions arrive early rather than late. I mean Benjamin Franklin said a lot of wise things but when he said, 'An ounce of prevention is worth a pound of cure', I mean that is the guiding light at Berkshire."[32]

SEEKER "So if wisdom lies in prevention—what should I do?"

LIBRARIAN "Prepare yourself."

MUNGER "If wisdom is what you want, you are going to get it sitting on your ass."

"If you had an observer with a time clock watching Warren, he would find that Warren spent most of his time sitting on his ass and reading...If you really want to be the outlier in terms of achievement, just sit down on your ass and read—and do it all the time."[33]

SEEKER   "So reading prepared you to make better decisions?"

LIBRARIAN "Yes—but not only by reading—but also by spending time thinking."

MUNGER   "Neither Warren nor I is smart enough to make...decisions with no time to think...We make actual decisions very rapidly, but that's because we've spent so much time preparing ourselves by quietly sitting and reading and thinking."[34]

BUFFETT   "A good part of our success is that we spend a lot of time thinking[35]... We think the best way to minimize risk is to think[36]...the best way to think about investments is to be in a room with no one else and just think."[37]

SEEKER   "But thinking is so hard to do. To paraphrase Ebenezer Blackadder, 'Sometimes I feel like my head is emptier than a hermit's address book.'"[38]

LIBRARIAN "There are actually studies done on how much people hate to think—many people would rather do something stupid than be left alone thinking."

BUFFETT   "Unfortunately, Bertrand Russell's observation about life in general applies with unusual force in the financial world: "Most men would rather die than think. Many do."[39]

SEEKER   "I usually act before I think but of course I know the result of that strategy. Thank god I met you guys."

"Ok, to be wiser I need to read and think."

MUNGER   "I don't know anyone who's wise who doesn't read a lot. But that's not enough: You have to have a temperament to grab ideas and do sensible things. Most people don't grab the right ideas or don't know what to do with them."[40]

"And if you get into the mental habit of relating what you're reading to the basic...underlying ideas being demonstrated, you gradually accumulate some wisdom."[41]

SEEKER   "But how do you get time to read? I always believed you guys were pretty busy all the time with meetings and all."

BUFFETT   "At Berkshire, we don't have any meetings or committees, and I can think of no better way to become more intelligent than sit down and read. In fact, that's what Charlie and I mostly do."[42]

"I hate meetings, frankly. I have created something that I enjoy: I happen to enjoy reading a lot, and I happen to enjoy thinking about things."[43]

MUNGER   "We both hate to have too many forward commitments in our schedules. We both insist on a lot of time being available almost every day to just sit and think…We read and think…We do that because we like that kind of a life. But we've turned that quirk into a positive outcome for ourselves."[44]

SEEKER   "I can't do that—I need to do something most of the time."

LIBRARIAN "There is a saying, 'Anyone who is too busy, never has time to think."

BUFFETT   "Pascal's observation seems apt: 'It has struck me that all men's misfortunes spring from the single cause that they are unable to stay quietly in one room.'"[45]

SEEKER   "I better spend some time on learning and thinking then."

MUNGER   "We schedule time to think. Most people schedule themselves like a dentist, and their happiest day is when they can manage to squeeze in one additional ten minute appointment."[46]

"I think you have to have time to think. And it's so easy to get so busy that you no longer have time to think—and you pay a huge price for that."[47]

LIBRARIAN "And when you think, think!"

MUNGER   "This modern generation, which has gotten so good at doing two or three things at once—multi-tasking, aided by electronic devices—I'll confidently predict will end up worse than people more like Warren Buffett with more solitary reading time and less trying to do three things at once."[48]

BUFFETT   "It personally gives me an edge when other people are not paying attention to reading and thinking, and are instead on their phones. It means that I gain knowledge from reading a few 10-K's while others are tweeting what they had for breakfast."[49]

LIBRARIAN "Attention is a limited resource. Rapidly switching our attention between tasks is also inefficient because it takes a lot of cognitive energy since our brain can only focus at one thing at a time. If you knew how much energy it takes—you would never multi-task; even if you eat a lot of sugar. Focus your attention on one thing—it's less effort."

MUNGER   "I think people that multi-task pay a huge price…I think when you multi-task so much, you don't have time to think about anything deeply. You're giving the world an advantage you shouldn't do. Practically everybody is drifting into that mistake."

"Concentrating hard on something that is important is…I can't succeed at all without doing it. I did not succeed in life by intelligence. I succeeded because I have a long attention span[50]…the idea of multitasking my way to glory has never occurred to me[51]…and when you multitask like crazy, none of the tasks will be done well."[52]

6

Seeker   "So, prepare me…how do you do it? What do you read and try to learn?"

If we understand what works and not, we know what to do

Munger   "We try to understand what works, what doesn't, and why."[53]

Librarian   "How else will you know what you should do or not do if you don't first learn and understand what works and not?"

Seeker   "I get it—if I had known what works and not—before I made some important decisions—I would have avoided what doesn't work and done what works."

Buffett   "We saw what worked and didn't work. And it made us appreciate a lot what did work and shy away from things that didn't…So we learned that it made a great deal of sense to figure out what pond to jump into—and that what pond you jumped into was actually probably more important than how well you could swim."[54]

Librarian   "And if something works then keep doing it."

Seeker   "Any way that works is OK?"

Munger   "Deng Xiaoping…said, 'I don't care whether the cat is black or white as long as it catches mice.'"[55]

Seeker   "Sounds simple."

Munger   "It is just that simple. We've had enough good sense when something was working well, keep doing it. The fundamental algorithm of life: repeat what works."[56]

"If the system you are using comes to an asinine answer that finally won't work, you throw out the system and find one that makes more sense[57]……You don't keep repeating what isn't working."[58]

Seeker   "Still, to learn all this…to do the right things and avoid all the big mistakes…I mean, you are brilliant and I am only an ordinary mortal with a low IQ. In fact, even my waistline exceeds my IQ."

It is better to try to be consistently not stupid than to be very intelligent

Munger   "You don't have to be brilliant, only a little bit wiser than the other guys, on average, for a long, long time."[59]

Buffett   "To some extent, the record of Berkshire—to the extent it's been good—has not occurred because we've done brilliant things, but because we've probably done fewer dumb things than most."[60]

Seeker   "Smart then?"

Buffett   "We didn't do all the smartest things. We didn't do anything really dumb."[61]

MUNGER "Lots of people are very smart in terms of passing tests and making rapid calculations. And yet they just make one asinine decision after another in life because in their quick-computing minds are these terrible streaks of nuttiness."[62]

BUFFETT "I do find it amazing how many people with high IQs get off the track. It's astounding to me how people who are really very smart manage to engage in so many self-destructive actions, and I'm not just thinking in terms of business."[63]

LIBRARIAN "Let me tell you a story about the great mathematical genius Évariste Galois that illustrates the difference between intelligence and wisdom:"

"'In a clash with political opponents, where also a girl was involved, in his own words 'an infamous prostitute' he accepted a duel with pistols. He was not a good shotsman and knew for certain that he would be killed in the duel. Therefore, he spent the night before the duel in writing down at a desperate speed his mathematical testament…The next day he was shot, and died the following day at the age of 21.'"[64]

MUNGER "The one thing that has surprised me all my life is how many people with high IQs do massively stupid things…It happens everywhere, but it is surprising how extreme the stupidity is and how talented the people are who do them….and it makes the world a very dangerous place because the man whom you trust because he's your physician, your doctor, your investment manager, what have you, can go plumb crazy."[65]

SEEKER "I always believed high IQ people were brilliant and smart and always made the right decisions."

LIBRARIAN "Someone once said, 'What most distinguishes the foolish and the intelligent is the foolish consistently commits the same stupidities, while the intelligent always find new ones.'"

BUFFETT "It's more interesting to see why smart people don't succeed, and to avoid [those errors of theirs]."[66]

MUNGER "We recognized early on that very smart people do very dumb things, and we wanted to know why and who, so we could avoid them."[67]

SEEKER "Why were they?"

BUFFETT "It's ego. It's greed. It's envy. It's fear. It's mindless imitation of other people. I mean, there are a variety of factors that cause that horsepower of the mind to get diminished dramatically before the output turns out."[68]

MUNGER "'Crowd folly,' the tendency of humans, under some circumstances, to resemble lemmings, explains much foolish thinking of brilliant men and much foolish behavior."[69]

LIBRARIAN "Or overconfidence—overestimating your abilities or know-it-all tendencies and underestimate what can go wrong. A disease especially common among experts and people who believe they are very smart."

MUNGER "Smart, hard-working people aren't exempted from professional disasters resulting from overconfidence. Often they just go aground in the more difficult voyages on which they choose to embark based on self-appraisals in which they conclude that they have superior talents and methods."[70]

LIBRARIAN "But sometimes overconfidence can have some good effects."

MUNGER "While an excess of self-regard is often counterproductive in its effects on cognition, it can cause some weird successes from overconfidence that happens to cause success. This factor accounts for the adage: 'Never underestimate the man who overestimates himself.'"[71]

BUFFETT "I would say if Charlie and I have any advantage it's not because we're so smart, it is because we're rational and we very seldom let extraneous factors interfere with our thoughts. We don't let other people's opinion interfere with it...we try to get fearful when others are greedy. We try to get greedy when others are fearful. We try to avoid any kind of imitation of other people's behavior. And those are the factors that cause smart people to get bad results."[72]

MUNGER "A lot of people with high IQs are terrible investors because they've got terrible temperaments. And that is why we say that having a certain kind of temperament is more important than brains. You need to keep raw irrational emotion under control. You need patience and discipline and an ability to take losses and adversity without going crazy. You need an ability to not be driven crazy by extreme success."[73]

BUFFETT "We don't think we are smarter than others, we just won't do stuff we don't understand. And we won't be jealous when others do well. That is what it is all about."[74]

MUNGER "Berkshire won't do better than others because we're smarter but because our systems are better."[75]

"It is remarkable how much long-term advantage people like us have gotten by trying to be consistently not stupid, instead of trying to be very intelligent. There must be some wisdom in the folk saying, 'It's the strong swimmers who drown.'"[76]

SEEKER "Now, tell me about your approach to wisdom."

If we know what doesn't work we don't go there

MUNGER "Buddha said, 'I only teach one thing. I teach the cause of human sorrow—and how to avoid some of it.' Now that isn't exactly what he said—it isn't word for word. However, that's the gist of it."

"Well, that is very much my approach to wisdom. In other words, if you go around figuring out what doesn't work and then avoid it—and you also learn, when you get that sorrow that you can't avoid, how to handle it (which is what Buddha was trying to teach), well that's pretty good encapsulated wisdom."[77]

SEEKER "That life is tough and filled with sorrow?"

MUNGER "No. If you want to avoid sorrow, you've got to know the cause of sorrow."[78]

LIBRARIAN "If something isn't working isn't it better to first try to find out why it doesn't work before you try to fix it?"

MUNGER "To decide what will cure bad cognition, it will help to know what causes it[79]…In other words, knowledge is very helpful and there are certain ways of understanding life that improve outcomes."[80]

SEEKER "Please tell me how you started your quest for wisdom."

MUNGER "I have long been very interested in standard thinking errors[81]… It was obvious to me for some reason, at an early age, that a great many very brilliant and disciplined people made perfectly screwy decisions that were disastrous—and that it happened, frankly, wherever I looked."

"I found this extremely curious, and somehow early in life I got the idea that I would never be able to play chess blindfolded against six Grandmasters and win. God just did not give Charlie Munger any such skill. But I said, 'Oh my gosh, I cannot be as asinine as all these other people if I just kind of work at it steadily for a long time,' and that is what I did."[82]

SEEKER "So how did you do it?"

MUNGER "I was greatly helped in my quest by two turns of mind. First, I had long looked for insight by inversion in the intense manner counseled by the great algebraist, Jacobi: 'Invert, always invert.' I sought good judgment mostly by collecting instances of bad judgment, then pondering ways to avoid such outcomes."[83]

BUFFETT "Charlie…has always emphasized the study of mistakes rather than successes, both in business and other aspects of life. He does so in the spirit of the man who said: 'All I want to know is where I'm going to die so I'll never go there.'"[84]

SEEKER "As Woody Allen said, 'It's not that I'm afraid to die, I just don't want to be there when it happens.'"[85]

"Back to inversion."

BUFFETT "He likes to invert…I mean, that's his approach generally is casting out a whole bunch of things."[86]

LIBRARIAN "Mr. Munger's friend Li Lu said the same, 'When Charlie thinks about things, he starts by inverting. To understand how to be happy in life,

Charlie will study how to make life miserable; to examine how business become big and strong, Charlie first studies how businesses decline and die; most people care more about how to succeed in the stock market, Charlie is most concerned about why most have failed in the stock market.'"[87]

Seeker   "What was the second turn of mind?"

Munger   "Second, I became so avid a collector of instances of bad judgment that I paid no attention to boundaries between professional territories...I could already see that real-world problems didn't neatly lie within territorial boundaries. They jumped right across."

"And I was as dubious of any approach that, when two things were inextricably intertwined and interconnected, would try and think about one thing but not the other. I was afraid, if I tried any such restricted approach, that I would end up, in the immortal words of John L. Lewis, 'with no brain at all, just a neck that had haired over.'"[88]

Seeker   "I love it."

Munger   "If I could just avoid all the folly, maybe I could get an advantage without having to be really good at anything...And so this process I have gone through life identifying folly and trying to avoid it has worked wonderfully for me."[89]

Seeker   "Still do?"

Munger   "I am a collector of inanities and I catalogue the inanities on structures in my head and it's been a wonderful thing to do...When you're collecting inanities there's never a shortage."[90]

"One day at a time I find new errors and add to my list."[91]

Seeker   "You both do this?"

Buffett   "We have been a student of other's folly, and it has served us well."[92]

"We want to see what has caused businesses to go bad[93]...I've often felt there might be more to be gained by studying business failures than business successes. In my business, we try to study where people go astray, and why things don't work."[94]

Seeker   "But isn't it better to learn from success?"

Munger   "A lot of success in life and business comes from knowing what you want to avoid: early death, a bad marriage, etc."

"Just avoid things like racing trains to the crossing, doing cocaine, etc. Develop good mental habits. ..Avoid evil, particularly if they're attractive members of the opposite sex."[95]

Librarian   "To first think about what to eliminate or exclude — what doesn't work etc. is also the way the mind of great chess players works."

Buffett   "There was a great article in the *New Yorker* magazine...when the Fischer/Spassky chess matches were going on. And it got into this

11

speculation of whether or not humans would ever be able to take on computers in chess. Here were these computers doing hundreds of thousands of calculations a second. And the article asked, 'When all you're really looking at is the results from various moves in the future, how can a human mind deal with a computer that's thinking at speeds that are so unbelievable?'"[96]

LIBRARIAN "In just the first four moves there are 318 billion ways you could play a chess game."

SEEKER "Yes, how could a mortal do that?"

BUFFETT "Well, it turns out a mind like...that of Fischer or a Spassky essentially was eliminating about 99.99% of the possibilities without even thinking about 'em. So it wasn't that they could outthink the computer in terms of speed, but they had this ability of what you might call 'grouping' or 'exclusion', where essentially they just got right down to the few possibilities out of these zillions of possibilities that really had any chance of success."[97]

SEEKER "Give me an example."

BUFFETT "If my job was to pick a group of 10 stocks in the Dow Jones average that would outperform the average itself, I would probably not start by trying to pick the 10 best. Instead, I would try to pick the 10 or 15 worst performers and take them out of the sample, and work with the residual. It's an inversion process...Start out with failure, and then engineer its removal."[98]

Thinking backwards is a great tool for solving problems

MUNGER "If you turn problems around into reverse, you often think better."[99]

LIBRARIAN "Let me illustrate this. Assume that a bacterium doubles every 24 hours and that it has infested a pond after 60 days. Can you now tell me on what day the pond was half-full of the bacteria?"

SEEKER "So now I need to be a calculus whiz—sorry, but I don't have a calculator handy."

LIBRARIAN "No advanced math is necessary—just do it backwards. Start at day 60 and remember it doubles every day."

SEEKER "I see what you mean—it is half-full the day before or day 59."
"More please."

MUNGER "Think in reverse like Jacobi. What must we avoid because we don't want it?"[100]

LIBRARIAN "For example, instead of asking how you can achieve a goal, ask the opposite question: What don't I want to achieve? What causes the non-goal? How can I avoid that? What do I now want to achieve? How can I do that?"

SEEKER   "Such as?"

MUNGER   "For instance, if you want to help India, the question you should consider asking is not: 'How can I help India?' Instead, you should ask: 'How can I hurt India?' You find what will do the worst damage, and then try to avoid it."[101]

"So think it through backward as well as forward. It's a trick that works in algebra and a trick that works in life."[102]

SEEKER   "Good tool this Jacobi observation."

MUNGER   "The mental process that really has worked for me my whole life, and I use it all the time, is turning everything into reverse. I figure out what I don't like instead of figuring out what I like in order to get what I like. I sometimes think straight forward too, of course. But thinking of what I didn't like and how I can avoid it has just worked wonders for me."[103]

SEEKER   "So even a fool like me can learn from studying folly?"

MUNGER   "If you…can just tune out the really easy-to-tune-out folly, you'll be surprised how well you do in life."[104]

SEEKER   "Come on, it must be more complicated than that."

MUNGER   "I think part of the popularity of Berkshire Hathaway is that we look like people who have found a trick. It's not brilliance. It's just avoiding stupidity."[105]

SEEKER   "Isn't that really the same thing?"

MUNGER   "You say it is the same thing just stated differently — well, maybe it is the same thing just stated differently. But you understand it better if you go at it the way we do, which is to identify the main stupidities that do bright people in and then organize your patterns for thinking and developments, so you don't stumble into those stupidities."[106]

SEEKER   "I always thought there was some secret formula behind your success?"

Keep it simple and make it easy for yourself

BUFFETT   "There's no magic to it[107]…We haven't succeeded because we have some great, complicated systems or magic formulas we apply or anything of the sort. What we have is just simplicity itself."[108]

MUNGER   "Our ideas are so simple that people keep asking us for mysteries when all we have are the most elementary ideas."[109]

BUFFETT   "I think a lot of people make things more complicated than they need to."[110]

LIBRARIAN "Yes, and especially among people who believe they are very intelligent and have a tendency to overcomplicate things so they can show how talented and smart they are. But in their chase towards elegant concepts they often get distracted from the simple truths. As François de La Rochefoucauld said, 'The desire to appear clever often prevents one from being so.'"[111]

BUFFETT "If you want to achieve a great time for swimming the 100 meters, it's a lot smarter to swim with the tide than it is to work on your stroke."[112]

SEEKER "But what you do seems pretty tough to do."

MUNGER "Part of the reason that we have a decent record is that we pick things that are easy. Other people believe they're so smart they can take on things that are really difficult. That proves to be more dangerous...We have ducked a lot of problems other people have willingly taken on."[113]

"We just look for no-brainer decisions."[114]

BUFFETT "Easy does it...Charlie and I have not learned how to solve difficult business problems. What we have learned is to avoid them... To the extent we have been successful, it is because we concentrated on identifying one-foot hurdles that we could step over rather than because we acquired any ability to clear seven-footers."

"In both business and investments it is usually far more profitable to simply stick with the easy and obvious than it is to resolve the difficult."[115]

MUNGER "One of the greatest ways to avoid trouble is to keep it simple."[116]

"We don't like complexity and we distrust others systems and think it many times leads to false confidence. The harder you work, the more confidence you get. But you may be working hard on something that is false. We're so afraid of that process so we don't do it."[117]

BUFFETT "Charlie and I don't like difficult problems. If something is difficult to figure...We'd rather multiply by 3 than by π."[118]

SEEKER "When I wrestle with tough problems or want to do something very difficult, I always turn to an expert."

MUNGER "So many people think that if they just hire somebody with the appropriate labels, they can do something very difficult. That is one of the most dangerous ideas a human being can have. All kinds of things can create problems by causing complexity. The other day I was dealing with a problem—it was a new building. And I said, 'This problem has three things I've learned to fear—an architect, a contractor and a hill.'

"If you go through life like that, I think you'll at least make fewer mistakes than people who think they can do anything, no matter how complex, by just hiring somebody with a credible label. You don't have to hire out your thinking if you keep it simple."[119]

SEEKER "Still, seems awfully tough what you've done."

MUNGER "I think what we've done all these years wasn't all that hard to do—and it's not all that hard to explain."[120]

"All that said and done, I think a lot of people just don't get it. As Samuel Johnson said, famously: 'I can give you an argument, but I can't give you an understanding.'"[121]

LIBRARIAN "Arthur Schopenhauer said, 'The wise in all ages have always said the same thing, and the fools, who at all times form the immense majority, have in their way too acted alike, and done just the opposite; and so it will continue'[122]...And to add a comment from a wise friend, 'And the percentages don't change, despite an ever increasing access to information.'"

SEEKER "But there must be some secret?"

The secret is ignorance removal

MUNGER "If there's any secret we have, it's ignorance removal. If it weren't for the fact that we were so good at removing ignorance, we'd be nothing today. And the nice thing is we still have a lot more ignorance left to remove."[123]

SEEKER "I like this already."

"Give me now some examples of things and behavior that will help me remove some ignorance."

LIBRARIAN "We will. In the following we will tell you some things that don't work—presented in the 'Jacobi' way—and what does work that may help you avoid some big mistakes."

"Some things may seem a little repetitious but as the saying goes, 'repetition is the mother of learning.'"

[Author's remark: Warning – the following is not for those who only read the headlines.]

PART TWO

ON WHAT DOESN'T WORK AND WHAT DOES

"The road to Hades is easy to travel; at any rate men pass away with their eyes shut."

– Bion of Borysthenes[124]

"What hits you affects you and wakes you up
more than what pleases you…
Death can surprise us in so many ways…
If I were a writer of books, I would compile a register,
with a comment, of the various deaths of men:
he who should teach men to die would at the same time
teach them to live."

- Michel Eyguem de Montaigne[125]

FIND AND MARRY A LOUSY PERSON

BUFFETT   "You should make right decisions, and one of the most important decisions you will make in your life is choosing a good spouse. You need everything to be stable, and if that decision isn't good, it may affect every other decision in life, including your business decisions."[126]

"My wife—my first wife, I was a mess when I met her. She did all kinds of things for me. I mean I'm not kidding. I would be an entirely different person if I hadn't married well. It's very important to marry well."[127]

SEEKER   "I didn't. 'My wife and I were happy for twenty years. Then we met.' Rodney Dangerfield said that. But it was my own fault. To paraphrase Groucho Marx, 'I don't want to have any wife that will have me as a husband.' I mean what kind of honorable woman will do that? It turned out she wasn't."

BUFFETT "Who you marry is enormously important—it'll affect everything."[128]

LIBRARIAN "Still, some people spend more time deciding what television set to buy than a life-changing decision like a marriage."

"Did you know that many people spend more time planning the wedding than their marriage?"

SEEKER "It sounds nuts when you put it like that."

"So help me, what qualities should I look for in a spouse?"

BUFFETT "Should I look for humor, character, intelligence, looks?... If you really want a marriage that will last, look for someone with low expectations[129]...That is the marriage that's going to last, if you both have low expectations."[130]

SEEKER "What else should I think about?"

BUFFETT "What's important is what your thoughts are on big things... make sure that your spouse has the same thoughts on the same big things... It would be crazy to get married when you differ on important points... Don't marry someone to change them[131]...Don't keep score. Keeping score doesn't build organizations, homes etc."[132]

MUNGER "What's the best way to get a good spouse...The best single way is to deserve a good spouse because a good spouse is by definition not nuts."[133]

SEEKER "Gosh, I guess I need to be the kind of person that she would want to have."

BUFFETT "Look for someone who will love you unconditionally and will subtly encourage you to be better than you thought you can be."[134]

"Marry someone who is a better person than you are. Always associate yourself with people who are better than you."[135]

MUNGER "What you want to maximize is a seamless web of deserved trust. And if your proposed marriage contract has 47 pages, my suggestion is that you not enter."[136]

LIBRARIAN "That is also a good advice in business dealings."

BUFFETT "I like to deal with people where I feel a one-page contract would do the job. If I have to have 50 pages in there to protect me against the guy I'm dealing with, I'll always wonder if I needed 51."[137]

LIBRARIAN "While we talk about contract—here is a lesson I learned the hard way."

BUFFETT "It is impossible to unsign a contract, so do all your thinking before you sign."[138]

LIBRARIAN "Another thing—If your past relationship was lousy, don't settle for a new one that seems slightly better—it may still be terrible."

SEEKER   "Why?"

LIBRARIAN   "Something may seem better than it really is depending on what you've been used to. Our minds are designed to detect and react to change. We don't experience or judge a thing by itself but in contrast to some anchor—something that is available, we've experienced recently, expected or got used to—and if the new thing is a slight improvement we see it as better than it objectively really is."

MUNGER   "In my generation, when women lived at home until they got married, I saw some perfectly terrible marriages made by highly desirable women because they lived in terrible homes. And I've seen some terrible second marriages which were made because they were slight improvements over an even worse first marriage."[139]

SEEKER   "Another thing—what's the secret to getting good kids?"

BUFFETT   "I married the right woman…They had a wonderful mother and fortunately they took on her great attributes."[140]

SEEKER   "Comes back to right spouse again…another thing…What is important to think about as a father?"

BUFFETT   "The greatest gift that my father ever gave me was unconditional love. Now, that doesn't mean that you get applauded for everything that you do. My father definitely told me if he didn't agree with my actions, but I always knew that he would be there for me."

"Throughout my life my father told me he supported me no matter what I wanted to do. It's an enormous factor. If you receive it from your parents that's great, if you don't, it's an uphill battle. That's why… choosing a spouse is the most important decision in your life. You need to choose a spouse who believes in you and will give you that unconditional love. The best way to find a spouse like this, I think, is to be lovable."[141]

TURN YOUR BODY AND MIND INTO A WRECK

BUFFETT   "Think of any car—a genie offers you any car in the world. The catch is that it's the only car you'll ever get."[142]

SEEKER   "What should I do?"

BUFFETT   "You read the manual 10 times, you change the oil twice as often as you need to, you take fastidious care, so that it remains the car of your dreams forever."

"You get only one mind and body—the same ones you'll have at 40, 60, etc. You need to take care of them and maximize their potential. It will be too late to take care of your body and mind later on. You can maintain them, but it's hard or impossible to undo big mistakes or negligence later on. You don't want to end up with a wreck on your hands."[143]

MUNGER   "The four closest friends of my youth were highly intelligent, ethical, humorous types, favored in person and background. Two are long

18

dead, with alcohol a contributing factor, and a third is a living alcoholic—if you call that living."

"While susceptibility varies, addiction can happen to any of us, through a subtle process where the bonds of degradation are too light to be felt until they are too strong to be broken. And I have yet to meet anyone, in over six decades of life, whose life was worsened by overfear and overavoidance of such a deceptive pathway to destruction."[144]

SEEKER   "Keep it coming."

ONLY LEARN FROM YOUR OWN TERRIBLE EXPERIENCES

MUNGER   "Learn everything you possibly can from your own personal experience, minimizing what you learn vicariously from the good and bad experience of others, living and dead. This prescription is a sure-shot producer of misery and second-rate achievement."

"I recommend as a memory clue to finding the way to real trouble from heedless, unoriginal error the modern saying: 'If at first you don't succeed, well, so much for hang gliding.'"[145]

SEEKER   "That really hit me."

MUNGER   "Many people have to learn the lessons of life the hard way through really terrible experience. Mark Twain said that a man who picks up a cat by the tail learns something in a way that's much more effective than any alternative way. But that's a terrible way to learn things…You shouldn't have to try it to learn not to pee on an electric fence."[146]

BUFFETT   "The trick is to learn most lessons from the experiences of others."[147]

MUNGER   "The more hard lessons you can learn vicariously rather than through your own hard experience, the better[148]…That is a much more pleasant way to learn."[149]

BUFFETT   "People always make the same mistakes."[150]

MUNGER   "You can see the results of not learning from others' mistakes by simply looking about you. How little originality there is in the common disasters of mankind—drunk driving deaths, reckless driving maimings, incurable venereal diseases, conversion of bright college students into brainwashed zombies as members of destructive cults, business failures through repetition of obvious mistakes made by predecessors, various forms of crowd folly, and so on."[151]

"The other aspect of avoiding vicarious wisdom is the rule for not learning from the best work done before yours. The prescription is to become as non-educated as you reasonable can."[152]

BUFFETT   "I think you can learn a lot from other people. In fact, I think if you learn basically from other people, you don't have to get too many new ideas on your own. You can just apply the best of what you see."[153]

LIBRARIAN "And the most efficient way is to learn from wise people—those who already have figured out what works and not and their lessons."[154]

BUFFETT "I would look for the best practices and I would discard the rest... Look at effective individuals and try to figure out why they're effective."[155]

SEEKER "Yes, like you guys."
"Anything else that is useful?"

MUNGER "I think history's very helpful. It enables you to keep things in perspective...So the history of civilization—and the history of finance and investing—is very useful."[156]

BUFFETT "I like history. I like financial history particularly...it's useful to realize how extraordinary things can happen occasionally."[157]

LIBRARIAN "And it help us to avoid thinking 'but this time it is different.' History mostly repeats itself even if it's never exact. As the Greek historian Thucydides wrote, 'The events which happened in the past and which (human nature being what it), will, at some time or other and in much the same ways, be repeated in the future.'"[158]

"But it seems that every generation forgets the misery of the past and this is maybe why some crisis occurs regularly. Every generation has to get its own head chopped off in its own way."

MUNGER "Why do we have to repeat the same old follies over and over again in a thin disguise? But evidently we do."[159]

BUFFETT "What we learn from history is that people don't learn from history."[160]

LIBRARIAN "And that everyone is wise after the event. As the proverb says, 'After the ship has sunk everyone knows how she might have been saved.'"

SEEKER "I told you so."

LIBRARIAN "Winston Churchill said it well, 'Want of foresight, unwillingness to act when action would be simple and effective, lack of clear thinking, confusion of counsel until the emergency comes, until self-preservation strikes its jarring gong—these are the features which constitute the endless repetition of history.'"[161]

SEEKER "I get the message."

LIBRARIAN "The French author André Gide said, 'Everything that needs to be said has already been said. But since no one was listening, everything must be said again.'"

SEEKER "Ok—enough."

LIBRARIAN "Learn from history and when you later see something ask, 'Have I seen this before or has this happened before and what happened then?' What normally happens in similar situations? Why should this be any different?'"

"But learn history's general lessons and don't draw the wrong conclusions based on some past events specific and unique circumstances. Take a lesson from Henry Kissinger, 'History is not, of course, a cookbook offering pretested recipes. It teaches by analogy, not by maxims. It can illuminate the consequences of actions in comparable situations, yet each generation much discover for itself what situations are in fact comparable.'"[162]

SEEKER   "Next misery, please. I think I got this one."

USE A HAMMER AS YOUR ONLY TOOL AND APPROACH EVERY COMPLEX PROBLEM AS IF IT WAS A NAIL

MUNGER   "You know the old saying: 'To the man with a hammer, the world looks like a nail.' This is a dumb way of handling problems."[163]

LIBRARIAN "The opposite is also true — If you define every problem as a nail, the only tool you look for is a hammer."

SEEKER   "Or like the saying, 'For every married woman every problem looks like a husband.'"

"Sorry, I couldn't resist but you better explain this — remember whom you talking to."

MUNGER   "One tends to use only models from one's own segment of a discipline, ignoring or under weighing others…too few denizens see the whole picture."[164]

LIBRARIAN "People often define problems in ways that fit their tools. They apply the same solution to every problem. And many times because they have a vested interest in using their own discipline to solve a problem."

MUNGER   "What happens is that people are trained in economics or engineering or marketing or investment management or something else. So they learn a few models and then they run around trying to solve all their problems with a limited number of models. And they don't really understand how their models intermix with other people's models."[165]

"Furthermore, the more powerful and useful is any model, the more error it tends to produce through overconfident misuse."[166]

LIBRARIAN "But you don't have to be that way."

MUNGER   If 'A' is narrow professional doctrine and 'B' consists of the big, extra-useful concepts from other disciplines, then, clearly, the professional possessing 'A' plus 'B' will usually be better off than the poor possessor of 'A' alone. How could it be otherwise?"[167]

"The only antidote for being an absolute klutz due to the presence of a man-with a-hammer syndrome is to have a full kit of tools. You don't have just a hammer. You've got all the tools."[168]

SEEKER   "And the tools are?"

MUNGER "You must know the big ideas in the big disciplines and use them routinely — all of them, not just a few[169]…and you're immensely wiser than others[170]…A, it gives perspective. B, it gives a way for you to organize and file away experience in your head, so to speak."[171]

"And because the really big ideas carry about 95% of the freight, it wasn't at all hard for me to pick up about 95% of what I needed from all the disciplines and to include use of this knowledge as a standard part of my mental routines."[172]

SEEKER "What big ideas?"

LIBRARIAN "Some big ideas and fundamental universal principles from all the big disciplines that describe how the world works and that help us consider the big picture or many aspects of an issue — ideas that can handle a wide range of problems, issues and situations."

MUNGER "You need the best 100 or so models from microeconomics, physiology, psychology particularly, elementary mathematics, hard science and engineering [and so on]."[173]

"Those are all great big, models of considerable generality that are useful over and over again."[174]

SEEKER "Why do I need so many models?"

MUNGER "Isn't reality multidisciplinary, so that you have to use the tools of all the disciplines to solve the complex problems?[175]…Broadscale problems, by definition, cross many academic disciplines. Accordingly, using a unidisciplinary attack on such problems is like playing a bridge hand by counting trumps while ignoring all else."[176]

"And I have worked hard to avoid that problem and of course if you grab the big ideas in all the disciplines by definition you're a man with multiple tools so you're less likely to commit the inanities of the people who twist every problem into being a nail."[177]

LIBRARIAN "Take psychology professors as an example of 'nail-twisters.'"

MUNGER "First, academic psychology…lacks intradisciplinary synthesis. In particular, not enough attention is given to lollapalooza effects coming from combinations of psychological tendencies."[178]

SEEKER "Lollapalooza?"

LIBRARIAN "Some extraordinary or extreme result."

MUNGER "In the social sciences, really extreme results almost always come from a confluence of factors operating in the same direction."[179]

SEEKER "Go on."

MUNGER "And, second, there is a truly horrible lack of synthesis blending psychology and other academic subjects[180]… each professor didn't even know the models of the other disciplines, much less try to synthesize those disciplines with his own[181]…But only an interdisciplinary approach will correctly deal with reality."[182]

"The lack of synthesis probably reflects the standard curse of academia that tends to reward what Jacob Viner, the great economist, called truffle hounds, animals trained to such a narrow purpose that they were no good at anything else."[183]

SEEKER   "Good lesson — I try avoid nail twisting then."

LIBRARIAN "Do you want to get smart?"

SEEKER   "Of course, don't we all?"

MUNGER   "If you want to get smart, the question you have to keep asking is 'why, why why?'[184]

LIBRARIAN "And when you try to find out the 'why', look for the most fundamental explanation. And, of course, to do that you got to know the main big ideas."

MUNGER   "I always liked Occam's razor. That is a wonderful way to think."[185]

"You can never make any explanation that can be made in a more fundamental way in any other way than the most fundamental way…the most fundamental ideas…the more fundamental body of knowledge."[186]

LIBRARIAN "Occam is also about not using complicated explanations or theories where simple ones will do — the one requiring the least assumptions needed to explain something or free of irrelevant factors or the simplest in the sense of the more obvious and natural explanation."

SEEKER   "To quote *Dr. House*, 'The simplest explanation is almost always somebody screwed up.'"[187]

LIBRARIAN "Similar to Hanlon's razor, 'Never attribute to malice that which is adequately explained by stupidity.' Just remember that Occam is a rule of thumb — not an absolute law."

MUNGER   "The tradition of always looking for the answer in the most fundamental way available[188]…to the more fundamental body of knowledge[189]… saves a lot of time in this world."[190]

LIBRARIAN "And this is very hard to do if you don't have some knowledge of some basic ideas of how the world works."

SEEKER   "Good point."

MUNGER   "You can argue that Einstein's whole career was just a marvelous demonstration of Occam's razor. $E = mc^2$ is a pretty simple idea but think of the power of it."[191]

LIBRARIAN "Just remember, there is often more than one cause. What we try to do is to understand the strongest influencers of an outcome — the fundamental causes or key factors — not all of them."

MUNGER "Einstein developed—some people say—a corollary, a counter-corollary to Occam's razor. I don't know if it is true but I have seen Einstein quoted with this observation over and over again. 'Everything should be made as simple as possible but not simpler.' Well, if Einstein didn't say that, he should have said it."[192]

LIBRARIAN "Call it Einstein's razor and as you can see this is similar to Occam's, with the addition that Einstein warns about over-simplifying complex matters—especially when we deal with complex systems—systems with a lot of interactions. For example, ecosystems, the human body, social organizations, infrastructures, or the economy."

MUNGER "Because this is a very sound idea, I later developed a supplement to that corollary. And my supplement to Einstein's corollary about Occam's razor was: In messy social science, if the result you are observing is a Lollapalooza, look for a confluence of multiple causes, multiple forces operating in the same direction."[193]

LIBRARIAN "An expanded version of the Occam trick is to always try to simplify things to their essence—the fundamental or most important aspect of something—the core."

"Even here Einstein's dictum is valid; simplify to the essence of the matter, but not further."

BUFFETT "Charlie's got the best 30-second mind in the world[194]...If I call him and describe a problem to him, any kind of a situation, he gets to the essence of it immediately."[195]

LIBRARIAN "You both have an amazing ability to see the essence of things quickly—to simplify complex matters and distill complex problems to its essentials—the critical things that really matter."

"You are the definition of what Douglas Hofstadter once told me was a great thinker, 'Being able to reliable 'sniff' what counts in a complex situation and to reliably put one's finger on it (and, conversely, to ignore what doesn't count) is the trick of thinking well.'"

SEEKER "I can see I have a lot to learn."

LIBRARIAN "There is a lesson here—just like we give you some key factors for what doesn't work and what does work—always try to determine what the key factors or causes for what you want to achieve are and then make sure you get them right. And you can't do this if you don't first get your toolbox of ideas."

"We also need to look for the Achilles heel—the key factor that could turn someone or a system into a catastrophe."

BUFFETT "When we make decisions, we focus on the most important thing."[196]

SEEKER "I get it. Independent of if I'm looking for investment success, getting a good job, great friends, a spouse or what have you, I should try to figure out what the one or two most important factors for success are and focus on them. Or to take the Jacobi approach – the key factors for misery in those areas."

LIBRARIAN "Often the case is that if you can find the key factors it answers everything. And if you can't, you get nowhere."

SEEKER "I like this Occam trick – seems very efficient."

LIBRARIAN "We focus on efficiency where it makes sense. When we know we are doing the right things and we know what we want to achieve, we focus on the most efficient way- efficient evaluations, processes, use of time, etc."

MUNGER "There's such a general efficiency with Berkshire...Berkshire's system of decentralization is the most efficient kind of organization you can possibly have."[197]

LIBRARIAN "As the late golfer Tommy Armour said, 'Simplicity, concentration, and economy of time and effort have been the distinguishing features of the great players' and great teachers' methods...the frustrated ones lost their way to glory by wandering in a maze of detail.'"[198]

SEEKER "I love this. Give me an example of some big ideas I need to know."

MUNGER "The engineering idea of a backup system is a very powerful idea. The engineering idea of breakpoints – that's a very powerful model, too. The notion of a critical mass – that comes out of physics – is a very powerful model."[199]

SEEKER "Earlier you said, 'psychology particularly,' why?"

BUFFETT "It is very important to know how human beings act."[200]

LIBRARIAN "And a lot of these psychological tendencies influence us subconsciously."

SEEKER "And some tendencies are..."

LIBRARIAN "For example, we want to be liked and matter, we reciprocate, imitate, hate losses and takeaways, and stick to our decisions and rationalize them."

SEEKER "Tell me more about, say, reciprocation."

LIBRARIAN "We give back what we have received – like favors, disfavors, concessions, information, attitudes and treatments."

SEEKER "Like the saying 'As you sow, so shall you also reap.'"

LIBRARIAN "Yes, so if people give back what they receive, what then works is to give people what we want in return from them."

"As Confucius said, 'Never impose on others what you would not choose for yourself.'"[201]

MUNGER "The concept is to treat the other fellow the way that you'd like to be treated if the roles were reversed."[202]

LIBRARIAN "Go first with the behavior you want in return. If you want a positive attitude, you give one first."

BUFFETT "Good behavior by each party begets good behavior in return[203]... Almost always good things come from good behavior."[204]

LIBRARIAN "You get out what you put in. Someone wiser than me once said, 'You can never get more out of your work, your surroundings, your friends, and of life itself than you put in. If you are generous, you will meet generosity. If you help others to solve their problems, they will help you. If you give trust, you meet trust.'"

SEEKER "And what doesn't work?"

LIBRARIAN "To do to others what you do not want them to do to you. To quote *Dr. House* again, 'What usually happens when you poke something with a stick? It pokes back.'"[205]

"As you can see — I follow Lord Peter Wimsey — 'I always have a quotation for everything — it saves original thinking.'"[206]

MUNGER "We see the extreme power of the tendency to reciprocate disfavors in some wars, wherein it increases hatred to a level causing very, brutal conduct."[207]

LIBRARIAN "Our obligation of giving back also creates the possibility of uninvited favors, bribes, unfair exchanges or concessions."

SEEKER "Uninvited favors?"

LIBRARIAN "Yes, some use the principle to manipulate you. For example, there is a reason why drug companies spend money on 'gifts' to doctors; suppliers on customers; or corporations on politicians. They all create an obligation to pay back."

MUNGER "Wise employers, therefore, try to oppose reciprocate-favor tendencies of employees engaged in purchasing. The simplest antidote works best: Don't let them accept any favors from vendors."

"Sam Walton agreed with this idea of absolute prohibition. He wouldn't let purchasing agents accept so much as a hot dog from a vendor."[208]

SEEKER "Some more big ideas — say from math?"

LIBRARIAN "Compound interest."

"Assume you have $100.000 to invest and you sit on your ass for 20 years. Company A give you a 10% compound annual return for 20 years and Company B, 20%. Which one do you choose?"

SEEKER "I will of course invest in Company B since it gives me twice the money after 20 years."

LIBRARIAN "Yes B—and this is the magic of compounding at hig[h]
the difference isn't double but close to 6 times. $100,000 inves[t]
compounded annually amount to roughly $673,000 after 20
at 20%, $3.8 million. After 30 years the difference increases to (
times."

BUFFETT "Such...geometric progressions illustrate the value of either
living a long time, or compounding your money at a decent rate[209] [or]...A
combination of both."[210]

"It is always startling to see how relatively small differences in
rates add up to very significant sums over a period of years[211]...Below are
shown the gains from $100,000 compounded at various rates:

	4%	8%	12%	16%
10 Years	$48,024	$115,892	$210,584	$341,143
20 Years	$119,111	$366,094	$864,627	$1,846,060
30 Years	$224,337	$906,260	$2,895,970	$8,484,940

"It is obvious that a variation of merely a few percentage points
has an enormous effect on the success of a compounding (investment)
program. It is also obvious that this effect mushrooms as the period
lengthens."[212]

LIBRARIAN "Patience needed."

BUFFETT "Compound interest is a little bit like rolling a snowball down a
hill. You can start with a small snowball and if it rolls down a long enough
hill...and the snow is mildly sticky, you'll have a real snowball at the
end[213]...It's better if you're not in too much of a hurry and keep doing
sound things."[214]

"Berkshire was a small business at one time. It just takes time. It
is the nature of compound interest. You can't build it in one day, or one
week."[215]

SEEKER "Amazing, I really need to learn this idea...And of course, other
ideas too—as you said, I need all the tools."

MUNGER "And you've got to have one more trick. You've got to use those
tools checklist-style because you'll miss a lot if you just hope that the right
tool is going to pop up unaided whenever you need it."[216]

SEEKER "OK, then, but what ideas should a guy like me learn—because
I for sure never learned anything useful at the university. To be honest
though, I never really listened."

MUNGER "A lot of what's taught in higher education isn't very useful to
those learning it, and a lot of the people who are taught wouldn't learn
anything anyways."[217]

SEEKER   "I deserved that one."

LIBRARIAN "Usefulness is a great criterion. Rousseau said, 'Real wisdom is not the knowledge of everything, but the knowledge of which things in life are necessary, which are less necessary, and which are completely unnecessary to know.'"

"And what could be more useful than learning the big and timeless principles that tell you how the world works—how reality works, how human nature works—so you know what to do or not do in different situations."

MUNGER   "All this stuff is really quite obvious and yet most people don't really know it in a way where they can use it."[218]

LIBRARIAN "Yes, and the reason is often that they don't really understand the idea. And as John Stobaeus said, 'What use is knowledge if there is no understanding?[219]...To know when and how to use an idea means you must really understand it. As George Santayana said, 'To understand...is to know what to do.'"[220]

"So learn what you need to learn in a way that is useful for you and learn it in a way so you know how, where and when to best use it. As Charles Spurgeon said, 'Wisdom is, I suppose, the right use of knowledge. To know is not to be wise. Many men know a great deal, and are all the more fools for what they know. There is no fool so great a fool as a knowing fool. But to know how to use knowledge is to have wisdom.'"[221]

SEEKER   "Good test."

LIBRARIAN "You also need judgment. Some people know a lot but they still do fatal things—their heads may be filled with knowledge but empty of judgment."

"One more thing, you need to understand how ideas within a discipline and between disciplines interact and combine."

MUNGER   "When four or five forces from these models come together to operate in the same direction...you get lollapalooza effects—which can make you rich or they can kill you."[222]

SEEKER   "The big effects again."

MUNGER   "Really big effects, lollapalooza effects, will often come only from large combinations of factors. For instance, tuberculosis was tamed, at least for a long time, only by routine combined use in each case of three different drugs."[223]

"This is the way you win big in the world—by getting two or three forces working together in the same direction."[224]

SEEKER   "Since I have lost big, tell me more about how I can win big."

MUNGER   "Extreme success is likely to be caused by some combination of the following factors:

a) Extreme maximization or minimization of one or two variables.

b) Adding success factors so that a bigger combination drives success, often in non-linear fashion, as one is reminded by the concept of breakpoint and the concept of critical mass in physics. Often results are not linear. You get a little bit more mass, and you get a lollapalooza result.

c) An extreme of good performance over many factors.

d) Catching and riding some sort of big wave."[225]

SEEKER   "What do you mean with 'big wave'?"

MUNGER   "When…new businesses come in, there are huge advantages for the early birds. And when you're an early bird, there's a model that I call 'surfing' — when a surfer gets up and catches the wave and just stays there, he can go a long, long time. But if he gets off the wave, he becomes mired in shallows…But people get long runs when they're right on the edge of the wave — whether it's Microsoft or Intel or all kinds of people, including National Cash Register in the early days."[226]

SEEKER   "I like your lollapalooza thinking."

MUNGER   "I've been searching for lollapalooza results all my life, so I'm very interested in models than explain their occurrence."[227]

LIBRARIAN "And often a couple of factors are so critical that if they are in place, much of the rest automatically follows."

SEEKER   "I better have an example — make it a bad Lollapalooza one."

LIBRARIAN "One example is Moonie conversions, where they brainwash normal kids and turn them into zombies."

MUNGER   "[They] manipulate targets into situations combining isolation and stress. The isolation strengthens the social proof…and the stress, often increased by fatigue, augments the targets' susceptibility to the social proof…One cult even used rattlesnakes to heighten the stress felt by conversion targets."[228]

SEEKER   "Social proof?"

LIBRARIAN "People have a tendency to be influenced by what other people do."

"Another tendency they use is 'liking' where the recruiters use various strategies to get you to like them."

SEEKER   "What's bad with that?"

LIBRARIAN "We trust and are easily influenced or mislead by people we like or love."

MUNGER   "It…makes the like or lover tend (1) to ignore faults of, and comply with wishes…(2) to favor people…merely associated with the object of his affection…and (3) to distort other facts to facilitate love."[229]

SEEKER   "So if I am more influenced by people I like, how do they do it…I mean, what makes us like someone?"

Librarian "For example, we like those who are similar or familiar to us, or people that flatter us—for example by making us feel special and welcome—and give us compliments."

"We also like those who are physically attractive, popular, cooperative, or people we have positive associations with."

Seeker "You mean I like and trust people more when they look attractive?"

Librarian "Yes, but don't be fooled by physical appearance—what you see isn't always what you get—in many cases where you strip away the outer layers you'll find an empty shell."

Seeker "Similar, in what way—you mean people who are like me?"

Librarian "Yes, like attracts like…people who are most like you—with the same background, attitudes on politics, lifestyle, interest, attitude, looks, and values."

"When people look like you, dress like you, talk like you and have the same hobbies as you—you like and trust them."

Munger "Who doesn't like his own image looking back at him?"[230]

Librarian "This tendency is really about our basic need to be liked. We like those who like us because we like to be liked, matter, be needed, recognized, appreciated and belonging—no one likes to be criticized or ignored. And when we feel people like us, we like them back."

"And our need to be liked contributes heavily to social conformity."

Buffett "Who doesn't like to be liked and…who does not want to avoid being a person they can't stand."[231]

Munger "Man…like and love being liked and loved…and man will generally strive, lifelong, for the affection and approval of many people not related to him."[232]

Librarian "Mary Kay Ash once said, 'It's so simple, yet makes such a difference. Pretend that every single person you meet has a sign around his or her neck that says, 'Make me feel important.'"[233]

Buffett "I like appreciation. I like the fact that by and large our shareholders are appreciative. I've got an audience that I like and that's what causes me to work when I don't need the money."[234]

Seeker "Assuming your managers I assume."

Munger "Everybody likes being appreciated and treated fairly, and dominant personalities who are capable of running a business like being trusted."[235]

Buffett "I like applause and if I like applause then I'm sure they like applause. And what they really like is intelligent applause from a real critic, and they get that when they get that from me."[236]

MUNGER   "All human beings work better if they get…reinforcement…If there are constant rewards for doing well…you will be driven to do more of the same."

"Don't you think it would maybe be a good idea to direct some of that reinforcement to the people who are important to you — because there's an old saying: If you want to be happy in marriage, improve yourself as a spouse before you try to improve your spouse's qualities as a spouse."[237]

LIBRARIAN   "Happy wife, happy life and miserable wife, miserable life."

SEEKER   "Guilty!"

"Anyway, imagine having your kid lost to the Moonies. This Lollapalooza stuff of how things combine is really important."

MUNGER   "They do four, five or six things at once — and the 'conversion' process works to create the 'snap' in a sadly high fraction of cases."[238]

SEEKER   "Is there any trick I can use to protect myself from being manipulated?"

MUNGER   "I've gotten so that I now use a kind of two-track analysis. First, what are the factors that really govern the interests involved, rationally considered? And second, what are the subconscious influences where the brain at a subconscious level is automatically doing these things –which by and large are useful, but which often misfunction."

"One approach is rationality — the way you'd work out a bridge problem: by evaluating the real interests, the real probabilities and so forth. And the other is to evaluate the psychological factors that cause subconscious conclusions — many of which are wrong."[239]

LIBRARIAN   "As Agatha Christie's Poirot says, 'There is always a motive.'"

SEEKER   "Just so I get the importance of this I would appreciate one more extreme example."

MUNGER   "It is the unlikely extremes in outcome — good and bad — that often instruct best."[240]

SEEKER   "Can you give me an example from the corporate world?"

LIBRARIAN   "Take for example, the institution of the board of directors."

MUNGER   "Well, the top guy is sitting there, he's an authority figure[241]… everybody defer — subconscious tendency number one[242]…He's doing asinine things, you look around the board, nobody else is objecting, social proof[243]…subconscious tendency number two."[244]

"In social proof, it is not only action by others that misleads but also their inaction. In the presence of doubt, inaction by others becomes social proof that inaction is the right course."[245]

SEEKER   "I assume 'authority figure' has a meaning?"

LIBRARIAN   "We tend to automatically believe and defer to authorities."

Munger   "We're all subject to control to some extent by authority figures, particularly authority figures who are rewarding us."[246]

"It's incredible the reciprocity that happens when CEOs keep recommending that directors get paid more, and then the directors raise the CEO's pay.[247]... He's flying you around in the corporate airplane to look at interesting plants, or whatever in hell they do, and you go and you really get extreme dysfunction as a corrective decision-making body in the typical American board of directors."[248]

Librarian   "And then you have the incentive and independence issue—are most directors really independent?"

Buffett   "The so-called independent directors are receiving $200,000 to $300,000 per year, but they are not independent. How would you feel about going to work 4-6 days per year with pleasant company, prestige, and pay of $300,000 per year? I'm assuming you'd like to get another job like that."[249]

Seeker   "Of course."

Buffett   "A director whose moderate income is heavily dependent on directors' fees—and who hopes mightily to be invited to join other boards in order to earn more fees—is highly unlikely to offend a CEO or fellow directors, who in a major way will determine his reputation in corporate circles."[250]

Munger   "A director who gets $150,000 per year from a company and needs the money is not independent."[251]

Buffett   "There are a number of directors at any company that are making two or three hundred thousand dollars a year, and that money is important to them. And what they really hope is they get invited to go on other boards. Now if a CEO comes to another CEO and says, I hear you've got so-and-so on the board, we need another woman or whatever it may be, oh, she will behave."[252]

Seeker   "It's a lot of money. I would keep quiet for less."

Buffett   "If they say she raises hell at every meeting, she's not going to be on the next board. On the other hand, if they say she's constructive, her compensation committee recommendations have been spot on, et cetera, she's got another $300,000 a year job. That's the real world."[253]

Seeker   "But surely these so called 'independent directors' understand they are not independent?"

Munger   "Maimonides said …'A man is always going to be straight in his own eyes'[254]…You squelch by denial what you've recognized would make you think ill of yourself or would interfere with your income[255]…It's human nature—people will rationalize all sorts of things to get paid."[256]

Seeker   "What is true independence then?"

BUFFETT   "Independence is a state of mind[257]…The willingness to challenge a forceful CEO when something is wrong or foolish…The place to look for it is among high-grade people whose interests are in line with those of rank-and-file shareholders — and are in line in a very big way."[258]

MUNGER   "I think you get better directors when you get directors who don't need the money. When it's half your income and all your retirement, you're not likely to be very independent. But when you have money and an existing reputation that you don't want to lose, then you'll act more independently."[259]

LIBRARIAN   "Like Berkshire's board."

BUFFETT   "Most of our directors have a major portion of their net worth invested in the company. We eat our own cooking."[260]

"The bottom line for our directors: You win, they win big; you lose, they lose big. Our approach might be called owner-capitalism. We know of no better way to engender true independence."[261]

LIBRARIAN   "We need more people like Elihu Root."

MUNGER   "Elihu Root, probably the greatest cabinet officer we ever had, said one of my favorite comments: 'No man is fit to hold public office who isn't perfectly willing to leave it at any time.'"[262]

"But the man who has a lot to lose from leaving his office is going to be very loathe to be an independent director[263]…Is a director really fit to make tough calls who isn't perfectly willing to leave the office at any time? My answer is no."[264]

SEEKER   "Are there any other qualities you think is important for a director to have?"

BUFFETT   "In addition to being independent, directors should have business-savvy, a shareholder orientation and a genuine interest in the company."[265]

"There are a lot of people on boards that are very smart people but they don't know anything about business….there are loads of those people on corporate boards in America that have big names and they have no idea how to run a lemonade stand. And it's nothing wrong with them — they know how to do very well what they do. So you need business savvy, you need a shareholder orientation, which is lacking in a great many directors. You need interest, they've gotta want to show up because they're actually interested in the business, and not because they're interested in the fee or something."[266]

SEEKER   "But you got the right people."

BUFFETT   "We have an extraordinarily knowledgeable and business-oriented board of directors…None took the job for the money…They receive their rewards instead through ownership of Berkshire shares and the satisfaction that comes from being good stewards of an important enterprise."[267]

SEEKER "And how common are these qualities in boards?"

BUFFETT "Over a span of 40 years, I have been on 19 public-company boards (excluding Berkshire's) and have interacted with perhaps 250 directors. Most of them were 'independent' as defined by today's rules. But the great majority of these directors lacked at least one of the three qualities I value. As a result, their contribution to shareholder well-being was minimal at best and, too often, negative. These people, decent and intelligent though they were, simply did not know enough about business and/or care enough about shareholders to question foolish acquisitions or egregious compensation."[268]

SEEKER "I always believed the board of directors did the right things. And now you tell me reality doesn't work that way?"

BUFFETT "I've never seen a director who needs the money oppose an acquisition or executive compensation."[269]

SEEKER "But you spoke?"

BUFFETT "My own behavior, I must ruefully add, frequently fell short as well: Too often I was silent when management made proposals that I judged to be counter to the interests of shareholders."[270]

SEEKER "You too? Why?"

BUFFETT "Boardroom atmosphere...collegiality trumped independence[271]...Boards are in part business organizations and in part social organizations...usually your people have achieved some standing, perhaps, in the community. So they've learned how to get along with other people. And they don't suddenly change their stripes when they come into a board meeting[272]...you feel that the group around you, in terms of social behavior, can only tolerate a certain amount of obnoxiousness on your part. So you have to ration it out. You save yourself for big ones. It's not necessarily an easy equation."[273]

"So there's a great tendency to behave in a socially acceptable way and not necessarily in a business maximization way. The motives are good; the behavior is formed by decades earlier."[274]

LIBRARIAN "And people don't want to reject the CEO."

BUFFETT "Relations between the Board and the CEO are expected to be congenial. At board meetings, criticism of the CEO's performance is often viewed as the social equivalent of belching."[275]

LIBRARIAN "Take for example when the CEO makes an acquisition proposal."

BUFFETT "The nature of acquisitions is that they get to the board at a point where if you turn them down you are rejecting the chief executive, you are embarrassing him in front of his troops, you're doing all kinds of things. So, it just doesn't happen."

"I have seen board after board approve deals that afterwards the board members say, 'you know, I really didn't think it was a very good idea but what could we do about it?'"[276]

LIBRARIAN "And you can imagine what can happen when you have the wrong figure at the top."

BUFFETT "The real issue is mediocrity—there are too many .240 hitters on boards. Businesses often settle for a notch or two above mediocrity—there are strong human instincts at work."[277]

"If Frank Solich at Nebraska has a mediocre quarterback or whatever, he's gotta do something about it or he won't be coaching next year. When a Fortune 500 company has a mediocre CEO—a perfectly decent guy, good family man, a friend of yours or picked you for the board, what's your incentive to, perhaps, you know, to get rid of him? It isn't going to happen."[278]

MUNGER "The obvious implication: Be careful whom you appoint to power because a dominant authority figure will often be hard to remove."[279]

SEEKER "But I always believed directors had a lot to say."

BUFFETT "As a director, you can't remotely tell management what to do. All of this stuff you read in the press about the board setting strategy is baloney. As a board member, you can do practically nothing. If a CEO thinks a director is smart and on his side, he'll listen to some degree, but ninety-eight percent of the time, he'll do what he wants to anyway."[280]

MUNGER "Averaged out, the CEO does what he wants to do—and the board says 'yes'. Anything else is rare. The culture just works that way."[281]

BUFFETT "In almost sixty years of investing, we've found it practically useless to give advice to anyone."[282]

SEEKER "I hear you saying this is what happens, but should it happen this way?"

BUFFETT "Well, no, obviously you know everybody would speak freely and all of that sort of thing, and dialogue would be encouraged and the chairman would love to hear reasons why his ideas were no good, but it isn't quite that way."[283]

MUNGER "If you're counting on the outside directors to fix bad management, you're in trouble."[284]

"The outside directors on a corporate board usually display the near ultimate form of inaction. They fail to object to anything much short of an axe murder until some public embarrassment of the board finally causes their intervention."[285]

BUFFETT   "Charlie and I have been on boards of companies in which we're among the largest shareholders—and even then—we've had very little luck changing behavior. So we think that if you buy stock in a company, you'd better not count on being able to change their course of action."[286]

"So as a matter of investment technique and maybe as a matter of avoiding stress in your life and all of that sort of thing…it's better to be in with a management you're sympatico with than simply to be in a great business where the management is bent on doing things that don't make sense to you."[287]

SEEKER   "This was news for me."

"At any rate, it seems awfully tough to learn all these models and stuff."

MUNGER   "Instead, it turns out that the truly big ideas in each discipline, learned only in essence, carry most of the freight. And they are not so numerous, nor are their interactions so complex, that a large and multidisciplinary understanding is impossible for many, given large amounts of talent and time."[288]

"I would argue that what Berkshire has done has mostly been using trivial knowledge[289]…The more basic knowledge you have the less new knowledge you have to get."[290]

SEEKER   "Please explain."

LIBRARIAN "There are a few timeless and time-filtered ideas or principles that account for a lot of observations."

MUNGER   "The trick is to have your brain work better than the other person's brain because it understands the most fundamental models—the ones that will do the most work per unit. In science, just a few formulas will correctly make an enormous percentage of all predictions. And similarly, in messy practical life, certain models will carry a lot of extra weight."[291]

"You just have to know a few things and know them very well."[292]

BUFFETT   "You really should understand human behavior if you're going to run a business."[293]

SEEKER   "Have you always used ideas from different disciplines?"

MUNGER   "For some odd reason, I had an early and extreme multidisciplinary cast of mind. I couldn't stand reaching for a small idea in my own discipline when there was a big idea right over the fence in somebody else's discipline. So I just grabbed in all directions for the big ideas that would really work."[294]

"I have this thing about always putting things in context and seeking synthesis. I've done this all my life. It has turned out to be very remunerative."[295]

SEEKER   "But how can I remember all the models or ideas that you tell me I need to learn?"

MUNGER "Once you have the ideas, of course, you must continuously practice their use. Like a concert pianist, if you don't practice you can't perform well. So I went through life constantly practicing a multi-disciplinary approach."[296]

"A wise man engaged in learning some important skill will not stop until he is really fluent in it."[297]

SEEKER "I see I have some work to do in front of me — if I can work up the energy."

LIBRARIAN "Wouldn't it be worth practising to reduce the chance of getting into all the mess you have experienced in life — wouldn't a little preparation and prevention have paid off?"

MUNGER "More important than the will to win is the will to prepare."[298]

BUFFETT "Predicting rain doesn't count; building arks does."[299]

LIBRARIAN "It's all about understanding the ideas that tell you how the world really works and then make sure you are aligned with those realities."

"On the other hand — I believe people end up getting the brain they deserve."

MUNGER "It's amazing how resistant some people are to learning."[300]

BUFFETT "Especially when it's in their own interest to learn."[301]

MUNGER "Most people are happy in the shallows. After all, there is always somebody that's in a shallower place."[302]

LIBRARIAN "You can't get something for nothing. You have to work at it. You need to put some time and energy in it."

"As the saying goes, 'The only free cheese is in the mousetrap. But who has ever seen a happy mouse in there.'"

SEEKER "Stop — I get the message — you have convinced me."

"Now tell me some more things that don't work."

GO THROUGH LIFE WITH UNREASONABLE EXPECTATIONS

MUNGER "It's much more fun going through life constantly exceeding your expectations instead of being disappointed, so the secret of human felicity is not vast ambition, it's low expectations."[303]

LIBRARIAN "And have proper expectations on the people that you influence."

MUNGER "What we don't like in modern capitalism is the expectations game. It's not the kissing cousin of evil; it's the blood brother."[304]

BUFFETT "People who predict precisely are either kidding themselves or others. We've seen people get their egos involved. And everyone in the organization knows what the CEO has promised in public. It's setting up a system that sets up financial or psychological pressure for people to do things they probably don't want to do. It's a terrible mistake."[305]

MUNGER "We try and talk down expectations. We don't want to be surrounded by people with unreasonable expectations. In a [romantic] relationship, how much sense would it make [to have the other person expecting a whole lot from you]?"[306]

SEEKER "Some other thing that cause folly?"

ONLY TAKE CARE OF YOUR OWN INTEREST

MUNGER "Another thing that often causes folly and ruin is the 'self-serving bias' often subconscious, to which we're all subject[307]... I've underestimated this phenomenon all my life."[308]

LIBRARIAN "As the saying goes, "Every bird sings its own song.'"

MUNGER "You think that 'the true little me' is entitled to do what it wants to do."[309]

SEEKER "What should I do then?"

MUNGER "Of course you...want to get self-serving bias out of your mental routines. Thinking that what's good for you is good for the wider civilization, and rationalizing foolish or evil conduct, based on your subconscious tendency to serve yourself, is a terribly way to think."

"And you want to drive that out of yourself because you want to be wise, not foolish, good, not evil."[310]

LIBRARIAN "Another thing to remember is that when you take care of others interests and needs, you often take care of your own. As the late Zig Ziglar said, 'You can get everything in life you want if you will just help enough other people get what they want.'"[311]

"The key to sustainable success in all kinds of relationships is to look for and make the relationship win/win. And win/win doesn't happen if one side doesn't see the deal as a win, even if the other party sees it as a win. It must be a win for all parties involved, when taken from each party's respective point of view."

BLINDLY TRUST AND FOLLOW THE RECOMMENDATIONS OF ADVISORS AND SALESMEN

MUNGER "You also have to allow, in your own cognition and conduct, for the self-serving bias of everybody else, because most people are not going to be very successful at removing such bias, the human condition being what it is."[312]

SEEKER "But shouldn't I at least trust my advisors?"

MUNGER "All commissioned salesmen have a tendency to serve the transaction instead of the truth."[313]

LIBRARIAN "We all see life from our own angle and that includes all wonderful advisors and salesmen like lawyers, accountants, doctors, consultants, etc. And what is good and harmless for them may not be good for you."

SEEKER "Even doctors?"

MUNGER "I can give an example that surprised me. I'm used to doctors who think a procedure that's good for them is good for you. They're wrong. But in Redding, California a couple of doctors rose who gave everybody who consulted them open heart surgery. They convinced themselves that everybody needed open heart surgery. A normal heart was a widow maker. If you replaced it with carbon or nylon or something, they were way better off. They did massive amounts of open heart surgery."

"They had the feeling they were doing the right thing and really helping the patients. That surprised me. I'm always being surprised by something like that. It seems impossible. How could anybody behave that way? How could it go on for year after year?"[314]

SEEKER "What a horrible story."

MUNGER "It's incentive-caused bias. They were making money and status, and they were demonstrating skills and so forth. It's so extreme, you'd think that couldn't happen. If it did happen, you'd think it would be identified by other people early. It ran on for years."[315]

SEEKER "Any other 'salesmen?'"

MUNGER "Consider the presentations of brokers selling commercial real estate and businesses. I've never seen one that I thought was even within hailing distance of objective truth. In my long life, I have never seen a management consultant's report that didn't end with the same advice: 'This problem needs more management consulting services.'"[316]

BUFFETT "People marketing one fad or another in management tend to make it a little bit more complicated than necessary so that you have to call in the high priest. If all that really counts is the Ten Commandments, then it's very tough on religious counselors — it just doesn't make it complicated enough… it's hard to write a 300-page book that just says, 'Listen to your customer.'"[317]

"After all, what witch doctor has ever achieved fame and fortune by simply advising 'Take two aspirins'?"[318]

LIBRARIAN "And then we have the action-encouraging stock brokers. They advise us what to buy and sell. Volume creates commissions. So they have a strong incentive to get us to trade and do deals regardless of what's in our best interest."

BUFFETT "One of the ironies of the stock market is the emphasis on activity[319]… Like the Doctor who gets paid on how often to get you to change pills. If he gave you one pill that cures you the rest of your life, he would make one sale, one transaction and that is it. But if he can convince you that changing pills every day is the way to great health, it will be great for him and the prescriptionists. You won't be any healthier and you will be a lot worse off financially. You want to stay away from any environment that stimulates activity."[320]

"If you go to a dentist who gets paid by the number of teeth he pulls out, you better think ahead about what teeth you want to be pulled out."[321]

SEEKER "I once invested 50% of my retirement savings with an investment advisor that promised to double my money in a year in something called the LHIW project with no chance of a loss. And his projections were wonderful."

"My advisor made a lot of money but sorry to say, I lost it all. I felt like Groucho Marx when he said, 'I worked myself up from nothing to a state of extreme poverty.'"[322]

"Afterwards I found out that LHIW was short for 'Let's Hope It Works.'"

BUFFETT "When someone with experience proposes a deal to someone with money, too often the fellow with money ends up with the experience, and the fellow with experience ends up with the money."[323]

LIBRARIAN "I love the saying, 'A fool and his money are soon parted.'"

SEEKER "My only excuse is that he was very persuasive."

BUFFETT "Those who cannot fill your pocket will confidently fill your ear[324]...Many helpers are apparently direct descendants of the queen in Alice in Wonderland, who said: 'Why, sometimes I've believed as many as six impossible things before breakfast.' Beware the glib helper who fills your head with fantasies while he fills his pockets with fees."[325]

"I think it's dangerous to get advice from people where their compensation—and maybe very large compensation—depends on a specific line of advice they give you."[326]

LIBRARIAN "And double your money in one year! If it seems too good to be true, you can bet it's too good to be true. What was it Kipling said, 'All is not gold that glitters, and two and two make four.'"[327]

BUFFETT "And when someone tells you how old-fashioned that math is— zip up your wallet."[328]

"When promised quick profits, respond with a quick 'no.'"[329]

MUNGER "The more anything sounds like easy, free money, the less I tend to believe it."[330]

SEEKER "After your convincing arguments I'll watch out."

MUNGER "If you don't allow for self-serving bias in the conduct of others, you are...a fool."[331]

Librarian "Whenever you ask a seller or advisor what he recommends or whenever someone tries to sell you something remember..."

Buffett "Don't ask the barber whether you need a haircut."[332]

Seeker "Or to use your hammer-syndrome, 'Don't ask a man with only a hammer what tool he recommends.' Hope I got that right."

Librarian "The former *Washington Post* journalist Daniel Greenberg has a variant on the 'hammer' when it comes to the use of technology, — which also, of course, is applicable to other things, — 'The creators of a technology constitute the worst possible source of advice as to whether it should be utilized.'"[333]

Munger "Incentive-caused bias requires that one should often distrust, or take with a grain of salt, the advice of one's professional advisor, even if he is an engineer....Especially fear professional advice when it is especially good for the advisor."[334]

Seeker "But surely subscribing to investment newsletters can't be bad?"

Librarian "The author John Train said it well, 'The man who discovers how to turn lead into gold isn't going to give you the secret for $100 a year.'"[335]

"Also watch out for situations when people tell you what you want to hear — when it's not in their own interest to tell you the truth — if they do they may lose their job, your friendship, support or whatever."

Seeker "Like my friend John, he couldn't afford to disagree with his boss. He's got a wife and kids to support and a mortgage to pay — he does what he is told and what his boss wants to hear. However dumb it is."

Munger "It reminds me of the saying, 'Whose bread I eat, his song I sing.'"[336]

Librarian "He has a lot to lose so he won't bite the hand that feeds him — he may get his head chopped off."

Munger "Generally, the employment relationship — the need for money — causes more terrible cognition than any other single factor."[337]

"We want more people who say, 'Well, you're my boss. If that is what you want to do, you'll have to get a different errand boy. I'm not going to do it.'"[338]

Seeker "Whose bread I eat...I like that...Like the so called 'independent board' members you mentioned earlier. They play the tune of their paymasters."

Buffett "The typical corporate organization is structured so that a CEOs beliefs and biases are reinforced. Staffs won't give you any contrary recommendations — they'll just come back with whatever the CEO wants. And the Board of Directors won't act as a check, so the CEO pretty much gets what he wants."[339]

LIBRARIAN "A variant of 'whose bread..' is Thomas Fuller's satire about the Vicar of Bray."

"'The vivacious vicar [of Bray] living under King Henry VIII, King Edward VI, Queen Mary, and Queen Elizabeth, was first a Papist, then a Protestant, then a Papist, then a Protestant again. He had seen some martyrs burnt (two miles off) at Windsor, and found this fire too hot for his tender temper. This vicar, being taxed by one for being a turncoat and an inconstant changeling, said, 'Not so, for I always kept my principle, which is this - to live and die the Vicar of Bray.'"[340]

SEEKER   "Any more things on your plate that don't work?"

MINDLESSLY IMITATE THE LATEST FADS AND FASHIONS

BUFFETT   "What doesn't work is when you start doing things that you don't understand or because they worked last week for somebody else."[341]

MUNGER   "One of my favorite stories is about the little boy in Texas. The teacher asked the class, 'If there are nine sheep in the pen and one jumps out, how many are left?' And everybody got the answer right except this little boy, who said, 'None of them are left.' And the teacher said, 'You don't understand arithmetic.' And he said 'No, teacher. You don't understand sheep.'"[342]

LIBRARIAN   "It's the social proof tendency we mentioned earlier — it's human nature to follow others. But remember the saying, 'When the blind lead the blind, both shall fall into the ditch.'"

BUFFETT   "It always amazes me how high-IQ people mindlessly imitate."[343]

LIBRARIAN   "Including most of the investment management profession."

BUFFETT   "Most managers have very little incentive to make the intelligent-but-with-some-chance-of-looking-like-an-idiot decision. Their personal gain/loss ratio is all too obvious: if an unconventional decision works out well, they get a pat on the back and, if it works out poorly, they get a pink slip. (Failing conventionally is the route to go; as a group, lemmings may have a rotten image, but no individual lemming has ever received bad press.)"[344]

MUNGER   "I'm afraid the investing class, the managerial class, and the banking class are more like the sheep then they are like the guy who was willing to say what Sam Goldwyn was reported to have said, which was: 'Include me out.' It's one of my favorite expressions."[345]

BUFFETT   "You have to forget about all those things. You have to do what works, what you understand, and if you don't understand it and somebody else is doing it, don't get envious or anything of the sort. Just go on and wait until you find something you understand."[346]

LIBRARIAN   "Josh Billings possibly said, 'Half of the troubles of this life can be traced to saying yes too quickly and not saying no soon enough.'"

SEEKER "I wish I had done that when I saw my neighbor buying internet stocks and making a lot of money. Unfortunately, I followed him."

LIBRARIAN "Poirot said, 'If you put your head in the mouth of the lion, you cannot complain if one day he bites it off, eh'?"[347]

BUFFETT "You can't stand to see your neighbor getting rich. You know you're smarter than he is, and he's doing these things and getting rich. And your wife says that you're smarter than he is and he's richer than you are, you know, so why aren't you doing it."[348]

SEEKER "My wife never said that but I see what you mean."

BUFFETT "Pretty soon you start doing it. And so you get what I call the natural progression, the three I's: the innovators, the imitators, and the idiots. And that's what happens. Everybody just kind of goes along. And you look kind of silly if you disagree."[349]

LIBRARIAN "And when everyone else starts doing it, we soon end up in bubble territory."

BUFFETT "But bubbles blown large enough inevitably pop. And then the old proverb is confirmed once again: 'What the wise man does in the beginning, the fool does in the end.'"[350]

SEEKER "I am the bigger fool here."

LIBRARIAN "As Alice said in *Alice's Adventures in Wonderland*, 'If you drink much from a bottle marked 'poison' it is almost certain to disagree with you, sooner or later.'"

BUFFETT "You don't know how big they will get and you don't know when they will pop. You don't know when midnight will hit, but when it does, it turns carriages to pumpkins and mice...Some people want to stick around for the last dance, and they thought that a bigger fool would be just around the corner tomorrow[351]...they...hate to miss a single minute of what is one helluva party. Therefore, the giddy participants all plan to leave just seconds before midnight. There's a problem, though: They are dancing in a room in which the clocks have no hands."[352]

SEEKER "And probably dancing in the ballroom of the Titanic."

"By the way, what creates...I mean, how do we get a bubble?"

BUFFETT "The only way you get a bubble is when basically a very high percentage of the population buys into some originally sound premise— and it's quite interesting how that develops—an originally sound premise that becomes distorted as time passes and people forget the original sound premise and start focusing solely on the price action."

"Ben Graham...said you can get in a whole lot more trouble in investing with a sound premise than with a false premise."[353]

MUNGER   "He had it right[354]...bad ideas are born good. A well-intentioned idea of some kind works fine for a while, then stops working and goes into reverse."[355]

"It is so easy for us all to push a really good idea to wretched excess, as in the case of the Florida land bubble or the 'nifty fifty' corporate stocks."[356]

LIBRARIAN   "But people rationalize it by the saying, 'it's different this time.' But it never is."

"Human behavior stays the same — only the objects of the folly changes."

MUNGER   "The panic that came as a predecessor of the Great Recession had common themes [with the past] that are always the same. The crazy greed, the crazy leverage, the crazy delusions."[357]

LIBRARIAN   "I have always liked the saying, 'The more it changes the more it's the same thing.'"

SEEKER   "Fascinating this how one can get in more trouble with a good idea than a bad one."

MUNGER   "It's not the bad idea that do you in — it's the good idea that is carried to excess."

"When you come across a bad idea you and everyone else know it's bad, it can't hurt you. But when you come across a good and important idea, it's easy to overdo it."[358]

BUFFETT   "People forget about the reasons and mathematical limitations of the original premise and what got them excited in the first place."[359]

SEEKER   "And as soon as I forget that, I'm doomed."

BUFFETT   "What starts out going up for sound fundamental reasons then starts going up for unsound speculative reasons."[360]

LIBRARIAN   "Yes, like the 2007 housing crisis."

BUFFETT   "Housing...created a bubble like we've never seen."[361]

SEEKER   "Yes, I mean how could that happen? Going from something sound to something really bad — take me through it."

BUFFETT   "It's a totally sound premise that houses will become, worth more over time because the dollar becomes worth less. It isn't because... construction costs go up. And it isn't because houses are so wonderful. It's because the dollar is worth less than a house that was bought 40 years ago."

"And since 66% or 67% of the people want to own their home and because you can borrow money on it and you're dreaming of buying a home, if you really believe that houses are going to go up in value you buy one as soon as you can."[362]

SEEKER   "Sounds like a sound premise, or?"

BUFFETT   "That's a very sound premise…So the sound premise it's a good idea to buy a house this year because it will probably cost more next year and you're going to want a home and the fact that you can finance it gets distorted over time if housing prices are going up 10% a year and inflation is a couple of percent a year."[363]

SEEKER   "I just wait for the 'but' here."

BUFFETT   "But a house can be a nightmare if the buyer's eyes are bigger than his wallet and if a lender — often protected by a government guarantee — facilitates his fantasy."[364]

"At the core of the folly was the almost universal belief that the value of houses was certain to increase over time and that any dips would be inconsequential. The acceptance of this premise justified almost any price and practice in housing transactions. Homeowners everywhere felt richer and rushed to 'monetize' the increased value of their homes by refinancings. These massive cash infusions fueled a consumption binge throughout our economy. It all seemed great fun while it lasted…In 2007, the bubble burst, just as all bubbles must."[365]

LIBRARIAN   "The great delusion."

BUFFETT   "Almost all of the country became possessed by the idea that home prices could never fall significantly. That was a mass delusion, reinforced by rapidly rising prices that discredited the few skeptics who warned of trouble."

"Delusions, whether about tulips or Internet stocks, produce bubbles. And when bubbles pop, they can generate waves of trouble that hit shores far from their origin."[366]

SEEKER   "And the lenders — shouldn't they have been more careful?"

BUFFETT   "The lender feels the same way. Doesn't really make difference if it's a liar's loan or you don't have the income or something because even if they have to take it over, it'll be worth more next year. Once that gathers momentum and it gets reinforced by price action the original premise is forgotten."[367]

"Lenders happily made loans that borrowers couldn't repay out of their incomes, and borrowers just as happily signed up to meet those payments. Both parties counted on 'house-price appreciation' to make this otherwise impossible arrangement work. It was Scarlett O'Hara all over again: 'I'll think about it tomorrow.'"[368]

LIBRARIAN   "And afterwards, everybody scratches their heads wondering why they did it."

BUFFETT   "Be careful that when you buy something for a sound reason, make sure that the reason stays sound."[369]

"In our activities, we will heed the wisdom of Herb Stein: 'If something can't go on forever, it will end.'"[370]

LIBRARIAN "And things can change fast. The late economist Rudiger Dornbusch's dictum was, 'In economics, things take longer to happen than you think they will, and then they happen faster than you thought they could.'"[371]

BUFFETT "You'd be amazed at just how fast things can change."[372]

SEEKER "I am well aware of that, thank you very much."

"Going back to the lenders or banks—I do find it amazing they continued lending like they did."

BUFFETT "Whatever the other guy did, the other 36 were like a bunch of lemmings in terms of following. That's what's gotten all the big banks in trouble for the past 15 years. Every time somebody big does something dumb, other people can hardly wait to copy it."[373]

LIBRARIAN "Which of course created a situation where risky and bad behavior drives out the prudent and good."

MUNGER "There's a lot of new-form Gresham's Law out there where the bad practice drives out the good. If you run a nice conservative bank and some other guy has a bank and does a lot of very aggressive things that appear to work, and he reports higher and higher profits – the pressure to join the crowd on the guy at the lagging bank is huge."[374]

LIBRARIAN "As P.T. Barnum said, 'Nothing draws a crowd like a crowd.'"

MUNGER "What happens finally is that your competitors, who are growth mad, reduce their loan standards enormously."[375]

BUFFETT "As Wall Streeter Ray DeVoe says: 'Fools rush in where angels fear to trade.'"[376]

LIBRARIAN "Reminds me of a story about the actor Robert Charles Benchley. He was horrified when his request for a bank loan was promptly and unconditionally granted. He immediately closed his account, 'I don't trust a bank that would lend money to such a poor risk', he said."[377]

MUNGER "The bad loans drive out the good…Bad lending drives out good. Think of how powerful that model is. Think of the disaster that it creates for everybody."[378]

BUFFETT "They behave like the fellow in a switchblade fight who, after his opponent has taken a mighty swipe at his throat, exclaimed, 'You never touched me.' His adversary's reply: 'Just wait until you try to shake your head.'"[379]

SEEKER "As the Klingon proverb from *Star Trek* goes, 'A fool and his head are soon parted.'"

MUNGER "The first chance you have to avoid a loss from a foolish loan is by refusing to make it; there is no second chance."[380]

LIBRARIAN "Another problem is believing the risk is low when the danger is greatest—for example, when banks determined bad debt reserves by past experience using actuarial techniques."

MUNGER "Well, what happens with that system after a long period of boom—when the real danger is greatest—is that the bad debt reserves of the bank go to near zero...that's insane. Anybody with any sense would know that the bad debt reserves should go up, not down...We should not have a system...where the bad debt reserves in a bank go to near zero at the top of every idiot boom."[381]

LIBRARIAN "This is what happens when the competitive juices flow over."

MUNGER "Most people in business can't stand their competitors running off in one direction, no matter how foolish—and leaving them just standing there alone."[382]

BUFFETT "The 'institutional imperative:' the tendency of executives to mindlessly imitate the behavior of their peers, no matter how foolish it may be to do so[383]...One of its main tenets is a copycat mechanism that decrees that any craving of a leader, however foolish, will be quickly supported by detailed rate-of-return and strategic studies prepared by his troops. For example, every time it becomes fashionable to expand into some new line of business, some companies will expand into it. Then they get out of it about five years later, licking their wounds."[384]

"I did not intuitively understand it when I entered the business world. I thought then that decent, intelligent, and experienced managers would automatically make rational business decisions. But I learned over time that isn't so. Instead, rationality frequently wilts when the institutional imperative comes into play."[385]

SEEKER "Other folly from this?"

BUFFETT "For example...As if governed by Newton's First Law of Motion, an institution will resist any change in its current direction...Just as work expands to fill available time, corporate projects or acquisitions will materialize to soak up available funds."

"Institutional dynamics, not venality or stupidity, set businesses on these courses, which are too often misguided."[386]

SEEKER "But you stay away from that, don't you?"

BUFFETT "After making some expensive mistakes because I ignored the power of the imperative, I have tried to organize and manage Berkshire in ways that minimize its influence. Furthermore, Charlie and I have attempted to concentrate our investments in companies that appear alert to the problem."[387]

LIBRARIAN "But sometimes it happens anyway."

BUFFETT "I ask the managers of our subsidiaries to unendingly focus on moat-widening opportunities, and they find many that make economic sense. But sometimes our managers misfire. The usual cause of failure is that they start with the answer they want and then work backwards to find a supporting rationale. Of course, the process is subconscious; that's what makes it so dangerous."[388]

SEEKER   "Give me an example how I can protect myself from doing what everybody else is doing?"

BUFFETT   "Every time you hear the phrase 'Everybody else is doing it' it should raise a huge red flag. Why would somebody offer such a rationale for an act if there were a good reason available?"[389]

"If anyone gives this explanation, tell them to try using it with a reporter or a judge and see how far it gets them."[390]

LIBRARIAN "But some do it anyway."

BUFFETT   "We couldn't get Salomon to stop doing business with Mark Rich. It's hard to get large organizations to not do what successful competitors are doing."[391]

MUNGER   "People hate seeing their business shrink because others are taking volume away[392]...and if some dumb thing has to be done to keep it from shrinking, why, they rationalize doing the dumb thing."[393]

BUFFETT   "Unusual managerial discipline will be required, as it runs counter to normal institutional behavior to let the other fellow take away business — even at foolish prices."[394]

"We set no volume goals in our insurance business generally... as virtually any volume can be achieved if profitability standards are ignored."[395]

MUNGER   "At Berkshire Hathaway we try and let the place shrink. We never fire anybody, we tell them to go out and play golf. We sure as hell don't want to make any dumb loans. But that is very hard to do if you sit in a leadership position in society with people you helped recruit, you meet their wives and children and so forth."[396]

BUFFETT   "A lot of places have a mortgage department or a real estate department. They have a budget - and put money out based on using up their budget. And they have a whole bunch of people that don't have a job unless they do that. That's not the way we operate at Berkshire. We're willing, if the deals are right, to do many billions. If the deals aren't right, we don't have anybody whose job is dependent on keeping busy in a field like that. We don't waste a lot of time on things."[397]

SEEKER   "How do you avoid being seduced by the investment crowd?"

LIBRARIAN "Mark Twain said, 'Whenever you find that you are on the side of the majority, it is time to pause and reflect.'"

MUNGER   "You have to practice the right decision-making process and be skeptical of conventional wisdom. Keep your head when everyone else is losing theirs[398]...You don't have to go crazy because everybody else is."[399]

LIBRARIAN "And it is very hard to do well in investments if you only do what others do. You need to have your own and correct reasons to buy or sell something, not because of vivid and screaming headlines or what others say or do."

"I've heard Mr. Buffett say more than one time that emotional stability is more important the high IQ."

BUFFETT   "By far, the most important quality is not how much IQ you've got. IQ is not the scarce factor. You need a reasonable amount of intelligence, but the temperament is 90 % of it."[400]

SEEKER   "Temperament — explain more."

BUFFETT   "You do have to have an emotional stability, and sort of an inner peace about your decisions — because it is a game where you get subjected to minute-by-minute stimuli where people are offering opinions all the time. You have to be able to think for yourself."[401]

"Toughness is important. There is a lot of temptation to cave in or follow others but it is important to stick to your own convictions. I have seen so many smart people do dumb things because of what everyone else is doing."[402]

MUNGER   "Why are we different? We're working harder at trying to be rational. If you don't work hard at it, and just float along, you will fall victim to the folly of the crowd — and there will always be folly of the crowd."[403]

SEEKER   "If I didn't know before, I sure know now — I will be careful and don't automatically follow others."

BUFFETT   "We derive no comfort because important people, vocal people, or great numbers of people agree with us. Nor do we derive comfort if they don't. A public opinion poll is no substitute for thought[404]...We don't read other people's opinions. We want to think. We want to get the facts, and then think."[405]

"You will not be right simply because a large number of people momentarily agree with you. You will not be right simply because important people agree with you..."[406]

SEEKER   "So when will I be right?"

BUFFETT   "You will be right, over the course of many transactions, if your hypotheses are correct, your facts are correct, and your reasoning is correct."[407]

LIBRARIAN "And make sure that your facts really are facts of reality and not just assumptions. Montaigne said, 'If you ask people to account for 'facts', they usually spend more time finding reasons for them than finding out whether they are true. They ignore the whats and expatiate on the whys... They skip over the facts but carefully deduce inferences. They normally begin thus: 'How does this come about?' But does it do so? That is what they ought to be asking.'"[408]

"Are the 'facts' really facts—Is it really so? Is this really true? Did this really happen? Some things you think are so may not be so. As Will Rogers observed, 'The trouble with most people is not that they don't know much, but that they know so much that isn't true.'"[409]

BUFFETT "Once you have the facts, you have to think about what they mean."[410]

LIBRARIAN "Yes, and making sure you don't err in your interpretations of them or your conclusions."

BUFFETT "And then ask, 'What else do I need to know?'"[411]

LIBRARIAN "And don't miss the forest for the trees—It is not the amount of information that counts but the relevant information. More information isn't necessarily better information but it may falsely increase our confidence. Another problem is that many people absorb too much information without thinking. As Gertrude Stein said, 'Everybody gets so much information all day long that they lose their common sense.'[412]

"Also don't wait for information that doesn't affect your decision anyway—What is not worth knowing is not worth knowing."

SEEKER "Some other thing that can cause a lot of misery?"

OVERLY CARE ABOUT WHAT OTHER PEOPLE THINK ABOUT YOU

BUFFETT "The big question about how people behave is whether they've got an Inner Scorecard or an Outer Scorecard. It helps if you can be satisfied with an Inner Scorecard."[413]

SEEKER "Please explain—I assume we're not talking about golf."

BUFFETT "I always pose it this way. I say: 'Would you rather be the world's greatest lover, but have everyone think you're the world's worst lover? Or would you rather be the world's worst lover but having everyone think you're the world's greatest lover?' Now, that's an interesting question."[414]

LIBRARIAN "The 4th Earl of Chesterfield said, 'Vanity, or to call it by a gentler name, the desire of admiration and applause, is, perhaps, the most universal principle of human actions.'"

SEEKER "I see what you mean—not an easy one for me."

BUFFETT "You always want to consider your inner scorecard—how you feel about your own performance and success. You should worry more about how well you perform rather than how well the rest of the world perceives your performance. The success of Berkshire has always been more important than my own personal success in terms of financial returns."[415]

SEEKER "And your recommendation is?"

LIBRARIAN "The French writer Nicolas Chamfort said, 'Men whose only concern is other people's opinion of them are like actors who put on a poor performance to win the applause of people of poor taste; some of them would be capable of good acting in front of a good audience. A decent man plays his part to the best of his ability, regardless of the taste of the gallery.'"[416]

BUFFETT "Unlike most individuals, who hunger for the world's approval, Charlie judges himself entirely by an inner scorecard—and he is a tough grader."[417]

LIBRARIAN "Don't live a life based on the approval from others. Be authentic—be and act in accordance with who you are, what you like and are good at, or one day your mask may fall off. As Seneca said, 'No one can persevere long in a fictitious character; for nature will soon reassert itself.'"

SEEKER "I believe Christie's Poirot said something along that line, 'For in the long run, either through a lie, or through truth, people were bound to give themselves away.'"[418]

BUFFETT "In teaching your kids, I think the lesson they're learning at a very, very early age is what their parents put the emphasis on. If all the emphasis is on what the world's going to think about you, forgetting about how you really behave, you'll wind up with an Outer Scorecard. Now my dad: He was a hundred percent Inner Scorecard guy."

"He was really a maverick. But he wasn't a maverick for the sake of being a maverick. He just didn't care what other people thought."[419]

LET OTHER PEOPLE SET YOUR AGENDA IN LIFE

BUFFETT "The difference between successful people and very successful people is that very successful people say 'no' to almost everything."[420]

"You've got to keep control of your time. And you won't keep control of your time unless you can say no. You can't let other people set your agenda in life."[421]

LIBRARIAN "We all have 24 hours in the day. We can't save time, only spend it wisely or foolishly. And life is too short to waste so use your time wisely—prioritize and learn to say no."

MUNGER "Both Warren and I have an amazingly open calendar and we're very reluctant to put new commitments in there—I like flexibility and it has worked for me."[422]

LIBRARIAN "Also remember that saying yes to what looks like a small favor may sometimes lead to bad effects. Take for example, Mr. Buffett's request to his managers. What do you write to them?"

BUFFETT   "Please turn down all proposals for me to speak, make contributions, intercede with the Gates Foundation, etc. Sometimes these requests for you to act as intermediary will be accompanied by 'It can't hurt to ask.' It will be easier for both of us if you just say 'no.' As an added favor, don't suggest that they instead write or call me. Multiply 80 or so businesses by the periodic 'I think he'll be interested in this one' and you can understand why it is better to say no firmly and immediately."[423]

SEEKER   "I get it—the danger of setting a precedent—I have to think through the consequences of saying yes—what else the 'yes' may mean."
   "I really must say I like your style. More nutty things, please."

LIVE ABOVE YOUR MEANS

MUNGER   "There once was a man who became the most famous composer in the world. But he was utterly miserable most of the time. And one of the reasons was that he always overspent his income. That was Mozart. If Mozart couldn't get by with this kind of asinine conduct, I don't think you should try it."[424]

SEEKER   "Mozart—I believe it was Victor Borge who said, 'Ah Mozart! He was happily married, but his wife wasn't.'"

BUFFETT   "Charlie and I have always been big fans of living within your income. And if you do that, you'll have a whole lot more income later on."[425]

MUNGER   "If you want to get rich, or make some serious money, you've got to underspend your income. And you've got to intelligently invest the money you haven't spent."[426]

BUFFETT   "There's nothing like the savings you accumulate before you start raising a family and the bills start coming in. Plus, the money will work for you for a longer period of time. You have to save. It's the only way you're going to acquire wealth unless you hit the lottery."[427]

LIBRARIAN   "And make sure you always have some ready reserve cash. I remember what Warren's grandfather Ernest once wrote in a letter to his youngest son, Fred: 'I feel that everyone should have a reserve…There has never been a Buffett who ever left a large estate, but there has never been one that did not leave something. They never spent all they made, but always saved part of what they made, and it has all worked out pretty well.'"[428]

SEEKER   "But it seems young people today are not taught the importance of saving money—only how to spend it. Just like what I have always done."

MUNGER   "I failed in this with some of my relatives. If you don't know how to save, I don't know how to help you."[429]

   "I admire the ability to suffer now in the hopes of making something better. I'm skeptical of the approach that never finds it necessary to suffer now to make it better. There's a lot to be said to seeking ways to suffer now to make things better. That's the way it is in investing — sacrifice now in the hopes of something better.[430]

BUFFETT   "Habits really make an incredible difference, in terms of where you end up in life...the importance of encouraging good habits in your children's lives, particularly about money[431]...such as learning not to spend more than you have, and saving for the unexpected, and not borrowing money unless you have a plan to pay it back[432]... is very important to encourage early in life."[433]

SEEKER   "What can the schools do?"

BUFFETT   "Anything you can do very early through the school system will have my vote."[434]

MUNGER   "I'm not sure the schools are at fault. I place most of the fault with the parents."[435]

BUFFETT   "Not everyone gets the right parents. How would you fix them?"[436]

MUNGER   "It is very hard to fix people who had the wrong parents...I don't think I'm good at that."[437]

SEEKER   "This is such great advice. Have it coming and I rub my own nose in it."

MUNGER   "I know I'll perform better in life if I'm constantly rubbing my own nose in my own previous mistakes. That is a wonderful trick, I cannot recommend it enough....And the nice thing about it is that...there is no shortage of opportunities to exercise this wonderful talent."[438]

LIBRARIAN   "Another thing, in most cases don't lend money to friends."

SEEKER   "Why?"

LIBRARIAN   "An old saying tells it all — 'Lend your money and lose your friend.' The ancient Roman playwright Plautus said, 'If you lend a person any money, it becomes lost for any purpose as one's own. When you ask for it back again, you may find a friend made an enemy by your kindness. If you begin to press still further...either you must part with that which you have entrusted, or else you must lose that friend.'"

MUNGER   "If you'd like to see how badly people are capable of behaving, simply loan them money when they're in a desperate situation. People stretched out to the edge tend not to behave very well."[439]

SEEKER   "What has money meant to you guys?"

BUFFETT   "I knew I wanted to make a lot of money. But that's because I knew I wanted to be independent[440]...Then I could do what I wanted to do with my life. And the biggest thing I wanted to do was work for myself. I didn't want other people directing me[441]...I was interested in being in a position to control the decision making process[442]...The idea of doing what

I wanted to do every day was important to me[443]…The money itself is all going to charity."[444]

MUNGER   "I wanted independence[445]… I liked being able to say what I thought instead of what was expected of me."[446]

SEEKER   "This is great stuff—more misery, please."

GO HEAVILY INTO DEBT

LIBRARIAN   "'Debt and Misery live on the same road,' says a Russian proverb."

BUFFETT   "The ability to borrow enormous amounts of money combined with the chance to get either very rich or very poor very quickly has historically been a recipe for trouble at some point."[447]

SEEKER   "But if I can get rich faster by borrowing?"

BUFFETT   "Unquestionably, some people have become very rich through the use of borrowed money. However, that's also been a way to get very poor. When leverage works, it magnifies your gains. Your spouse thinks you're clever, and your neighbors get envious. But leverage is addictive. Once having profited from its wonders, very few people retreat to more conservative practices."[448]

"Borrowed money can magnify your mistakes, and it may magnify them to the point where they wipe you out[449]…Leverage is what causes people trouble so don't put yourself in a position where somebody can pull the rug out from under you."[450]

LIBRARIAN   "Even smart people go broke that way."

MUNGER   "Smart men go broke three ways: liquor, ladies and leverage"[451]

BUFFETT   "Whenever a bright and rich person goes broke, it's usually because of leverage."[452]

"And as we all learned in third grade—and some relearned in 2008—any series of positive numbers, however impressive the numbers may be, evaporates when multiplied by a single zero. History tells us that leverage all too often produces zeroes, even when it is employed by very smart people[453]…No matter how many winners you've got, if you either leverage too much or do anything that gives you the chance of having a zero in there, it'll all turn to pumpkins and mice."[454]

SEEKER   "I know the feeling."

BUFFETT   "One of the things you will find, which is interesting and people don't think of it enough, with most businesses and with most individuals, life tends to snap you at your weakest link. So it isn't the strongest link you're looking for among the individuals in the room. It isn't even the average strength of the chain. It's the weakest link that causes the problem."[455]

"You can have somebody whose aggregate performance is terrific, but if they have a weakness, maybe it's with alcohol, maybe it's susceptibility to taking a little easy money, it's the weak link that snaps you. And frequently, in the financial markets, the weak link is borrowed money."[456]

LIBRARIAN "And you even sold some financial stocks when you noticed the danger flag of heavy leverage."

BUFFETT "They were trying to and proclaiming that they could increase earnings per share in some low double digit range or something of the sort. And any time a large financial institution starts promising regular earnings increases you're going to have trouble."[457]

MUNGER "Warren and I get nervous with vast amounts of leverage unless we're 100% confident that risk-taking won't creep into the culture."

"It reminds me of a guy running a company who fired his top producer. The guy asked him, 'Why are you firing me? I'm your top producer.' To which he responded, 'You make me nervous. I'm a rich old man. Why should I be nervous?"[458]

BUFFETT "We feel that there is so much about a financial institution that you don't know just by looking at the figures that if anything bothers us a little bit, we're never sure whether it's an iceberg situation or not."[459]

MUNGER "Where you have complexity, by nature you can have fraud and mistakes. You'll have more of that than in a company that shovels sand from a river and sells it. This will always be true of financial companies, including ones run by governments. If you want accurate numbers from financial companies, you're in the wrong world."[460]

"We're quite sensitive to financial risks…We're exceptionally goosey of leveraged financial institutions. If they start talking about how good risk management is, it makes us nervous. We fret way earlier than other people. We've left a lot of money on the table through early fretting. It's the way we are."[461]

LIBRARIAN "You even sat down and tried to talk sense with one of the CEO's of a financial institution."

MUNGER "We told the CEO he needed to make sound loans on sound property to sound people, to only do loans on home mortgages, and to not talk to any Wall Street bankers. The guy had a Ph.D. in economics. All they had to do was to behave the way an engineer would behave."[462]

SEEKER "But take a non-financial business then—doesn't huge debt force a manager to be more efficient?"

BUFFETT "Huge debt, we were told, would cause operating managers to focus their efforts as never before, much as a dagger mounted on the steering wheel of a car could be expected to make its driver proceed with intensified care. We'll acknowledge that such an attention-getter would produce a very alert driver. But another certain consequence would be a deadly — and unnecessary — accident if the car hit even the tiniest pothole or sliver of ice. The roads of business are riddled with potholes; a plan that requires dodging them all is a plan for disaster."[463]

SEEKER   "What about Berkshire and leverage?"

MUNGER   "One of the very interesting things about Berkshire Hathaway is how chicken it is, how cautious, how low is its leverage."[464]

BUFFETT   "We basically never borrow money[465]...We only use borrowed money in our utility business."[466]

SEEKER   "I always believed you financial guys wanted to maximize your return?"

BUFFETT   "Good business or investment decisions will eventually produce quite satisfactory economic results, with no aid from leverage. Therefore, it seems to us to be both foolish and improper to risk what is important (including, necessarily, the welfare of innocent bystanders such as policyholders and employees) for some extra returns that are relatively unimportant."[467]

"Why be exposed to ruin and disgrace and embarrassment for some extra return that's not meaningful."[468]

MUNGER   "It's really crazy if you're very comfortable and secure to leverage. The incremental value of getting a little extra return is not that great...I have a friend who says, 'I've been to 'go'. And I never want to go back there.'"[469]

BUFFETT   "However, we are not phobic about borrowing...We are willing to borrow an amount that we believe — on a worst-case basis — will pose no threat to Berkshire's well-being."[470]

SEEKER   "Privately?"

BUFFETT   "I never borrowed money even when I had $10,000 basically, what difference did it make? I was having fun as I went along. It didn't matter whether I had $10,000 or $100,000 or $1,000,000 unless I had a medical emergency come along."[471]

"I've never borrowed money of any significant amount because I just didn't want to go back to go."[472]

SEEKER   "On to the next misery."

GO DOWN AND STAY DOWN WHEN BAD THINGS HAPPEN

MUNGER   "[A] prescription for misery is to go down and stay down when you get your first, second, or third severe reverse in the battle of life. Because there is so much adversity out there, even for the lucky and wise, this will guarantee that, in due course, you will be permanently mired in misery."[473]

SEEKER   "But it is so hard not to."

MUNGER   "It's…necessary to accommodate a lot of failure, and because no matter how able you are, you're going to have headwinds and troubles… If a person just keeps going on the theory that life is full of vicissitudes and just does the right thinking and follows the right values it should work out well in the end. So I would say, don't be discouraged by a few reverses."[474]

SEEKER   "Easier said than done."

LIBRARIAN "You can't sit around and dwell on bad things, regret the past or feel like a victim."

SEEKER   "I can't just discard my feelings."

MUNGER   "It's natural to grieve when life is tough, but one thing that is asinine is self-pity."[475]

"I think the attitude of Epictetus helps guide one to the right reaction. He thought that every mischance in life, however bad, created an opportunity to behave well. He believed every mischance provided an opportunity to learn something useful. And one's duty was not to become immersed in self-pity, but to utilize each terrible blow in a constructive fashion."[476]

LIBRARIAN "Also try to keep things in perspective and accept that some circumstances cannot be changed. See life's obstacles as temporary setbacks, not disasters."

MUNGER   "I think most lives work best when you simply react intelligently to the opportunities and difficulties you encounter, and just take the results as they fall."[477]

SEEKER   "How can one cope with it better?"

MUNGER   "What works best for me in coping with all disappointment is what I call the Jewish method: humor."[478]

"The three things I have found helping in coping with its challenges are: (1) Have low expectations. (2) Have a sense of humor. (3) Surround yourself with the love of friends and family. Above all live with change and adapt to it[479]…Human beings are resilient. They adapt."[480]

SEEKER   "I'll try."

MUNGER   "I have found that life is easier to handle if you employ just one simple mental trick. Just assume something will be really tough and you think, 'Can I bear it if that happens?' If you reach the conclusion yes, you just smile and go on."[481]

LIBRARIAN "As Descartes wrote to Princess Elisabeth of Germany, 'In truth, the most important thing for curing illnesses and maintaining health is good humor and joy.'"[482]

SEEKER   "How do you handle or prepare for adversity and shocks in your business affairs?"

MUNGER "We try to run our affairs so that no matter what happens, we'll never have to 'go back to go.'"[483]

"In my lifetime, I've seen interest rates range from 1% to 20%. We try to operate so that really extreme interest rates in either direction wouldn't be too bad for us."[484]

BUFFETT "We really want to run Berkshire so that if the world isn't working tomorrow the way it's working today—and is working in a way that nobody expected—we won't have a problem. We do not want to be dependent on anybody or anything else."[485]

SEEKER "Give me some examples."

BUFFETT "We concentrate on conservatively financed businesses with strong competitive strengths, run by able and honest people. If we buy into these companies at sensible prices, losses should be rare."[486]

MUNGER "We stick to a few simple pieces of ethos and particularly the engineering ethos—like having a margin of safety in the whole system[487] … In engineering, people have a big margin of safety.[488]… I think our operation is safer, because we think like engineers. We want these margins of reliability."[489]

BUFFETT "We think about worst cases all the time and add on a margin of safety…always leaving some extra room for things."[490]

MUNGER "Everybody understands that if you're building a bridge, you don't want a bridge that will handle exactly the maximum load and no more. You want a bridge that will handle a lot more than the maximum load. And that margin of safety is just enormously important in bridge-building."[491]

LIBRARIAN "For example, when the engineer John Roebling designed the Brooklyn Bridge people asked him if the bridge couldn't collapse like so many others. He replied, 'No, because I designed it six times as strong as it needs to be, to prevent that from happening.'"[492]

MUNGER "I have a rule in life, if there is a big whirlpool you don't want to miss it with 20 feet—you round it with 500 feet."[493]

BUFFETT "We have all kinds of extra levels of safety that we maintain at Berkshire[494]…We build in layers of safety others may think is foolish."[495]

LIBRARIAN "As the saying goes, 'The mouse that has but one hole is quickly taken.'"

MUNGER "Systems need duplicative safety features—backup system one, backup system two, and so on."[496]

BUFFETT "We will never become dependent on the kindness of strangers[497]… We never want to get dependent on banks or other people's money."[498]

MUNGER "We are ridiculously conservative by the standards of Wall Street. The reserves have reserves. The leverage is tiny. We don't have to renew our credit every Monday morning in order to keep going. Berkshire tries to behave in such a way that nobody would ever deny it credit. And then we have a backup system so that if they ever did, we still won't need it."[499]

BUFFETT   "Charlie and I believe in operating with many redundant layers of liquidity, and we avoid any sort of obligation that could drain our cash in a material way. That reduces our returns in 99 years out of 100. But we will survive in the 100th while many others fail. And we will sleep well in all 100."[500]

"Cash or available credit is a lot like oxygen. You don't notice it 99.9% of the time, but when it is absent, it is the only thing you notice. We don't want to be in that position[501]…American business provided a case study of that in 2008. In September of that year, many long-prosperous companies suddenly wondered whether their checks would bounce in the days ahead. Overnight, their financial oxygen disappeared."[502]

SEEKER   "But you have plenty of oxygen."

BUFFETT   "Markets can behave in extraordinary ways, and we have no interest in exposing Berkshire to some out-of-the-blue event in the financial world that might require our posting mountains of cash on a moment's notice."[503]

"Financial staying power requires a company to maintain three strengths under all circumstances: (1) a large and reliable stream of earnings; (2) massive liquid assets and (3) no significant near-term cash requirements. Here's how we will always stand on the three essentials. First, our earnings stream is huge and comes from a vast array of businesses. Our shareholders now own many large companies that have durable competitive advantages, and we will acquire more of those in the future. Our diversification assures Berkshire's continued profitability, even if a catastrophe causes insurance losses that far exceed any previously experienced."[504]

LIBRARIAN   "And not only does financial strength help you sleep better, it also gives you opportunities—especially in times of turmoil or when others are scared."

MUNGER   "Have maximum financial flexibility to face both hazards and opportunities."[505]

BUFFETT   "The most attractive opportunities may present themselves at a time when credit is extremely expensive—or even unavailable. At such a time we want to have plenty of financial firepower[506]…Our basic principle is that if you want to shoot rare, fast-moving elephants, you should always carry a loaded gun."[507]

"But we also know we've got the managers that can deliver on the properties once we own them. And that's a huge, huge advantage."[508]

Seeker "By the way, how do you invest your available cash?"

Buffett "We keep our cash largely in U.S. Treasury bills and avoid other short-term securities yielding a few more basis points...We agree with investment writer Ray DeVoe's observation, 'More money has been lost reaching for yield than at the point of a gun.'"[509]

Librarian "As Oscar Wilde said, 'When the gods wish to punish us they answer our prayers.'"

Seeker "I see—you seem very conservative."

Munger "Our culture of conservatism runs pretty deep...We are more disaster-resistant than most other places[510]...Everything must withstand great stresses."[511]

Librarian "Even your accounting is conservative."

Munger "We're so horrified by aggressive accounting [that is rampant in Corporate America] that we reach for ways to be conservative. It helps our business decisions and protects Berkshire."[512]

Seeker "But can't you be too conservative?"

Munger "The risk from having some over-conservatism is just about zero."[513]

Seeker "Regarding out-of-the-blue events—I assume most people don't want to think about worst cases?"

Buffett "People don't want to think about it until it happens, but it is best thought about before it happens[514]...We think about worst cases all the time."[515]

Seeker "Does stress-testing for worst cases help?"

Librarian "It depends on your assumptions. If you rely on worst-case scenarios from the past, you assume that what has happened in the past will be the worst that you can expect to happen in the future."

"So how can you stress-test for worst cases given that we can't include events that haven't happened yet and may be worse than past events or worse event than has happened but isn't in our sample space?"

Buffett "Everything that can happen will happen...it's Berkshire's job to be absolutely prepared for the very worst."[516]

Munger "We don't think because it's never happened that it won't...We just try to be conservative."[517]

Librarian "A few years before John Edward Smith became the captain of the Titanic—on the maiden voyage of the Adriatic ship—he said, 'I cannot imagine any condition which would cause a ship to founder. I cannot conceive of any vital disaster happening to this vessel. Modern shipbuilding has gone beyond that.'"[518]

MUNGER "We naturally have minds that think about tidal waves in California where they've never had one in modern California civilization. Can you image what a 60-foot tidal wave would do in California? There's nothing physically impossible in having a 60-foot tidal wave in an earthquake zone, which California is in."[519]

LIBRARIAN "As Shakespeare said, 'There are more things in heaven and earth, Horatio, than are dreamt of.'"

BUFFETT "Though practically all days are relatively uneventful, tomorrow is always uncertain. (I felt no special apprehension on December 6, 1941 or September 10, 2001.) And if you can't predict what tomorrow will bring, you must be prepared for whatever it does.[520]

"People tend to underestimate low probability events when they haven't happened recently, and overestimate them when they have[521]…We think about low probabilities events all the time[522]…We think more about big events in the financial arena than the natural arena. Financial markets have vulnerabilities that we try to think of and build in ways to protect us against them—and even some capabilities where we might profit in a huge way."[523]

LIBRARIAN "To paraphrase something I picked up from Nassim Taleb. 'What most people seem to miss is that every worst past had to be a surprise, since it had no precedent and if the worst case in the past didn't have a predecessor so why should the future worst?'

"'If you go back through history and look at large crisis—the worst war, recession, financial event or any shock—they all exceeded the worst shock in the past—they were all surprises.'"[524]

SEEKER "I get it. If I for example use history's worst financial crash as an anchor for the worst possible future crash I may be in for a surprise since this worst-case event, when it happened, exceeded the worst historical crash at the time."

LIBRARIAN "Yes, Taleb calls this the Lucretius problem after the Latin philosopher who wrote that the fool believes that the tallest mountain in the world will be equal to the tallest one he has observed."[525]

SEEKER "You mentioned the Titanic—I believe it was Lord Grantham in the television drama *Downton Abbey* who said about the Titanic, 'Every mountain is unclimbable until someone climbs it; so every ship is unsinkable until it sinks.'"[526]

"But it is tough to imagine the future."

LIBRARIAN "That is why Berkshire, when they were looking for some investment managers, wanted some very special people."

BUFFETT "Over time, markets will do extraordinarily, even bizarre things. A single, big mistake could wipe out a long string of successes. We therefore need someone genetically programmed to recognize and avoid serious risks, including those never before encountered. Certain perils that lurk in investment strategies cannot be spotted by use of the models commonly employed today by financial institutions."[527]

MUNGER "I do think that over time, perfectly strange things happen in the investment world. I mean, who would have predicted the World Trade Center collapse? Who of us would have predicted interest rates at their present levels?"[528]

LIBRARIAN "It can always get worse than you think. I love this story from Howard Marks: 'I tell my father's story of the gambler who lost regularly. One day he heard about a race with only one horse in it, so he bet the rent money. Halfway around the track, the horse jumped over the fence and ran away. Invariably things can get worse than people expect. Maybe 'worst-case' means 'the worst we've seen in the past.' But that doesn't mean things can't be worse in the future.'"[529]

SEEKER "Once more—it shows the need for safety margins or to stay away from certain things."

LIBRARIAN "And as history demonstrates, very extreme events can and will happen—even worse than seen to date."

BUFFETT "You never know what's going to happen in finance—you've got to be prepared for extraordinary things. And if you're going to last a hundred years, it means you have to last every day of the hundred years. It isn't good enough to last 99.9 percent. So we're prepared for that[530]… I believe the chance of any event causing Berkshire to experience financial problems is essentially zero. We will always be prepared for the thousand-year flood."[531]

"It pays to conduct your affairs so that no matter how foolish other people get, you're still around to play the game next day."[532]

LIBRARIAN "That advice also includes considering counterparty risk. That your business' customers and suppliers have the resilience and financial strength to survive 'stormy weather'—because if terrible problems happen to them, terrible things may happen to you or what may kill them may kill your business."

BUFFETT "A single weak link can pose trouble for all."[533]

"The best thing you can do is count on your own resources. That's what we do at Berkshire."[534]

MUNGER "You may well say, 'Who wants to go through life anticipating trouble?' Well, I did, trained as I was. All my life I've gone through life anticipating trouble…It didn't make me unhappy to anticipate trouble all the time and be ready to perform adequately if trouble came. It didn't hurt me at all. In fact it helped me."[535]

LIBRARIAN "Confucius had the same experience, 'The superior man, when resting in safety, does not forget that danger may come. When in a state of security he does not forget the possibility of ruin. When all is orderly, he does not forget that disorder may come. Thus his person is not endangered, and his States and all their clans are preserved.'"

"And when trouble comes, don't feel like a victim of events."

WHEN IN TROUBLE FEEL SORRY FOR YOURSELF

MUNGER   "In general, it's totally non-productive to get the idea that the world is unfair."[536]

"Self-pity can get pretty close to paranoia. And paranoia is one of the very hardest things to reverse."[537]

SEEKER   "But if something happens that's ruining my life?"

MUNGER   "One idea is that whenever you think something or some person is ruining your life, it's you."[538]

LIBRARIAN "It only makes you bitter, takes energy and make others to like us less."

MUNGER   "I had a friend who carried a thick stack of linen-based cards. And when somebody would make a comment that reflected self-pity, he would slowly and portentously pull out his huge stack of cards, take the top one and hand it to the person."

"The card said, 'Your story has touched my heart. Never have I heard of anyone with as many misfortunes as you.'"[539]

SEEKER   "What works?"

MUNGER   "I…think that when something bad happens, it's always partly your own fault[540]…Feeling like a victim is a perfectly disastrous way to go through life. If you just take the attitude that however bad it is in any way, it's always your fault and you just fix it as best you can—the so-called 'iron prescription'—I think that really works. I love spreading around corny stuff like that. Just because it's corny doesn't mean it isn't true. In fact, Warren and I often say, 'If it trite, it's right.'"[541]

SEEKER   "I love it!"

MUNGER   "I don't like any feeling of being victimized. I think that is a counterproductive way to think. And I am not a victim. I am a survivor."[542]

SEEKER   "Anything more?"

MUNGER   "I think it's usually a mistake to think only about your probable misfortunes. You should also think about what's good about your situation."[543]

BUFFETT   "There is no reason to look at the minuses in life. It would be crazy. We count our blessings."[544]

MUNGER   "I wouldn't have done a lot in my life different. I think I've been a very fortunate man and I don't think I should be complaining about how my life has worked out."[545]

SEEKER   "Ok, on to the next misery."

GET EVEN AND TAKE REVENGE EVEN IF YOU HURT YOURSELF

MUNGER   "Resentment…I cannot recommend it highly enough to you if you desire misery."[546]

SEEKER   "But shouldn't I get back at people who hurt me?"

LIBRARIAN "Remember the proverb, 'Before setting off on revenge, you first dig two graves.'"

MUNGER   "It's reasonable to clobber someone to prevent them from doing something wrong again or to set an example. But to hurt someone else for revenge is just dumb."[547]

LIBRARIAN "This is how conflicts can escalate into unending anger, destruction, and violence."

MUNGER   "Disraeli, as he rose to become one of the greatest Prime Ministers, learned to give up vengeance as a motivation for action, but he did retain some outlet for resentment by putting the names of people who wronged him on pieces of paper in a drawer."

"Then, from time to time, he reviewed these names and took pleasure in noting the way the world had taken his enemies down without his assistance."[548]

BUFFETT   "Forty years ago, Tom [Capital Cities/ABC former CEO Tom Murphy] gave me one of the best pieces of advice I've ever received. He said, 'Warren, you can always tell someone to go to hell tomorrow'…You haven't missed the opportunity. Just forget about if for a day. If you feel the same way tomorrow, tell them then—but don't spout off in a moment of anger."[549]

LIBRARIAN "As Groucho Marx is reported to have said, 'If you speak when angry, you'll make the best speech you'll ever regret.'"[550]

SEEKER   "Not a good idea, then to get angry."

BUFFETT   "I do think it's a mistake to get angry with people that disagree with you… it does not help when you demonize or get too violent with the people you're talking to."[551]

MUNGER   "I would argue that you don't want to make important decisions in anger. You want to display as much ruthlessness as your duty requires, and you do not want to add one single iota because you're angry."[552]

SEEKER   "More sources of misery?"

BE ENVIOUS

MUNGER   "Envy, of course, joins chemicals in winning some sort of quantity prize for causing misery[553]…I think envy is one of the major problems of the human condition, and that's why it figured so prominently in the laws of Moses. Remember, he said you couldn't even covet your neighbor's donkey."[554]

"Generally speaking, envy, resentment, revenge and self-pity are disastrous modes of thoughts[555]...Resentment is crazy. Revenge is crazy. Envy is crazy. If you get those things out of your life early, life works a lot better."[556]

LIBRARIAN "Envy and jealousy has caused many ruined friendships, marriages, sibling relationships and coworker relations."

BUFFETT "The real way the rich are different is that they can be so much meaner if they want to be. If you get mad at your brother in-law and you are poor you just don't go to Thanksgiving dinner, if you get mad and you are rich you have lawyers that go to work at 7 in the morning to cause you trouble, you have private detectives, and all kinds of things."

"Many years ago a woman called me from a big publishing family, they are all rich in the family, and they were in a huge fight. She called me up and I had never met her and she said 'I'd like you to come down to this town, you understand newspaper properties and we would trust you to work out a solution to our families problems with regards to this very valuable property'. I said to her I just have one question: do you want to win or do you just want your brother to lose? She paused for a long time and said don't bother coming. I mean she wanted pain for him. If you are thinking about how to cause pain for somebody else rather than creating a situation that benefits yourself you are going to get a terrible result over time."[557]

MUNGER "I've heard Warren say a half a dozen times, 'It's not greed that drives the world, but envy.'"[558]

BUFFETT "Our experience is that envy is what really drives people. You can give someone a $2 million bonus and they're happy until they see the next guy got $2.1 million and then they're miserable."[559]

LIBRARIAN "One reason is people's obsession with relative status."

MUNGER "Yale can't stand Harvard making more money, and vice versa."[560]

LIBRARIAN "Some people even choose to be worse off as long as those we envy have even less."

"There is an old Russian story where a farmer finds a magic lamp. He rubs it, and a genie appears who promises to grant him one wish. The farmer thinks for a moment then says: 'My neighbor has a cow. I don't have a cow. I wish my neighbor's cow dead.'"

SEEKER "Guilty! I remember a guy at work that did roughly the same job as me—still, he got paid $10,000 more. I would rather have taken less salary, but only if the other guy had made less than I got."

"Now, when I am thinking about it—it sounds crazy—maybe I'm wising up."

BUFFETT   "Envy is the silliest [of all the sins], because you feel worse and the other people feel fine; maybe they feel better. Rule out envy as part of your repertoire."[561]

MUNGER   "Generally speaking, I think envy is the most destructive damn thing. I try and drive it out of my own system. I'm very good at it, too. I just wish my fellow citizens were less consumed by it, particularly the politicians."[562]

SEEKER   "But if I also want to be on top?"

MUNGER   "If you're comfortably rich and someone else is getting richer faster than you by…so what?! Someone will always be getting richer faster than you. This is not a tragedy[563]…someone else is always going to be doing better at any human activity you can name."[564]

SEEKER   "If by any remote chance someone should be envious of me, what then?"

MUNGER   "The best way to avoid envy, recognized by Aristotle, is to plainly deserve the success we get."[565]

SEEKER   "This is getting better and better. More dumb things I should avoid?"

BE UNRELIABLE AND UNETHICAL

MUNGER   "One certain path to failure is being unreliable[566]…Do not faithfully do what you have engaged to do. If you will only master this one habit you will more than counterbalance the combined effect of all your virtues, howsoever great."[567]

SEEKER   "I have sinned here."

LIBRARIAN   "We all have chapters we rather would have been unpublished."

BUFFETT   "None of us are perfect, you know? I always say that, 'Every saint has a past, every sinner has a future.'"[568]

MUNGER   "Reliability is essential for progress in life[569]…If you become very reliable and stay that way, it will be very hard to fail in doing anything you want."[570]

"Our model is a seamless web of trust that's deserved on both sides[571]…When you get a seamless web of deserved trust, you get enormous efficiencies…Who…would…want to be in a family without a seamless web of deserved trust?"[572]

SEEKER   "I wouldn't."

MUNGER   "It's not rocket science; it's elementary. Why more people don't do it, I don't know. Perhaps because it's so elementary."[573]

LIBRARIAN "A common reason."

MUNGER "Conduct yourself in a way that allows other people to trust you. It helps even more if other people are right in trusting you."[574]

"I think track records are very important. If you start early trying to have a perfect one in a some simple thing like honesty, you're well on your way to success in this world."[575]

BUFFETT "Gianni Agnelli [former chairman of Fiat] once time told me, 'When you get older, you'll have the reputation you deserve.' You can fool people some of the time but not forever. I believe the same is true for companies."[576]

LIBRARIAN "Being dishonest and unethical is a sure-proof way to sorrow."

MUNGER "Peter Kaufman says something very smart: 'If all these crooks and promoters knew how much money there was in being honest, there'd be more people who did it.'"[577]

BUFFETT "It takes twenty years to build a reputation and five minutes to ruin it. If you think about that, you'll do things differently."[578]

"Never trade reputation for money."[579]

LIBRARIAN "Don't you even send out a memo to your managers on this?"

BUFFETT "Every two years, I write them a very simple letter. It's a page and a half. I don't believe in 200page manuals because you put out a 200page manual, everybody's looking for loopholes basically."[580]

SEEKER "What do you tell them?"

BUFFETT "Berkshire can afford to lose money, even lots of money; it can't afford to lose reputation, even a shred of reputation…And in the long run we will have whatever reputation we deserve."[581]

MUNGER "Getting a good reputation in life can have remarkably favorable outcomes[582]…You just have to get the best reputation you can in the years and time you have available. It may work out well and it may work out poorly but it's a good use of time. I've seen so many times where the opportunity people got was because of reputation, so I think hardly anything is more important than behaving well as you go through life."[583]

BUFFETT "And a great reputation, as I say, is like virginity, it can be preserved, but it can't be restored. At least that's what my dad told me."[584]

MUNGER "We actually have tried to behave better as we've grown more prosperous. I recommend you follow those old-fashioned principles. You'd be crazy if you didn't."[585]

SEEKER "I was crazy but fortunately you are on the way to cure some of my deficiencies."

MUNGER "We learned good lessons when we were young. We've been more selective. I don't think we've ever regretted not making a lot of easy money when we decided it was beneath us[586]…There should be a huge area between what you're willing to do and what you can do without significant risk of suffering criminal penalty or causing losses. We believe you shouldn't go anywhere near that line. You ought to have an internal compass."[587]

"We don't claim to have perfect morals, but at least we have a huge area of things that, while legal, are beneath us. We won't do them."[588]

LIBRARIAN "Some do it anyway."

MUNGER "This combination of envy and self-serving bias makes people to go to the edge[589]...There's enormous money and happiness, and better service to be gained, by just deciding, 'I'm going to do without that.' Warren used to say, when we were brokers at Salomon, 'I'm waiting for a list of the business that we have declined because it was morally beneath us even though it was legal.' People are just so competitive they just want to do every damn thing that can be done, profitably, whereas, we need something beyond that."[590]

"Foregoing money, because it's sort of tainted, or too close to tainted, or too close to gaming, is a very good thing."[591]

LIBRARIAN "Didn't the founder of Price Club, Sol Price do something like that?"

MUNGER "Sol Price used to say, success in business came from deciding which business you could intelligently do without. He had a list of business he didn't want. He didn't want business from people who wrote bad checks. He didn't want business of people who shoplifted. He didn't want business of people who clogged-up his parking lot without buying very much. He carefully invented a system where he kept those people out, and succeeded by deciding what he would be better off without and avoiding it. This is a very good way to think, and it's not all that common."[592]

SEEKER "So how do I know if something I do is ethical?"

BUFFETT "The simple test of good ethics, is how would you feel about any act, if a reasonably intelligent, but unfriendly reporter were to write it up and put it in tomorrow's paper for everyone to see. If it passes that test, it's okay, and if you have to think about it, it probably isn't the right thing to do."[593]

SEEKER "Since one of the jobs I've had was in advertising, it reminds me of what the genius David Ogilvy said, 'Never write an advertisement which you wouldn't want your own family to read. You wouldn't tell lies to your own wife. Don't tell them to mine.'"[594]

MUNGER "There's money in being trusted. It's such a simple idea. Yet, everybody rushes into every goddamn scummy activity that seems to work."[595]

"I'm proud to be associated with the value system at Berkshire Hathaway…I think you'll make more money in the end with good ethics than bad."[596]

SEEKER   "What is the best way to teach ethics?"

MUNGER   "I think the best single way to teach ethics is by example. And that means if you take in people who demonstrate in all their daily conduct an appropriate ethical framework, I think that has enormous influence on the people who watch it. Conversely, if your ethics slip, and if people are being rewarded for ethical slips, then I think your ethics cascade downward at a very, very rapid rate."[597]

LIBRARIAN   "Try to follow the Cadet Honor Code: 'A Cadet will not lie, cheat, or steal, or tolerate those who do.'"

MUNGER   "When I was an officer in the military, we had a rule called Conduct Unbecoming an Officer. It was not specific, but it said there were certain ways to behave as an example for others. I don't see why we shouldn't have this for our corporate executives."

"If you rise high in a corporation or elsewhere in life, you have a duty to be an exemplar — you have a duty to take less than you deserve, to set an example."[598]

LIBRARIAN   "If the rule is 'what you send out you get back' then you should be extra careful what signals you send out when you're in a position of power."

SEEKER   "This shows the importance of doing right as a parent."

MUNGER   "The best method for training your children is to be the proper example."[599]

LIBRARIAN   "You don't want to be what the crime fiction writer Catherine Aird once wrote about someone, 'If you can't be a good example, then you'll just have to be a horrible warning.'"[600]

BUFFETT   "The most important job you have is to be the teacher to your children. You are the big, great thing to them. You don't get a rewind button. You don't get to do it twice. You teach with what you do, not what you say."[601]

MUNGER   "Whatever values you want your children to have you better be demonstrating to them day after day after day."[602]

"The younger people are going to adopt to whatever the ethos is that suffuses the place[603]… if you see people you respect behaving in a certain way, especially under stress, [that has a real impact]."[604]

LIBRARIAN   "Children are also influenced a lot by their friends so make sure the right 'peer group' surrounds them."

MUNGER "Judith Rich Harris...demonstrated that peer pressure on the young is far more important, and parental nurture is much less important, than had been commonly recognized."[605]

"This makes it wise for parents to rely more on manipulating the quality of the peers than on exhortations to their own offspring."[606]

BUFFETT "If you take any large group, you will have some kind of bell-shaped curve where you will find a lot of people in the middle, who, under most conditions, will behave well, but when they are in really difficult situations, they won't. You will find people who are just outstanding on the right-hand side of the curve and those are the people who are my heroes, frankly. I don't think it has changed much over the years...I don't think the human animal changes too much. I think the only way humans change is if they get into a new culture and adopt the mores of that culture. I think it's easier to drop down, unfortunately, if you get into a kind of jungle-type culture, than to move up if you are in some monastic-type culture."[607]

"I learned that it pays to hang around with people better than you are, because you will float upward a little bit. And if you hang around with people that behave worse than you, pretty soon you'll start sliding down the pole. It just works that way."[608]

LIBRARIAN "As the ancient Greek dramatist Menander said, 'Bad company corrupts good character.'"

BE A JERK AND TREAT PEOPLE REALLY BADLY

BUFFETT "When you see some guy that should have everything going for him and everybody in town hates him, you want to make sure you don't have any of the qualities that make him hated."[609]

MUNGER "Warren and I know many businessmen who have not a friend on earth—and rightly so. Once you have friends and find friends, hang on to them."[610]

"You don't want to be like the motion picture executive who had so many people at his funeral, but they were there just to make sure he was dead."[611]

LIBRARIAN "Like Woody Allen says, 'What a world. It could be so wonderful if it wasn't for certain people.'"[612]

SEEKER "I assume a jerk is always a jerk—with or without money."

LIBRARIAN "As someone said, 'Even if you win the rat race, you're still a rat.' But remember the saying, 'It's nice to be important, but more important to be nice.'"

BUFFETT "Be a nice person...Look around at the people you like. If you like traits of other people, doesn't it follow that other people would like you if you have those same traits?"[613]

"One thing you learn in life and business...life circles back around...you're going to meet a lot of people that you think will be one-stop shops initially in your life but they aren't."[614]

LIBRARIAN "Schopenhauer said, 'It is a wise thing to be polite; consequently, it is a stupid thing to be rude.'"[615]

BUFFETT "You should always try to be a good person."[616]

MUNGER "At the end of the day—if you live long enough—most people get what they deserve.[617]...Ask the question: How can you best get what you want? The answer: Deserve what you want! How can it be any other way?"[618]

"You want to deliver to the world what you would buy if you were on the other end...the people who've had this ethos win in life, and they don't just win money and honors. They win the respect, the deserved trust of the people they deal with. And there is huge pleasure in life to be obtained from getting deserved trust."[619]

SEEKER "What is success to you?"

BUFFETT "I am so blessed. I get to do what I like to do with people that I love. That is happiness. I am happy day after day after day. How could I be any happier? Someone once said success is getting what you want and happiness is wanting what you get."[620]

"When you get to be my age you will be successful if the people who you hope to have love you, do love you. Charlie and I know people who have buildings named after them, receive great honors, etc. and nobody loves them—not even the people who give them honors."[621]

SEEKER "How do you get people to love you then?"

BUFFETT "The only way to be loved is to be lovable. You always get back more than you give away. If you don't give any you won't get any."[622]

"Some people never learn that. They're busy cheating people, cutting corners, lying to them, all kinds of things and they think they're a success because they have tens of millions of dollars later in life. I don't think they are a success[623]...Ultimately, money is not the ultimate measure of success, but rather, it is how many loved ones you have around you."[624]

LIBRARIAN "And start early to become the right person."

BUFFETT "Ben Graham...When he was twelve years old, he sat down and made a list of the qualities he admired in other people; and he made a list also of the qualities that he found unattractive in other people. He decided that it was just an act of will and then habit to develop those attractive qualities and to get rid of the unattractive qualities."

"Anybody can show up on time; they cannot claim credit for ideas that are not their own; they cannot cut corners; they can avoid envy. All of those things are doable and they make an enormous difference in how you function, not only in your job, but in society, subsequently."[625]

Seeker   "I'll try."

Buffett   "They are simply a matter of deciding what you are going to do and what kind of person you are going to make out of yourself, and then doing it[626]…You choose what kind of human being you're going to be, and then other people choose whether they'll associate with you or not."[627]

"I would do the same thing in terms of looking at businesses… I'd try and look for what I admire and emulate it. And I'd make sure that I tried very hard not to let thing that are distasteful creep into my own system."[628]

Librarian   "It helps to have the right heroes in life."

Buffett   "I think it's very important to have the right heroes…So I say, choose your heroes carefully, and then figure out what it is about them that you admire. Then you figure out how to do the same thing. It's not impossible."[629]

Seeker   "The importance of doing right as a parent again."

Buffett   "Of course, virtually everybody starts out with their initial models being their parents. So they are the ones that are going to have a huge effect on 'em. And if that parent turns out to be a great model, I think it's going to be a huge plus for the child. I think it beats a whole lot of other things in life to have the right models around."[630]

Munger   "The best legal experience I ever got was when I was very young. I asked my father why he did so much work for a big blowhard, an overreaching jerk, rather than for his best friend Grant McFayden. He said, 'That man you call a blowhard is a walking bonanza of legal troubles, whereas Grant McFayden, who fixes problems promptly and is nice, hardly generates any legal work at all.' My dad was teaching me a lesson and it worked."[631]

Seeker   "Did it change your behavior?"

Munger   "Considering its size, Berkshire has supported fewer lawyers than any company I can think of. We've gone through the world like Grant McFayden, the pioneering Omaha Ford dealer."[632]

"That's an example of teaching by inversion. Figure out what you don't want and you'll get to what you do want[633]…Warren had the same instincts I had. We haven't had our share of disappointed, angry people that ruin so many lives."[634]

Librarian   "I just thought about what Benjamin Franklin wrote in *Rules for Making Oneself a Disagreeable Companion*: 'Talk much of your-self, your education, your knowledge, your circumstances, your successes in business, your victories in disputes, your own wise sayings and observations on particular occasions, etc. etc. If when you are out of breath, one of the company should seize the opportunity of saying something; watch his words, and, if possible, find somewhat either in his sentiment or expression, immediately to contradict and raise a dispute upon. Rather than fail, criticise even his grammar.'"[635]

SEEKER   "Your inversion/slash thinking backwards trick again. It is amazing how much it clarifies what not to do."

"What are your views on choice of occupation?"

HAVE A JOB THAT MAKES YOU FEEL MISERABLE

LIBRARIAN "Do what you hate, for a company you hate, with people that you hate and who hate you back."

SEEKER   "Ok, I know what not to do then."

BUFFETT   "The big thing you want to do is you want to enjoy every day. So you want to have a job you love and you want to work with people that you like and admire and trust."[636]

"You want to ask the question, 'Where am I going to have most fun?'[637]…If it turns you on, then you'll do well at it."[638]

SEEKER   "Do you mean that I have a higher chance to succeed if I'm passionate about my job?"

BUFFETT   "Having passion for something is far from an automatic guarantee of success, but I think it helps. It's hard to imagine very many athletes succeeding without a passion for their sport, though obviously many who are equally passionate fall on their face (count me among those)."

"I tell the college students who visit Omaha to try to find the job that they'd take if they didn't need a job (easier said than done but still the right goal). They may not enjoy wild success but they will certainly enjoy life more than if they go to a job they find uninteresting. And, on balance, I believe they will enjoy more success."[639]

MUNGER   "You have to do something that you really like doing and that you are very interested in. In my whole life I've never been good at something I wasn't very interested in. It just doesn't work."[640]

"It's very hard to succeed until you take the first step in what you're strongly interested in. There's no substitute for strong interest."[641]

SEEKER   "I always had jobs that I didn't like very much."

BUFFETT   "If you are in a job that you are not enthusiastic about, find something else. You're not doing yourself any favor, and you're not doing your employer any favor and you're going to make a change anyway at some point."[642]

SEEKER   "How about looking for something that pays me well?"

BUFFETT   "Don't look for the money. Look for something you love, and if you're good, the money will come[643]…If you think you will be happier getting 2x instead of 1x, you are probably making a mistake. You will get in

73

trouble if you think making 10x or 20x will make you happier because then you will borrow money when you shouldn't or cut corners on things."[644]

"I know lots of people who are not rich in financial terms but they are still happy. I know plenty of unhappy rich people."[645]

MUNGER "I have three basic rules. Meeting all three is nearly impossible, but you should try anyway: (1) Don't sell anything you wouldn't buy yourself. (2) Don't work for anyone you don't respect and admire. (3) Work only with people you enjoy."[646]

BUFFETT "It just doesn't work if you don't admire or trust them. I do not hire people I would not want as friends or as neighbors. I work with people who make my life easier. You can't work with people who make your stomach grind."[647]

SEEKER "Like my former boss."

MUNGER "You particularly want to avoid working directly under somebody you don't admire and don't want to be like. It's dangerous."[648]

BUFFETT "You really want to be working for somebody you admire. If you're working for somebody who causes your stomach to turn, maybe you have to keep doing it to keep eating for a while but don't settle for it...If something goes wrong, if you find yourself working for the wrong employer and they're doing things you don't approve of or they're not treating you fairly, the world isn't over yet. You just go out and find somebody else."[649]

SEEKER "Anything else I should think about?"

BUFFETT "Make yourself a person that you would want to hire. We look for people with not necessary the highest IQs, but people who have a good work ethic, are loyal, honest and reliable."[650]

MUNGER "I first look for trust, regardless of talent. First you need trust and then good judgment[651]...Trustworthiness is more important than brains. We wouldn't hire anyone—no matter how able they were—if we didn't trust them."[652]

WORK WITH SOMETHING THAT GOES AGAINST YOUR NATURE AND TALENT

MUNGER "If you try and do something that is against the grain of your nature—even if you succeed at it—it is going to be a very painful life."[653]

LIBRARIAN "We are all prisoner of our talents."

SEEKER "How can I best find out what I have any talent for?"

BUFFETT "It is a question of being self-realistic...Being realistic in appraising your own talents and shortcomings, and some are a whole lot better at it than others...The best really know when they are playing the game that they're going to win."[654]

LIBRARIAN "Try to understand what you enjoy and then you should also try to combine what you enjoy with what you're good at. Ask, 'What am I good at and what do I like? What's working for me and what's not working? What comes easy for me?"

"Know your limitations—as Benjamin Franklin advised, 'If your head is wax, don't walk in the sun.'"

MUNGER "Well, I'm really better at determining my level of incompetency and then just avoiding that...I prefer to think that question through in reverse."[655]

SEEKER "Jacobi again."

BUFFETT "Learning what you don't want to do is just as important as learning what you do want to do."[656]

MUNGER "I don't think it's as difficult to figure out your competence as it may appear. If you're 5' 2", you don't have much future in the NBA. If you are 92 years old, you are not going to be the romantic lead in Hollywood. If you weigh 350 pounds, you shouldn't dance in the Bolshoi ballet. If you can hardly count cards at all, you shouldn't compete in blackjack."[657]

SEEKER "I guess professional basketball is out of the question."

MUNGER "You need to recognize where nature has been kind and play a game where nature has given you the greatest talent. Man is the prisoner of his talents. I'm afraid that's the hand we're given to play in life. If you're 5' 2", I don't think you want to play basketball?"[658]

BUFFETT "What I am is a realist...perhaps it would have been nice to be a major league baseball player, but that's where the realism comes in."[659]

MUNGER "You'll do better if you have passion for something in which you have aptitude. If Warren had gone into ballet, no one would have heard of him."[660]

LIBRARIAN "And set up a system and environment that plays to your strengths and minimizes your weaknesses."

SEEKER "Tell me something more useful."

BELIEVE YOU KNOW EVERYTHING ABOUT EVERYTHING

MUNGER "You've got to know what you know and what you don't know. What could possibly be more useful in life than that?"[661]

LIBRARIAN "Unfortunately, most of us don't know what we don't know. Instead we tend to overestimate how much we know and have opinions on things when in reality we don't know what we really are talking about. Like the wise Maimonides said, 'Every person thinks his mind...more clever and more learned that it is.'"

SEEKER "You mean I think I know something when I really don't?"

BUFFETT "In Darwin's words, 'Ignorance more frequently begets confidence than does knowledge.'"[662]

LIBRARIAN "Yes, we are often ignorant about our own ignorance — we don't know what we don't know. This means that we must first realize that we are ignorant on a subject or an issue before we can stop being ignorant, and instead say we don't know or try to get some genuine knowledge."

"Ignorance and high confidence is not a good combination. So knowing what you don't know is the hallmark of a wise person."

SEEKER "Hmm."

LIBRARIAN "And if you believe you are an expert on a subject or very intelligent the more over-confident you are about the depths of your knowledge."

MUNGER "You're a disaster if you don't know the edge of your competency. Warren frequently says, 'I'd rather deal with a guy with an IQ of 130 who thinks it's 125 than a guy with an IQ of 180 that thinks it's 200. That second guy will kill you."[663]

SEEKER "And the trick is?"

BUFFETT "The important thing in your circle of competence is not how big the circle is. It isn't the area of it. It's how well you define the perimeter. So you know when you are in it, and you know when you are outside of it."[664]

MUNGER "I do think that knowing the edge of your competency is important. If you think you know a lot more than you do, you will get in trouble."[665]

BUFFETT "If I have any advantage, it's probably that I know when I know what I'm doing, and I know when I don't know what I'm doing."[666]

MUNGER "Warren and I know the edge of our own competency better than other people do."[667]

SEEKER "But take opinions as an example. It is so hard to admit 'I don't know.' I always feel I have a need to have an opinion on every subject."

BUFFETT "You don't have to have an opinion on everything."[668]

"Charlie and I are competent to make judgments on certain things, and not on other things. We try to focus on what we can understand."[669]

LIBRARIAN "As Ludwig Wittgenstein said, 'Whereof one cannot speak, thereof one must be silent.'"[670]

"Also, listen and make sure you really understand a question or an issue before you answer or comment on it. You need to answer two questions: A) Do I truly have the competence needed and B) Do I truly understand the issue? Like the man behind Peter's Principle, Laurence Peter said, 'Some problems are so complex that you have to be highly intelligent and well informed just to be undecided about them.'"[671]

SEEKER "I have to think about that one."

MUNGER   "I try to get rid of people who always confidently answer questions about which they don't have any real knowledge. When you don't know and you don't have any special competence, don't be afraid to say so...Nobody expects you to know everything about everything."[672]

LIBRARIAN   "'You know everybody is ignorant, only on different subjects.'"

MUNGER   "A crotchet that says, 'This is too hard for me. I'm not going to try to understand it.' That's a very useful crotchet."[673]

LIBRARIAN   "Confucius had it right, 'Real knowledge is to know the extent of one's ignorance.'"

SEEKER   "Still, some very successful people have opinions of all kind of subjects?"

MUNGER   "My old Harvard Law classmate, Ed Rothschild, always called such a popping-off 'the shoe button complex,' named for the condition of a family- friend who spoke in oracular style on all subjects after becoming dominant in the shoe button business."[674]

"His father commuted daily with the same group of men...One of them had managed to corner the market in shoe buttons — a really small market, but he had it all. He pontificated on every subject, all subjects imaginable. Cornering the market on shoe buttons made him an expert on everything. Warren and I have always sensed it would be a big mistake to behave that way."[675]

BUFFETT   "For us to think that just because we made a lot of money, we're going to be better at giving advice on every subject—well, that's just crazy...I'm very suspect of the person who is very good at one business—it also could be a good athlete or a good entertainer—who starts thinking they should tell the world how to behave on everything."[676]

MUNGER   "I frequently tell the apocryphal story about Max Planck when he won the Nobel Prize and went around Germany giving the same standard lecture on the new quantum mechanics. The chauffeur gradually memorized the lecture and said, 'would you mind Professor Planck, because it's so boring to stay in our routine, if I gave the lecture in Munich and you just sat in front wearing my chauffeur's hat?' Planck said, 'why not.'"[677]

SEEKER   "Did the chauffeur do it?"

MUNGER   "The chauffeur got up and gave this long lecture on quantum mechanics. After which a physics professor stood up and asked a perfectly ghastly question. The speaker said, 'Well, I'm surprised in that in advanced city like Munich I get such an elementary question. I'm going to ask my chauffeur to reply.'"[678]

SEEKER   "Great story."

MUNGER   "Well…In this world I think we have two kinds of knowledge: One is Planck knowledge, that of the people who really know. They've paid the dues, they have the aptitude. Then we've got chauffeur knowledge. They have learned to prattle the talk. They may have a big head of hair. They often have fine timbre in their voices. They make a big impression. But in the end what they've got is chauffeur knowledge masquerading as real knowledge."[679]

LIBRARIAN   "They are what John Cleese calls an articulate incompetent, 'A person who speaks clearly and cogently and persuasively about something, without actually understanding anything about the reality that their words are intending to describe.'

   "He continues, 'Such a person is dangerous to an organization because they can sound very persuasive, despite the fact that they have absolutely no clue what they are talking about.'"[680]

SEEKER   "Like my investment advisor — so well-spoken and nice to talk to on all kinds of subjects but as I later found out, to quote Aesop, 'A splendid head, and yet no brain.'"

LIBRARIAN   "What was it someone said, 'A dog is not considered good because of his barking; a man is not considered clever because of his ability to talk.' So beware of the articulate incompetent."

   "As the former chairman of Random House, Robert Bernstein said, 'That's what frightens me about business schools…They train their students to sound wonderful. But it's necessary to find out if there's judgment behind their language.'"[681]

MUNGER   "You're going to have the problem in your life of getting as much responsibility as you can into the people with the Planck knowledge, and away from the people who have the chauffeur knowledge. And there are huge forces working against you."[682]

LIBRARIAN   "Another dangerous version to avoid is the twaddler — full of empty talk, rubbish and nonsense."

MUNGER   "Man, as a social animal who has the gift of language, is born to prattle and to pour out twaddle that does much damage when serious work is being attempted."[683]

SEEKER   "But you two for sure don't suffer from that. Back to the circle — have you gone outside?"

BUFFETT   "Charlie and I worry about ourselves getting outside of our circle of competence. And we've done it. It is very tempting. It's probably part of the human condition — in terms of hubris or something."[684]

LIBRARIAN   "Take for example acquisitions — many CEO's overestimate the returns they can produce, they get blind to difficulties or the risks involved, and they underestimate their opponents or competition."

BUFFETT "Everything looks rosy…when you first are looking at a deal. You don't see the downsides. You don't see the execution problems, you don't see the people who are going to leave."[685]

SEEKER "Why does it happen?"

BUFFETT "The heads of many companies are not skilled in capital allocation. Their inadequacy is not surprising. Most bosses rise to the top because they have excelled in an area such as marketing, production, engineering, administration or, sometimes, institutional politics. Once they become CEOs, they face new responsibilities. They now must make capital allocation decisions, a critical job that they may have never tackled and that is not easily mastered. To stretch the point, it's as if the final step for a highly- talented musician was not to perform at Carnegie Hall but, instead, to be named Chairman of the Federal Reserve."[686]

MUNGER "[The] guy who invented the Peter Principle is right: You know we all get promoted in hierarchies and, of course, half the time some guy gets one category too high and of course half the time you have someone who is utterly unqualified for this spot he is sitting in and yet he has the power. He's got a big ego and everything else."[687]

BUFFETT "They've never bought a business in their life. They don't know what it's all about. So they usually do one or two things. Either they set up an internal department, hire a bunch of guys and have them tell him something to do. Of course, the guys know if they don't tell him something to do, then there will be no jobs. So you can imagine what activity takes place then. Or they go out and hire investment bankers who get paid by the transaction."[688]

MUNGER "When you promote the General Sales Manager to CEO making unrelated business acquisitions, you naturally cause more trouble that you earlier did when you made a less substantive change by promoting the Sales Manager of some territory to General Sales Manager."[689]

SEEKER "But why do some managers think they can do…"

MUNGER "An extreme optimism based on an inflated self-appraisal is one[690]…They thought they were so smart they could do something difficult[691]…In self-appraisals of prospects and talents, it is the norm…for people to be ridiculously over-optimistic."[692]

LIBRARIAN "But many CEO's believe they are the exception—that they are different and can pull it off. As the saying goes, 'The downfall of a magician is the belief in his own magic.'"

MUNGER "I think that many CEOs get carried away into folly. They haven't studied the past models of disaster enough and they're not risk-averse enough."[693]

LIBRARIAN "And CEO's like to do deals."

BUFFETT "CEOs aren't shrinking violets. They like to make deals, and they have big goals. Investment bankers will be calling on them, there are all these forces that push toward deals, and if you push toward deals you get a lot of dumb deals."[694]

MUNGER "It's in the nature of successful corporations to be talked into dumb deals."[695]

BUFFETT "They rely on Wall Street, which of course recommends doing deals because they get paid X if the deal doesn't go through and 20X is the deal does."[696]

LIBRARIAN "And when a CEO want to make a deal, he make sure the deal looks great on paper."

BUFFETT "While deals often fail in practice, they never fail in projections [697]...If a CEO is enthused about a particularly foolish acquisition, both his internal staff and his outside advisors will come up with whatever projections are needed to justify his stance. Only in fairy tales are emperors told that they are naked."[698]

SEEKER "But you are different."

MUNGER "Berkshire, by design...never had the equivalent of a 'department of acquisitions' under pressure to buy. And it never relied on advice from 'helpers' sure to be prejudiced in favor of transactions."[699]

BUFFETT "We've tried very hard to not be eager to do deals, just to be eager to do deals that make sense."[700]

MUNGER "Two-thirds of acquisitions don't work. Ours work because we don't try to do acquisitions — we wait for no-brainers."[701]

SEEKER "How do you evaluate a possible acquisition?"

MUNGER "We're light on financial yardsticks; we apply lots of subjective criteria: Can we trust management? Can it harm our reputation? What can go wrong? Do we understand the business? Does it require capital infusions to keep it going? What is the expected cash flow?"[702]

SEEKER "I love this stuff, more please."

MUNGER "All I can say is we have a good batting average, and that is probably because we're probably a little more competent than we think we are. There's some modesty in what we're doing."[703]

SEEKER "Any advice on friends, business associates or people in general? By the way what is real friendship?"

BUFFETT "I know a woman in her 80's, a Polish Jew woman forced into a concentration camp with her family but not all of them came out. She says, 'I am slow to make friends because when I look at people, I have one question in mind; would they hide me?'"

"If you get to be my age, or younger for that matter, and have a lot of people that would hide you, then you can feel pretty good about how you've lived your life[704]…That can't be bought. I know people that have billions of dollars and their children would say, 'he's in the attic.'"[705]

ASSOCIATE WITH ASSHOLES

MUNGER   "Avoid dealing with people of questionable character."[706]

LIBRARIAN "Walk away if you can. Remember the saying, 'Don't fight with a pig, you'll just get dirty and the pig likes it.'"

MUNGER   "Our basic rule has always been that we don't deal with assholes."[707]

BUFFETT   "I have turned down business deals that were otherwise decent deals, because I didn't like the people that I would have to work with."[708]

"If I can add one percent or five percent to my net worth by being around people…who make me want to throw up, I'm not interested."[709]

MUNGER   "We don't want low grade people around us…Our experience has been that low grade people kill you."[710]

SEEKER   "But sometimes crooks get better and improve."

LIBRARIAN "Crooks don't retire. They are vultures. They just change trees now and again."

BUFFETT   "And the bad actor will try to tantalize you in one way or another. But you won't win. It pays to just avoid him."[711]

MUNGER   "You want to avoid other people who are total rat poison, and there are a lot of them."[712]

BUFFETT   "You will move in the direction of the crowd that you associate with[713]…You want to associate with first-class people."[714]

MUNGER   "The high quality people you interact with, clutch them to your bosom. And the low quality people just get them the hell out of your life."[715]

"Dealing with people you can trust and getting all the others the hell out of your life, it ought to be taught as a catechism."[716]

BUFFETT   "One of the best things you can do in life is to surround yourself with people who are better than you are…If you hang around with people who behave worse than you, pretty soon you'll start being pulled in that direction."[717]

MUNGER   "We just try to operate in a seamless web of deserved trust and be careful whom we trust[718]…Basically, I've had a very favored life. I've got wonderful associates…I've been very lucky or wise…in the people I've trusted in life."[719]

SEEKER   "But how do I know whom to trust?"

MUNGER   "It's hard to judge the combination of character and intelligence and other things. It's not at all simple, which explains why we have so many divorces. Think about how much people know about the person they marry, yet so many break up. It's not easy."[720]

BUFFETT "There is no way to eliminate the possibility of error when judging humans."[721]

SEEKER "That doesn't help me."

MUNGER "When you have doubts about a person, you can pass. There's enough nice people to interface with."[722]

BUFFETT "Charlie and I have had very good luck buying businesses and putting our trust in people—it's been overwhelmingly good, but we filter out a lot of people. People give themselves away and maybe it's an advantage being around awhile and seeing how people give themselves away by what they talk about and what's important and not important to them."

"We rule out people 90% of the time. Maybe we're wrong sometimes, but what's important is the ones we let in."[723]

SEEKER "I assume it is important for you guys in investing and managing to spot bad people?"

BUFFETT "We do not wish to join with managers who lack admirable qualities, no matter how attractive the prospects of their business. We've never succeeded in making a good deal with a bad person...After some other mistakes, I learned to go into business only with people whom I like, trust, and admire."[724]

SEEKER "Let's say I want to hire someone—what is important to think about?"

BUFFETT "You look for the logical things—passion, an interest in running the business, honesty. Such as, do they love the business, or do they love the money? This is the first filter. I mean real passion...If temperament is the most important personal asset in managing money, in business, it's passion."[725]

SEEKER "More?"

BUFFETT "First and foremost, you have to feel good around them, you must enjoy their company, like a friend or a family member. If you feel good around them, it means they have characteristics you admire and are moving in the direction you want to associate with."[726]

LIBRARIAN "And integrity."

BUFFETT "One friend of mine said that in hiring they look for three things: intelligence, energy, and character. If they don't have the last one, the first two will kill you because, it's true, if you are going to hire somebody that doesn't have character, you had really better hope they are dumb and lazy, because, if they are smart and energetic, they'll get you in all kinds of trouble."[727]

"I am looking for people that function very, very well. And that means not having any weak links."[728]

SEEKER   "I understand now that trust is extremely important."

LIBRARIAN "Think how much life is simplified and improved when you are around and deal with people you can trust. Or to invert — think about the misery of being around people you can't trust."

MUNGER   "Good character is very efficient. If you can trust people, your systems can be way simpler. There's enormous efficiency in good character and dis-efficiency in bad character."[729]

"We have less paperwork and more trust than most places... Most people underestimate the pleasure that comes from trust[730]... Complex bureaucratic procedure does not represent the highest form civilization can reach. One higher form is a seamless, non-bureaucratic web of deserved trust. Not much fancy procedure, just totally reliable people correctly trusting one another."[731]

SEEKER   "You talk about trust — still, I assume you believe in having contracts, or?"

BUFFETT   "We are not big believers in contracts. We hand people hundreds of millions of dollars, or billions in some cases, to sell us their business. And the decision we have to make is, 'Are they going to have the same passion for the business after they hand us the stock certificate and we hand them the money that they had beforehand.' And if we're wrong on that, no contract is going to save us...We don't want relationships that are based on contracts. I can't really think of a formal contract we have."[732]

MUNGER   "If everybody distrusts everybody and tries to protect himself with contracts and procedure, you don't have the best human culture, you have the worst."[733]

BUFFETT   "If I need a team of lawyers and accountants, it isn't going to be a good deal.... We've never had an extended negotiation with anybody about anything. That's just not our style. If it's going to be that way, I don't want to deal with them — because it's going to ruin my life sooner or later. So we just walk away."[734]

SEEKER   "Lawyers...as Chico Marx said, 'Whenever you got business trouble, the best thing to do is to get a lawyer. Then you got more trouble, but at least you got a lawyer.'"[735]

SEEKER   "What about incentive contracts?"

BUFFETT   "We have a whole bunch of different arrangements on that, but we don't try to hold people by contracts. It wouldn't work. And we basically don't like engaging in 'em."[736]

"They have to go to work every day because they want to go to work, not because there's some contract, or because they need the money.

So I try to create the conditions that would cause them to really rather be at work than on some yacht someplace which they could easily afford."[737]

Seeker   "But how do you get people that don't need more money to work?"

Buffett   "Treat them fairly and in the manner that we would wish to be treated if our positions were reversed."[738]

"Why would you jump out of bed and be excited about going to work that day? And we try to apply that to the people who work with us[739]...It doesn't require a 150 I.Q. or anything to do that. It does require a certain sensitivity as to why people get up in the morning and why they want to do what they do."[740]

Seeker   "Such as?"

Buffett   "We try to provide an environment for them which is exactly like what we'd want if we were running a business. The main thing we would want is we would not want a lot of second guessing, we would not want a lot of home office meetings, we would not want a lot of supervision from some group Vice President at headquarters. We just would not want a lot of nonsense. We would like to run our own business in our own way."[741]

"If I had people second-guessing me all day, I would get sick of it. I would say, 'What the hell do I need this for?' And, that's exactly the way our managers would feel if I went around second-guessing them or telling them how to run their business."[742]

Munger   "We have decentralization just short of abdication in handling our subsidiaries."[743]

Buffett   "The extraordinary delegation of authority now existing at Berkshire is the ideal antidote to bureaucracy. In an operating sense, Berkshire is not a giant company but rather a collection of large companies. At headquarters, we have never had a committee nor have we ever required our subsidiaries to submit budgets (though many use them as an important internal tool). We don't have a legal office nor departments that other companies take for granted: human relations, public relations, investor relations, strategy, acquisitions, you name it."[744]

"We will never allow Berkshire to become some monolith that is overrun with committees, budget presentations and multiple layers of management. Instead, we plan to operate as a collection of separately-managed mediumsized and large businesses, most of whose decision-making occurs at the operating level."[745]

Munger   "Most of what we do...is just not to interfere in a counterproductive way."[746]

Seeker   "That's not what most other businesses do, is it?"

Buffett   "Gillette, the oil companies, etc. all went out and bought a lot of businesses and tried to run them themselves. We're under no illusions that we can do that. We think that having lots of Executive Vice Presidents, directives from headquarters, centralized Human Resources etc. can destroy the incentives of the people who've already gotten rich, and we're counting on them making us rich."[747]

MUNGER "Our contribution to See's Candies has been limited to leaving it alone. When we bought it, it already had a wonderful culture, a wonderful trademark and a wonderful reputation. Our contribution was not screwing it up. There are a lot of people who would have bought it and would have screwed it up. They would have thought that headquarters knows best."[748]

BUFFETT "The whole idea of Berkshire is that managers are responsible for their businesses and we don't tell them what to do."[749]

MUNGER "We like it—that's the way we would want it of we were the manager."[750]

BUFFETT "We let successful companies keep running the way they've run in the past. That's what made them successful and that's what will keep them successful[751]...We don't have, and don't expect to have, operating people in our parent organization. All of the businesses we own are run autonomously to an extraordinary degree. In most cases, the managers of important businesses we have owned for many years have not been to Omaha or even met each other. When we buy a business, the sellers go on running it just as they did before the sale; we adapt to their methods rather than vice versa."[752]

MUNGER "The business management record of Warren is pretty damn good, and I think it's frequently underestimated. He is a better business executive for spending no time engaged in micromanagement."[753]

LIBRARIAN "It reminds me of something your friend Tom Murphy said, '[Warren Buffett and I] are both proponents of a decentralized management philosophy: of hiring key people carefully; of pushing decisions down the organization; and of setting overall principles and resisting temptation to be involved with details. In other words, don't hire a dog and try to do the barking.'"[754]

BUFFETT "I believe the GEICO story demonstrates the benefits of Berkshire's approach. Charlie and I haven't taught Tony a thing—and never will—but we have created an environment that allows him to apply all of his talents to what's important. He does not have to devote his time or energy to board meetings, press interviews, presentations by investment bankers or talks with financial analysts."

"Furthermore, he need never spend a moment thinking about financing, credit ratings or 'Street' expectations for earnings per share. Because of our ownership structure, he also knows that this operational framework will endure for decades to come. In this environment of freedom, both Tony and his company can convert their almost limitless potential into matching achievements."[755]

MUNGER "Our approach has worked for us. Look at the fun we, our managers, and our shareholders are having. More people should copy us. It's not difficult, but it looks difficult because it's unconventional — it isn't the way things are normally done. We have low overhead, don't have quarterly goals and budgets or a standard personnel system, and our investing is much more concentrated than average. It's simple and common sense."[756]

SEEKER "But don't your companies need some kind of control and direction?"

BUFFETT "We can obtain a better management result through non-control than control."[757]

MUNGER "We buy businesses that don't require a lot of control. That's the beauty of the system we've created."[758]

BUFFETT "Every now and then you have a disappointment but overwhelmingly if you put trust in the equation with people that have already showed that they have a lot of ability running their business, there's real trust."[759]

"We think giving managers this degree of freedom allows them to accomplish a lot more — our lack of supervision does mean we miss some things...but on balance it is a benefit."[760]

MUNGER "Our success has come from the lack of oversight we've provided, and our success will continue to be from a lack of oversight."[761]

BUFFETT "But if you're going to provide minimal oversight, you have to buy carefully."[762]

SEEKER "With so many employees aren't you worried something might go wrong?"

BUFFETT "With so many employees something can always go wrong. It will happen. But we try to create a culture and incentives that minimize that."[763]

MUNGER "In terms of intellectual content, I think this place tries harder to be rational than most places. And I think it tries harder than most places to be ethical — meaning to tell the truth and to not be abusive. Now with [so many employees] at Berkshire, I'll bet as I sit here at least one of them is doing something that I would very much regret. However, despite the presence of some human failing, we've had an amazingly low amount of litigation or scandal or anything of that sort over a vast number of decades."[764]

SEEKER "So you say mistakes happen?"

BUFFETT "This approach produces an occasional major mistake that might have been eliminated or minimized through closer operating controls. But it also eliminates large layers of costs and dramatically speeds decision-making."[765]

"We would rather suffer the visible costs of a few bad decisions than incur the many invisible costs that come from decisions made too slowly — or not at all — because of a stifling bureaucracy."[766]

MUNGER "By the standards of the rest of the world, we over-trust — but I think a lot of places work better where there is a culture of trust. And so far, our results have been far better, because we carefully selected people who should be over-trusted."[767]

BUFFETT "Culture, more than rule books, determines how an organization behaves."[768]

"I think we have a very good culture virtually everyplace in Berkshire. I hope it's everyplace. This is what we are looking for, and it's more a question of culture than controls. If you have a good culture, I think you can make the rules pretty simple."[769]

LIBRARIAN "You really seem to have a wonderful culture in Berkshire."

BUFFETT "Berkshire's culture runs as deep as any large company's (culture) could. It's a vital part of Berkshire to have a clearly defined, deeply embedded culture that pervades the company. I expect it will continue and become even stronger. Once Charlie and I aren't around it will be so clear that it's not a force of personality but institutionalized…It will continue for decades and decades and decades to come. Culture is everything at Berkshire."[770]

SEEKER "By the way, how does a company create a great culture?"

BUFFETT "Culture has to come from the top. It has to be consistent…part of written communications…lived, be followed, and rewarded when followed and punished when not. It has to be done for a very long time. It's much easier to inherit a culture, and it's easier in small firms."

"It seems to be more what you do rather than what you say. Just as your child sees what you do rather than what you say, it's the same thing in business. People see how those above them behave and they move in that direction."[771]

MUNGER "Berkshire's culture could go on for a long, long time because we've decentralized power to people who deserve it."[772]

SEEKER "It works for you then."

BUFFETT "We think giving our managers the degree of freedom we do works well for us. There may be downsides to our style, but what they won't be able to measure is how much we've been able to achieve on the positive side with dozens and dozens of people because we gave them that leeway."[773]

MUNGER "Places work better when they create a culture of deserved trust. Too much tight controls and monitoring, I think will do more harm than good."[774]

BUFFETT "Our trust is in people rather than process. A 'hire well, manage little' code suits both them and me."[775]

SEEKER "What do you do to gain the trust of those who sold to you?"

BUFFETT "We've kept our word to them. We have to be very careful what we promise. We can't promise there will be no layoffs, but we can promise not to sell the business unless there is the prospect of unending losses or labor problems. If we didn't keep our promises, word would get around."[776]

SEEKER "Must be an advantage when a family wants to sell their business."

BUFFETT "Our long-avowed goal is to be the 'buyer of choice' for businesses—particularly those built and owned by families. The way to achieve this goal is to deserve it. That means we must keep our promises; avoid leveraging up acquired businesses; grant unusual autonomy to our managers; and hold the purchased companies through thick and thin (though we prefer thick and thicker)."

"Our record matches our rhetoric. Most buyers competing against us, however, follow a different path. For them, acquisitions are 'merchandise.' Before the ink dries on their purchase contracts, these operators are contemplating 'exit strategies.' We have a decided advantage, therefore, when we encounter sellers who truly care about the future of their businesses."[777]

MUNGER "I think our life works better and we attract a better class of businesses in Berkshire because we aren't buying things to resell."[778]

BUFFETT "We have a unique asset in Berkshire, and we'll maintain it as long as we behave ourselves."[779]

LIBRARIAN "And that your entry is the right one—for example, the right kind of seller."

BUFFETT "We find it meaningful when an owner cares about whom he sells to. We like to do business with someone who loves his company, not just the money that a sale will bring him (though we certainly understand why he likes that as well). When this emotional attachment exists, it signals that important qualities will likely be found within the business: honest accounting, pride of product, respect for customers, and a loyal group of associates having a strong sense of direction."

"The reverse is apt to be true, also. When an owner auctions off his business, exhibiting a total lack of interest in what follows, you will frequently find that it has been dressed up for sale, particularly when the seller is a 'financial owner.' And if owners behave with little regard for their business and its people, their conduct will often contaminate attitudes and practices throughout the company."[780]

SEEKER   "Anything more on trust."

MUNGER   "We like it when our companies have long-term relationships with really excellent and reliable suppliers. I think capitalism works better when there's a lot of deserved trust in the system...and of course, your customers have to trust you."[781]

SEEKER   "Thanks for your exposé on the importance of trust. Anyway, I will be more careful—only deal with people I can trust and be careful whom I trust."

MUNGER   "No matter how smart you are, there are smart people out there who can fool you if they really want to. So, be sure you can trust the smart people you work with."[782]

LIBRARIAN "And don't forget yourself—be a person that can be trusted."

BUFFETT   "We want to be a good partner ourselves because we want to attract good partners."[783]

MUNGER   "The right way to get a good spouse is to deserve one. The same goes for getting a good business partner...If you just behave yourself correctly, it's amazing how well it works."[784]

SEEKER   "While we talk about friends and associates, I must say—you two seem to have a wonderful partnership—and have fun together."

BUFFETT   "Charlie and I have had a lot of fun together[785]...You've got to enjoy it...I would have had a lot of fun over the years, but not nearly as much fun without Charlie."[786]

SEEKER   "After listening to you guys, it seems to me that having fun is an important ingredient in life."

LIBRARIAN "You're right—like someone said, 'Enjoy life—there are no reruns.'

BUFFETT   "We're here on earth only one time, unless Shirley MacLaine is right, so you ought to be doing something that you enjoy as you go along, and can be enthusiastic about."[787]

MUNGER   "It's very peculiar for two people this old to be doing something this long. But Warren likes doing it. And I like doing it. It's much more fun, two than one. When something good happens, everybody wants to call somebody. It's a human need—we're social animals."[788]

BUFFETT   "One plus one with Charlie and me certainly adds up to more than two."[789]

MUNGER   "I hardly know anybody who's done very well in life in terms of cognition that doesn't have somebody trusted to talk to. Einstein would not have been able to do what he did without people to talk to…You organize your own thoughts as you try and convince other people."[790]

LIBRARIAN "Like the physicist Niels Bohr did—he needed to talk with other physicist 'in order to sharpen his own thoughts…he simply needed somebody to talk to in order to find out what he was thinking.'"[791]

SEEKER "I assume it also helps to talk things over with each other—maybe to get a different viewpoint or to have someone that point out possible flaws in ones thinking."

MUNGER "Well, going through the process of talking to someone else about your ideas requires you to put them together in a certain kind of format and manner that can be articulated to the other person. And that process is useful in seeing some flaws in your argument."[792]

LIBRARIAN "Garrett Hardin had some wise words on the matter, 'It would be an enormous error to assume that our picture of the world is built only on logic. No matter how hard-headed one tries to be, one's thinking is shaped by the biases of all-encompassing worldviews derived from assumptions of which one is barely (if at all) conscious. (One's opponent often sees these assumptions more clearly. Since the relation is mutual, it is obvious that we need each another as critics, if nothing else.)'"[793]

BUFFETT "Charlie is my canary in the coal mine[794]…He sees any valid weakness in 60 seconds[795]…People believe what they want to believe. Everyone rationalizes their actions. A partner like Charlie can point it out to me. If we have a strength, it is that we think things through and we have the advantage of having each other. We are not influenced by other people."[796]

"To have someone that you respect enormously say, 'you know, you're really out in an area where you don't belong, Warren'. I mean, I will pay attention to him when he says that, and he'll say it. So there's real utility in our functions together, for one to simply just say, 'are you sure you know what you're talking about?'"[797]

LIBRARIAN "A truth-teller."

BUFFETT "You have to have someone who tells the truth…There's just no way that Charlie would not tell me the truth[798]…Charlie…immediately… thinks, he sees the facts so fast and thinks so fast, and he doesn't waste any time making arguments just for the hell of it."[799]

SEEKER "Do you two ever disagree?"

BUFFETT "We sometimes don't agree. In 56 years, however, we've never had an argument. When we differ, Charlie usually ends the conversation by saying: 'Warren, think it over and you'll agree with me because you're smart and I'm right.'"[800]

"If we disagree, we probably won't do a deal, but if I decide to do it, that's fine. He is behind me one hundred percent."[801]

MUNGER   "We ordinarily come to an agreement. Once in a blue moon, there's something I would have done that he doesn't do. Very seldom does he do anything that I wouldn't do. We get along very well. And I think once in a while, we may actually change one another's view on a close issue."[802]

SEEKER   "But if something doesn't work out as expected?"

BUFFETT   "In fifty years...the guy has never second-guessed me in any way, shape, or form. There's never any 'I told you so,' or anything like that. He has absolutely no problem being number two with me."[803]

MUNGER   "It's not letting ego or jealousy or your own personality take over...Intelligence takes over."[804]

   "That's one of the beauties of the partnership...I am in so many activities where I am the dominant personality. Most people do not 'fit into' that mode—they can only operate in that mode. Yet I am particularly willing to play the secondary role. Warren's a more able man in doing what we're doing, so it's the appropriate response. There are some times you should be first, some times you should be second, and some times you should be third."[805]

SEEKER   "What keeps you up at night—what worries you?"

BUFFETT   "If it's going to keep me awake at night, I am not going to go there."[806]

   "We really don't worry. If we were worried about something in the business, we'd correct it."[807]

MUNGER   "I don't think it's terribly constructive to spend your time worrying about things you can't fix. I'm all for, as long as when you're managing your money, recognize that terrible things can happen. In the rest of your life, you can be a foolish optimist."[808]

SEEKER   "What about stress?"

BUFFETT   "I've been very fortunate in that I have no stress whatsoever...I tap dance on the way to work. I do believe in working at something you enjoy."[809]

SEEKER   "Any more things that don't work?"

MUNGER   "The standard sin of not recognizing what's unpleasant to recognize[810]...The tendency to distort reality so that it's endurable."[811]

DISTORT YOUR PROBLEMS SO THEY FIT YOUR WISHES

MUNGER   "A lot of people distort reality so it fit their wishes[812]...If you turn on the television, you'll find the mothers of the most obvious criminals that man could ever diagnose, and they all think their sons are innocent. That's simple psychological denial...The reality is too painful to bear, so one distorts the facts until they become bearable."[813]

LIBRARIAN "Most of us avoid the truth when it hurts. It is easier to choose the truth we want to hear. I think Queen Elizabeth One said, 'I like to know what the truth is so I can decide whether to believe it or not.'"

MUNGER "The tendency's most extreme outcomes are usually mixed up with love, death, and chemical dependency. In chemical dependency, wherein morals usually break down horribly, addicted persons tend to believe that they remain in respectable condition, with respectable prospects. They thus display an extremely unrealistic denial of reality as they go deeper and deeper into deterioration."[814]

SEEKER "Like a former friend of mine—as soon as things went against him a little, he escaped to the bottle."

LIBRARIAN "Isaac Asimov said, 'The easiest way to solve a problem is to deny it exists.'"[815]

MUNGER "After all, centuries before Christ, Demosthenes noted, 'what a man wishes, he will believe'"[816]

LIBRARIAN "Of course, it would be a nicer world if your wishes could make things come true—but the world doesn't work that way. You should make decisions based on reality, not what you wish it to be."

BUFFETT "Wishing makes dreams come true only in Disney movies; it's poison in business."[817]

LIBRARIAN "Something you don't have to tell GEICO's CEO, Tony Nicely."

BUFFETT "Everything he does makes sense. He never engages in wishful thinking or otherwise distorts reality, as so many managers do when the unexpected happens."[818]

SEEKER "Personally, I have an amazing ability to filter out inconvenient reality."

MUNGER "Part of enjoying life is just seeing and facing it like it is and adapt to the reality as it is whether you like it or not."[819]

LIBRARIAN "But unfortunately, that's not how we treat a lot of problems—if we don't look at them they don't exist."

BUFFETT "It doesn't go away just because they don't want to think about it."[820]

"Charlie calls this sort of behavior 'thumb-sucking.'"[821]

MUNGER "Sitting there thinking and dogging, musing, and consulting."[822]

LIBRARIAN "But as the author Alex Haley said, 'If you don't deal with reality, then reality will deal with you.'"[823]

BUFFETT "When a problem exists, whether in personnel or in business operations, the time to act is now."[824]

SEEKER "But what if it's really not a problem yet?"

MUNGER "Just because the full consequences haven't yet hit, doesn't mean there isn't a huge problem. It's as if someone jumped out of a window on the 42nd floor. As you go by the 20th floor, you're still OK, but that doesn't mean you don't have a real problem."[825]

BUFFETT "Our inability to quantify or time the risk does not mean we should ignore it[826]…You have to build the ark before the rains come."[827]

LIBRARIAN "Don't kick the problem down the road , hoping it will go away or use bandage for a serious problem but address it at its core—otherwise you may 'live' today but 'die' another day."

MUNGER ""If you won't attack a problem while it's solvable and wait until it's unfixable, you can argue that you're so damn foolish that you deserve the problem."[828]

SEEKER "Like my grandfather always said, 'you can avoid reality, but you cannot avoid the consequences of avoiding reality.' I should have listened to him."

MUNGER "Wise people step on big and growing troubles early."[829]
"All I know is I've always been better able to cope with my problems if I brutally face them the way they are."[830]

BUFFETT "When you have a problem, get it right, get it fast, get it out and get it over…It does take some delays at the time, you have to gather the information and make sure it is right."[831]

LIBRARIAN "Great advice even in a real crisis."

BUFFETT "State clearly that you do not know all the facts. Then promptly state the facts you do know. One's objective should be to get it right, get it quick, get it out, and get it over. You see, your problem won't improve with age."[832]

LIBRARIAN "Of course, sometimes you don't see what the problem is because you don't know about it—sometimes because people are afraid of telling you."

SEEKER "Why should people be afraid of telling me about a problem?"

LIBRARIAN "The Pavlovian Messenger syndrome—We associate bad news with the messenger so most people don't want to be the carrier of bad news. It is safer to be quiet."

MUNGER "Ancient Persians actually killed some messengers whose sole fault was that they brought home truthful bad news, say, of a battle lost. It was actually safer for the messenger to run away and hide, instead of doing his job as a wiser boss would have wanted it done."[833]

SEEKER "But this was then, what about today?"

MUNGER "Persian Messenger Syndrome is alive and well in modern life, albeit in less lethal versions. It is actually dangerous in many careers to be a carrier of unwelcome news. Union negotiators and employer representatives often know this, and it leads to many tragedies in labor relations. Sometimes lawyers, knowing their clients will hate them if they recommend an unwelcome but wise settlement, will carry on to disaster."

"CBS, in its late heyday, was famous for occurrence of Persian Messenger Syndrome because Chairman Paley was hostile to people who brought him bad news. The result was that Paley lived in a cocoon of unreality, from which he made one bad deal after another."[834]

LIBRARIAN "But shooting the messenger doesn't change reality."

SEEKER "And the antidote?"

BUFFETT "At Berkshire, we believe in Charlie's dictum—'Just tell me the bad news; the good news will take care of itself'—and that is the behavior we expect of our managers when they are reporting to us."[835]

MUNGER "It also helps to be so wise and informed that people fear not telling you bad news because you are so likely to get it elsewhere[836]...So people trust us in that, and that helps prevent mistakes from escalating into disasters."[837]

LIBRARIAN "During World War II, Winston Churchill followed the same recipe. He created the statistical office—entirely outside the normal chain of command—whose principal function was to bring him the unfiltered facts—good or bad. As he said, 'I...had no need for cheering dreams. Facts are better than dreams.'"[838]

BUFFETT "We can handle bad news, but we don't like them late."[839]

"A reluctance to face up immediately to bad news is what turned a problem at Salomon from one that could have easily been disposed of into one that almost caused the demise of a firm with 8,000 employees."[840]

LIBRARIAN "Denying reality is also a way for people to go broke."

SEEKER "You're talking about me? Please, tell me more."

STICK TO, JUSTIFY AND RATIONALIZE YOUR ACTIONS NO MATTER HOW DUMB THEY ARE

MUNGER "Deprival-Superreaction Tendency and Inconsistency-Avoidance Tendency often join to cause one form of business failure. In this form of ruin, a man gradually uses up all his good assets in a fruitless attempt to rescue a big venture going bad."[841]

SEEKER "Hey, stop, what do you mean with the deprival and Inconsistency tendency?"

LIBRARIAN "This is two of the principles you should have in your repertoire since they explain how reality works—in this case human nature. In fact, they have a lot in common—that we don't like to lose whatever feels rewarding."

94

SEEKER "So tell me—take it slow and start with the inconsistency principle."

LIBRARIAN "We all see ourselves and want others to see us as reasonable nice, honest and smart—we don't do dumb things or want to look stupid, weak or dishonest. We believe we make good decisions and do things for a good reason."

"We are therefore consistent with our actions and beliefs—and justify them—especially when we have invested a lot of time, physical and mental effort, money or reputation into them. Or made them public."

SEEKER "Of course I stick to what I have done—why should I have put in so much effort or whatever in something if it isn't worth it?"

"What's so bad with that?"

MUNGER "Inconsistency-Avoidance…has many good effects in civilization. For instance, rather than act inconsistently with public commitments, new or old public identities, etc., most people are more loyal in their roles in life as priests, physicians, citizens, soldiers, spouses, teachers, employees, etc."[842]

LIBRARIAN "Another good use is the learning method for acquiring medical skills."

MUNGER "In clinical medical education, the learner is forced to 'see one, do one, and then teach one,' with the teaching pounding the learning into the teacher[843] …When you do one, you learn better and when you teach one, you're announcing your commitment[844]…Boy, does that pound in what you want pounded in. Again, the consistency and commitment tendency. And that is a profoundly correct way to teach clinical medicine."[845]

SEEKER "And the downside of being consistent?"

LIBRARIAN "The human tendency to stick to, justify or rationalize our decisions—however wrong they are. It can make us throw good money after bad or hang on to bad ideas, unhappy relationships, and losing investments."

BUFFETT "Ben Franklin…Said…'So convenient a thing it is to be a reasonable creature, since it enables one to find or make a reason for everything one has a mind to do.'"[846]

LIBRARIAN "And J.P. Morgan said, 'A man always has two reasons for what he does—a good one, and the real one.'"

SEEKER "So what happens as soon as we've made a decision?"

LIBRARIAN "As soon as we have made a decision we convince ourselves that we were right by seeing what we want to see and finding what we want to find—we notice and favor what agrees with our decision, and ignore, don't look for or undervalue or criticize what doesn't."

SEEKER   "Of course I want to make sure I was right—not to prove myself wrong."

LIBRARIAN "What was it Baron Molson said, 'I will look at any additional evidence to confirm the opinion to which I have already come.'"[847]

SEEKER   "It comes natural to me to pick the evidence that support my own view and ignore what's against it."

BUFFETT   "What the human being is best at doing, is interpreting all new information so that their prior conclusions remain intact."[848]

SEEKER   "Hmm, in other words not very objectively."

LIBRARIAN "And as Mr. Munger showed in his example, we even 'invest' more to prove to ourselves and others we are right. And the more committed we are or the more we have 'invested', the harder it is to back off."

SEEKER   "I know the feeling."

MUNGER   "It is easy to see that a quickly reached conclusion…combined with a tendency to resist any change in that conclusion, will naturally cause a lot of errors in cognition for modern man."[849]

SEEKER   "But if it later turns out we are clearly wrong?"

LIBRARIAN "The more we have justified an action or 'invested' in a decision, the harder it is to admit we were wrong and change course. E.O. Wilson said it well, 'Old beliefs die hard even when demonstrably false.'"[850]

MUNGER   "No matter how bad some humans have handled things, they are just keeping their previous conclusions. It's the normal way of handling things for humans."[851]

SEEKER   "Yes, but don't we at one point have to admit we were wrong?"

LIBRARIAN "We don't like to admit we we're wrong—even when we are shown to be wrong. So we come up with rationalizations and excuses, assign blame or sometimes we even cover things up."

"Cardinal de Retz said, 'One of man's greatest failings is that he looks almost always for an excuse, in the misfortune that befalls him through his own fault, before looking for a remedy—which means he often finds the remedy too late."[852]

BUFFETT   "As Goethe observed, "When ideas fail, words come in very handy."[853]

MUNGER   "If you call people up in front of you who are in a state of trauma and hanging on to shreds of their former dignity and ask them to account for their failure, by and large, they're going to blame anyone but themselves. That's human nature…And people come up with self-serving explanations."[854]

LIBRARIAN "Rudyard Kipling said, 'I never made a mistake in my life; at least, never one that I couldn't explain away afterwards.'"[855]

SEEKER "I get it, I justify my wrong decision as a way to keep on believing I am a smart guy — to keep my image as a good decision maker."

MUNGER "A tendency to avoid or promptly resolve cognitive dissonance."[856]

LIBRARIAN "Yes, self-justification — and you sleep better when you rationalize your earlier decision by convincing yourself it was the best thing you could have done at the time and anybody else would have done the same."

SEEKER "Amazing how we human creatures are."

LIBRARIAN "People's fear of looking foolish or losing reputation has caused many stupidities. And the more successful people are — reputation wise — the more they are afraid of appearing foolish or losing face."

BUFFETT "We are willing to look foolish as long as we don't feel we have acted foolishly."[857]

LIBRARIAN "Our 'fear-of-losing-face'-tendency also partly explains why so many bad ideas are preserved."

BUFFETT "The famous physicist, Max Planck, was talking about the resistance of the human mind, even the bright human mind, to new ideas — particularly in the face of ones that had been developed carefully over many years and were blessed by others of stature and so on. And he said, 'Science advances one funeral at a time.' I think there's a lot of truth to that. It's certainly been true in the world of finance."[858]

"What happens is that you spend years getting your Ph.D. in finance. And in the process, you learn theories with a lot of mathematics that the average layman can't do. So you become sort of a high priest. And you wind up with an enormous amount of yourself in terms of your ego — and even professional security — invested in those ideas. Therefore, it gets very hard to back off after a given point."[859]

LIBRARIAN "A person who is rewarded for holding a certain opinion is not going to change it."

MUNGER "It's very hard to change people when the incentives are in the opposite direction."[860]

BUFFETT "Resistance among the powerful is natural when change clashes with their self-interest. Business, politics, and, yes, religions provide many examples of such defensive behavior."[861]

MUNGER "Why is man-with-a-hammer syndrome always present? Well if you stop to think about it, it's incentive-caused bias. His professional reputation is all tied up with what he knows. He likes himself and he likes his own ideas, and he's expressed them to other people — consistency and commitment tendency. I mean you've got four or five of these elementary psychological tendencies combining to create this man-with-a-hammer syndrome."[862]

"When a better tool comes along (idea or approach), what could be better than to swap it for your old, less useful tool? Warren and I routinely do this, but most people, as Galbraith says, forever cling to their old, less useful tools."[863]

LIBRARIAN "Now you understand why it's so hard to change people or get them to admit mistakes or why it is so hard to say we're sorry or why people stick to and justify certain things no matter how wrong they are."

MUNGER "I find it amazing how difficult intelligent people have to change their minds—no matter how wrong they are."[864]

LIBRARIAN "Yes, some people only want to have their ideas confirmed and others are open to different views. Unfortunately, most people belong to the first category."

SEEKER "Regarding the bad side of being consistent, any advice?"

MUNGER "Spend no time arguing with people whose idea you know to be stupid."[865]

SEEKER "No, I mean for me personally."

LIBRARIAN "Remember that merely because you made the wrong decision isn't equal to being stupid. Only wiser than before. When you find out that you are wrong—accept it—you have only done something we all do—a mistake. Remember the saying, 'A wise man changes his mind, but a fool never does.'"

"Also, since reality and circumstances change there is no need to feel ashamed or feel obligated to make excuses or give reasons for changing your mind. And if you think about it, is it not better to do what agrees with reality than to be proved right when you really are wrong? As Dickson Watts said, 'Fools try to prove that they are right. Wise men try to find when they are wrong.'"

SEEKER "I would still feel dumb."

LIBRARIAN "Take a lesson from George Soros, 'I recognize that I may be wrong…I am a very critical person who looks for defects in myself as well as in others. But, being so critical, I am also quite forgiving. I couldn't recognize my mistakes if I couldn't forgive myself. To others, being wrong is a source of shame; to me, recognizing my mistakes is a source of pride. Once we realize that imperfect understanding is the human condition, there is no shame in being wrong, only in failing to correct our mistakes.'"[866]

MUNGER "It is a great habit to be willing to change your mind."[867]

LIBRARIAN "Also, when you do something dumb or when you are wrong, say you're sorry. Accept responsibility. Apologies matter. Remember the saying, 'A fault confessed is half forgiven.'"

"And don't minimize it or say 'I am very sorry…but due to…it wasn't my fault.' Apologize honestly without the 'but' — a sincere apology and not a self-serving or flimsy one."

SEEKER "But it is so hard to do."

MUNGER "What…so terrible about that? Why get your ego so involved… that you can't ever admit a little failure?"[868]

SEEKER "Anything that may help here to make me more objective?"

MUNGER "Darwin's result was due in large measure to his working method, which violated all my rules for misery and particularly emphasized a backward twist in that he always gave priority attention to evidence tending to disconfirm whatever cherished and hard-won theory he already had."[869]

SEEKER "When something I believe is disconfirmed I rescue it — I just change my assumptions."

MUNGER "Most people early achieve and later intensify a tendency to process new and disconfirming information so that any original conclusion remains intact. They become people of whom Philip Wylie observed: 'You couldn't squeeze a dime between what they already know and what they will never learn.'"[870]

SEEKER "I really need to wise up."

LIBRARIAN "Force yourself to actively look for counter-evidence."

BUFFETT "Studying counter-evidence is a highly useful activity, though not one always greeted with enthusiasm at citadels of learning."[871]

"Charlie and I believe that when you find information that contradicts your existing beliefs, you've got a special obligation to look at it — and quickly."[872]

LIBRARIAN "In fact, history shows that the really great scientists of the past had a habit of changing their minds when they found contradictory evidence. As H.L. Mencken said, 'The essence of science is that it is always willing to abandon a given idea, however fundamental it may seem to be, for a better one.'"[873]

BUFFETT "I consider myself a journalist, to some extent. I assign myself a story. I say, is the Washington Post company worth $22 a share in 1973? I say, is the BNSF Railroad worth us paying $34 billion? I assign myself the story. It's my working hypothesis that it is, but then I go and look for the facts, and I try not to be selective about the facts that I use as input… always observe that rule about not letting the hypothesis determine the story…you have to give up that hypothesis if it turns out not to be correct or if it's misleading."[874]

MUNGER   "If you minimize objectivity, you ignore not only a lesson from Darwin but also one from Einstein. Einstein said that his successful theories came from 'Curiosity, concentration, perseverance, and self-criticism'…By self-criticism, he meant becoming good at destroying your own best-loved and hardest-won ideas."[875]

LIBRARIAN "Like when you bought some stocks in Western Insurance Services."

BUFFETT   "I went down to the Nebraska Insurance Department, and I got the convention reports on their insurance companies, and I read Best's. I didn't have any background in insurance. But I knew I could understand it if I worked at it for a while. And all I was really trying to do was disprove this thing. I was really trying to figure out something that was wrong with this. Only there wasn't anything wrong. It was a perfectly good insurance company, a better than average underwriter, and you could buy it at one times earnings."[876]

LIBRARIAN "So, to avoid fooling yourself from seeing things that aren't there, criticize yourself, ask why you might be wrong or what evidence may lead you to change your mind. Try to find evidence against what you want to achieve."

"Another thing to ask is, 'what evidence should exist if my hypothesis or argument is correct?' The absence of something we expect to see or happen is information and a clue in itself. Negative evidence and events that don't happen, matter when something implies they should be present or happen."

SEEKER   "I have to think about that last one."

LIBRARIAN "Also, when you think you have arrived to a correct decision, consider that the opposite of what you want to happen, could happen. And then try to think about what factors can cause what you don't want to happen to happen."

SEEKER   "The Jacobi trick again! Like we have done today—looking at ways I could 'die'."

LIBRARIAN "Yes, there is actually a variant of the 'all-I-want-to know…' called pre mortem analysis or where you assume you have already 'died.'"[877]

SEEKER   "Please tell me."

LIBRARIAN "Imagine a future catastrophe today. Assume you want to do X and then your Crystal ball tells you that a year or two down the road your decision turned into a catastrophe. Then try to find out possible reasons to why that happened and see if you can find ways to prevent or defend against it or if it is better just to avoid it."

Seeker   "I see what you mean—once more I see the value of your idea of trying to identify lethal problems in advance."

Librarian "Another thing is to surround yourself with smart people who don't always agree with you—especially when you're wrong."

"Abraham Lincoln, when he was elected, appointed to his cabinet some of his toughest political opponents—including Edwin Stanton (appointed by Lincoln as Secretary of War), who reportedly earlier had called him a 'long-armed ape'—and listened to them very carefully."[878]

Munger   "Similarly, other modern decision makers will often force groups to consider skillful counterarguments before making decisions."[879]

Seeker   "I must be better at welcoming people who call me an idiot—assuming of course they tell me why."

Munger   "The ability to take criticism constructively and learn from it is very useful."[880]

Librarian "Yes, and sometimes you can even turn a bad decision into a good one."

Munger   "I spoke earlier about the desirability of removing ignorance piece by piece."[881]

Seeker   "Yeah, your so called secret."

Munger   "Another trick is scrambling out of your mistakes, it is enormously useful."[882]

"We've done a lot of that—scrambled out of wrong decisions. I would argue that that's a big part of having a reasonable record in life. You can't avoid wrong decisions. But if you recognize them promptly and do something about them, you can frequently turn the lemon into lemonade."[883]

Librarian "Similar to what the author Jack London is supposed to have said, 'Life is not always a matter of holding good cards, but sometimes, playing a poor hand well.' So play the hand you're dealt. Be flexible in adapting to changing circumstances."

Munger   "I think we've adapted pretty well to changes in our circumstances. Since change is inevitable, adapting to change in our circumstances is necessary."[884]

"Keynes used to say, 'When I get new facts or new insights, I'd change my mind. What do you do?'"[885]

Seeker   "Change?"

Munger   "Well, of course you do. That's what we did. Our circumstances were different and our opportunities were different, so we behaved differently."[886]

Librarian "Keynes's advice reminds me of the game of bridge—a game that has a lot of things common with investing."

BUFFETT "The approach and strategies are very similar in that you gather all the information you can and then keep adding to that base of information as things develop. You do whatever the probabilities indicated based on the knowledge that you have at that time, but you are always willing to modify your behavior or your approach as you get new information."

"Investing is not as tough as being a top-notch bridge player. All it takes is the ability to see things as they really are."[887]

LIBRARIAN "There is a story about the British politician George Brown that is apt here. Brown was interviewed after he helped Britain to join the common market. Something he had earlier publicly said that he would never do. So a BBC reporter asked him, 'And how do you reconcile these statements?' His quick reply was, 'It is easy. I have just changed my bloody mind.'"

"It is all about realism and living in the present — to not be addicted to the past but to update beliefs, adapt and change if something doesn't agree with reality…when you get new facts or better understanding."

"Now you understand why there is a downside to long range master plans."

SEEKER "No, I don't but I am sure you will tell me."

MUNGER "I have a deep distrust in master planning. People get to believing the plan because they created it. What is needed is the kind of propensity to disbelieve by changing your previous conclusions. And we're very good at that, thank God."[888]

"There has never been a master plan. Anyone who wanted to do it, we fired because it takes on a life of its own and doesn't cover new reality."[889]

LIBRARIAN "Unfortunately, too many people try to change reality to fit their plan or favorite solution. It reminds me of something Mike Tyson said, 'Everybody has a plan until they get punched in the mouth.'"

MUNGER "The guy who wrote the master plan wasn't facing the new reality. He was just guessing forward as well as he could. And we want people taking the new information into account."[890]

LIBRARIAN "Unfortunately a lot of 'planners' mistake their maps — plans or accounting — for the world as it actually is but forget the map is not reality. And when the map and reality don't match, reality rules. Always stick to reality and follow the old military expression, 'If the terrain and the map disagree, follow the terrain.'"

SEEKER "Reminds me of an internet date a female friend had. The man's description of himself disagreed with the real man when he appeared so my friend followed reality and ran away."

LIBRARIAN "As the saying goes, 'One look is worth a thousand words.' It also helps us to get an independent source of information."

"Furthermore, to emphasize what Mr. Munger says, since reality or the terrain is continually changing, don't reject or distort it but accept it as it is and adapt and adjust to it. Follow the prescription of the ancient philosopher Bion of Borysthenes: 'We should not try to alter circumstances but to adapt ourselves to them as they really are, just as sailors do. They don't try to change the winds or the sea but ensure that they are always ready to adapt themselves to conditions. In a flat calm they use the oars; with a following breeze they hoist full sail; in a head wind they shorten sail or heave to. Adapt yourself to circumstances in the same way.'"[891]

BUFFETT   "I would say that more dumb acquisitions are made in the name of strategic plans than any other."

"I would be very wary if a board went through some elaborate process where a strategic plan was reviewed in great detail and then they endorse it and then the management went on to make acquisitions and then they came and said, 'But we made it in accord with a strategic plan.'"[892]

SEEKER   "And your strategic plan is?"

BUFFETT   "We do have a few advantages, perhaps the greatest being that we don't have a strategic plan. Thus we feel no need to proceed in an ordained direction (a course leading almost invariably to silly purchase prices) but can instead simply decide what makes sense for our owners."[893]

"We have no more master plan now than we did when we bought a textile mill [Berkshire Hathaway] in 1965. Charlie and I don't sit around and talk about the future of industries. We have no reports or staff. We just review what comes in and look for companies with a durable competitive advantage at an attractive price."[894]

"Our experience has been [big ideas] pop up occasionally. (How's that for a strategic plan?)"[895]

MUNGER   "It wasn't just Berkshire Hathaway that got this attitude about master planning…The modern John Hopkins [hospital and medical school] was created by Sir William Osler who quoted over and over again one line from Carlyle: 'The task of man is not to see what lies dimly in the distance, but to do what lies clearly at hand.'"[896]

"I think master plans do more harm than good. Anyway, we don't allow them at Berkshire, so you don't have to worry about them."[897]

SEEKER   "Ok, back to what you said earlier on putting in more money to rescue something. You mentioned another tendency—deprival super-reaction syndrome?"

LIBRARIAN   "We don't like losses. And we hate losing much more than we enjoy gaining—losses, negative news or information feels much worse than gains, positive news or information feels good."

MUNGER   "The quantity of man's pleasure from a ten dollar gain does not exactly match the quantity of his displeasure from a ten-dollar loss. That is, the loss seems to hurt much more than the gain seems to help. Moreover, if a man almost gets something he greatly wants and has it jerked away from him at the last moment, he will react much as if he had long owned the reward and had it jerked away."[898]

"I include the natural human reactions to both kinds of loss experience—the loss of the possessed reward and the loss of the almost-possessed reward—under one description, Deprival-Superreaction Tendency[899]…that makes 'take-aways' so hard to get in any type of negotiation and helps make most gamblers so irrational."[900]

LIBRARIAN   "Or take relationships – getting criticized by your boss or spouse feels much worse than getting praise feels good. In fact, someone said about marriages that positive interactions must outnumber negative interactions by about five to one for a marriage to succeed."

SEEKER   "Wow! If I had known that a word of criticism is five times more powerful than a word of encouragement or praise I could have had a better marriage instead of no marriage at all."

"And I assume some people are more loss averse than others."

LIBRARIAN   "Yes, we tend to be more loss averse the older we get. It is also based on our recent experiences and state of mind. But as with all other human traits—there is lot of individual variation."

"And the larger the impact of a potential loss, the more loss adverse people are."

SEEKER   "Of course, there is a difference between losing $100 and being ruined."

"Ok, back to you."

MUNGER   "Huge insanities can come from just subconsciously over-weighing the importance of what you're losing or almost getting and not getting."[901]

"A man ordinarily reacts with irrational intensity to even a small loss, or threatened loss, of property, love, friendship, dominated territory, opportunity: status, or any other valued thing."[902]

SEEKER   "That's me! It doesn't matter if I lose something big or small—I just hate it!"

MUNGER   "When you take away something people like you get this overwhelmingly silly reaction[903]…man…will often compare what is near instead of what really matters. For instance, a man with $10 million in his brokerage account will often be extremely irritated by the accidental loss of $100 out of the $300 in his wallet."[904]

"People are really crazy about minor decrements down[905]…Even a one-degree loss from a 180-degree view will sometime create enough

Deprival-Superreaction Tendency to turn a neighbor into an enemy, as I once observed when I bought a house from one of two neighbors locked into hatred by a tiny tree newly installed by one of them."[906]

LIBRARIAN "If we can only gain from a situation, we avoid risk, but when we feel threatened or are in really deep trouble, we fight a lot harder and take larger risks. No one is as dangerous as the opponent who fights for his survival. It is like the story about the rabbit and the fox. Why does a rabbit run faster than a fox?"

SEEKER   "You tell me."

LIBRARIAN "Aesop said, 'The rabbit runs faster than the fox, because the rabbit is running for his life while the fox is only running for his dinner.' And many studies of animals show that 'defenders of a territory almost invariably overcome intruders of the same species who try to take over their territory. Residents who face the risk of losing their territory exert more effort than challengers who try to gain new territory.'"[907]

"As Baltasar Gracián said, 'Never contend with a man who has nothing to lose.' Or someone who has everything to lose. So you can imagine what happens in a negotiation where one party can only gain and the other one has everything to lose. Or when both parties face losses."[908]

SEEKER   "It increases the chance of conflict. If I had faced a choice between losing for sure and 'surviving by fighting'—even if the chance was miniscule—I pick the fight."

LIBRARIAN "Then you can understand how difficult it is to reach some agreement in cases where both parties have to give up something or make a concession to get something else. We'd rather take a conflict than make a concession."

SEEKER   "Let me have a try on concessions—getting one feels like a gain but giving one feels like a loss. And since we hate losses more than we like equal gains it will be tough to reach a 'fair' agreement since both parties see it as unfair."

LIBRARIAN "Yes, and our loss aversion explains why we always undervalue what we get relative to what we give."

"Instead, try to see things from your counterparty's point of view and don't mind to make concessions on minor matters if that more easily leads to the more important matters settled to your advantage. Only take a firm stand on really important things."

SEEKER   "What's your view of negotiations?"

BUFFETT "People have different styles of negotiation. I don't want to be in a negotiation where it 'has to end' at some point. I don't want them to have me by the throat while I have them by the throat. Either we give up or one strangles the other…You don't want to get in a negotiation that you can't afford to walk away from. Bargaining with people you love is a terrible mistake. It's destructive."[909]

SEEKER   "Thanks. Anyway, I see now what you meant with your initial example—putting in more money to avoid a loss. Not a good idea to put in more resources to rescue something if it has no chance of recovering."

LIBRARIAN "Don't throw good money after bad. Still, many do and the more they stand to lose, the more risk they take."

MUNGER   "That's the reason so many people are ruined by gambling—they get behind and then they feel like they have to get it back the way they lost it. It's a deep part of human nature."[910]

LIBRARIAN "Do you remember the trader Nick Leeson?"

SEEKER   "Wasn't he the guy who caused the downfall of Barings Bank?"

LIBRARIAN "Yes, he had over the years accumulated huge losses but instead of admitting them, he said that he 'gambled on the stock market to reverse his mistakes and save the bank.'[911] Naturally things only got worse and he ended up losing $1.4 billion."

SEEKER   "You've got me again! I got into a venture and lost some money and felt I had to win it back. I couldn't face my wife and tell her that I had lost all this money. The more I lost…I just got deeper and deeper in it…I was so embarrassed."

BUFFETT   "You don't have to make it back the way you lost it. A stock doesn't know you own it."[912]

        "You buy 100 shares of General Motors (GM). Now all of a sudden you have this feeling about GM. It goes down, you may be mad at it. You may say, 'Well, if it just goes up for what I paid for it, my life will be wonderful again.' Or if it goes up, you may say how smart you were and how you and GM have this love affair. You have got all these feelings…. The stock just sits there; it doesn't care what you paid or the fact that you own it."[913]

SEEKER   "And the antidote is?"

MUNGER   "One of the best antidotes to this folly is good poker skill learned young[914]…fold early when the odds are against you[915]…rethink and say, 'I can afford to write this one off and live to fight again. I don't have to pursue this thing as an obsession—in a way that will break me.'"[916]

BUFFETT   "Whatever the outcome, we will heed a prime rule of investing: You don't have to make it back the way that you lost it."[917]

LIBRARIAN "Ask: Based on what I want to achieve, if I hadn't already done this, knowing what I now know, would I do it today? If not, change."

        "Decisions should be based on the present and where you want to be. Not where you've been."

Seeker "Reminds me of your earlier Keynes quote, to change when I get new facts or insights."

Librarian "Yes — realism."

Seeker "I see now that consistency and deprival is very linked together. I mean, I assume one of the reasons why we stick to certain things including bad ideas is because we don't want to lose something that feels rewarding to us."

"I understand that it is very hard to change someone's mind but why can't I just tell him or her they suffer from the consistency tendency or whatever?"

Munger "If you and a friend are discussing Old Joe and that he suffers from some of these tendencies it is Ok but if you tell Joe directly he is suffering from some of these tendencies he will become very hostile."[918]

Librarian "It's like telling him you know what's right and he doesn't — how would you like someone telling you that you're wrong and foolish and he is right and smart?"

"Telling people they are wrong, often makes them more resistant and defensive and only makes them justify their actions more and more."

Munger "His reputation is tacking a whack, we get deprival superreaction and then we get the reciprocation tendency."[919]

"You don't just reciprocate affection, you reciprocate animosity, and the whole thing can escalate."[920]

Librarian "He will criticize or dismiss it or he will tell you to get lost."

"Another thing, always avoid personal attacks and be careful not to publicly criticize someone. It also helps to acknowledge you could be wrong."

Buffett "Praise by name, criticize by category."[921]

Seeker "I see what you mean. Everyone loves to be praised and no one likes criticism."

"Anyway, I understand now that changing minds is very hard."

Buffett "I'd say that the history that Charlie and I have had of persuading decent, intelligent people who we thought were doing unintelligent things to change their course of action has been poor…When people want to do something, they want to do something."[922]

Seeker "Is that why you only invest in businesses where you don't have to change people?"

Buffett "Management changes, like marital changes, are painful, time-consuming and chancy."[923]

"We don't try to change people. It doesn't work well…We accept people the way they are."[924]

MUNGER   "The failure rate at trying to change a culture is likely to be 100%."[925]

BUFFETT   "Changing cultures is really tough. I've had a little experience with that. The trick in business is to get in with a culture that's already the right kind."[926]

LIBRARIAN "Yes, like for example, not only a culture of trust but also one where people face and deal with reality."

BUFFETT   "We want people joining us who already are the type that face reality and that basically [not only] tell us the truth, but tell themselves the truth—which is even more important. Once you get an organization that lies to itself—and there are plenty that do—I just think you get into all kinds of problems. And people know it throughout the organization and they adopt the norms of what they think is happening up above them."[927]

MUNGER   "By and large, we've chosen people we admire enormously to have the power beneath us. It's easy for us to get along with them on average because we love and admire them. And they create the culture for whatever invention and reality recognition is going on in their businesses. And included in that reality recognition is the recognition that previous conclusions were incorrect."[928]

SEEKER   "Ok, I get it—don't invest in companies to change them."

BUFFETT   "We don't buy into companies to change them. We think that has all the efficacy of marrying somebody to change them. Before the ceremony takes place, we try to make sure that they'll be happy with us and more importantly that we'll be happy with them. And we try to behave in a way that they'll be happy with us."[929]

MUNGER: "If you want to guarantee yourself a life of misery, marry somebody with the idea of changing them."[930]

BUFFETT   "Marrying someone to change them is crazy and I would say hiring someone to change them is just as crazy. Life is so much fun this way to. Who does want to spend their life trying to change people from their natural approaches?"[931]

LIBRARIAN "It reminds me of your Chuck Huggins story."

BUFFETT   "Someone once asked See's chairman, Chuck Huggins, 'How do you get them [the employees] to be so friendly?' Chuck's reply was, 'The most important thing is to hire friendly people.'"

   "And that's obvious, but it's the single most important thing to do. It's sort of like marrying. You don't want to marry to change somebody. Similarly, it's a lot easier to hire the right person than to change them."[932]

SEEKER   "Once more I learn that changing people is really tough."

LIBRARIAN "As Judge Jacob Braude said, 'Consider how hard it is to change yourself and you'll understand what little chance you have in trying to change others.'"

SEEKER "It reminds me of a song from one of the Marx movies, [the Seeker starts singing] *'I don't know what they have to say / It makes no difference anyway / Whatever it is, I'm against it. / No matter what it is or who commenced it, I'm against it! / Your proposition may be good / But let's have one thing understood: / Whatever it is, I'm against it. / And even when you've changed it or condensed it, I'm against it!'*"[933]

LIBRARIAN "What a talent we have here, guys."

SEEKER "Thanks, but seriously there must be some way that is more effective than others in changing people's opinions or behavior, or?"

MUNGER "Appeal to interest and not to reason if you want to change conclusions."[934]

LIBRARIAN "And people's interests are not only financial. They could also be social or moral. For example, avoiding social punishment like public embarrassment, exclusion/ostracism, or based on superstition. Also, conscience, shame or guilt may cause people to change or stop some undesirable behavior."

SEEKER "Aha, now it is coming—maybe I can have an example?"

LIBRARIAN "Give him the Salomon case."

MUNGER "I watched the brilliant and worthy Harvard-Law-Review-trained general counsel of Salomon Brothers lose his career there. When the able CEO was told that some underling had done something wrong, the general counsel said, 'Gee, we don't have any legal duty to report this, but I think it's what we should do, it's our moral duty.'"

"The general counsel was technically and morally correct. But his approach didn't persuade. He recommended a very unpleasant thing for the busy CEO to do and the CEO, quite understandably, put the issue off, and put it off, and not with any intent to do wrong. In due course, when powerful regulators resented not having been promptly informed, down went the CEO and the general counsel with him."[35]

SEEKER "Instead he should have appealed to the CEO's interest."

BUFFETT "It takes real, effective pressure to change behavior where the behavior is in the self interest of that person. People do not give up self interest easily."[936]

MUNGER "The self-serving bias of man is very extreme and should have been used in attaining the correct outcome[937]...You want to persuade somebody, you really tell them why...Incentives... matter...Vivid evidence...works."[938]

SEEKER "Tell them 'why'?"

LIBRARIAN "People will be better persuaded and do better if they are told and understand 'why.'"

MUNGER "In general, learning is most easily assimilated and used when, life long, people consistently hang their experience, actual and vicarious, on a latticework of theory answering the question: Why?"

"Few practices…are wiser than not only thinking through reasons before giving orders but also communicating these reasons to the recipient of the order. No one knew this better than Carl Braun, who designed oil refineries with spectacular skill and integrity. He had a very simple rule…: You had to tell Who was to do What, Where, When, and Why. And if you wrote a communication leaving out your explanation of why the addressee was to do what was ordered, Braun was likely to fire you because Braun well knew that ideas got through best when reasons for the ideas were meticulously laid out."[939]

LIBRARIAN "And since the fear of loss is stronger and more motivating than the desire to gain, we stand a better chance changing someone if we appeal to their fear of losing what they value."

BUFFETT "The way to change behavior is to have the fear among those doing wrong, the fear that it's going to come home to them and hit them hard."[940]

LIBRARIAN "And most people have something they fear more than anything else."

MUNGER "Telling the client in vivid terms that he was very likely to be clobbered to smithereens if he didn't behave as his counsel recommended."[941]

"'You're likely to ruin your life and disgrace your family and lose your money[942]…your job[943]…your status[944]…your reputation, your standing in the community, your wife will be mad at you, and your kids will be embarrassed to admit you're their dad[945]…My recommendation will prevent a likely disaster from which you can't recover'[946]…I know both men. That would've worked."[947]

LIBRARIAN "And we stand an even better chance to influence someone if the message is coming from an authority figure since we have a tendency to overly respect and trust authorities and experts. Of course, it also works if you are a friend the recipient trust and likes."

"Or assign a person a trait label—like a good reputation to uphold—that motivates the person to behave consistently with that trait—an image to live up to. For example, 'You are widely known to be trustworthy, cooperative and fair'. This of course assuming it's true."

SEEKER "While we discuss our tendency to be consistent—anything more I need to know?"

LIBRARIAN "Yes, for example how Benjamin Franklin used the tendency to win the respect and friendship of an opponent."

MUNGER "As he was rising from obscurity in Philadelphia and wanted the approval of some important man, Franklin would often maneuver that man into doing Franklin some unimportant favor, like lending Franklin a book. Thereafter, the man would admire and trust Franklin more because a nonadmired and nontrusted Franklin would be inconsistent with the appraisal implicit in lending Franklin the book."[948]

LIBRARIAN "Asking a favor of someone is likely to increase that person's liking for us since people want to be consistent with their behavior."

SEEKER "I see what you mean—he couldn't have lent a book to a guy he didn't like—that would have been inconsistent so he justified it by telling himself he did it because he liked Franklin."

LIBRARIAN "Franklin also tells us about an old maxim: 'He that has once done you a kindness will be more ready to do you another, than he whom you yourself have obliged.'"

MUNGER "The practice of Franklin, whereunder he got approval from someone by maneuvering him into treating Franklin favorably, works viciously well in reverse. When one is maneuvered into deliberately hurting some other person, one will tend to disapprove or even hate that person."[949]

SEEKER "This has all been very enlightening, especially how hard it is to change people. So in most situations it seems better go with what you said earlier—don't try to change people or enter situations where one has to change people."

LIBRARIAN "Benjamin Franklin said it well, 'He that would live in peace and at ease, must not speak all he knows, nor judge all he sees.'

"And what says that your opinion or solution is the correct one."

SEEKER "Or we may both be wrong."

MUNGER "I think it's unreasonable to expect perfect agreement with all of one's own ideas."[950]

LIBRARIAN "The American car manufacturer Henry Ford is quoted as having said: 'If there is any one secret of success, it lies in the ability to get the other person's point of view and see things from that person's angle as well as from your own.'

"Change perspective—don't believe others see the world as you do—instead try to see the world through the other side's eyes—from their perspective. Many times, if we could see the world the way others see it, we more easily understand why they do what they do."

MUNGER "Ask yourself what are the arguments on the other side[951]...The study of the law is good for people in that it constantly asks you to consider one side and then consider the other—what arguments can be made on one side and then on the other as you seek to determine which rule of law would be better and why. That process sort of forces objectivity...It's a huge plus."[952]

Librarian "And start defining what the both of you really mean so you talk about the same thing. A lot of conflicts are due to the wrong assumptions and misunderstandings. As Goethe said, 'Misunderstandings and neglect create more confusion in this world than trickery and malice. At any rate, the last two are certainly much less frequent.'"[953]

Seeker "I have realized that."

Librarian "And especially if there are a lot of lawyers or advisors involved."

"Also, you can't fight all battles so pick your battles carefully—don't fight the ones you can't do anything about anyway or that aren't in your long term interest. If you take a stand, do it only on important things."

"Nietzsche said, 'The value of a thing sometimes lies not in what one attains with it, but in what one pays for it—what it costs us.'"[954]

Seeker "I see what you mean—it takes energy, time and stress."

Librarian "Don't get so caught up in the heat of the moment you lose sight of what matters and what you want to achieve in the end."

"Knowing what you ultimately want to accomplish makes it easier to decide what is important and not. Will you be better or worse off by going to war? Will it really benefit your overall objective? As they said in the movie *Broken City*, 'There are some wars you fight and there are some wars you walk away from.'"

Buffett "I don't think going to war is a very good idea in most situations."[955]

"There's only so many bullets you can use in the gun. If you start objecting to this and this and this, pretty soon people don't pay any attention to you. You want to save your bullets for when they really count."[956]

Librarian "As someone said, 'you don't have to attend every argument you're invited to.'"

Buffett "People need to pick their spots or they will not only be ignored, but not heard on other issues. It's not even a bad thought to keep in mind for marriage. It's hard to change others' behavior, and it's not helped by shouting."[957]

Munger "I think the general idea that people should shout about everything they disapprove of is just suspect."[958]

"In life you have to choose your battles and pick your spots. And, if we all screamed about everything we disapproved of, we wouldn't be able to hear each other."[959]

LIBRARIAN "And as the saying goes 'Sometimes peace is better than being right. And sometimes you must know when to accept a loss and quit."

SEEKER "Anything else?"

LIBRARIAN "Ideology—what John Adams once described as, 'the science of idiocy…taught in the school of folly.'"[960]

BE AN EXTREME IDEOLOGUE

MUNGER "Another nutty idea is to be an extreme ideologue…it absolutely destroys cognition if you get this intense loyalty to a particular identity."[961]

LIBRARIAN "Take for example, intense left or right political beliefs. The more important they are to us the more we turn blind to evidence suggesting we may be wrong."

MUNGER "Who can really know for sure who the best president for the republic is? Yet many people are totally confident they know the answer."[962]

LIBRARIAN "Not everything comes in black and white—reality is often more complex."

MUNGER "I argued that intense political animosity should be avoided because it causes much mental malfunction, even in brilliant brains. Since then, political animosity has increased greatly, both on the left and right, with sad effects on the ability of people to recognize reality, exactly as I would have expected."[963]

"Avoid intense ideology—it turns you into a lousy thinker."[964]

LIBRARIAN "And the deprival syndrome also comes into play."

SEEKER "How?"

MUNGER "Deprival-Superreaction Tendency often protects ideological or religious views by triggering dislike and hatred directed toward vocal nonbelievers. This happens, in part, because the ideas of the nonbelievers, if they spread, will diminish the influence of views that are now supported by a comfortable environment including a strong belief-maintenance system."

"University liberal arts departments, law schools, and business organizations all display plenty of such ideology-based groupthink that rejects almost all conflicting inputs."[965]

LIBRARIAN "And young people need to be especially aware of the dangers of extreme ideology."

MUNGER "When you announce that you're a loyal member of some cult-like group and you start shouting out the orthodox ideology, what you're doing is pounding it in, pounding it in, pounding it in."[966]

"Envy, huge self-pity, extreme ideology, intense loyalty to a particular identity—you've just taken your brain and started to pound on it with a hammer."[967]

SEEKER   "Any antidotes?"

MUNGER   "I have what I call an 'iron prescription' that helps me keep sane when I drift toward preferring one intense ideology over another. I feel that I'm not entitled to have an opinion unless I can state the arguments against my position better than the people who are in opposition. I think that I am qualified to speak only when I've reached that state."[968]

SEEKER   "That's a tough one."

LIBRARIAN "For example, take our strong and passionate views on complex issues — the economy, climate change, crime, energy, health care, foreign policy, you name it. We think we know the correct solution but do we really? As Peter Medawar said, 'The intensity of a conviction that a hypothesis is true has no bearing over whether it is true or not.'"[969]

SEEKER   "When you phrase it like that, I assume we don't."

MUNGER   "What I'm against is being very confident and feeling that you know, for sure, that your particular intervention will do more good than harm given that you're dealing with highly complex systems wherein everything is interacting with everything else."[970]

LIBRARIAN "As a good friend says, 'Don't mess with complex systems if you're not fluent.' We don't know what the causal chain looks like."

SEEKER   "But what about curing policies based on scary scenarios from computer models?"

LIBRARIAN "How can a computer model reflect reality given, as Mr. Munger said, we're dealing with complex systems no one fully understand? And how can you make a policy based on what you can't know? Reality is more complicated than the models. And getting the reality right is the basis for good actions. Diseases must be diagnosed before they can be cured. And if the diagnosis is wrong, the prescription will be wrong.

        "Unfortunately, instead of following the medical maxim, 'First do no harm', some scares have done more harm than good. As Molière said, 'Nearly all men die of their remedies, and not of their illnesses.'"

MUNGER   "These mathematical techniques have created a lot of false confidence."[971]

SEEKER   "But these models seem so precise?"

LIBRARIAN "Henri Matisse said, 'Exactitude is not truth'[972]…and as John von Neumann is reported to have said, 'There is no sense in being precise, when you don't even know what you're talking about.'"[973]

        "Unfortunately, many issues involve a lot of ideological verbiage where many of the participants have vested interests in believing things that aren't true — it may get them a lot of publicity, grants and power."

SEEKER   "Anything else I should be thinking about?"

114

LIBRARIAN "Since sometimes there is little or no scientific or well-supported evidence to support a lot of publicized policies or claims, we once more have to ask the Montaigne question, 'Yes, but is it true?' Some people create their own facts and conveniently leave out the real facts. To paraphrase a saying by financier and statesman Bernard Baruch, 'Everyone's entitled to their own opinions, but not to their own facts.'"

SEEKER "I hadn't thought about that—which of course is natural since I haven't been known to do much thinking."

LIBRARIAN "We should all try to do what true scientists do—strive for objectivity—trying to describe the world as it is, accepting uncertainty and leaving room for doubt and questioning our beliefs and conclusions. It is so easy to make mistakes and fool ourselves. To paraphrase Bertrand Russell, 'The whole problem with the world is that fools and fanatics are always so certain of themselves, but wiser people so full of doubts.'"[974]

MUNGER "I think the mindset of science is very useful outside of science... because it tries harder than any other discipline not to fool itself...The ethos of not fooling yourself is one of the best ethos that you can possibly have."[975]

BUFFETT "Apply logic to help avoid fooling yourself. Charlie will not accept anything I say just because I say it, although most of the world will."[976]

LIBRARIAN "The way science is supposed to be done—by forming hypotheses and testing them—is a great way to avoid fooling yourself."

"One thing that often shows us and our 'opponent' that none of us understand as much as we think we do is to take the 'explain HOW-would-that-work-test.'"[977]

SEEKER "I can't wait, please tell me."

LIBRARIAN "When you want to question someone's opinion on a complex policy, don't ask them to give you reasons for why they believe as they do—it only makes them defensive and often they stick to their beliefs even harder. Instead ask them to explain in detail how the policy would actually work in reality to accomplish the desired goals—how it step by step could be implemented—the steps and mechanisms involved in getting it done. And also if they have thought through other effects."

"This often makes us all realize that we don't understand as much as we think we do."

SEEKER "It seems right—at least for me. There are so many times I have found out that I had strong opinions on what is right or should be done without having a clue on the 'how.'"

LIBRARIAN "Another thing could be for example to show your 'opponent' the absurd or negative consequences or implications that would follow if what they say would be true. Or, the absurd or negative consequences that would follow if what you say would not be true. You can also show them the unlikely conditions under which an idea makes sense or how hard it is to be implemented."

Seeker   "Give me a simple example."

Librarian "Assume you say, 'We need discipline in schools.' What would be the consequences if this statement weren't true? Negative or unbelievable? Suppose there was no discipline in schools, wouldn't there be more of the behavior we don't want?"

"Of course, merely because we can't spot a flaw in an argument doesn't automatically mean it is true."

Seeker   "Or just because I can spot a flaw doesn't mean it's false."
"Sorry, I couldn't help myself."

Librarian "On the other hand, our experience is that in most cases it doesn't matter what facts you present—you can't change people with arguments that contradict their ideological views. So in many cases it is better not to."

Seeker   "Not even objective facts?"

Librarian "I am sorry but when our beliefs are threatened or when the truth becomes inconvenient, we close our ears to the facts."

Seeker   "More on what doesn't work?"

Librarian "Before we go over to the next folly, let's us take an interlude to emphasize some things—relevant for understanding, thinking and communicating. It is our friend simplicity again."

"Whenever you try to explain the why and how, keep it as simple and clear as possible. Assuming of course you really understand it—as a physicist friend of mine told me many years ago, 'You haven't really understood an idea if you can't in a simple way describe it to almost anyone.' As Cicero said, 'No one can speak well, unless he thoroughly understands his subject.'"

Seeker   "I get it—I need to understand whatever I'm talking about."

Librarian "And knowing definitions or the name of something doesn't mean you understand it. Comprehension isn't about words—there is a difference between knowing the name of something and understanding what it means. So make sure you really understand the meaning—for example, by looking at what happens, the effect that is produced or what is accomplished."

Seeker   "I assume this is also a good test for me to know I really understand the big ideas and how to apply them—since I can't use what I can't understand."

Librarian "Another 'trick' is to write—writing is a kind of thinking. Writing helps you to clarify your thoughts—because to write clearly you must first think clearly."

116

BUFFETT "If you understand an idea, you can express it so others can understand it. I find that every year when I write the report. I hit these blocks. The block isn't because I've run out of words in the dictionary. The block is because I haven't got it straight in my mind yet. There's nothing like writing to force you to think and to get your thoughts straight"[978]

LIBRARIAN "Lee Iacocca said, 'In conversation you can get away with all kinds of vagueness and nonsense, often without even realizing it. But there's something about putting your thoughts on paper that forces you to get down to specifics. That way, it's harder to deceive yourself - or anybody else.'"[979]

BUFFETT "I learn while I think when I write it out. Some of the things I think I think, I find don't make any sense when I start trying to write them down and explain them to people...And if it can't stand applying pencil to paper, you'd better think it through some more."[980]

SEEKER "I think I get it—To write clearly is to clear up my thinking so writing helps me clarify my thinking."

LIBRARIAN "And know what you want to achieve. Many times simplicity is hard to achieve because to simplify we need to know where we are going."

"As we've said—if your thinking is clear you can also express things in a clear and simple way—but don't assume that the other party knows the same as you about the subject."

MUNGER "I have this friend who is really not very smart at all. He makes everybody explain things until he understands it... But he does have incredible patience. He doesn't do anything unless he understands it."[981]

SEEKER "Any trick?"

LIBRARIAN "Richard Feynman had a great question to the speaker when he listened to a talk in a field he didn't know well. 'Can you give me a really simple example of what you're talking about?' If the speaker couldn't oblige, Feynman got suspicious...Did this person really have something to say, or was this just fancy technical talk parading as scientific wisdom?'"[982]

SEEKER "A great test."

LIBRARIAN "Take as an example what Einstein said on relativity, 'When a man sits with a pretty girl for an hour, it seems like a minute. But let him sit on a hot stove for a minute and it's longer than any hour. That's relativity.'"[983]

SEEKER "Even I get that."

LIBRARIAN "The lesson—always be as clear and concrete as possible. A good thing to remember is Mr. Munger's Orangutan theory."

SEEKER "We're going to talk about apes now?"

MUNGER "If a smart person goes into a room with an orangutan and explains whatever his or her idea is, the orangutan just sits there eating his banana, and at the end of the conversation, the person explaining comes out smarter."[984]

LIBRARIAN "Just assume you're explaining something to an orangutan."

BUFFETT "There's something about smart people explaining ideas to an orangutan that makes their decision-making better."[985]

LIBRARIAN "It forces us to organize our thoughts, speak simpler, and cut the clutter and crap to get to the key point. In short—it clarifies your thinking and message. And explaining even helps the learning process."

"To emphasize once again the importance of clarity I will use the wise words of the Swedish bishop and author Esaias Tegnér who in a poem 200 years ago wrote, 'What you cannot clearly say, you don't know: To tongue of man his thought brings word: What's said obscurely is what's thought obscurely.'"[986]

SEEKER "Ok, to speak obscurely is to think obscurely, to speak clearly is to think clearly. I need to improve here—in most cases my tongue outruns my thoughts."

LIBRARIAN "The unclearly said is the unclearly thought. As the saying goes, 'Sometimes it is good if what comes out of the mouth is first allowed to pass the brain.'"

"And with clear thought comes simplicity. As the Chinese writer and inventor Lin Yutang said, 'Simplicity...is the outward sign and symbol of depth of thought...How difficult is clarity of thought, and yet it is only as thought becomes clear that simplicity is possible.'"[987]

SEEKER "I really like this keep it simple ethos you guys have. You really are great in your ability to make things less complicated and clearer and reducing things to their essence."

LIBRARIAN "I have always liked Douglas Hofstadter's guiding principles, 'Clarity, simplicity, and concreteness have coalesced into a kind of religion for me—a set of never-forgotten guiding principles.'"[988]

"Always when I hear Mr. Buffett and Mr. Munger, I am thinking about Einstein's reply to a student. The student had challenged Einstein's statement that the laws of physics should be simple by asking: 'What if they aren't simple?' Einstein replied, 'Then I would not be interested in them.'"[989]

"So don't go searching for complications where there are none— admire simplicity."

SEEKER "But clear thinking and simplicity is not easy."

LIBRARIAN "No—nothing good comes easy. Like everything else it takes effort, patience and practice. It is like Steve Jobs said, 'You have to work hard to get your thinking clean to make it simple.'"[990]

SEEKER "This is so so good. Ok I'm ready for the next folly."

MAKE IT EASY FOR PEOPLE TO CHEAT, STEAL AND BEHAVE BADLY

MUNGER   "If you run a business where it's easy to steal because of your methods, you're working a great moral injury on the people who work for you.[991]…you will cause a lot of good people to go bad."[992]

BUFFETT   "They usually behave worse if they find out they can get away with something."[993]

LIBRARIAN "And then they rationalizes their bad behavior."

MUNGER   "One more sad example of evil rewarded dying hard, as a great many people conclude that something can't be evil if they are profiting from it."[994]

LIBRARIAN "And as soon as they start to behave badly, they do it again since we repeat what worked for us the last time. That is how bad habits form."

MUNGER   "As these things are paid off—when this fraud and folly is rewarded—of course, you get more of it."[995]

BUFFETT   "It's like stealing five bucks from the cash register and promising yourself you'll pay it back. You never do. You end up the next time stealing ten bucks. Once you start that kind of game, it draw's everybody in. The organization picks up on it, people get cute and clever, and it snowballs."[996]

MUNGER   "Not everyone…resists the social contagion of bad behavior. And, therefore, we often get 'Serpico Syndrome,' named to commemorate the state of a near-totally corrupt New York police division joined by Frank Serpico[997]…You know, everybody else is doing it and you are a sucker if you don't go along and so on and so on[998]…He was then nearly murdered by gunfire because of his resistance to going along with the corruption in the division. Such corruption was being driven by social proof plus incentives, the combination that creates Serpico Syndrome."[999]

BUFFETT   "Once you get a significant number of important players benefiting from any kind of corruption in any kind of system, you're going to have a terrible time changing it. That's why it should be changed early."[1000]

MUNGER   "To rephrase Burke, 'For folly and evil to triumph in the world all that is necessary is for the wise and good men to do nothing.'"[1001]

SEEKER   "What works?"

MUNGER   "Because both bad and good behavior are made contagious by Social-Proof Tendency, it is highly important that human societies (1) stop any bad behavior before it spreads and (2) foster and display all good behavior."[1002]

"A system that can be easily defrauded ruins a civilization[1003]… You are not going to be helped by contrition and shame—human being as they are—you've got to have civilized procedures to prevent people going crazy[1004]…I think you've got to have whole lines of activity that people simply aren't allowed to engage in."[1005]

BUFFETT   "You better not have a system that is dependent on the absence of fraud. It will be with us."[1006]

MUNGER   "You have to set up a system in which it's not easy for human beings to cheat or delude themselves."[1007]

SEEKER   "Such as?"

MUNGER   "Making humans system as cheating-proof as practicable, even if this leaves some human misery unfixed. After all, the people who create rewarded cheating on a massive scale leave a trail of super-ruin in their wake, since the bad conduct spreads by example and is so very hard to reverse."[1008]

LIBRARIAN   "Just remember to not set a policy on the margin — irritating the 99 honest to catch the 1 rotten."

   "If opportunity makes the 'thief' then reduce the opportunities. What do you think will happen if we make if effortless, seen as not risky, very rewarding and no or little penalty if caught?"

SEEKER   "I get it. Anything more?"

MUNGER   "It's hard to fix human systems without fixing human incentives[1009]…If the incentives are wrong, the behavior will be wrong. I guarantee it. Not by everybody, but by enough of a percentage that you won't like the system."[1010]

SEEKER   "Give me an example."

MUNGER   "Early in the history of Xerox, Joe Wilson…had to go back to Xerox because he couldn't understand why its new machine was selling so poorly in relation to its older and inferior machine. When he got back to Xerox, he found out that the commission arrangement with the salesmen gave a large and perverse incentive to push the inferior machine on customers, who deserved a better result."[1011]

   "You don't want to be in a perverse incentive system that's rewarding you if you behave more and more foolishly, or worse and worse[1012]…If you get in a place with a lot of perverse incentives it's hard to keep your sanity."[1013]

SEEKER   "So how do you two avoid crazy incentives?"

MUNGER   "We carefully structured our life and system so we didn't have to be under crazy incentives…I do not trust myself well enough and I behave better than most to have a lot of perverse incentives on myself to do bad things…much better to set yourself up so that the temptations are low."[1014]

SEEKER   "Give me one more example on incentives."

MUNGER   "One of my favorite cases about the power of incentives is the Federal Express case. The integrity of the Federal Express system requires that all packages be shifted rapidly among airplanes in one central airport each night. And the system has no integrity for the customers if the night work shift can't accomplish its assignment fast. And Federal Express had one hell of a time getting the night shift to do the right thing."[1015]

SEEKER   "So what did they do?"

MUNGER   "They tried moral suasion. They tried everything in the world without luck. And, finally, somebody got the happy thought that it was foolish to pay the night shift by the hour when what the employer wanted was not maximized billable hours of employee service but fault-free, rapid performance of a particular task. Maybe, this person thought, if they paid the employees per shift and let all night shift employees go home when all the planes were loaded, the system would work better. And, to and behold, that solution worked."[1016]

SEEKER   "Brilliant!"

MUNGER   "The iron rule of nature is that you get what you reward for—if you want ants to come, put sugar on the floor."[1017]

LIBRARIAN "Since people go where there is a reward and we get what we reward for, what do you think will happen if we reward what we don't want?"

SEEKER   "We get it."

BUFFETT   "If you have behavior you want to get rid of it's probably not the smartest idea to reward it. If you have a dog peeing on your carpet, you do not want to start giving it a bunch of dog biscuits."[1018]

"You…have to have the right rewards and penalties for behavior. That's how you get decent behavior."[1019]

MUNGER   "It's all about the incentives… Always follow the incentives as far as you can, and there you'd find solutions and truth."[1020]

"It is almost a general rule of…life that, when incentives are all wrong, controls (even criminal law controls) can't fix our troubles."[1021]

SEEKER   "I assume when we talk about rewards, we're not only talking about money?"

MUNGER   "Although money is the main driver among rewards, it is not the only reward that works. People also change their behavior and cognition for sex, friendship, companionship, advancement in status, and other nonmonetary items."[1022]

LIBRARIAN "Money, vanity, reputation, power…we are all motivated by different things."

BUFFETT   "There are certain assets—sports teams, newspapers, movie studios—that have a 'psychic income'—power, ego, influence—and that's something that people will pay for."

"If you want to spend $1 billion on something that has value beyond its economic value, you could buy the New York Yankees, and you would immediately become important. If you buy the New York Times, you become even more important. People will do things and spend money to become important — it's part of human nature."[1023]

LIBRARIAN "And as you know we hate when something we like is or threatens to be, taken away. Avoiding losses and what's painful is its own reward."

"And remember that different people are rewarded by different things and we also need to identify a person's total reward system. Someone may do something that doesn't seem to make sense but sometimes the positive reinforcement of the bad behavior outweigh the negative reinforcement of some punishment — which many times isn't certain to happen anyway."

SEEKER "Regarding incentives — more things that are important to think about?"

LIBRARIAN "Make sure the decision maker has the same interests as you so people do what you want because it is also what they want. As Jean de La Bruyère said, 'The shortest and best way of making your fortune is to let people clearly see that it is in their interests to promote yours.'"[1024]

MUNGER "Upton Sinclair said, 'It is difficult to get a man to understand something when his salary depends upon him not understanding it.'"[1025]

"To set up incentives which reward A and then tell people that you want B...is always going to cause a lot of A."[1026]

LIBRARIAN "Never expect people to act against self-interest."

MUNGER "It is hard to be wise when the messages which drive you are wrong messages produced by a mal-designed system."[1027]

BUFFETT "A large system cannot ask many individuals to behave contrary to what they perceive to be in their own self-interest...Any system with that built in as a premise contains the seeds of its own destruction."[1028]

LIBRARIAN "Tie incentives to performance and to the factors that determine the result you want to achieve. If you for example have a business that measures and reward performance by the amount of steel produced, they will get a lot of steel produced. But the amount of produced steel is only one part of the equation. Is this really what ultimately creates what we want to achieve in the end — value?"

"Thomas Sowell illustrates this well, 'When Soviet nail factories had their output measured by weight, they tended to make big, heavy nails, even if many of these big nails sat unsold on the shelves while the country was 'crying for small nails'.'"[1029]

"So first ask: what factors cause what we want to achieve?"

SEEKER "How do you incentivize your managers?"

BUFFETT   "Berkshire employs many different incentive arrangements, with their terms depending on such elements as the economic potential or capital intensity of a CEO's business. Whatever the compensation arrangement, though, I try to keep it both simple and fair."[1030]

"When capital invested in an operation is significant, we also both charge managers a high rate for incremental capital they employ and credit them at an equally high rate for capital they release."[1031]

MUNGER   "They're very simple and we don't tend to change them often. It's amazing how well it has worked."[1032]

BUFFETT   "We want to have compensation policies that are both easy to understand and in sync with what we wish our associates to accomplish."[1033]

"It's not highly complex, but you have to understand the business…We do not bring in compensation consultants and we don't have a human resources department, legal department, etc. That makes life way to complicated, and people get vested in going to conferences."[1034]

MUNGER   "I'd rather throw a viper down my shirt front than hire a compensation consultant."[1035]

SEEKER   "How about a cyclical type of business—say an oil business?"

BUFFETT   "If oil goes from $30 to $60, there's no reason to pay [an oil company executive] for that. If they have low finding costs, which they can control, I'd pay them like crazy for that. That is the job you hire them for. To hand them huge checks for something they have no control over is crazy, and it's equally crazy to penalize them if oil prices go down. If oil prices went down and my CEO had low finding costs, we'd pay him like crazy."[1036]

SEEKER   "Anything else on compensation?"

BUFFETT   "They are always tied to the operating results for which a given CEO has authority. We issue no lottery tickets that carry payoffs unrelated to business performance. If a CEO bats .300, he gets paid for being a .300 hitter, even if circumstances outside of his control cause Berkshire to perform poorly. And if he bats .150, he doesn't get a payoff just because the successes of others have enabled Berkshire to prosper mightily."[1037]

MUNGER   "Perhaps the most important rule in management is 'Get the incentives right.'"[1038]

BUFFETT   "That makes a difference. It doesn't solve everything, I mean, you can still get terribly optimistic managements that will do very stupid things and all that."[1039]

LIBRARIAN   "And have a responsible system."

SEEKER   "Responsible?"

LIBRARIAN   "For example, what do you think happens when people are protected from the consequences of bad behavior?"

SEEKER   "They will behave badly."

LIBRARIAN "No one wants to stop what is rewarded — especially if they don't pay any price for being wrong."

MUNGER   "We have to have people subject to carrots and sticks. You take away the stick and that whole system won't work."[1040]

BUFFETT   "In our book, alignment means being a partner in both directions, not just on the upside. Many 'alignment' plans flunk this basic test, being artful forms of 'heads I win, tails you lose.'[1041]...The Kiewit Company [is] the most successful construction company in the world and it has been for decade... and it's got a set of management principles and basically it started with Pete Kiewit saying that arranging a compensation system so when the company got in trouble not only he went broke but all the people that got him in trouble went broke."[1042]

"When an executive only has upside and no downside, it will always lead to excessive risk-taking[1043]...You have to create a downside... There have to be incentives — not only to get rich, but to behave well."[1044]

SEEKER   "But you have a downside in your Berkshire shares."

BUFFETT   "I'm making the decisions at Berkshire. When I make the decisions at Berkshire, I'm thinking about the fact that a) I've got 99% of my net worth in it and it's all going to charities so I mean, if I cause this place to go broke, there's a lot of downside to me. And there's a lot of downside to the Kiewit Company if they do silly things in their construction business. And I think that downside has an effect on people."[1045]

LIBRARIAN "Yes — it is a responsible system — just as the philosopher Charles Frankel recommended."

MUNGER   "He said the system is responsible in proportion to the degree that the people who make the decisions bear the consequences.[1046]

"The best cure is to have a system where the people who make the decisions bear the consequences."[1047]

LIBRARIAN "Ask, 'Who benefits? Who bear the consequences?'"
"Tell him about the Roman system."

MUNGER   "An example of a really responsible system is the system the Romans used when they built an arch. The guy who created the arch stood under it as the scaffolding was removed. It's like packing your own parachute."[1048]

SEEKER   "Like eating my own cooking."

LIBRARIAN "Let us now turn it around — what do you think will happen if you put decisions in the hands of those who don't pay any price for being wrong, reward people for what you don't want and set up the system so the chance of being caught if people cheat is minimal?"

SEEKER   "This inversion stuff always clarifies things."

MUNGER "Everybody relearns the same lessons over and over again. Human nature is such that you have to have tough systems[1049]...a system which minimizes human weakness and builds a culture of accountability."[1050]

BUFFETT "You have to build in human nature, and then you have to counteract where human nature takes you, when it takes you some place that you don't want it to go."[1051]

LIBRARIAN "Yes, you better not design a system that counts on people not being human."

BUFFETT "That is not the way the world works."[1052]

LIBRARIAN "We can't change human nature — like someone once said, 'You can shoot the tiger, or stay out of his way, but you cannot pronounce him a vegetarian.'"

MUNGER "You can't blame the tiger for being a tiger. But you need a gamekeeper[1053]...It is insane to blame the tiger when he gets out of the cage and goes on a rampage. The cage has to be stronger and the keepers should know better than to leave the door unlocked."[1054]

LIBRARIAN "You just have to create an environment with the right systems in place to get the behavior you want — systems that are aligned with human nature. And remember Maimonides observation that to understand human behavior, just watch it — people move towards what they find agreeable, and away from what they find disagreeable."

SEEKER "Anything more that is important to consider?"

MUNGER "Another generalized consequence of incentive caused bias is that man tends to 'game' all human systems...Antigaming features... constitute a huge and necessary part of almost all system design. Also needed in system design is an admonition: Dread, and avoid as much you can, rewarding people for what can be easily faked[1055]...If I were running the world I wouldn't pay off anything that can be easily faked."[1056]

LIBRARIAN "Another thing needed is to sometimes make some systems a little bit unfair."

MUNGER "The craving for perfect fairness causes a lot of terrible problems in system function."[1057]

SEEKER "I always believed we all want to be treated fairly?"

LIBRARIAN "We do — in fact, we react strongly to unfairness."

BUFFETT "Nobody wants to work in an environment where they feel they're being treated unfairly."[1058]

LIBRARIAN "But fairness is not always about treating every system the same."

MUNGER "Some systems should be made deliberately unfair to individuals because they'll be fairer on average for all of us. Thus, there can be virtue in apparent non-fairness."

"I frequently cite the example of having your career over, in the Navy, if your ship goes aground, even if it wasn't your fault. I say the lack of justice for the one guy that wasn't at fault is way more than made up by a greater justice for everybody when every captain of a ship always sweats blood to make sure the ship doesn't go aground. Tolerating a little unfairness to some to get a greater fairness for all is a model I recommend."[1059]

LIBRARIAN "Give him the workers' compensation example on cheating and justice."

MUNGER "Let's say you have a desire to do public service. As a natural part of your planning, you think in reverse and ask, 'What can I do to ruin our civilization?' That's easy. If what you want to do is to ruin your civilization, just go to the legislature and pass laws that create systems wherein people can easily cheat. It will work perfectly."[1060]

"Is the system sound when obvious fraud goes on a massive scale? I would say no. And it spreads. You get what you reward for. That's why the claims keep coming and coming and coming."[1061]

LIBRARIAN "Of course, we can never totally eliminate the risk of cheating or 'catch' all the crooks. As the old expression goes, 'Show me a ten-foot wall and I'll show you an eleven-foot ladder.'"

SEEKER "Reminds me of the saying, 'Make it foolproof, and someone will make a better fool'"

LIBRARIAN "A zero-tolerance policy doesn't work and only take resources from other things—what you want is as small risk as possible."

SEEKER "Any final words on the subject of cheating."

MUNGER "I once heard of child-teaching method so effective that the child remembered the learning experience over fifty years later. The child later became Dean of the USC School of Music and then related to me what father said when he saw his child taking candy from the stock of his employer with the excuse that he intended to replace it later. The father said, 'Son, it would be better for you to simply take all you want and call yourself a thief every time you do it.'"[1062]

LIBRARIAN "Just remember not to complicate your system—make it simple."

MUNGER "One of the greatest ways to avoid trouble is to keep it simple. When you make it vastly complicated—and only a few high priests in each department can even pretend to understand it—what you're going to find out all too often is that those high priests don't really understand it at all. They understand how to game the system, so they do pretty well—but the system often goes out of control."[1063]

SEEKER   "One learns something every minute here."
          "Any more craziness?"

RISK WHAT YOU HAVE AND NEED, TO GET WHAT YOU DON'T NEED

BUFFETT   "The idea of risking what you need and is important to you for something that you don't need and is unimportant is just craziness. And we try to run Berkshire with that principle in mind."[1064]

MUNGER   "I've always felt that people were crazy to risk what they have and need—namely, wonderful jobs—for tiny, little, incremental advantages or to avoid tiny, little, incremental detriments."[1065]

SEEKER   "You better give me an example."

LIBRARIAN "Long Term Capital Management [LTCM] was a hedge fund with a team of top traders and 'Nobel' laureates that used complex mathematical models combined with high financial leverage."

          "In 1998 LTCM lost more than 90% of its $4.8 billion of assets—their models fell apart."

MUNGER   "LTCM was a classic example of smart people doing dumb things—their IQ got in the way. People that know the edge of their competency are safe, those that don't are dangerous."[1066]

BUFFETT   "If you take the 16 of them, they have about as high an IQ as any 16 people working together in one business in the country…An incredible amount of intellect in one room. Now you combine that with the fact that those people had extensive experience in the field they were operating in."

          "They had in aggregate, the 16, had 300 or 400 years of experience doing exactly what they were doing and then you throw in the third factor that most of them had most of their very substantial net worth's in the businesses. Hundreds and hundreds of millions of their own money up (at risk), super high intellect and working in a field that they knew. Essentially they went broke. That to me is absolutely fascinating."[1067]

MUNGER   "They relied too much on mathematical formulas and too little on common sense."[1068]

BUFFETT   "It is like Henry Kauffman said, 'The ones who are going broke in this situation are of two types, the ones who know nothing and the ones who know everything.' It is sad in a way."[1069]

LIBRARIAN "Reminds me of something William Osler said, 'One of the most delightful sayings of antiquity is the remark of Heraclitus upon his predecessors—that they had much knowledge but no sense.'"[1070]

MUNGER   "People were actually making decisions about how much risk to take, based on the application of correct math[1071]…There was only one trouble with the math: The assumption was wrong… too many extreme things happened that the math didn't correctly predict."[1072]

BUFFETT "The guys at Long-Term Capital Management were extremely intelligent, but they just didn't contemplate what could happen — they thought the future would look like the past."[1073]

SEEKER "Once more I learn that high IQ doesn't always help one from falling."

MUNGER "The problem isn't getting rich, it's staying sane."[1074]

BUFFETT "Charlie and I have run into more dysfunctional people with 160 IQs than most people, probably…We've seen people self-destruct in pursuit of making money they didn't really need because they were already rich."[1075]

LIBRARIAN "Still, there are people who risk everything for something they can't possibly need."

BUFFETT "But to make money they didn't have and didn't need, they risked what they did have and what they did need. That is just plain foolish; it doesn't matter what your IQ is. If you risk something that is important to you for something that is unimportant to you it just doesn't make sense."

"The downside, especially if you are managing other people's money, is not only losing all your money, but it is disgrace, humiliation and facing friends whose money you have lost."[1076]

SEEKER "A friend of mine was comfortably rich but he always felt he never had enough so during the internet craze he saw a great opportunity to make more by leveraging up because it looked so easy. And it started well, in fact so well that he convinced himself that he knew what he was doing. But reality caught up with him and in the end, he lost most of his money."

"Afterwards he told me he felt like Mr. E. Blackadder when he said, 'Goodbye, Millionaire's Row. Hello, Room 12 of the Budleigh Salterton Twilight Rest Home for the Terminally Short of Cash!'"[1077]

MUNGER "I knew a guy who had $5 million and owned his house free and clear. But he wanted to make a bit more money to support his spending, so at the peak of the internet bubble he was selling puts on internet stocks. He lost all of his money and his house and now works in a restaurant."[1078]

LIBRARIAN "Yes, history repeats over and over again — some people never know when they are rich enough. They always look up to someone else as being richer so the higher their bar goes."

BUFFETT "There was a lousy book with a great title written by Walter Gutman — You Only Have to Get Rich Once. Now that seems pretty fundamental."[1079]

SEEKER "What a great truth."

MUNGER "I think the people who say, 'I need more' and therefore try to get more than they need, are likely to get into terrible trouble."[1080]

BUFFETT "If you have $100 million at the beginning of the year and you will make 10% if you are unleveraged and 20% if you are leveraged 99 times out of a 100, what difference if at the end of the year, you have $110 million or $120 million? It makes no difference."

"If you die at the end of the year, the guy who makes up the story may make a typo, he may have said 110 even though you had a 120. You have gained nothing at all. It makes absolutely no difference. It makes no difference to your family or anybody else."[1081]

SEEKER "More please."

LIBRARIAN "What we just talked about ties in with something else."

ONLY LOOK AT THE SUNNY UPSIDE

LIBRARIAN "How about we play a game of Russian Roulette? Here, take this revolver with six chambers and one bullet."

SEEKER "Are you nuts?"

LIBRARIAN "No, it's a perfectly reasonable deal. Pull it once and if you win, you get $1 million. There are 6 equally likely possible outcomes when you pull the trigger—empty, empty, empty, empty, empty, bullet. It is an 83% chance that you get $1 million. Pretty good isn't it?"

SEEKER "You ask me if I want to play a lottery with 6 tickets where one ticket is lethal?"

LIBRARIAN "Yes, the probability is only 17% that you lose."

BUFFETT "$83\frac{1}{3}\%$ of the time it works to play Russian Roulette with one bullet and six chambers."[1082]

SEEKER "Thanks for the offer, but I decline."

LIBRARIAN "How about if I make the price $10 million?"

SEEKER "Now you're talking. $10 million is an awful lot of money and as you say, the chance is 83% that I win."

LIBRARIAN "Are you really sure? Let's look at the consequences if you bet 'no bullet' but you turn out wrong."

SEEKER "I'll die—you're right, no money is worth the risk of getting killed."

MUNGER "You only get to live once."[1083]

BUFFETT "I don't care if the odds you succeed are 99 to 1 or 1000 to 1 that you succeed. If you hand me a gun with a million chambers with one bullet in a chamber and put it up to your temple and I am paid to pull the trigger, it doesn't matter how much I would be paid. I would not pull the trigger. You can name any sum you want, but it doesn't do anything for me on the upside and I think the downside is fairly clear. Yet people do it financially very much without thinking."[1084]

LIBRARIAN "I would never play Russian Roulette just as I would never play around with alligators."

BUFFETT "In our view, it is madness to risk losing what you need in pursuing what you simply desire."[1085]

LIBRARIAN "So the lesson here is that we can't only look at how likely or unlikely something is—which is hard to know anyway—by definition you can't know in advance what will happen. We must always consider how severe the consequences of being wrong are."

SEEKER "Explain."

BUFFETT "You've got to make sure that the mistakes don't kill you."[1086]

LIBRARIAN "'A single slip may cause lasting sorrow' says a Chinese proverb."

BUFFETT "Anything times zero is zero and I don't care how good the record is in every other year if one year there's a zero…Charlie and I have seen guys go broke or close to it because 99 of 100 of their decisions were good, but the 100th did them in."[1087]

LIBRARIAN "All that matters is if a decision or an event are consequential— its immediate and long-term consequences. What happens if you make the wrong decision or something happens that you didn't expect? Does it matter? How does it affect you—its downside/upside or costs/benefits? And as we've said before, mistakes or events don't matter if they are harmless."

BUFFETT "If we can't tolerate a possible consequence, remote though it may be, we steer clear of planting its seeds."[1088]

LIBRARIAN "If a catastrophic outcome is possible or you can't judge the downside, stay away."

BUFFETT "I try to operate in a way where I can't lose significant sums over time. I might not make the most money this way, but I will minimize the risk of permanent loss. If there's 1 in 1000 chance that an investment decision can threaten permanent loss to other people, I just won't do it."[1089]

SEEKER "I wish I had known something about this way of reasoning before. I tell you why. Ten years ago I was employed by a company that was under investigation by the authorities."

LIBRARIAN "Because of something you did?"

SEEKER "No, my boss—I had nothing to do with it. But it was such a bad situation I was thinking of resigning. Unfortunately, I decided to stay and even after I was cleared people assumed I also was guilty and treated me like a criminal."

"Now, how would you reason in a case like this?"

BUFFETT   "I always start from a position of fear…I always look at the downside first in anything."[1090]

LIBRARIAN "Is a catastrophic outcome possible? If yes, what option gives me the lowest chance of a catastrophe?"

"What are my options—resign or stay. If I resign because I bet that my boss is as crook but I'm wrong—he is innocent—I will look stupid and lose my friends."

"If I stay because I bet that my boss is innocent but I'm wrong—he is a crook—I will be guilty by association and treated like a criminal. In which alternative do I lose less? What option gives me the lowest downside?"

SEEKER   "I made the wrong call, I should have resigned—that option was the least harmful."

LIBRARIAN "In making 'to do or not to do' choices always weigh the consequences of being wrong in each case."

BUFFETT   "Individually, we probably worry more about the downside than just about any manager you can find. Collectively, it's Armageddon around here every day. But we care about that."[1091]

LIBRARIAN "Another problem is the 'so far, so good' trap or when you play Russian Roulette but you don't know it. For example, you do something that has the potential to turn into a catastrophe but you are fooled into a false sense of security by the success so far. But as the saying goes, 'Don't think there are no crocodiles because the water is calm.' Merely because a catastrophe hasn't happened yet doesn't mean it won't happen. As Richard Feynman said in connection with the Challenger investigation, 'When playing Russian roulette the fact that the first shot got off safely is little comfort for the next.'"[1092]

BUFFETT   "The fundamental principle of auto racing is that to finish first, you must first finish. That dictum is equally applicable to business and guides our every action at Berkshire."[1093]

SEEKER   "Interesting this approach to first focus on what can go wrong or the downside and if and what can turn something into a catastrophe. That's not how I did it, for sure."

LIBRARIAN "There is a story attributed to George Bernard Shaw. It goes something like this: A foreign actress wrote to Mr. Shaw as follows: 'My dear Mr. Shaw: I beg to remind you that as you have the greatest brain in the world, and I have the most beautiful body, it is our duty to posterity to have a child.' Whereupon Mr. Shaw replied: 'My dear: I admit that I have the greatest brain in the world and that you have the most beautiful body, but it might happen that our child would have my body and your brain. Therefore, I respectfully decline.'"

"I don't know if this story is true or not but Mr. Shaw claimed that he once received a comparable 'strange offer' from a 'foreign actress', and that he did make that reply."[1094]

SEEKER   "I have to remember this—to first look at the downside."

LIBRARIAN "Another benefit of first looking at the downside or what can go wrong is efficiency. Take investments as an example—If you first eliminate what doesn't work or what won't achieve what you want, you don't have to spend a lot of time and attention of analyzing the company. If there is a huge downside—for example a catastrophe risk or the key factors that are needed for success aren't there or any other disqualifying factors like no sustainable advantage, bad and untrustworthy management or something else—just say 'no thank you.'"

SEEKER   "The backward approach again—to first focus on what to avoid/ what not to do or to paraphrase what you said earlier, 'All I want to know if there are any factors that can cause me to die, so I'll never go there.'"

BUFFETT   "Understand the downside not just today but five to ten years from now."[1095]

LIBRARIAN "As Cardinal de Retz said, 'The most ordinary cause of people's mistakes are their being too much frightened at the present danger, and not enough so at that which is remote.'"[1096]

SEEKER   "Assuming the downside is bearable, what about the upside?"

BUFFETT   "When I see something that looks attractive, I start getting greedy...but I'm always looking at the downside on something first."[1097]

LIBRARIAN "Didn't your investments in Korean stocks look pretty good on those criteria?"

BUFFETT   "We found some securities in Korea a few years ago that were ridiculously cheap[1098]...good balance sheets and trading at 2 times or 3 times earnings and a business that wouldn't go obsolete."[1099]

"There was almost no chance that you don't make money... unless war breaks out or there's a major disaster, but you run that risk investing anywhere."[1100]

LIBRARIAN "The other side of the consequential coin is if the upside makes a difference. How much does your wealth change? Does it have a real impact?"

BUFFETT   "Though there are as many good businesses as ever, it is useless for us to make purchases that are inconsequential in relation to Berkshire's capital. (As Charlie regularly reminds me, 'If something is not worth doing at all, it's not worth doing well.')"[1101]

MUNGER   "We don't spend a lot of time thinking about things that will make practically no money."[1102]

LIBRARIAN "If you have little to lose but much to gain from a certain action —
do it. But run away — and quickly — from anything with a big downside
and little upside or an unprotected downside."

SEEKER "Give me an example of how I can protect myself from unbearable
consequences."

LIBRARIAN "There is a story about Napoleon's mother, Letizia. She couldn't
understand why Napoleon should take on the British since things were
going so well."

"So she sold all of her French holdings and exchanged them for
British pounds."[1103]

SEEKER "Why?"

LIBRARIAN "If her son won, she should have a good life in the victorious
nation. But if he lost, she would not be wiped out but still be ok since she
had the pounds."

"She hedged or protected her assets."

SEEKER "Smart lady...I understand now — I think so anyway."

"Now, I would like us to move over more to business and
investing — part from what you've told me so far, what else works and
does not work?"

–PART THREE–

ON WHAT ELSE DOESN'T WORK AND WHAT DOES IN BUSINESS AND INVESTING

"I am a better investor because I am a businessman and a better businessman because I am an investor."

–Warren E. Buffett

INVEST YOUR MONEY IN OVERPRICED ASSETS – PREFERABLY BUSINESSES WITHOUT ANY COMPETITIVE ADVANTAGES OR FUTURE AND WITH LOUSY AND CROOKED MANAGEMENT

If you are a businessman think like an investor and if you're an investor think like a businessman

MUNGER "I think that business experience and investment experience both help in making investments."[1104]

LIBRARIAN "They interact."

BUFFETT "Being an investor you're buying pieces of a business so you better understand business. And being a businessman, you better understand alternatives for money in terms of allocating capital – and therefore you are partially an investor[1105] …because investments are simply business decisions in terms of capital allocation."[1106]

MUNGER "I understood reality better when I approached the study of business from the viewpoint of a person considering investing in it[1107]…I think it's very useful to have a capitalistic perspective on products, namely how do you make this thing work for the people that own it?"[1108]

"I think corporate managers ought to study investing more, because they'd be better managers. And I think that everyone who thinks through the investment process learns more about how the world really works."[1109]

BUFFETT "In what I think is by far the best book on investing ever written – 'The Intelligent Investor', by Ben Graham – the last section of the last chapter begins with, 'Investment is most intelligent when it is most businesslike.' (This section is called 'A Final Word', and it is appropriately titled.)"[1110]

"I'd advise you to get exposure and experience in a number of businesses—whether it´s a part time, full time or anything else—because there´s nothing like seeing how businesses operate to build your judgment. When you understand what kind of things are more competitive and what kind of things are less competitive and why things work as they do, all of those things add to your knowledge."[1111]

SEEKER   "I've been working in different businesses so maybe I have some knowledge there, even though things didn't work out too well. I better listen carefully to what you say."

"By the way, what is investing really about?"

Investing is about where to allocate your capital

BUFFETT   "The only reason for making an investment and laying out money now is to get more money later on, right?[1112]...And obviously, you're looking for the highest interest rate."[1113]

SEEKER   "Yes—even if I seem to have gotten it backward."

BUFFETT   "That's what investing is all about."[1114]

"The question is how much you get back, when you expect to get it back, and how sure you are that you'll get it back[1115]...and what interest rates are."[1116]

SEEKER   "Interest rates?"

BUFFETT   "The value of every business—the value of a farm, an apartment house or any other economic asset—is 100% sensitive to interest rates. That's because all you're doing when you're investing is transferring money to someone now in exchange for a stream of money which you expect to come back in the future. And the higher interest rates are, the less that present value will be. "[1117]

SEEKER   "So the lower rates are, the higher the value, or?"

BUFFETT   "Interest rates are to asset prices sort of like gravity to the apple. When interest rates are low there is little gravitational pull on asset prices... Interest rates power everything in the economic universe."[1118]

SEEKER   "I assume profits are worth a lot now since interest rates are so low?"

BUFFETT   "Obviously profits are worth a whole lot more when the government bond is 1% than if the government bond yield is 5%...I look at those numbers, but I also look at them in the context of the fact that we're living in a world that has incredibly low interest rates and the question is how long will those interest rates prevail? Will it become like Japan where it's gone on for decades and decades?"[1119]

SEEKER   "Confusing."

MUNGER   "If you aren't confused I don't think you understand it very well."[1120]

SEEKER   "I read some countries even have negative rates — as I said confusing."

MUNGER   "It's new territory...I think something so strange and so important is likely to have consequences. I think it's highly likely that the people who confidently think they know the consequences down in the economics profession, none of them predicted this...I don't know what's going to happen. I regard it all as very weird, if interest rates go to zero, and all of the governments in the world print money like crazy, and prices are going down. Of course I'm confused. Anybody who's intelligent and is not confused doesn't understand the situation very well. I think in fact that, if you find it puzzling, your brain is working correctly."[1121]

SEEKER   "This is the first time anyone has complemented me on having a confused mind."

"Going back to what investing is, you mean, it doesn't matter what I invest in — it is the same way of reasoning?"

BUFFETT   "It's true whether if you're buying a farm, it's true if you're buying an apartment house, any financial asset...oil in the ground, you're laying out cash now to get more cash back later on. And the question is how much are you going to get, when are you going get it, and how sure are you?"[1122]

"You'd try to figure out what you were laying out currently and what you're likely to get back over time, how certain you felt about getting it and how it compared to other alternatives."[1123]

SEEKER   "I had never thought about investing this way."

BUFFETT   "All I can tell you is what I do basically — and that's to try to figure out what a business is worth."[1124]

SEEKER   "Please, continue — tell me how I can go astray here and what works."

LIBRARIAN   "Buy a popular broker-recommended bad business you don't understand that operates in an industry with brutal competition and that lack any competitive advantage operated by a management that lacks integrity, intelligence, experience and dedication and buy it at a ridiculously high price."

SEEKER   "This inversion stuff really works — at least I get that I shouldn't overpay."

Buy "wrongly" cheap productive assets you understand

Buffett "Price is all important[1125]...The first law of capital allocation... is that what is smart at one price is dumb at another[1126]...Long ago, Ben Graham taught me that 'Price is what you pay; value is what you get.' Whether we're talking about socks or stocks, I like buying quality merchandise when it is marked down."[1127]

"We want to buy things we understand, and we want to buy them very cheap. If we don't understand them, we don't buy them. If they're not cheap, we don't buy them."[1128]

Librarian "But remember that a cheap business may be cheap for the right reason—so full of problems that it turns out to be no bargain at all—so ask if it is cheap for the right or wrong reason."

Buffett "The original purchase 'bargain' price probably will not turn out to be such a steal after all. In a difficult business, no sooner is one problem solved than another surfaces—never is there just one cockroach in the kitchen."[1129]

Librarian "You never want to catch a falling knife that keeps on falling—you'll only get hurt."

Buffett "If you are in a lousy business for a long time, you will get a lousy result even if you buy it cheap. If you are in a wonderful business for a long time, even if you pay a little bit too much going in you will get a wonderful result if you stay in a long time."[1130]

"Our goal is to find an outstanding business at a sensible price, not a mediocre business at a bargain price. Charlie and I have found that making silk purses out of silk is the best that we can do; with sow's ears, we fail."[1131]

Seeker "Based on experience, I assume."

Buffett "More than 50 years ago, Charlie told me that it was far better to buy a wonderful business at a fair price than to buy a fair business at a wonderful price. Despite the compelling logic of his position, I have sometimes reverted to my old habit of bargain-hunting, with results ranging from tolerable to terrible."[1132]

Munger "The investment game always involves considering both quality and price, and the trick is to get more quality than you pay for in price. It's just that simple."[1133]

Buffett "We usually feel we are paying too much...we could have paid significantly more money for some businesses and it still would have been a good decision. In general, if you get a chance to buy a good business where you think there is a high degree of certainty that it has economic characteristics that they will earn unusually high rates over time, or, better yet, can reinvest to grow, you should probably stretch a little."

"It happened with See's Candies. We were paying 5% more than I wanted and Charlie said, 'For god's sakes Warren write the check.' We always think it is too expensive."[1134]

SEEKER   "But it turned out to be a great deal."

BUFFETT   "To date, See's has earned $1.9 billion pre-tax, with its growth having required added investment of only $40 million. See's has thus been able to distribute huge sums that have helped Berkshire buy other businesses that, in turn, have themselves produced large distributable profits. (Envision rabbits breeding.) Additionally, through watching See's in action, I gained a business education about the value of powerful brands that opened my eyes to many other profitable investments."[1135]

SEEKER   "But how do you know when a stock is rightly cheap?"

BUFFETT   "Most stocks at one time or another sell at very silly prices, and it doesn't take a high IQ to figure out that they're cheap[1136]...After all, you need not know a man's precise age to know that he is old enough to vote nor know his exact weight to recognize his need to diet."[1137]

LIBRARIAN   "Like your investment in the oil company Petro China."

BUFFETT   "With something like Petro China, my reaction is similar to seeing somebody who weighs somewhere between 300 and 350 pounds. I might not know how much they weigh, but I know they're fat."

"And that's all I'm looking for—knowing if an opportunity is financially fat. And whether Petro China weighed $95 billion or $105 billion, it didn't make much difference. It was selling for $35 billion...any further refining of analysis would've been a waste of time."[1138]

LIBRARIAN   "No need for extra analysis—just know what you need to know."

SEEKER   "So exactness is not necessary?"

BUFFETT   "We are very inexact...How certain we are is the most important part...You'd be amazed at how inexact we are[1139] ...Using precise numbers is, in fact, foolish; working with a range of possibilities is the better approach."[1140]

MUNGER   "We never sit down, run the numbers out and discount them back to net present value...The decision should be obvious."[1141]

SEEKER   "How did you think when you looked at Petro China?"

BUFFETT   "When you get a company that is producing 2-1/2 million barrels a day, that's 3% or more of the world's oil production, and they're selling based on U.S. prices using WTI (West Texas Intermediate) as a base price, and where they have a significant part of the marketing and refining in a country where the tax rate's 30% and they say they're going to pay out 45% of earnings to you in dividends, and they don't have unusual amounts of leverage—if you're buying something like that at well under half, or

138

maybe a third, of what comparable oil companies are selling for, it's not rocket science[1142]...You just have to do the work."[1143]

MUNGER   "But when you were buying, no-one else was. It required uncommon sense."[1144]

SEEKER   "By the way, what's the key factor to look at in an oil company?"

BUFFETT   "The most important metric, over time is finding costs per MCF [million cubic feet of gas] or barrel [of oil][1145]...I'd measure the cost of finding new reserves over time—the ability to discover and extract oil at low unit costs."[1146]

SEEKER   "Ok, I get it, low finding costs. Resonates with what you said was important when deciding compensation for executives in the oil industry."
"And if the asset is not cheap?"

LIBRARIAN "You wait."

SEEKER   "Patience has never been my strong side. I always wanted to get rich quickly."

BUFFETT   "People want to get rich—especially without working."[1147]

MUNGER   "Basically, I think the desire to get rich fast is pretty dangerous. My own system was to get rich slow, and it protracts a rather pleasant process."[1148]

BUFFETT   "No matter how great the talent or efforts, some things just take time. You can't produce a baby in one month by getting nine women pregnant."[1149]

MUNGER   "It takes character to sit there with all that cash and do nothing. I didn't get to where I am by going after mediocre opportunities."[1150]

BUFFETT   "You have to wait for the fat pitch. There's no use running if you're on the wrong road."[1151]

SEEKER   "How long do you wait?"

MUNGER   "You have to wait until something comes along, which, at the price you're paying, is easy."[1152]

LIBRARIAN "Sit still until you find a no-brainer."

MUNGER   "If you have a big edge, back it heavily because you don't get a big edge often. Opportunity comes, but it doesn't come often, so seize it when it does come[1153]...being prepared, on a few occasions in a lifetime, to act promptly in scale in doing some simple and logical thing will often dramatically improve the financial results of that lifetime."[1154]

LIBRARIAN "To quote a line from Shakespeare's *Julius Caesar*, 'There is a tide in the affairs of men, which, taken at the flood, leads on to fortune.'"

MUNGER   "Really good investment opportunities aren't going to come along too often and won't last too long, so you've got to be ready to act and have a prepared mind."[1155]

"And if you can't think fast and act resolutely, it does you no good. So you're like a man standing by a stream trying to spear a fish. And if the fish just comes by once a week or once a month or once every ten years, you've got to be there to throw that spear fast before the fish swims on."[1156]

BUFFETT   "Some days it's raining gold. Not very often, but when it is, you've got to be out there. And that will happen periodically. It'll happen, but you can't make it happen. In the meantime, you let the cash pile up if that's what happens."[1157]

MUNGER   "I think the record shows the advantage of a peculiar mind-set — not seeking action for its own sake, but instead combining extreme patience with extreme decisiveness."[1158]

"That's contrary to human nature. Just to sit there all day doing nothing but waiting. It's easy for us. We've got a lot of other things to do. For an ordinary person, can you imagine just sitting for five years doing nothing?"[1159]

SEEKER   "Impossible for me."

MUNGER   "It's so contrary to human nature. You don't feel active, you don't feel useful, so you do something stupid."[1160]

"It's waiting that helps you as an investor, and a lot of people just can't stand to wait. If you didn't get the deferred-gratification gene, you've got to work very hard to overcome that."[1161]

BUFFETT   "The trick is, when there is nothing to do, do nothing[1162]...You don't get paid for activity. You only get paid for being right."[1163]

SEEKER   "When are things really cheap?"

Things are often cheapest when people are fearful and pessimistic

BUFFETT   "You make your best buys when people are overwhelmingly fearful[1164]...The most common cause of low prices is pessimism — some times pervasive, some times specific to a company or industry."[1165]

MUNGER   "When everybody is totally discouraged and think the world is going to hell, that's when we like to be buying."[1166]

SEEKER   "I always bought when it was sunny and when the market was going up. My optimism was flourishing."

BUFFETT   "Charlie and I don't expect to win...you over to our way of thinking — we've observed enough human behavior to know the futility of that — but we do want you to be aware of our personal calculus. And here a confession is in order: In my early days I, too, rejoiced when the market rose."[1167]

SEEKER   "But it looked so easy — the market was going up and up."

BUFFETT "Remember the late Barton Biggs' observation: 'A bull market is like sex. It feels best just before it ends.'"[1168]

LIBRARIAN "Good times, booms, temporary tailwinds or lousy competition can also fool you that business or management performance is better than it really is—or vice versa during the opposite."

"There is a saying, 'In the land of the blind, the one-eyed man is king.' And it is very easy for managers to fool themselves believing they are really good when their competitors are blind."

BUFFETT "A rising tide lifts all yachts[1169]...you only see who's being swimming naked when the tide goes out."[1170]

SEEKER "My investments didn't have a thread on their body when the market turned."

"Stupid me!—but I was so caught up in the game."

BUFFETT "It's just the scope of human beings to do crazy things, self-destructive things...most people, even smart people, have trouble not getting caught up in the game and thinking I'll just dance one more dance like Cinderella at five minutes till twelve or something like that because they think they are smarter than the rest of the public...Or they don't protect themselves against something that will come totally from right field."[1171]

SEEKER "And we never seem to learn—at least not me. I'll do more crazy things."

BUFFETT "Human beings do crazy things from time to time...You can't rule out human emotions. When people get greedy as a pack, strange things happen. When they get fearful as a pack, strange things happen... Confidence is not going to exist when fear exists. Fear is very contagious. It spreads very quickly."[1172]

LIBRARIAN "And because of our loss aversion, fear motivates us more than greed does."

BUFFETT "A climate of fear is your friend when investing; a euphoric world is your enemy."[1173]

"Attractive opportunities come from observing human behavior...It's just capitalizing on human behavior...It's people that make opportunities when others are frozen by fear or excited by greed. Human behavior allows for success if you are able to detach yourself emotionally."[1174]

MUNGER "If you stay rational yourself, the stupidity of the world helps you."[1175]

LIBRARIAN "And things may change but human nature stays the same. I think it was the trader Jesse Livermore who said, 'Wall Street never changes. The pockets change, the suckers change, the stocks change, but Wall Street never changes because human nature never changes.'"[1176]

BUFFETT "People will always behave in a manic-depressive way over time[1177]...When people panic, when fear takes over, or when greed takes over, people react just as irrationally as they have in the past[1178]...Occasional outbreaks of those two super-contagious diseases, fear and greed, will forever occur in the investment community. The timing of these epidemics will be unpredictable. And the market aberrations produced by them will be equally unpredictable, both as to duration and degree. Therefore, we never try to anticipate the arrival or departure of either disease."[1179]

SEEKER "And what do you do instead?"

BUFFETT "Our goal is more modest: we simply attempt to be fearful when others are greedy and to be greedy only when others are fearful."[1180]

"The less the prudence with which others conduct their affairs, the greater the prudence with which we should conduct our own affairs."[1181]

SEEKER "What type of assets do you prefer?"

Be opportunistic and adapt and change when the facts and circumstances change

BUFFETT "We will look at any category of investment, so long as we understand the business we're buying into and believe that price and value may differ significantly."[1182]

MUNGER "We don't have a master theory of asset allocation. We're simply opportunity driven—individual opportunity driven."[1183]

BUFFETT "Our acquisition technique at Berkshire is simplicity itself: We answer the phone."[1184]

"Moreover, we are free of historical biases created by lifelong association with a given industry and are not subject to pressures from colleagues having a vested interest in maintaining the status quo. That's important: If horses had controlled investment decisions, there would have been no auto industry."[1185]

LIBRARIAN "And you don't need that many opportunities."

MUNGER "I just had the idea that maybe we could find a few, often enough so it would serve our lifetime needs, and we were patient and we waited and we occasionally made a few investment decisions."[1186]

BUFFETT "Yeah. As I've said before, you wait for the fat pitch."[1187]

SEEKER "How many do I need in a lifetime?"

MUNGER "If you took our top fifteen decisions out, we'd have a pretty average record. It wasn't hyperactivity but a hell of a lot of patience. You stuck to your principles and when opportunities came along, you pounced on them with vigor."[1188]

BUFFETT "Charlie and I decided long ago that in an investment lifetime, it's just too hard to make hundreds of smart decisions...Therefore, we adopted a strategy that required our being smart—and not too smart at that—only a very few times."[1189]

"An investor needs to do very few things right as long as he or she avoids big mistakes."[1190]

MUNGER "Through this practice of concentration of investments, we seek to better understand the few decisions we make."[1191]

LIBRARIAN "And sometimes even one investment is good enough. Benjamin Graham said about his investment in GEICO, 'Ironically enough, the aggregate of profits accruing from this single investment decision far exceeded the sum of all the others realized through 20 years of wide-ranging operations in the partners' specialized fields, involving much investigation, endless pondering, and countless individual decisions…one lucky break, or one supremely shrewd decision—can we tell them apart?—may count for more than a lifetime of journeyman efforts.'"

"Graham continues, 'But behind the luck, or the crucial decision, there must usually exist a background of preparation and disciplined capacity'"[1192]

MUNGER "We made some of our luck by being curious and seeking out wisdom and we certainly recommend that."[1193]

LIBRARIAN "Assuming of course one is smart enough to recognize and take advantage of the opportunity."

SEEKER "And some money available—anyway, I get it—from now on I will practice patience and wait for the really big opportunity."

BUFFETT "There will always be opportunities in the market because of people doing extreme things…The future won't be exactly the same, but it rhymes."[1194]

"Periodically, financial markets will become divorced from reality—you can count on that."[1195]

SEEKER "But what is all this talk that the market is efficient?"

BUFFETT "When the price of a stock can be influenced by a herd on Wall Street with prices set at the margin by the most emotional person, or the greediest person, or the most depressed person, it is hard to argue that the market always prices rationally."[1196]

MUNGER "If I were managing $2 million (which, by the way, I once did) I certainly would be looking in a lot of smaller places where I could find more extreme and easy-to-diagnose mispricings."[1197]

"You don't get that many great opportunities in a lifetime. When life finally gave me one, I blew it."[1198]

SEEKER "Tell me."

MUNGER "Many decades ago I made a big mistake caused in part by subconscious operation of my Deprival-Superreaction Tendency. A friendly broker called and offered me 300 shares of ridiculously underpriced, very thinly traded Belridge Oil at $115 per share, which I purchased using cash I had on hand."

"The next day, he offered me 1,500 more shares at the same price which I declined to buy, partly because I could only have made the purchase had I sold something or borrowed the required $173,000. This was a very irrational decision. I was a well-to-do man with no debt; there was no risk of loss; and similar no risk opportunities were not likely to come along. Within two years, Belridge Oil sold out to Shell at a price of about $3,700 per share, which made me about $5.4 million poorer than I would have been had I then been psychologically acute. As this tale demonstrates, psychological ignorance can be very expensive."[1199]

SEEKER   "Maybe it wasn't a missed opportunity—even if you believed you couldn't lose—one never knows."

MUNGER   "There was no risk. I could have borrowed. There wasn't the slightest risk in borrowing money to buy Belridge Oil. The worst that would happen was I would get out with a small profit. It was a really dumb decision."[1200]

"It reminds me, I asked Carl Reichardt when he was running Wells Fargo why he made some dumb decision. He said, 'Charlie, I had my head up my ass.' That is why I made that decision. It was crazy...It didn't take due diligence, I just had to take my head out of a place where it shouldn't be."[1201]

SEEKER   "It seems I've had my head up there most of the time."

MUNGER   "You're not going to get that many really good ones — don't blow your opportunities. They're not that common, the ones that are clearly recognizable with virtually no downside and big upsides."[1202]

"Don't be too timid, when you really have a cinch. Go at life with a little courage."[1203]

SEEKER   "Ok, back again, I know you talked about pessimism and pricing but what is wrong with something popular?"

LIBRARIAN "What glitters is not always gold."

BUFFETT   "Our investments will be chosen on the basis of value, not popularity."[1204]

SEEKER   "But surely a good tip from my broker can't hurt?"

BUFFETT   "What is good for the croupier is not good for the customer."[1205]

"There are fads in Wall Street. And Wall Street will sell what it can sell...It's one of the most important things you should remember in investing."[1206]

LIBRARIAN "Have you already forgotten what we talked about earlier?"

SEEKER   "You're right."

"This is too much information at one time. I need a break and some pie. Man can't live on wisdom alone."

[Author's remark: My wife just entered my study with a homemade blueberry pie with ice cream. So rich and tasty I can hardly finish a second slice.]

SEEKER   "Ok, back again, you talked about how brokers can fool me."

BUFFETT   "The people selling you securities are often selling you things they make a lot of money in. The first question you should ask of anybody selling you securities is, 'How are you getting paid and how much are you getting paid?'"

"And when somebody comes around to you and says, I'm going to sell you this wonderful security but there's this big chunk in it for me, get suspicious. As they say, when a person with experience meets a person with money, the person with the money gets the experience and the person with the experience gets the money."[1207]

SEEKER   "I'll be careful—what about understanding—you mentioned businesses you understand?"

Stick to businesses where you can assess that their economics is good and getting better

BUFFETT   "We try to stick to businesses we believe we understand[1208]... And our definition of understanding is thinking that we have a reasonable probability of being able to assess where the business will be in 10 years... It's not a question of understanding the product they turn out, the means they use to distribute it—all of that sort of thing—it's the predictability of the economics of the situation 10 years out."[1209]

"We try to figure out whether its economics—meaning its earning power over the next five or ten or fifteen years—are likely to be good and getting better or poor and getting worse. And we try to evaluate its future income stream[1210]...'Does it look like it has good economics? Has it earned high returns? Does it strike me as something that's likely to do that?'[1211]... It's all about evaluating the economic potential, the economic future of a given business."[1212]

LIBRARIAN   "Take See's as an example."

BUFFETT   "When we bought See's Candy 1972, we had to come to a judgment about whether we could figure out the competitive forces that would operate, the strengths and the weaknesses of the company and how it would look over a 10- or 20- or 30-year period."[1213]

SEEKER   "So if the economics is good you buy?"

BUFFETT   "Of course, a business with terrific economics can be a bad investment if it is bought for too high a price."[1214]

SEEKER   "Isn't it pretty hard to figure out the future?"

BUFFETT   "Seeing the future is impossible in many cases, in our view, and difficult in others. But sometimes it's relatively easy. And those are the ones that we're looking for."[1215]

"That means they must be relatively simple and stable in character. If a business is complex or subject to constant change, we're not smart enough to predict future cash flows."[1216]

SEEKER   "Give me an example."

BUFFETT   "I know what the chewing business will look like ten years from now[1217]...The internet isn't going to change the way people chew gum. It isn't going to change which gum they chew. If you own the chewing gum market in a big way, and you've got Doublemint, and Spearmint, and Juicy Fruit, those brands will be there 10 years from now."[1218]

"We don't want to own things where the world is going to change rapidly because I don't think I can see change that well or any better than the next fellow. So, I really want something that I think is going to be quite stable, that has very good economics going for it."[1219]

LIBRARIAN   "There has to be some reasonable predictability of the economics."

BUFFETT   "We favor businesses and industries unlikely to experience major change. The reason for that is simple...we are searching for operations that we believe are virtually certain to possess enormous competitive strength ten or twenty years from now. A fast-changing industry environment may offer the chance for huge wins, but it precludes the certainty we seek[1220]...A business that constantly encounters major change also encounters many chances for major error."[1221]

SEEKER   "But don't all businesses change?"

BUFFETT   "Obviously all businesses change to some extent. Today, See's is different in many ways from what it was in 1972 when we bought it: It offers a different assortment of candy, employs different machinery and sells through different distribution channels."

"But the reasons why people today buy boxed chocolates, and why they buy them from us rather than from someone else, are virtually unchanged from what they were in the 1920s when the See family was building the business. Moreover, these motivations are not likely to change over the next 20 years, or even 50[1222] ...We are best at evaluating businesses where we can come to a judgment that they will look a lot like they do now in five years. The businesses will change, but the fundamentals won't."[1223]

SEEKER   "Ok, I understand that certain businesses are more resistant to change than others."

BUFFETT   "You have to understand when competitive advantages are durable and when they're fleeting."[1224]

"So I focus on the absence of change. So, when I look at the Internet, for example, and I look at a new business, I try and figure out how

146

that industry or that company can be hurt or changed, and I avoid that…I don't think the Internet is going to change…whether people shave or how they shave."[1225]

SEEKER "Going back to what you talked about earlier on the consistency tendency and how hard it is to change people. Doesn't this also mean that if people are reluctant to change it is hard for a new product to displace another one?"

LIBRARIAN "There is a form of Occam principle in physics that is as valid for us humans — the principle of least action. And just as nature finds the shortest path for a beam of light, we humans naturally do things in a way that require minimal effort and time."

SEEKER "Now you've lost me — what has this to do with me changing products?"

LIBRARIAN "Trying to change our habits demands effort and effort takes energy — which is a cost. And our brains constantly look for ways to save effort. Furthermore, a change creates an uncomfortable feeling so naturally we try to avoid this feeling by not changing. That's why we take the easy way, favor shortcuts, and default options and stick to our habits. And the more emotional a decision is or the more choices we have, the more we prefer the status quo."

BUFFETT "People's habit patterns are very strong. I shave my face on the same side every morning and put on the same shoe first and people are creatures of habit. And the product that they have been receiving every day for great many years has an enormous advantage."[1226]

"I never like to bet on something reversing that has gone in one direction for a long time."[1227]

LIBRARIAN "And then add our natural aversion for losses — we know what we have but we don't know if that we get by switching is better so staying with the status quo feels less risky."

"So it is very hard to change habits or ways of doing things — like for example to displace an existing product people like and have been used to."

MUNGER "Biological creatures…don't like the removal of long-enjoyed benefits."[1228]

LIBRARIAN "Of course, products get replaced when someone comes along that can offer a better, simpler or cheaper alternative."

SEEKER "Ok, back to understanding."

BUFFETT "A lot of businesses I can't understand. I can understand Gillette. I can understand Coca-Cola. I can understand Wrigley's chewing gum. When I say I can understand it, it means I have a pretty good idea of what they're going to look like 10 or 15 years from now. That's understanding a business."[1229]

LIBRARIAN "Understanding is filter number one."

BUFFETT "Risk comes from not knowing what you are doing."[1230]

SEEKER "If you understand the business, then what?"

Buy assets protected with a durable competitive advantage run by able and honest people

BUFFETT "If it passes through that filter, it's whether a company can have a sustainable edge…If we can't understand it, obviously, it's not going to happen. We can't determine whether it has a sustainable edge. And, if we can understand it, we very often conclude that it's not the kind of business that has a sustainable edge."[1231]

SEEKER "Tell me more about sustainable edge—what is needed?"

BUFFETT "In business, I look for economic castles protected by unbreachable 'moats.'"[1232]

SEEKER "You mean like the one that surrounds King Arthur's castle—a defense against threats?"

BUFFETT "'Moats'—a metaphor for the superiorities they possess that make life difficult for their competitors[1233]…We like businesses that are protected in some way from competition."[1234]

"In capitalism, you have these economic castles. Apple, Microsoft, etc. Some have smaller castles. If you have a castle in capitalism, people are going to try to capture it. You need 2 things—a moat around the castle, and you need a knight in the castle who is trying to widen the moat around the castle[1235] …There are some businesses that have very large moats around them and they have crocodiles and sharks and piranhas swimming around them. Those are the kind of businesses you want…Johnny Weissmuller in a suit of armor could not make across the moat."[1236]

SEEKER "I assume this means that the larger the edge a company has, the more protected it is, or the larger the moat or the barriers that stop invaders from entering are."

BUFFETT "The dynamics of capitalism guarantee that competitors will repeatedly assault any business 'castle' that is earning high returns."[1237]

"We try to figure out why the castle's still standing and what's going to keep it standing or cause it not to be standing five, ten or twenty years from now. What are the key factors? How permanent are they? And how much do they depend on the genius of the lord in the castle? Then if we feel good about the moat, we try to figure out whether the lord is going to try to take it all for himself or whether he's likely to do something stupid with the treasure, etc."[1238]

Understand why it has a moat—the key factors and their permanence

MUNGER "You really have to understand the company and its competitive positions."[1239]

LIBRARIAN "Why does the business have an edge against its competitors? Ask, 'why can't company A do what company B does?' 'What stops some competitor from entering the market?'"

BUFFETT "The best way to understand this is to study businesses that have achieved it."[1240]

"I want to understand the moat around the business and how sticky their customers are versus their competitors. I ask customers, 'how often do you compare prices?'"[1241]

SEEKER "The question is then, how does a company get this edge?"

LIBRARIAN "By having something that differentiates them from their competitors."

BUFFETT "Because it's the low cost producer in some area, because it has a natural franchise due to its service capabilities, because of its position in the consumer's mind, because of a technological advantage or any kind of reason at all[1242]...some times through patents, and/or real estate location."[1243]

SEEKER "And a really good moat is...?"

BUFFETT "One of the best moats in many respects is to be a low-cost producer[1244]...Being a low-cost producer of something that's essential to people is going to be a very good business usually."[1245]

"We're the low-cost producer at GEICO in auto insurance among big companies. And when you're the low-cost producer—whether it's copper, or in banking—it's huge."[1246]

SEEKER "So low cost is the key in banks?"

BUFFETT "With banking, low cost money is the key[1247]... It's like comparing a copper producer whose costs are $2.50 a pound with a copper producer whose costs are $1 a pound. Those are two different kinds of businesses. One is going to go broke at $1.50 a pound, and the other one's going to still be doing fine."[1248]

"I love the idea of being into the low-cost producer[1249]...I always have been attracted to the low cost operator in any business and, when you can find a combination of (i) an extremely large business, (ii) a more or less homogenous product, and (iii) a very large gap in operating costs between the low cost operator and all of the other companies in the industry, you have a really attractive investment situation."[1250]

LIBRARIAN "As you said, like your auto insurance company GEICO with its underlying cost advantage."

BUFFETT   "People have to buy auto insurance so everyone is going to have one auto insurance policy per car basically."

"What are they going to buy it on (based on what criteria)? They (customers) will buy based on service and cost. Most people will assume the service is identical among companies or close enough. So they will do it on cost."[1251]

SEEKER   "Yes, saving some money is always good."

BUFFETT   "So they're buying a product they really don't like very well. It costs them a significant part of their family budget. Therefore, cost becomes very important…And saving significant money makes a real difference in a lot of household budgets[1252]…and only a low-cost operation can deliver these."[1253]

SEEKER   "What does this mean — what is the moat?"

BUFFETT   "I have to be a low cost producer — that is my moat[1254]…We're the low-cost producer. And if you're the low-cost producer of something that people have to buy — and it's roughly a $1,500 item — then you've got a terrific, terrific business. And we have durable competitive advantages there."[1255]

"The company's low costs create a moat — an enduring one — that competitors are unable to cross."[1256]

SEEKER   "You mean the reason you make money selling insurance is because you deliver a necessary product at a price people like and the reason you can sell your product at a low price is because you run an extremely efficient and low-cost operation relative to the competition?"

BUFFETT   "Efficiency is the key to low cost[1257]…GEICO's unusual profitability results from its extraordinary operating efficiency and its careful classification of risks, a package that in turn allows rock-bottom prices for policyholders[1258]…and low prices attract and retain good policyholders. The final segment of a virtuous circle is drawn when policyholders recommend us to their friends."[1259]

"The sustainable competitive advantage at GEICO is to be the low-cost producer providing very good service."[1260]

SEEKER   "I love the GEICO commercials."

BUFFETT   "A brand is a promise. And we're getting the promise in people's minds that there's a good chance they can save money if they check with GEICO. And we'll never stop."[1261]

LIBRARIAN   "Another example of a company that is very cost-efficient is your furniture company — The Nebraska Furniture Mart."

BUFFETT   "They buy brilliantly, they operate at expense ratios competitors don't even dream about, and they then pass on to their customers much of the savings. It's the ideal business — one built upon exceptional value to the customer that in turns translates into exceptional economics for its owners."[1262]

SEEKER "Assume I have a business—what is important to think about regarding my customers?"

LIBRARIAN "Think like a customer and make sure you can simply explain your 'product' and why it is different."

BUFFETT "You either figure out what's in your customers' mind and decide you are going to serve them; or you are not going to be in business…Just keep taking care of the customer…In the end, nobody that's ever taken good care of the customer has ever lost…that is the name of the game."[1263]

LIBRARIAN "Take ISCAR as an example."

BUFFETT "ISCAR's products are small, consumable cutting tools that are used in conjunction with large and expensive machine tools. It's a business without magic except for that imparted by the people who run it."

"But Eitan, Jacob and their associates are true managerial magicians who constantly develop tools that make their customers' machines more productive. The result: ISCAR makes money because it enables its customers to make more money. There is no better recipe for continued success."[1264]

LIBRARIAN "There is only one judge of great service and great products—the customer."

"Like Sam Walton once said, 'There is only one boss—the customer—and he or she can fire everybody in the company from the chairman down, simply by spending his or her money elsewhere.'"[1265]

BUFFETT "No company ever does well ignoring its customer."[1266]

LIBRARIAN "Or arguing with them about what they want or should have."

"Like someone said, 'If you don't care about your customers, someone else will.'"

MUNGER "Never abuse current clients by trying to get new ones. Think how this would work in matrimony—if you ignore your current wife while you pursue another one."[1267]

"You would be surprised at the people in life that don't practise that rule."[1268]

BUFFETT "Every day, in countless ways, the competitive position of each of our businesses grows either weaker or stronger. If we are delighting customers, eliminating unnecessary costs and improving our products and services, we gain strength. But if we treat customers with indifference or tolerate bloat, our businesses will wither. On a daily basis, the effects of our actions are imperceptible; cumulatively, though, their consequences are enormous."[1269]

MUNGER "One of the directors [Daily Journal] said very simply, we should make a list of everything that irritates a customer, and then we should eliminate those defects one by one."[1270]

LIBRARIAN "And preferable, have someone without commitment to the past but with a fresh pair of eyes, make the list."

SEEKER "Great! Any ways I can test how strong a moat is?"

One test of the strength of a moat is essentiality and pricing power

BUFFETT "The single most important decision in evaluating a business is pricing power. If you've got the power to raise prices without losing business to a competitor, you've got a very good business. And if you have to have a prayer session before raising the price by a tenth of a cent, then you've got a terrible business."[1271]

LIBRARIAN "And where you have pricing power you have essentiality."

SEEKER "What do you mean?"

LIBRARIAN "It is something the late media mogul Walter Annenberg who owned *The Daily Racing* Form and *TV Guide* explained was one of the reasons for his success."

"He said, 'As to investment techniques, as related to the publishing business, I have had a keen awareness of one aspect which I regard as absolutely fundamental — is this publication essential? The fact is that we have, in our Country, a surprising number of publications, some of them well edited, that have no true essentiality. That is why, as a publisher, I have tried to be careful relative to the element of essentiality in starting a publication or in investing in a publication.'"[1272]

SEEKER "Essential, you mean something people need or want?"

LIBRARIAN "Yes, something you must have or feel you can't be without — the company has something that would be highly missed if it were gone tomorrow — the product is essential to customers and there is no substitute. So two questions to ask are: Is the need that the business is serving likely to go away? Can what the company offer be copied or replaced?"

"I remember Mr. Buffett back in 1991 told students about something that illustrates this. So let's go back in time and see what Mr. Buffett said then."

BUFFETT "The highest priced daily newspaper in the United States, with any circulation at all, is the *Daily Racing Form*…You can charge $2.00 for *The Form*, you can charge $1.50, you can charge $2.50 and people are going to buy it…Why? There is no substitute. If you go to the track, assuming you're a forms player, you don't want 'Joe's Little Green Sheet', you want *The Form*. And it doesn't make any difference what it costs! There is no substitute. And that's why they've got a 65% pretax margin. It doesn't take a genius to figure it out".

"It's an essential business. It will be an essential business five or 10 years from now. You have to decide whether horse racing will be around five or 10 years from now, and you have to decide whether there's any way people will get their information about past performances of different horses from different sources. But you've only got about two questions to answer, and if you answer them, you know the business will make a lot of money."[1273]

SEEKER "This is not like the average newspaper today."

BUFFETT "They were absolutely essential to a very high percentage of the American public 20, 30, or 40 years ago...So they were a product that had pricing power and which was essential to the customer as well as the advertiser. And they've lost that essential nature...they were only essential to the advertiser as long as they were essential to the reader."[1274]

"Now...the number of both print and electronic advertising channels has substantially increased. As a consequence, advertising dollars are more widely dispersed and the pricing power of ad vendors has diminished[1275]...Almost all newspaper owners realize that they are constantly losing ground in the battle for eyeballs. Simply put, if cable and satellite broadcasting, as well as the internet, had come along first, newspapers as we know them probably would never have existed."[1276]

SEEKER "Another 'essential'?"

MUNGER "Reed-Elsevier got rich on one of the greatest business models ever created. They published scientific journals. They didn't pay a dime for the content, because people want to be published. They didn't pay a dime for the reviewing and editing, because the people wanted to do the reviewing and editing as part of their duty to science."

"With content totally free, they published the journal and every library had to buy them, and every leading scientist. It was just a total racket, and every year they raised the price by 15 percent."[1277]

LIBRARIAN "Another essential business is Berkshire's rail and energy operations."

BUFFETT "Society will forever need massive investments in both transportation and energy."[1278]

SEEKER "Tell me some more good things about your energy business."

BUFFETT "The first is common to all utilities: recession-resistant earnings, which result from these companies offering an essential service on an exclusive basis. The second is enjoyed by few other utilities: a great diversity of earnings streams, which shield us from being seriously harmed by any single regulatory body."[1279]

SEEKER "And the railroad?"

BUFFETT "Our BNSF operation...has certain important economic characteristics that resemble those of our electric utilities. In both cases we provide fundamental services that are, and will remain, essential to the economic well-being of our customers, the communities we serve, and indeed the nation."[1280]

"The moat of railroad companies are that no one can build anymore because of saturation."[1281]

MUNGER   "We're not going to create another transcontinental railroad. Do you have any idea what it would cost to duplicate Burlington-Northern's structure based on replacement cost? And this is something we now need — it's not a replacement cost for something that we wouldn't replace."[1282]

SEEKER   "Do you have any more 'essentials'?"

BUFFETT   "Homes and autos will remain central to the lives of most families. Insurance will continue to be essential for both businesses and individuals."[1283]

SEEKER   "Essentiality and pricing power — have to remember that."

BUFFETT   "Any time you can charge more for a product and maintain or increase market share against well entrenched, well known competitors, you know that you have something very special in people's minds."[1284]

"You can almost measure the strength of a business over time by the agony its managers go through in determining whether a price increase can be sustained. You can learn a lot about the durability of the economics of a business by observing the price behavior."[1285]

LIBRARIAN   "And some businesses even have some untapped pricing power — where you can raise the price with no negative effects on unit volume."

BUFFETT   "In our See's purchase, Charlie and I had one important insight: We saw that the business had untapped pricing power."[1286]

"Essentially, every year for 19 years I've raised the price of candy on December 26. And 19 years goes by and everyone keeps buying candy. Every ten years I tried to raise the price of linings a fraction of a cent, and they'd throw the linings back at me. Our linings were just as good as our candies. It was much harder to run the linings factory than it was to run the candy company."[1287]

SEEKER   "You were into linings too?"

LIBRARIAN   "The foundation of today's Berkshire — their textile operation."

BUFFETT   "Nobody ever went into a men's clothing store and said, 'I'd like to buy a pinstriped suit with a Hathaway lining.' Never. They say 'I want a coat' all over the world…The product was undifferentiated. The candy product is differentiated."[1288]

LIBRARIAN   "I remember one company where they raised the prices substantially, and still had as much volume as before. Partly because the users loved their products and partly because it wasn't the user who paid for them anyway. So one question to ask is: 'Who ultimately decides what to buy and how that person measured and rewarded and who pays?'"

BUFFETT "You also see pricing power in efficiencies. For example Burlington Northern rail transport compared to truck transport is three times more cost efficient and competitive. Products that are more cost efficient are able to demand higher prices. Their product has pricing power because their consumers are willing to pay more to capture those efficiencies."[1289]

SEEKER "But moats change, don't they?"

BUFFETT "Every day with every product, the moat widens or narrows[1290]... Our managers of the businesses we run, I have one message to them...we want to widen the moat. We want to throw crocs, sharks and gators—I guess—into the moat to keep away competitors[1291]...And doing that is essential if we are to have the kind of business we want a decade or two from now[1292]...If you do this, everything else follows."[1293]

"Any business that has a widening moat is going to make a lot of money over time."[1294]

MUNGER "Just keeping your eye on the ball of widening the moat—being a steward of the competitive advantage that came to you, and being able to deliver it in a stronger form to those that come after—is such a simple idea... At the Kiewit Company, the had a rule: 'If you can't deliver a subordinate who's capable of taking over from you—if you haven't trained that into your system—were not going to promote you.'"

"These things are all so simple. Yet, instead, we have endless jumbo mumbo, and everybody tries to make it so damned complicated when it's not all that complicated."[1295]

BUFFETT "There seems to be some perverse human characteristic that likes to make easy things difficult."[1296]

"Ben Graham taught me 45 years ago that in investing it is not necessary to do extraordinary things to get extraordinary results. In later life, I have been surprised to find that this statement holds true in business management as well. What a manager must do is handle the basics well and not get diverted."[1297]

SEEKER "Your simplicity ethos again...Anyway, I understand a little better now why you prefer businesses where lack of change is a key ingredient."

BUFFETT "Our own emphasis is on trying to find businesses that are predictable in a general way as to where they'll be in 10 or 15 or 20 years. That means we look for businesses that in general aren't going to be susceptible to very much change. We view change as more of a threat... We're looking for the absence of change to protect ways that are already making a lot of money and allow them to make even more in the future."[1298]

"With See's Candy we don't think things will change much, even though the real profitability is limited to West Coast. We do not see a competitor taking the business."[1299]

LIBRARIAN "Compare this with the car industry."

BUFFETT "There appear to have been at least 2,000 car makes, in an industry that had an incredible impact on people's lives. If you had foreseen in the early days of cars how this industry would develop, you would have said, 'Here is the road to riches.' So what did we progress to by the 1990s? After corporate carnage that never let up, we came down to three U.S. car companies — themselves no lollapaloozas for investors. So here is an industry that had an enormous impact on America — and also an enormous impact, though not the anticipated one, on investors."[1300]

SEEKER "It's less predictability here — more change, too many variables. Hard to guess the winners."

BUFFETT "If you'd taken the heads of the five largest auto companies in 1970, 1975, 1980 and 1985 and put them under sodium pentothal and have them tell you who they thought would be number one 5 years later — or even 2 or 3 — they would have been way off."[1301]

"I've always said the easier thing to do is figure out who loses. And what you really should have done in 1905 or so, when you saw what was going to happen with the auto is you should have gone short horses. There were 20 million horses in 1900 and there's about 4 million horses now. So it's easy to figure out the losers, you know the loser is the horse. But the winner was the auto overall. But 2000 companies just about failed, a few merged out and so on."[1302]

LIBRARIAN "And then we have the T.V. set and radio-industry."

BUFFETT "I think there's, I don't know, 20-25 million sets a year sold in the United States. I don't think there's one of them made in the United States anymore. You'd say, T.V. set manufacturer, what a wonderful business. Nobody had a T.V. in 1950, thereabouts, '45-'50. Everybody has multiple sets now. Nobody in the United States has made any real money making the sets; they're all out of business."

"Radio was the equivalent in the 20s. Over 500 companies making radios in the 1920s. Again, I don't think there's a U.S. radio manufacturer at the present time."[1303]

SEEKER "And just look at the present landscape — young people today doesn't even have a T.V. or a radio — just a computer and a smart phone."

"There is a lesson here."

BUFFETT "Charlie and I avoid businesses whose futures we can't evaluate, no matter how exciting their products may be. In the past, it required no brilliance for people to foresee the fabulous growth that awaited such industries as autos (in 1910), aircraft (in 1930) and television sets (in

1950). But the future then also included competitive dynamics that would decimate almost all of the companies entering those industries. Even the survivors tended to come away bleeding."[1304]

SEEKER "But still, they all looked like they had the prospect of dramatic growth."

BUFFETT "Just because Charlie and I can clearly see dramatic growth ahead for an industry does not mean we can judge what its profit margins and returns on capital will be as a host of competitors battle for supremacy. At Berkshire we will stick with businesses whose profit picture for decades to come seems reasonably predictable. Even then, we will make plenty of mistakes."[1305]

SEEKER "So the key…"

BUFFETT "The key to investing is not assessing how much an industry is going to affect society, or how much it will grow, but rather determining the competitive advantage of any given company and, above all, the durability of that advantage. The products or services that have wide, sustainable moats around them are the ones that deliver rewards to investors."[1306]

"The trick is to have no competitors. That means having a product that truly differentiates itself[1307]…advantages that other people can't copy[1308]…You can develop a good restaurant and somebody can come along and copy it the next day and figure out something new to add to the menu or add a little more parking. People are always looking at successful models and going after them. That's terrific for the consumer. It can be very brutal to be in those kinds of businesses"[1309]

SEEKER "What about pharma companies—surely they have an edge with their different drugs?"

BUFFETT "The question is how you pick a pharma company when you haven't got the faintest idea what your competitor in 6 or 7 years will be offering."[1310]

SEEKER "What about investing in things like Facebook?"

BUFFETT "I really don't know what that business is going to look like ten years from now. I certainly don't know what… [their] competitors will look like ten years from now."[1311]

MUNGER "I don't invest in what I don't understand. And I don't want to understand Facebook."[1312]

"It just doesn't interest me at all to gab all the time on the Internet with people and I certainly hate the idea of young people putting in permanent form the dumbest thoughts and the dumbest reports of action that you can ever imagine[1313]…There is a time in your existence of when your folly ought to be hidden."[1314]

BUFFETT "Understanding the economic characteristics of a business is different than predicting the fact that an industry is going to do wonderfully.

So when I look at the internet businesses or I look at tech businesses, I say this is a marvelous thing and I love to play around on the computer, and I order my books from Amazon and all kinds of things. But I don't know who's going to win. Unless I know who's going to win, I'm not interested in investing; I'll just play around on the computer."[1315]

MUNGER "The question of how long your period in the sun will be is a very good one."[1316]

BUFFETT "In the end, the better mousetrap usually wins. But the people with the second or third best mousetrap will try to keep that from happening. We try to stay away from that sort of thing. We know there will be change, but we don't know who the winners will be."[1317]

LIBRARIAN "Tell him about your rough enterprise-classification and their characteristics."

BUFFETT "Franchise is another way of expressing the moat concept[1318]... An economic franchise arises from a product or service that: (1) is needed or desired; (2) is thought by its customers to have no close substitute and; (3) is not subject to price regulation. The existence of all three conditions will be demonstrated by a company's ability to regularly price its product or service aggressively and thereby to earn high rates of return on capital."

"Moreover, franchises can tolerate mis-management. Inept managers may diminish a franchise's profitability, but they cannot inflict mortal damage."[1319]

MUNGER "Of course you prefer a business that will prosper even if it is not managed well...We are not looking for mismanagement. We like the capacity to stand it if we stumble into it."[1320]

BUFFETT "The test of a franchise is what a smart guy with a lot of money could do to it if he tried...The real test of a business is how much damage a competitor can do, even if he is stupid about returns."[1321]

SEEKER "Franchise — in contrast to what?"

BUFFETT "In contrast, 'a business' earns exceptional profits only if it is the low-cost operator or if supply of its product or service is tight. Tightness in supply usually does not last long. With superior management, a company may maintain its status as a low-cost operator for a much longer time, but even then unceasingly faces the possibility of competitive attack. And a business, unlike a franchise, can be killed by poor management."

"Keep...in mind, however, that many operations fall in some middle ground and can best be described as weak franchises or strong businesses."[1322]

SEEKER "What about if the business is so-so but has a great manager?"

BUFFETT "Of course, a terrific CEO is a huge asset for any enterprise...But if a business requires a superstar to produce great results, the business itself cannot be deemed great. A medical partnership led by your area's premier brain surgeon may enjoy outsized and growing earnings, but that tells little about its future. The partnership's moat will go when the surgeon goes. You can count, though, on the moat of the Mayo Clinic to endure, even though you can't name its CEO."[1323]

SEEKER "Turnarounds?"

BUFFETT "Literally hundreds of turnaround possibilities in dozens of industries have been described to us over the years and, either as participants or as observers, we have tracked performance against expectations. Our conclusion is that, with few exceptions, when a management with a reputation for brilliance tackles a business with a reputation for poor fundamental economics, it is the reputation of the business that remains intact."[1324]

"Good jockeys will do well on good horses, but not on broken-down nags."[1325]

LIBRARIAN "And some industries and businesses have permanently poor economics and a high mortality rate and as the proverb says, 'No matter how hard you throw a dead fish in the water, it still won't swim.'"

"But separate a permanent problem from a temporary setback — assuming it's a fundamentally sound business."

MUNGER "We own a lot of companies that have temporary reversals."[1326]

BUFFETT "A great investment opportunity occurs when a marvelous business encounters a one-time huge, but solvable, problem as was the case many years back at both American Express and GEICO."

"Overall, however, we've done better by avoiding dragons than by slaying them."[1327]

LIBRARIAN "And some businesses may have more problems than you expect and want."

"Take Tesco as an example — bad news often comes to the surface in doses — one problem surface and then another etc. Or we solve one problem and another one soon thereafter arises."

BUFFETT "During 2014, Tesco's problems worsened by the month. The company's market share fell, its margins contracted and accounting problems surfaced. In the world of business, bad news often surfaces serially: You see a cockroach in your kitchen; as the days go by, you meet his relatives."[1328]

SEEKER "As you said earlier, 'In a difficult business, no sooner is one problem solved than another surfaces — never is there just one cockroach in the kitchen.'"[1329]

LIBRARIAN "Didn't you experience that in MidAmerican's mining venture?"

BUFFETT "Last year [2003] MidAmerican wrote off a major investment in a zinc recovery project that was initiated in 1998 and became operational in 2002. Large quantities of zinc are present in the brine produced by our

California geothermal operations, and we believed we could profitably extract the metal. For many months, it appeared that commercially— viable recoveries were imminent. But in mining, just as in oil exploration, prospects have a way of 'teasing' their developers, and every time one problem was solved, another popped up. In September, we threw in the towel."[1330]

LIBRARIAN "And sometimes the first problems may just be the tip of the iceberg. As someone once said, 'behind every little problem there's a larger problem, waiting for the little problem to get out of the way.'"

SEEKER "Tell me about some more businesses and their type of moats. For example consumer products."

BUFFETT "When you get into consumer products, you´re really interested in finding out, or thinking about, what´s in the mind of how many people throughout the world about a product now—and what´s likely to be in their minds five or ten or 20 years from now[1331]... If you are selling a consumer product you want it to be in as many minds as possible with as favorable connotations as possible."[1332]

SEEKER "Like See's Candy."

BUFFETT "See's Candies creates a moat in the minds of consumers[1333]... We bought See's Candy in 1972...What we did know was that they had share of mind in California. There was something special. Every person in California has something in mind about See's Candy and overwhelmingly it was favorable[1334]... It´s associated with pleasant experiences...So it´s not share of market, but share of mind, that counts...The question then becomes what does that name stand for five or ten or 20 years from now?"[1335]

"How did Coca-Cola build their moat? They deepened the thought in people's minds that Coca-Cola is where happiness is. The moat is what's in your mind[1336]...Coca-Cola is associated with people being happy around the world. Everyplace—Disneyland, the World Cup, the Olympics—where people are happy. Happiness and Coke go together."[1337]

LIBRARIAN "To summarize some of what we talked about. Let's translate it into a simple question: Does the business have something people need or want now and in the future (fundamental demand), that no one else has (competitive advantage) or can copy, take away or get now and in the future (sustainable) and can these advantages be translated into business value?"

SEEKER "More on good businesses please—I want to learn more."

BUFFETT "A really wonderful business is very well protected against the vicissitudes of the economy and competition over time[1338]...If you see a business take a lot of adversity and still do well, it tells you something about its underlying strength."[1339]

MUNGER   "The margin of safety in a great business is that it will stand a fair amount of mismanagement if that unfortunate circumstance happens to come along."[1340]

BUFFETT   "The best businesses by far for owners continue to be those that have high returns on capital and that require little incremental investment to grow[1341]...Return on capital employed determines how good a given business is...The question is how much does it need and how much does it get in return."[1342]

"There's a huge difference between the business that grows and requires lots of capital to do so and the business that grows and doesn't require capital...if you're investing, you should pay a lot of attention to that."[1343]

SEEKER   "Other wonderful businesses?"

BUFFETT   "A business is also wonderful if it takes money, but where the rate at which you reinvest the money is very satisfactory."[1344]

"The worst sort of business is one that grows rapidly, requires significant capital to engender the growth, and then earns little or no money."[1345]

"To sum up, think of three types of 'savings accounts.' The great one pays an extraordinarily high interest rate that will rise as the years pass. The good one pays an attractive rate of interest that will be earned also on deposits that are added. Finally, the gruesome account both pays an inadequate interest rate and requires you to keep adding money at those disappointing returns."[1346]

SEEKER   "I assume you shun capital intensive businesses then."

BUFFETT   "Anticipating...that Berkshire will generate ever-increasing amounts of cash, we are today quite willing to enter businesses that regularly require large capital expenditures. We expect only that these businesses have reasonable expectations of earning decent returns on the incremental sums they invest. If our expectations are met—and we believe that they will be—Berkshire's ever-growing collection of good to great businesses should produce above-average, though certainly not spectacular, returns in the decades ahead."[1347]

SEEKER   "I assume that is why you invested in the utility field...are there any capital intensive businesses you rather stay away from?"

BUFFETT   "I would say the capital intensive businesses that scare me more are the ones outside of the utility field where you just pump in more money without knowing that you're going to get—within a range, anyway—a more or less guaranteed return. So there's no way we get rich on our utility investments, but there's no way we get poor either....But on balance, if you can find a good business that's not capital intensive, you're going to be better off in it than in a capital intensive business over time."[1348]

SEEKER   "Anything else that separates the good and the bad?"

MUNGER   "I've heard Warren say since very early in his life that the difference between a good business and a bad one is that a good business throws up one easy decision after another, whereas a bad one gives you horrible choices — decisions that are extremely hard to make: 'Can it work?' 'Is it worth the money?'"

"One way to determine which is the good business and which is the bad one is to see which one is throwing management bloopers — pleasant, no-brainer decisions — time after time after time. For example, it's not hard for us to decide whether or not we want to open a See's store in a new shopping center in California. It's going to succeed. That's a blooper."[1349]

LIBRARIAN "In contrast to the tough airline business. Here you are forced to make investments without really knowing if you're going to make money or not."

BUFFETT   "It's labor intensive, capital intensive and largely a commodity type business[1350]...The airline industry's demand for capital...has been insatiable[1351]...If you are an airline today and you try to raise your prices, an hour later, you will be lowering them because of competition[1352]...In a business selling a commodity-type product, it's impossible to be a lot smarter than your dumbest competitor."[1353]

"I made a mistake when I bought US Air Preferred some years ago. I had a lot of money around. I make mistakes when I get cash. Charlie tells me to go to a bar instead. Don't hang around the office. But I hang around the office and I have money in my pocket, I do something dumb. It happens every time. So I bought this thing...We bought it because it was an attractive security. But it was not in an attractive industry[1354]...But we then got very lucky. In one of the recurrent, but always misguided, bursts of optimism for airlines, we were actually able to sell our shares in 1998 for a hefty gain. In the decade following our sale, the company went bankrupt. Twice."[1355]

SEEKER   "Tell me some common traits for a commodity business."

BUFFETT   "Hundreds of competitors, ease of entry, and a product that cannot be differentiated in any meaningful way."[1356]

MUNGER   "It's very, very hard to avoid being commoditized in high powered competition in the modern world...Many businesses that you thought were hugely advantaged can be hugely commoditized."[1357]

BUFFETT   "When a company is selling a product with commodity-like economic characteristics, being the low-cost producer is all-important."[1358]

SEEKER   "Ok, back again — more tough businesses?"

MUNGER   "For years, I was a director of an International Harvester dealership...That is a really tough business. And there's never any cash.

As the saying goes, at the end of the year, your profit is sitting out in the yard — in the form of your used equipment. And struggling with a business that never produces any cash...is no fun."[1359]

BUFFETT "Our acquisition preferences run toward businesses that generate cash, not those that consume it[1360]...You don't want a business that's like 'a horse that never runs, but eats."[1361]

"In his class, Ben Graham used the example of a hypothetical company he called the Frozen Corporation — which was a company whose charter prohibited it from ever paying out anything to its owners or ever being liquidated or sold....And Ben's question was, 'What is such an enterprise worth?' It's a theoretical question. However, it forced you to think about the realities of what business is all about — which is putting out money today to get back more money later on."[1362]

SEEKER "Any other tough ones?"

BUFFETT "A business that must deal with fast-moving technology is not going to lend itself to reliable evaluations of its long-term economics."[1363]

"That's the problem in high tech — a few will profit, but a lot will have problems, and it's hard to see who does what in advance. We know that Snickers bars will still be sold and do well in 10 years. That doesn't make candy a better business; it's just that we know who the winner is."[1364]

MUNGER "I was in an electronic business where we had what I would call style changes. However, they were really technology changes. Our main product was obsoleted by magnetic tape. And nobody told me that magnetic tape was going to be invented and that it was going to obsolete my main product. And I found it a very unpleasant experience."[1365]

"Technological change is one of the hardest things to cope with, which is why so many people fail at it."[1366]

BUFFETT "I have avoided technology sectors as an investor because in general I don't have a solid grasp of what differentiates many technology companies. I don't know how to spot durable competitive advantage in technology...Technology is based on change; and change is really the enemy of the investor."[1367]

"Our criterion of 'enduring' causes us to rule out companies in industries prone to rapid and continuous change...A moat that must be continuously rebuilt will eventually be no moat at all."[1368]

MUNGER "I am not an expert on the moats of technology companies. The reason, by and large, I don't own them is because I do not understand whether or not their moats will last or not...I'm not sure anybody else knows either."[1369]

"Berkshire of course has consciously avoided rapid technological obsolescence. We own a railroad, we own a lot of utilities, we own big insurance companies...I don't think we're going to hang coal in the sky in balloons or something. I think a railroad doesn't require that much technology, a utility isn't going to have a lot of technological stuff, and neither will an insurance company."[1370]

BUFFETT   "We understand technology, how businesses can apply it, its benefits, impact on society, etc. It's the predictability of the economics of the situation 10 years out that we don't understand. We would be skeptical that anyone can."[1371]

SEEKER   "Anything else that is important to judge the staying quality of the business?"

BUFFETT   "I always ask myself how much it would cost to compete effectively with a business."[1372]

    "You give me a billion dollars and tell me to go into the chewing gum business and try to make a real dent in *Wrigley's*. I can't do it. That is how I think about businesses. I say to myself, give me a billion dollars and how much can I hurt the guy?"[1373]

LIBRARIAN   "The CEO of Intel, Andy Grove had another question—the silver bullet."

SEEKER   "Are we going to kill werewolves now?"

BUFFETT   "When I'd interview managers, I'd ask what their business nightmare is[1374]...If you had a silver bullet and you could put it through the head of one competitor, which competitor and why? You will find who the best guy is in the industry."[1375]

MUNGER   "I think it's important to know which competitor is most likely to do you in."[1376]

LIBRARIAN   "If possible, you can also get some clues on business strength from asking various players in the industry."

BUFFETT   "Ask the management of each company which competitor they would be willing to put their net worth in for the next 10 years. Then ask which of their competitors they would short. This will provide important insights into the industry that even those who work their whole life in the industry would not realize."[1377]

    "I would also always ask, 'If our roles were reversed, what questions would you ask me if I were running your business?'"[1378]

SEEKER   "We talked earlier about missed opportunity and Belridge Oil. Are there some opportunities you wished you had missed?"

BUFFETT   "A few years back, I spent about $2 billion buying several bond issues of Energy Future Holdings, an electric utility operation serving portions of Texas. That was a mistake—a big mistake."[1379]

SEEKER   "So where did you go wrong?"

BUFFETT   "A fundamental assumption—that gas prices would go higher—was wrong. That was a basic error[1380]...I totally miscalculated the gain/loss probabilities when I purchased the bonds."[1381]

MUNGER   "I once knew a man who had a nice wife and children. And in five minutes between trains, he managed to conceive an illegitimate child by some woman he met in the club car. When asked why he did it, he said, 'It seemed like a good idea at the time.'"[1382]

BUFFETT   "A line from a country song seems apt: 'I wish I didn't know now what I didn't know then.'"[1383]

SEEKER   "Any more mistakes?"

BUFFETT   "We bought what we thought was a second-rate department store in Baltimore[1384]...[Hochschild Kohn]... at a third-rate price, but we found out very quickly that we bought a fourth-rate department store at a third-rate price. And we failed at it, and we failed..."[1385]

MUNGER   "Quickly. "[1386]

BUFFETT   "Yeah, quickly. That's true. We failed other times in retailing. Retailing is a tough, tough business, partly because your competitors are always attempting and very frequently successfully attempting to copy anything you do that's working. And so the world keeps moving. It's hard to establish a permanent moat that your competitor can't cross. And you've seen the giants of retail, the Sears, the Montgomery Wards, the Woolworth's, the Grants, the Kresges. I mean, over the years, a lot of giants have been toppled."[1387]

MUNGER   "Buying Hochschild Kohn was like the story of a man who buys a yacht. The two happy days are the day he buys it and the day he sells it."[1388]

BUFFETT   "After ending our corporate marriage to Hochschild Kohn, I had memories like those of the husband in the country song, 'My Wife Ran Away With My Best Friend and I Still Miss Him a Lot.'"[1389]

MUNGER   "I think retailing is going to get tougher and tougher and tougher...Costco got one of the major toothpaste manufacturers of the world to make their toothpaste in Costco's tube at a very low price. This is not good for the Procter and Gambles, the Unilevers of the world, and the Colgates of the world. So, generally speaking, that's one threat. Then you add the Amazon threat...where you just punch a button and it comes the next day. You don't have to drive through traffic; you don't have to look for a parking spot. You don't have to wait in line."[1390]

BUFFETT   "Amazon...could affect a lot of businesses who don't think they will be affected. For Amazon, it is very hard to find unhappy customers. A business that has millions and millions of happy customers can introduce them to new items, it will be a powerhouse and could affect a lot of businesses."[1391]

MUNGER   "It is almost sure to hurt a lot of businesses a lot. Anything that can be easily bought with a home computer or iPad. I think it will hugely affect a lot of people—it's terrible for most retailers. It is not slightly terrible, but really terrible."[1392]

BUFFETT   "If I were buying a retail business, I would think about what people will try to do to that business through the internet."[1393]

MUNGER   "Then you add the fact that we have too damn many stores that are the natural over-optimism of both lenders and real estate developers and merchants and so forth."[1394]

BUFFETT   "If you substitute 5% of the retail volume via the internet where real estate is essentially free, you can have a store in every town in the world through the internet without having any rental expense…I would give a lot of thought to that if I were owning a lot of retail rental space."[1395]

SEEKER   "One more."

BUFFETT   "I spent $244 million for shares of two Irish banks that appeared cheap to me[1396]…I was wrong on the Irish banks in a very big way. I simply didn't understand, and it was available for me to understand, the incredible exposure they'd gotten to land-development-type loans…For a country with 4+ million people, they had money lent for developing properties and homes that would extend just forever in the future. It was a terrible mistake—by me. Nobody lied to me or gave me any bad information. I just plain wasn't paying attention."[1397]

"Upon leaving, our feelings about the business mirrored a line in a country song: 'I liked you better before I got to know you so well.'"[1398]

MUNGER   "One of Berkshire's greatest mistakes was when we gave two percent of Berkshire for a wonderful shoe business [Dexter Shoe] in Maine, which was the wonderful, most trusted supplier of J. C. Penney and so on and so on…Berkshire got clobbered by the Chinese competition in shoes."[1399]

BUFFETT   "We don't buy businesses with much thought of world trends, but we do think about businesses subject to foreign competition, with high labor content and a product that can be shipped in."[1400]

MUNGER   "If you're in any business of a manufacturing nature that China can do well, after you consider transport, then you're in the crosshairs of a very formidable opponent. Why didn't we recognize this with the shoe business? Well, as a German philosopher once said, 'Too soon old and too late smart.'"[1401]

BUFFETT   "Nobody misled me, I just looked at it and came to the wrong answer[1402]…I assessed the future competitive position inappropriately… What I had assessed as durable competitive advantage vanished within a few years[1403]…because of foreign competition."[1404]

MUNGER   "Basically I would say we gave two percent of Berkshire. What we got was hardly anything. It was a big mistake. On the other hand, it just impaired Berkshire's performance by two percent once in one year out of many…we remember the mistake we made in the hope of not repeating it."[1405]

"There's one good side to these things. It does make you more careful. It really refreshes your attention to get banged on the nose like that."[1406]

BUFFETT "A line from Bobby Bare's country song explains what too often happens with acquisitions: 'I've never gone to bed with an ugly woman, but I've sure woke up with a few.'"[1407]

MUNGER "The most extreme mistakes in Berkshire's history have been mistakes of omission. We saw it, but didn't act on it…Since mistakes of omission [aren't visible], most people don't pay attention to them. We rub our noses in mistakes of omission[1408]…There's nothing that improves wisdom more than having your own nose whacked pretty hard."[1409]

BUFFETT "We've had a lot of experience with bad businesses and that makes you appreciate good ones, and to some extent it helps you distinguish the two. And we had a lot of fun doing it, though. If you're enjoying what you're doing, it helps a lot than if you're going to work with your teeth clenched all the time."[1410]

SEEKER "When you made mistakes, was there a common reason?"

BUFFETT "These errors came about because I misjudged either the competitive strength of the business I was purchasing or the future economics of the industry in which it operated."[1411]

SEEKER "But wouldn't due diligence have helped avoid some of these mistakes?"

BUFFETT "We've been burned only when we've made mistakes in judging the future economics of a business—which has nothing to do with due diligence[1412]…Dexter shoe was a disaster. It wasn't the leases or clauses, I was just wrong about the shoe business[1413]…Business judgment about economics—and people, to some extent, but primarily business economics—is 99% of deal making. As for the rest—people may go into it for their protection. Too often, they do it as a crutch—just to go through with a deal that they want to go through anyway. And, of course, all of the professionals know that. So believe me—they come back with the diligence whether it's due or not."[1414]

"And we don't kid ourselves by having lots of studies and reports made. They're going to support whatever they think the guy who pays 'em wants anyway. So they don't mean anything. They're nonsense."[1415]

LIBRARIAN "It is all about the advantages and their durability—a lot of companies seem to have forgotten that."

BUFFETT "When we got the call on Mars-Wrigley I wasn't going to look at labor costs or leases. The value of Wrigley does not depend on the value of the lease or an environmental problem. There is a whole lot of trivia that doesn't mean anything."[1416]

"The idea of due diligence at most companies is to send lawyers out, have a bunch of investment bankers come in and make presentations and things like that. And I regard that as terribly diversionary—because the board sits there entranced by all of that, by everybody reporting how wonderful this thing is and how they've checked out the patents and all of that. But, meanwhile, all too often, nobody's focusing on where the business is going to be in 5 or 10 years."[1417]

SEEKER   "I bet you don't make any more mistakes now."

BUFFETT   "I will make mistakes in the future, that is guaranteed. But, we will not make anything like 'bet the company' decisions that will ever cause us real anguish. That just doesn't happen at Berkshire. You're not going to make a lot of decisions without making an occasional mistake."[1418]

"You cannot be active in a big business without making some mistakes. And sometimes there will be big ones, but you have to look at the whole record[1419]...In the past 50 years, we have only once realized an investment loss that at the time of sale cost us 2% of our net worth. Twice, we experienced 1% losses. All three of these losses occurred in the 1974–1975 period, when we sold stocks that were very cheap in order to buy others we believed to be even cheaper."[1420]

"Fortunately, my mistakes have usually occurred when I made smaller purchases[1421]... our large purchases have generally worked well—extraordinarily well in a few cases."[1422]

SEEKER   "Always good to know that I can make some stupid investments and still end up well."

LIBRARIAN "Don't draw the wrong conclusion. What you have to understand is that no one can really be involved in investments without making occasional mistakes. What's important though is to avoid the big or lethal ones. Small mistakes don't matter."

"One of the things the financial manager Stanley Druckenmiller said he learned from George Soros was that, 'It's not whether you're right or wrong that's important, but how much money you make when you're right and how much you lose when you're wrong.'"[1423]

SEEKER   "I see what you mean, even considering mistakes, Mr. Buffett's and Mr. Munger's accomplishments and long time record is really out of this world—amazing. They did the big things right."

LIBRARIAN "So true, so true. As Mr. Buffett said, you have to look at the whole record over time."

"The other thing we talked about is to acknowledge and act on your mistakes and not fight the wrong or not important battles. And the benefit of acknowledging your mistakes is that hopefully you learned something from them."

BUFFETT   "It's a learning process, and mistakes made in one year often contribute to competence and success in succeeding years."[1424]

"Agonizing over errors is a mistake. But acknowledging and analyzing them can be useful, though that practice is rare in corporate boardrooms...triumphs are trumpeted, but dumb decisions either get no follow-up or are rationalized."[1425]

SEEKER   "I can clearly see I have some work in front of me."

BUFFETT   "Try to learn about who's got good businesses and why they're good businesses. And learn about the businesses that went out of business and why they went out of business."[1426]

MUNGER   "Somebody like Warren or myself can't enter an automobile agency without thinking, 'Is this a good business or a bad business? If it's a bad business, why is it a bad business? If it's a good business, why is it a good business?'"[1427]

BUFFETT   "Charlie is ungodly smart about business and human behavior. He observes a lot."[1428]

SEEKER   "Your 'why?' question again."

MUNGER   "I have a habit in life. I observe what works and what doesn't and why."[1429]

"I do it automatically...If you have that temperament, you will gradually learn. If you don't, then I can't help you."[1430]

BUFFETT   "Yogi Berra said, 'You can observe a lot just by watching.'"[1431]

LIBRARIAN "That is how you get smarter. Open your eyes and look around you and notice what happens and ask 'why?' Is this working or not—why or why not? And if you then understand what works and not and why, you know what to do or not do in different situations."

"You can learn a lot by keeping your mouth shut and your eyes and ears open."

BUFFETT   "If I drive by a McDonald's stand or a Kentucky Fried Chicken stand I will automatically think to myself, 'What is this business worth? How many customers do walk in the door? What kind of gross margins can they have? How many people do they need? How likely it is that another chicken stand opens across the street.' All of those things."

"That's true of the chicken stand and it's true of Google or you name the business. It's all about evaluating the economic potential, the economic future of a given business."[1432]

MUNGER   "You need to have a passionate interest in why things are happening. That cast of mind, kept over long periods, gradually improves your ability to focus on reality. If you don't have the cast of mind, you're destined for failure even if you have a high I.Q."[1433]

SEEKER   "And then use the Occam or Lollapalooza trick, assuming I know some basic ideas—you see, I listen to you guys."

"Give me an example of a successful business and why."

MUNGER   "I'm a director of Costco. It's easy to understand. In the history of the world, few companies have succeeded on a 12% mark-up. They make it up with high volume. Costco has the right culture. They promote from within. It's a wonderful place to work."[1434]

SEEKER   "Anything else I should think about?"

LIBRARIAN "You should also try to understand if the business or management result is due to skill or to chance."

MUNGER   "As you occupy some high-profit niche in a competitive order, you must know how much of your present prosperity is causes by talents and momentum assuring success in new activities, and how much merely reflects the good fortune of being in your present niche."[1435]

BUFFETT   "In a bull market, one must avoid the error of the preening duck that quacks boastfully after a torrential rainstorm, thinking that its paddling skills have caused it to rise in the world."[1436]

"I think the duck can only take the credit (or blame) for his own activities. The rise and fall of the lake is hardly something for him to quack about[1437]...A right-thinking duck would instead compare its position after the downpour to that of the other ducks on the pond."[1438]

MUNGER   "I recall one story when Arco was celebrating making a lot of money on its oil fields. Their house counsel was an Irish guy who could get away with saying things, so he said: 'I want to toast the guy who really deserves the credit for our success: Here's to King Faisal! All the predictions we made were wrong, costs were way over budget, etc. But along came King Faisal, who formed a cartel [OPEC], caused the price of oil to soar, and made us a fortune.'

"That is the kind of toast you seldom hear in corporate life, because it'll get you fired. But I love the kind of man who'll make a toast like that—a credit to the human race and an ornament to the civilization. Anyone who can join that [group], do so."[1439]

LIBRARIAN "Unfortunately, when times are good, too many of us say we are geniuses and when times are bad, very few of us admit we are fools."

MUNGER   "Some of the most important miscalculations come from what is accidentally associated with one's past success."[1440]

SEEKER   "Any recipe for that?"

MUNGER   "The proper antidotes to being made...a patsy by past success are (1) to carefully examine each past success, looking for accidental, noncausative factors associated with such success that will tend to mislead as one appraises odds implicit in a proposed new undertaking and (2) to

170

look for dangerous aspects of the new undertaking that were not present when past success occurred."[1441]

SEEKER   "Except for what you just told me, generally I assume the track record of the business is a good guide and simplifies the evaluation?"

MUNGER   "We tend to judge by the past record. By and large, if it has a lousy past record and a bright future, we're going to miss the opportunity."[1442]

BUFFETT   "[It's true that] most of our decisions relate to things where we expect the future not to change much[1443]…Obviously the current figures — particularly in the kind of businesses that we buy — tend to be representative, we think, of what might happen in the future."[1444]

LIBRARIAN "But it is not as simple as that."

BUFFETT   "If merely looking up past financial data would tell you what the future holds, the Forbes 400 would consist of librarians."[1445]

LIBRARIAN "And I can assure you it isn't."

BUFFETT   "Future profitability of the industry will be determined by current competitive characteristics, not past ones[1446]…The company should be viewed as an unfolding movie, not as a still photograph. Those who focused in the past on only the snapshot of the day sometimes reached erroneous conclusions."[1447]

SEEKER   "What about projections from the seller, surely they help?"

BUFFETT   "Too often, the words from *HMS Pinafore* apply: 'Things are seldom what they seem, skim milk masquerades as cream.' Specifically, sellers and their representatives invariably present financial projections having more entertainment value than educational value."[1448]

MUNGER   "Projections generally do more harm than good — especially when they are prepared by people who desire a certain outcome."[1449]

BUFFETT   "Why potential buyers even look at projections prepared by sellers baffles me. Charlie and I never give them a glance, but instead keep in mind the story of the man with an ailing horse. Visiting the vet, he said: 'Can you help me? Sometimes my horse walks just fine and sometimes he limps.' The vet's reply was pointed: 'No problem - when he's walking fine, sell him.'"

"We face the inherent problem that the seller of a business practically always knows far more about it than the buyer and also picks the time of sale — a time when the business is likely to be walking 'just fine.'"[1450]

MUNGER   "Usually, I don't use formal projections. I don't let people do them for me because I don't like throwing up on the desk, but I see them made in a very foolish way all the time, and many people believe in them, no matter how foolish they are. It's an effective sales technique in America to put a foolish projection on a desk."[1451]

BUFFETT "When they make these offerings, investment bankers display their humorous side: They dispense income and balance sheet projections extending five or more years into the future for companies they barely had heard of a few months earlier. If you are shown such schedules, I suggest that you join in the fun: Ask the investment banker for the one-year budgets that his own firm prepared as the last few years began and then compare these with what actually happened."[1452]

"I've never seen an investment banker's book in which future earnings are projected to go down. But many businesses' earnings go down. We made this mistake with Dexter shoes—it was earning $40 million pretax and I projected this would continue, and I couldn't have been more wrong."[1453]

LIBRARIAN "The barber and Mark Twain quotes come in handy as default positions when you look at projections."

BUFFETT "Don't ask the barber whether you need a haircut."[1454]

MUNGER "Mark Twain, talked of the promoters of his day. He said, 'A mine is a hole in the ground owned by a liar.' That's the way I've come to look at projections."[1455]

LIBRARIAN "Also, when it comes to the past record—what worked before may not work in the future—conditions, environments, circumstances and opponents change—industry conditions and technologies change, customers change their behavior, habits, needs, tastes and preferences, good times turn to bad times, competition gets tougher and the quality of management deteriorates."

BUFFETT "Anyone ignoring these differences makes the same mistake that a baseball manager would were he to judge the future prospects of a 42-year-old center fielder on the basis of his lifetime batting average."[1456]

"You can compare that to going out to the racetrack and betting on a 13-year-old horse that had a great record up to then."[1457]

LIBRARIAN "You don't want to end up betting on a horse that is ready for the glue factory."

"I remember one case from the summer of 2001 where a European company A acquired company B. One month later B lost their biggest customer. The purchase price was based on past good figures that never returned."

"What people bought for the right reason in the past you may buy for the wrong reason today."

BUFFETT "Keynes anticipated a perversity of this kind in his 1925 review. He wrote: 'It is dangerous ... to apply to the future inductive arguments based on past experience, unless one can distinguish the broad reasons why past experience was what it was.' If you can't do that, he said, you may fall into the trap of expecting results in the future that will materialize only if conditions are exactly the same as they were in the past."[1458]

"We don't get paid for the past, only the future [profitability of a business]. The past is only useful to give you insights into the future, but sometimes there's no insight."[1459]

LIBRARIAN "You just have to make sure that the conditions that caused past result are relatively unchanged."

BUFFETT "You have to ask yourself, 'Is there anything about the past record that makes it a poor guidelines as a forecaster of the future?'"[1460]

MUNGER "Frequently, you'll look at a business having fabulous results. And the question is, 'How long can this continue?' Well, there's only one way I know of to do that. And that's to think about why the results are occurring now — and then to figure out the forces that could cause those results to stop occurring."[1461]

BUFFETT "Ben [Graham] had various little games he would play with us. For example, sometimes he would give us a whole bunch of figures about Company A and Company B and have us evaluate them. And only after we'd finished the exercise would we learn that Company A and Company B were the same company at different points in its history."[1462]

SEEKER "As you said before — change happens to all businesses."

BUFFETT "All businesses should think about what can mess up their business model and position. We look at all of our businesses as subject to change…We want managers who are thinking about change, and what's going to be needed for their business model in the future. We know it won't look the same."

"Our businesses are strong and are generally not subject to rapid change, but sometimes slow change can be harder to see and lull you to sleep easier versus rapid change which you can see."[1463]

LIBRARIAN "And slow change can go unnoticed for a long time — until it's too late."

MUNGER "If it comes to you in small pieces, you're likely to miss it[1464]…A bridge-playing pal of mine once told me that a frog tossed into very hot water would jump out, but that the same frog would end up dying if placed in room-temperature water that was later heated at a very slow rate. My few shreds of physiological knowledge make me doubt this account. But no matter because many businesses die in just the manner claimed by my friend for the frog. Cognition, misled by tiny changes involving low contrast, will often miss a trend that is destiny."

"One of Ben Franklin's best-remembered and most useful aphorisms is 'A small leak will sink a great ship.' The utility of the aphorism is large precisely because the brain so often misses the functional equivalent of a small leak in a great ship."[1465]

LIBRARIAN "Many businesses have been killed by failing to adapt to a changing market need. Many times caused due to people's vested interest in preserving the status quo—addicted as they are to their present skills, procedures, positions and money."

MUNGER "Those who will not face improvements because there are changes will face changes that are not improvements."[1466]

LIBRARIAN "It is easy to get carried away when all things are great and not to anticipate any change. Machiavelli said that 'it is human nature when the sea is calm not to think of storms.'"[1467]

BUFFETT "If the business changes in a material way, you better change your business model or somebody else will — in which case you'll have even more changes facing you."[1468]

SEEKER "What usually kills a business?"

BUFFETT "The ABCs of business decay, which are arrogance, bureaucracy and complacency. When these corporate cancers metastasize, even the strongest of companies can falter[1469] …Sears had them all. When you build an organization that has been incredibly successful, you have to work extremely hard to fight off arrogance, bureaucracy and complacency."[1470]

"The biggest thing that kills them is complacency. You want a restlessness, a feeling that somebody's always after you, but you're going to stay ahead of them. You always want to be on the move."[1471]

LIBRARIAN "A lot of companies get very self-satisfied after a long string of success. As an ancient proverb says, 'Whom the gods want to destroy, they send forty years of success.' A good reminder comes from what the Soviet chess grandmaster Alexander Kotov called 'Dizziness due to success', 'When your head is spinning with success that is the time when blunders occur.'"[1472]

MUNGER "Successful places tend to get bloated, fat, complacent. It's the nature of human life[1473]…Most places when they get rich get sloppy."[1474]

BUFFETT "The idea that you run a fat operation because your making money is wrong…I don't think you can ever find a statement that Charlie or I have ever made for the Berkshire companies or anyone else that there should be more people employed than needed in the business."[1475]

LIBRARIAN "It may also have imitating and dangerous consequences."

BUFFETT "Thirty years ago Tom Murphy, then CEO of Cap Cities, drove this point home to me with a hypothetical tale about an employee who asked his boss for permission to hire an assistant. The employee assumed that adding $20,000 to the annual payroll would be inconsequential. But his boss told him the proposal should be evaluated as a $3 million decision, given that an additional person would probably cost at least that amount over his lifetime, factoring in raises, benefits and other expenses."[1476]

LIBRARIAN "Reminds me of Parkinson's Law of Multiplication of Subordinates, 'An official wants to multiply subordinates, not rivals.'"

MUNGER "Yeah...normally if you're just super successful, if the sky just rains gold, every vice president gets an assistant. Then pretty soon the assistant has an assistant. It's just the way human nature works. It's sort of like cancer."[1477]

BUFFETT "I think you'll see our attitude about excess people is expressed in our headquarters where we have 25 people and Charlie's office in LA which has two people."[1478]

"Our experience has been that the manager of an already high-cost operation frequently is uncommonly resourceful in finding new ways to add to overhead, while the manager of a tightly-run operation usually continues to find additional methods to curtail costs, even when his costs are already well below those of his competitors."[1479]

SEEKER "So if I had a business, how should I then run it?"

BUFFETT "What should you be doing in running your business? Just what you always do: Widen the moat, build enduring competitive advantage, delight your customers, and relentlessly fight costs."[1480]

LIBRARIAN "And keeping things simple helps."

BUFFETT "I really believe in keeping things simple. We have no inside counsel. We have no public relations people. We have no guards. We have no cafeteria. And it's a lot easier to run that way. Frankly, I think way more gets done than if you have floor after floor of people that are reporting to people on the floor above them. I see so much waste in most companies and once it gets there, it is very hard to get rid of. It's much easier never to get there...a large organization. I mean, that would be business death as far as I'm concerned; so we're not going to get there."[1481]

SEEKER "Any other thing that often kills a business?"

LIBRARIAN "We often underestimate competition because we think we are alone and unique. We are too focused on our own skills and plans—what we can do and want to do—and are blind to our competitors' abilities and actions. But as we all know, our outcome also depends on present and future competition. Joe Roth, former chairman of *Walt Disney Studios* expressed this well: 'Hubris. Hubris. If you only think about your own business, you think, 'I've got a good story department, I've got a good marketing department, we're going to go out and do this.' And you don't think that everybody else is thinking the same way.'"[1482]

"Maybe they have the same plans as we do, chase the same customers, markets and business opportunities—or they may already be ahead of us in some areas."

MUNGER "In business, I commonly see people underappraise both the competency and morals of competitors they dislike. This is a dangerous practice, usually disguised because it occurs on a subconscious basis."[1483]

SEEKER "More?"

MUNGER "It's in the nature of things that most small businesses will never be big businesses. It's also in the nature of things that most big businesses eventually fall into mediocrity or worse[1484]...Look at the history of big companies in the world and the record is not good...We think we are doing well because we have a better system than most people."[1485]

BUFFETT "Size seems to make many organizations slow-thinking, resistant to change and smug. In Churchill's words: 'We shape our buildings, and afterwards our buildings shape us.'"[1486]

"In their glory days, General Motors, IBM, Sears Roebuck and U.S. Steel sat atop huge industries. Their strengths seemed unassailable. But the destructive behavior I deplored above eventually led each of them to fall to depths that their CEOs and directors had not long before thought impossible. Their one-time financial strength and their historical earning power proved no defense."[1487]

LIBRARIAN "And the real danger may come from new competitors that turn up from unexpected places. Andrew Carnegie once said, 'It is not the rich man's son that the young struggler for advancement has to fear in the race of life, nor his nephew, nor his cousin. Let him look out for the 'Dark Horse' in the boy who begins by sweeping out the office.'"[1488]

MUNGER "Almost all great records eventually dwindle[1489]...I think that's the natural consequence of competitive life...that it gets tough."[1490]

LIBRARIAN "Nothing lasts forever — some businesses and industries die and other rise."

BUFFETT "Capitalism can be tough...Capitalism is constantly looking to get people what they want at a price they want, and to do so efficiently. The problem is someone else gets hurt. There used to be lots of farmers in America, and then you had the tractor, and then the combine, etc. This is good for consumers, it has made food cheap. If you look at inflation for food over the last couple hundred years, it is down. But if horses could have voted, they would have voted down tractors."[1491]

LIBRARIAN "As Joseph Schumpeter said on how companies can die, 'In capitalist reality as distinguished from its textbook picture, it is not... [price]...competition which counts but the competition from the new commodity, the new technology, the new source of supply, the new type of organization (...) — competition which...strikes not at the margins...of the existing firms but at their foundations and their very lives.'"[1492]

MUNGER "I think it's in the nature of things for some business to die. It's also in the nature of things that in some cases, you shouldn't fight it, there's no logical answer in some cases except to wring the money out and go elsewhere."[1493]

SEEKER   "Do people usually do that?"

BUFFETT   "There are often obstacles to the rational movement of capital… capital withdrawals within the textile industry that should have been obvious were delayed for decades because of the vain hopes and self-interest of managements. Indeed, I myself delayed abandoning our obsolete textile mills for far too long."

"A CEO with capital employed in a declining operation seldom elects to massively redeploy that capital into unrelated activities. A move of that kind would usually require that long-time associates be fired and mistakes be admitted. Moreover, it's unlikely that CEO would be the manager you would wish to handle the redeployment job even if he or she was inclined to undertake it."[1494]

LIBRARIAN "But as you say, some do."

MUNGER   "There was this huge grocery store…Sam Walton of Wal-Mart announced that he was opening a much bigger, better grocery store with a lot of other…products at incredibly low prices. And the existing and successful chain…just closed their store right away."[1495]

SEEKER   "Why didn't they fight Walmart?"

LIBRARIAN "There is an old African proverb, 'When elephants dance, it is best for the mice to step aside.'"

BUFFETT   "We must heed Woody Allen: 'While the lamb may lie down with the lion, the lamb shouldn't count on getting a whole lot of sleep.'"[1496]

LIBRARIAN "Walmart was the equivalent of the Northern Pike."

MUNGER   "One of the models in my head is the 'Northern Pike Model'. You have a lake full of trout. But if you throw in a few northern pike, pretty soon there aren't many trout left but a lot of northern pike. Wal-Mart in its early days was the northern pike. It figured out how the customer could be better served and just galloped through the world like Genghis Kahn."[1497]

SEEKER   "So the lesson seems to be to get out of what hasn't any chance of recovering or surviving."

BUFFETT   "The most important thing to do when you find yourself in a hole is to stop digging."[1498]

LIBRARIAN "But most people don't, aided by wishful thinking, consistency and their aversion to losses."

MUNGER   "There is a time to fight and a time to not — not wasting resource… so don't fight the inevitable but milk it and go some other direction."[1499]

BUFFETT   "Should you find yourself in a chronically-leaking boat, energy devoted to changing vessels is likely to be more productive than energy devoted to patching leaks."[1500]

MUNGER "Berkshire extracted a lot of capital out of it [the textile business] and put it elsewhere. And if Berkshire had tried to keep fighting the decline of that business with more and more money, it would have blown most of its capital."[1501]

LIBRARIAN "As Kenny Rogers sang, 'You got to know when to hold em, know when to fold em, know when to walk away, know when to run.'"[1502]

BUFFETT "Whatever the outcome, we will heed a prime rule of investing: You don't have to make it back the way that you lost it."[1503]

SEEKER "Ok, do you sell a business if its fundamentals have permanently changed?"

BUFFETT "When we buy a business, it's for keeps. And we make only two exceptions: when they promise to start losing money indefinitely, or if we have major labor problems.

"But with stocks and bonds, we sell them...if the competitive advantage disappears, if we really lose faith in the management, if we were wrong in the original analysis — and that happens — or if we find something more attractive, we will sell."[1504]

SEEKER "What about if the price falls? I mean, assume I have bought a stock at $10 because I believed it was a good deal but then it falls to $2— shouldn't I sell then?"

BUFFETT "When I do invest, I don't care if the stock price goes from $10 to $2 but I do care about if the value went from $10 to $2."[1505]

SEEKER "Back to the business side—even if you prefer a great business, I assume management can make a big difference?"

MUNGER "Getting the right people into your system can frequently be more important than anything else."[1506]

BUFFETT "After some other mistakes, I learned to go into business only with people whom I like, trust, and admire."[1507]

"Character is crucial: A Berkshire CEO must be 'all in' for the company, not for himself...it's important that neither ego nor avarice motivate him to reach for pay matching his most lavishly-compensated peers, even if his achievements far exceed theirs. A CEO's behavior has a huge impact on managers down the line: If it's clear to them that shareholders' interests are paramount to him, they will, with few exceptions, also embrace that way of thinking."[1508]

SEEKER "How can I measure if the management is good or not?"

BUFFETT "See how they treat themselves versus how they treat the shareholders. And look at what they accomplished considering the hand they were dealt when they took over relative to the rest of their industry."[1509]

MUNGER "There are two different kinds of agency costs—one in which a manager favors himself at the expense of the shareholders and the other where he's not trying to favor himself, but where he does foolish things because he's just foolish by nature. Either way, it's very costly to you as the shareholder. So you have to judge those two aspects of human character. And they're terribly important."[1510]

SEEKER "Anything that can help me here?"

MUNGER "Immoral and stupid, not a good combination."[1511]

SEEKER "Seriously?"

BUFFETT "When people get their ego involved, people sometimes do things they normally wouldn't do. We try to eliminate incentives that would cause people to misbehave not only for financial rewards but also for ego satisfaction."[1512]

MUNGER "A rough rule in life is that an organization foolish in one way in dealing with a complex system is all too likely to be foolish in another."[1513]

LIBRARIAN "Reminds me of the Zen saying, 'The way you do anything, is the way you do everything.' The qualities an organization or management expresses in one part show up in other parts. When they do one thing poorly, they will do other things poorly. This is of course not a natural law but a good rule of thumb."

BUFFETT "A cumulation of small managerial stupidities will produce a major stupidity — not a major triumph."[1514]

SEEKER "You seem to have been very successful in judging management."

BUFFETT "We're successful because of simplicity itself: We let people who play the game very well keep doing it."[1515]

"We buy businesses with great management in place. We've seen their record. They come with the business."[1516]

MUNGER "The paper record is usually a better indicator of talent."[1517]

BUFFETT "The past record is the best single guide."[1518]

MUNGER "We don't train executives, we find them. If a mountain stands up like Everest, you don't have to be a genius to figure out that it's a high mountain."[1519]

BUFFETT "It would be tough to evaluate a class of MBAs and pick which ones would prove to be the best managers, just like it would be tough to pick the best golfer by watching them hit on the practice range. We haven't tried to evaluate, before they have a record, who will be superstar managers. Instead, we find people who've batted .350 for 10-50 years. We just assume we won't screw it up by hiring them. We take people who play the game very well and allow them to play."[1520]

LIBRARIAN "And they seem to stay."

BUFFETT "Our job is not so much to select great managers…Our job is to retain them…to make sure that they have the same enthusiasm, excitement, and passion for their job after the stock certificate changes hands that they had before."[1521]

"I can't put passion into someone. But I can create a structure that takes the passion away. We focus on not messing up something that is already good."[1522]

LIBRARIAN "Tell him about your model."

BUFFETT "My managerial model is Eddie Bennett, who was a batboy. In 1919, at age 19, Eddie began his work with the Chicago White Sox, who that year went to the World Series. The next year, Eddie switched to the Brooklyn Dodgers, and they, too, won their league title. Our hero, however, smelled trouble. Changing boroughs, he joined the Yankees in 1921, and they promptly won their first pennant in history. Now Eddie settled in, shrewdly seeing what was coming. In the next seven years, the Yankees won five American League titles."[1523]

SEEKER "I believed we talked about management?"

BUFFETT "What does this have to do with management? It's simple — to be a winner, work with winners. In 1927, for example, Eddie received $700 for the 1/8th World Series share voted him by the legendary Yankee team of Ruth and Gehrig. This sum, which Eddie earned by working only four days (because New York swept the Series) was roughly equal to the full-year pay then earned by batboys who worked with ordinary associates."

"Eddie understood that how he lugged bats was unimportant; what counted instead was hooking up with the cream of those on the playing field. I've learned from Eddie. At Berkshire, I regularly hand bats to many of the heaviest hitters in American business."[1524]

SEEKER "You work with winners."

BUFFETT "I know they're winners, they've been winning for years, so all I have to do is figure out how to keep them going. That's a lot easier to do, frankly, than interviewing 20 business school graduates and picking 19 winners. It's much better to go into something where people have been successful a long time."[1525]

SEEKER "When I want to buy some stocks in a company — if possible — does it help to talk to the management?"

BUFFETT "We do not find it particularly helpful to talk to managements... The numbers tell us a lot more than the managements."[1526]

MUNGER "If you sit down and talk to the key manager for an hour and you're a smart person, I think that could be a significant plus. But a smart person might be right 60% of the time and, for the balance, be misled. If you have some specific questions that the management is going to answer, obviously that would be helpful."[1527]

LIBRARIAN "Just as you need to find out how a business performs during turbulent or bad times, you need to do the same with management. You can only evaluate real management performance and their character when 'the tide goes out.'

"Another thing, some managers may be great in one business but lousy in another."

MUNGER "Just because you run one business well don't mean you will run another one well. You may be a great ballet dancer but a lousy weight lifter."[1528]

LIBRARIAN "I think it's time to repeat and further clarify some things — circle of competence and competitive edge — things relevant for both an individual and a business."

SEEKER "Good!"

"But first, I need to get some more sugar — I need a lot of energy to follow you guys. Any chance you have any Dairy Queen ice cream around?"

Go in a field, in which you have no interest, not any competence or talent for, no edge in and where the competition is huge

MUNGER "The secret to being successful in any field is getting very interested in it[1529]...I could force myself to be fairly good in a lot of things, but I couldn't excel in anything in which I didn't have an intense interest."[1530]

BUFFETT "You have to love something if you want to do well at it. This passion adds to your productivity."[1531]

LIBRARIAN "And in a field in which you have competence. Know what you can do and what you can't do."

BUFFETT "I think that is the biggest thing in business, figuring out where you are good and where you are not[1532]...If you're good at one thing, you're not necessarily good at another. You ought to use your talents where they're most useful and get others to use theirs."[1533]

"Adam Smith talks about 'Specialization of Labor '...allowing countries to specialize and work on what they are good at. Mike Tyson doesn't try to run Berkshire, and I don't try to get in the ring with Mike Tyson[1534]... When my wife and I had a baby, we hired an obstetrician — I didn't try to do it myself. When my tooth hurts, I don't turn to Charlie[1535]... The idea that you let other people do what they're best at and you do what you're best at, I've carried from lawn moving to philanthropy."[1536]

SEEKER "Oh, how wrong I have been — believing I could do it all by myself."

BUFFETT "When we formed Buffett Associates, Ltd...I passed out to the seven limited partners something called 'The Ground Rules'. And I said, 'Here's what I can do. Here's what I can't do. And here are some things

I don't know whether I can do or not… But the idea of setting out to do something that you know you can't do…That's got to lead to problems."[1537]

LIBRARIAN "Just figure out what you're good at and stay in that game. This is something good managers understand. They…"

BUFFETT "Stick with what they understand and let their abilities, not their egos, determine what they attempt. (Thomas J. Watson Sr. of IBM followed the same rule: 'I'm no genius,' he said. 'I'm smart in spots - but I stay around those spots.')"[1538]

LIBRARIAN "And you can't do the same thing everybody else does and expect to be better than others — you need to do something different — you need an edge."

BUFFETT "I don't want to play in a game where the other guy has an advantage. Somebody asked, 'How do you beat Bobby Fisher?' The answer was 'you play him any game except chess'[1539]…That ability to know when your odds are good versus playing outside that game is a huge asset."[1540]

MUNGER "If it is a very competitive business, and it requires competitive abilities you lack, you should look elsewhere. I took thermodynamics at Caltech and I immediately knew I would not be as smart as the professor. I did this in field after field and soon there were only a few left."[1541]

SEEKER "How do I find my edge?"

MUNGER "I would be looking for a place where I could figure out something very useful that other people didn't know[1542]…I don't think anything that any ordinary person can do easily is likely to work that well."[1543]

LIBRARIAN "Do correct things that other people aren't doing. Ask, 'Do I have an edge or an insight no one else has?' Understand yourself — what you can do and can't do and then enter the 'niche' where your advantages can be used and your weaknesses doesn't really matter."

"And you don't have to outshine everybody in the world, only those in the field in which you have chosen to play. Also, you may understand one field but another one better and/or you may be good in one field but lack the necessary edge. So go in the field you understand best and where you bring something special to the game."

MUNGER "If you're going to do well you need a competitive advantage — a moat."[1544]

"We don't even look at other places where we feel we don't have much of a competitive advantage…You have to do the same thing…we all have a limited amount of time and talent and we have to allocate it in a way so it will work better."[1545]

BUFFETT "One of the best moats in many respects is sometimes…having more talent. If you're the heavyweight champion of the world and you keep knocking out people, or if you're Steven Spielberg and can turn out great motion pictures, you've got a competitive advantage as long as you can keep doing it. It has enormous economic value."[1546]

SEEKER   "Ok, enough—I get it—before my head starts to spin."

"Assume I know what I can do and cannot do and where I have an edge, what's next?"

BUFFETT   "You want to work where there is little competition[1547]...One of the secrets of life is weak competition."[1548]

MUNGER   "The basic idea is that if you want to succeed in life in a capitalistic world, go where the competition is low... I went where there was dumb competition."[1549]

BUFFETT   "The unusual records—and there have been few that have been maintained—have been achieved by those who have worked relatively neglected fields in which competition was light...Your win-loss percentage in tennis will not be determined by the absolute level of ability that you possess. Rather, it will be determined by your ability to select inferior opponents...Application of this principle is the key element in bridge, poker, or investments."[1550]

LIBRARIAN   "Let me tell you a story a smart friend told me."

"Imagine you're playing poker in Vegas—what table should you sit down at? At the table with the best players or the one with the oilmen from Texas, betting big who don't even know if a straight flush beats a full house?"

SEEKER   "The way you frame it, obviously the Texas table."

LIBRARIAN   "Yes, what you want is being in a niche with no, dumb or very weak competitors—not strong competitors—just like you don't play Bobby Fisher in chess."

MUNGER   "I know of a place with a little poker game. And some of the other players love to play a lot of very complicated games because the less skilled card players...are even more patsies for the superior players. And, therefore, the superior players win faster."[1551]

LIBRARIAN   "You don't want to be the patsy. And the same is valid in business."

MUNGER   "Competence is a relative concept. I realized that what I needed to get ahead was to compete against idiots, and luckily for me there was a large supply."[1552]

LIBRARIAN   "So where do you stand the best chance of making the most money with the least risk? By selecting your market niche based on the largest possible beneficial contrast in terms of both advantage and extinction risk i.e. be the hottest source in the coldest possible niche with the coldest possible field of competitors. Try to align your own niche as far away from hot niches and hot competitors as possible. And then try to make sure you are enough differentiated — hard to copy or hunt down."

"Another thing when finding the right niche is getting on the right business train — one that is moving in the right direction."

BUFFETT "One of the lessons your management has learned — and, unfortunately, sometimes re-learned — is the importance of being in businesses where tailwinds prevail rather than headwinds."[1553]

"When I got out of Columbia one of my best friends was a terrific talent and he went to work in the steel business. He did OK, but it was the wrong business to be in. It's very important to be on the right train. you want to get on a train that's going 90 miles an hour and not one that's going 30 miles an hour and you're gonna push it along a little faster. So it really does make a huge difference. There are some businesses that are inherently far more opportunity than others. So you want to give a lot of thought to which train you're getting on."[1554]

LIBRARIAN "Tell him about your experience as the 50% owner of Sinclair gas station."

BUFFETT "It was a lousy business. We had a guy right next to us and he kept selling more gallons of gas than we did. He would cut our prices and everything. I don't care if you're a combination of Steve Jobs and Larry Ellison and everyone else; you're not going to succeed if you have a guy selling gas below cost next to you. It's important to get on the right train."[1555]

LIBRARIAN "And preferably an 'easy-to-succeed-train.'"

MUNGER "I have a habit in life. I observe what works and what doesn't and why[1556]...and I have seen so many idiots get rich in easy businesses... actually I wanted to be in an easier business."[1557]

BUFFETT "It is comforting to be in a business where some mistakes can be made and yet a quite satisfactory overall performance can be achieved."[1558]

LIBRARIAN "And practice getting better."

MUNGER "Obviously if you want to get good at something which is competitive, you have to think about it and practice a lot. You have to keep learning because world keeps changing and competitors keep learning."

"You have to go to bed wiser than you got up. As you try to master what you are trying to do — people who do that almost never fail utterly. Very few have ever failed with that approach. You may rise slowly, but you are sure to rise."[1559]

SEEKER "See if I got what you told me right."

"I need to do something I have an interest in and that agrees with my nature and my talent and then assuming I have an edge others can't copy, I should go where there is least competition or what your friend called, 'be the hottest source in the coldest niche with the coldest competitors.'"

Librarian "You got it."

Think about where the business is going to be in the future — not macro factors

Seeker "Another thing, how important is it to look at macro factors when investing?"

Buffett "Forming macro opinions or listening to the macro or market predictions of others is a waste of time. Indeed, it is dangerous because it may blur your vision of the facts that are truly important."[1560]

Munger "I have never taken a single course in economics, nor tried to make a single dollar, ever, from foreseeing macroeconomic changes."[1561]

"There's too much emphasis on macroeconomics and not enough on microeconomics. I think this is wrong. It's like trying to master medicine without knowing anatomy and chemistry."[1562]

Buffett "I pay no attention to economic forecasting. I worry about being in good businesses with good people. That's all I focus on… I've never based a decision on expansion of a business or anything like that based on an economic forecast because A) it's not reliable and B) it's not important[1563]…What you have to look at is where you expect the business to be 5, 10 or 20 years from now[1564]…What matters is the average earnings power and the sustainability of its competitive advantage."[1565]

Munger "Macroeconomics people…are often wrong because of extreme complexity in the system they wish to understand."[1566]

"If you're an agnostic about macro factors and, therefore, devote all of your time to thinking about the individual businesses and the individual opportunities, it's a way more efficient way to behave."[1567]

Buffett "In the 54 years we have worked together, we have never forgone an attractive purchase because of the macro or political environment, or the views of other people. In fact, these subjects never come up when we make decisions."[1568]

Librarian "One thing you can do whenever something 'negative' happens in the 'macro world' is to ask, 'X happens — what are the consequences for the value of the business — how will this event impact the key factors that create value in this business — unit volume, prices, costs, invested capital, opportunity costs? Will it make a difference now or over time? '"

"In most cases you will find it doesn't make much of difference — whatever the vivid headlines say."

Seeker "So you don't worry when there is some political or economic crisis?"

BUFFETT "That doesn't play a role in our decision to buy. We're going to be around for a hundred years. I've been buying companies for 50 years and we've seen all kinds of things…We want to buy good businesses that are run by good people in good places. It's like getting married. If you're getting married tomorrow, you're not going to worry about a headline today. You've just got to be sure you're marrying the right person."[1569]

SEEKER "Going back to forecasts again—take economists, surely they should know what is going to happen with the economy and the stock market?"

"For example, just the other day some expert economist said that the U.S. economy will start growing with 3% a year—and he looked very confident on television."

LIBRARIAN "How can they know that? They can't. Look at their past predictions—just look at what they said a year ago and compare this with what actually happened and you will find they were all wrong. And since their past predictions were wrong why should their present forecasts be right? If they didn't know back then, why should they know the future now?"

"So don't believe them—No one can predict the economy."

BUFFETT "I should note that the cemetery for seers has a huge section set aside for macro forecasters."[1570]

MUNGER "Macroeconomics people…are often wrong because of extreme complexity in the system they wish to understand."[1571]

"And we haven't seen great successes by others involved in macroeconomic predictions. They get a lot of air time but not much else. The trouble with making all these macroeconomic predictions is that people start to think they know something. It's much better to just say you're ignorant."[1572]

LIBRARIAN "To paraphrase what someone once said, 'Economic forecasts are like treasure maps; if you really have the real one, why spread it?'"

"Just look at these two gentlemen—they are living proofs that you don't need to be a macro forecaster to get outstanding results."

SEEKER "Yes, but…"

LIBRARIAN "It is understandable that you want to know the future. It is part of human nature to dislike uncertainty."

BUFFETT "People love predictions."[1573]

MUNGER "People have always had this craving to have someone tell them the future. Long ago, kings would hire people to read sheep guts. There's always been a market for people who pretend to know the future. Listening to today's forecasters is just as crazy as when the king hired the guy to look at the sheep guts. It happens over and over and over."[1574]

186

BUFFETT "Why spend talking about something you don't know anything about? People do it all the time, but why do it?... To ignore what you know to listen to what someone else says who doesn't know, doesn't make sense."[1575]

LIBRARIAN "Just assume that the foresights of the experts are a poor guide to the future."

MUNGER "It's kind of a snare and a delusion to outguess macroeconomic cycles...very few people do it successfully and some of them do it by accident. When the game is that tough, why not adopt the other system of swimming as competently as you can and figuring that over a long life you'll have your share of good tides and bad tides."[1576]

BUFFETT "Our macro factor is the country will do better over time. That guides us in everything we do."[1577]

SEEKER "But times don't look too rosy at the present."

BUFFETT "Don't let that reality spook you. Throughout my lifetime, politicians and pundits have constantly moaned about terrifying problems facing America. Yet our citizens now live an astonishing six times better than when I was born."[1578]

SEEKER "But it has been a lot of ups and downs during the journey."

BUFFETT "Though the path has not been smooth, our economic system has worked extraordinarily well over time. It has unleashed human potential as no other system has, and it will continue to do so. America's best days lie ahead."

"Charlie and I love investing large sums in worthwhile projects, whatever the pundits are saying. We instead heed the words from Gary Allan's new country song, 'Every Storm Runs Out of Rain.'"[1579]

LIBRARIAN "Or in the American Bishop John H. Vincent's word, 'There can be no rainbow without a cloud and a storm.'"[1580]

Common sense is better than advanced math and computer models

SEEKER "Do I need to know any advanced math in business or to calculate the value?"

BUFFETT "You don't have to understand higher mathematics. In fact, higher mathematics may actually be dangerous, because it will lead you down pathways that are better left untrod..."[1581]

MUNGER "You don't need higher math in business and if you learn it you feel tempted to use it—to your detriment[1582]...You really have to understand the company and its competitive positions....That's not disclosed by the math."[1583]

"I think you can do it without the fancy math[1584]...There is something to be said for 'keeping it simple'"[1585]

SEEKER   "That reminds me of a class reunion some years ago. Arriving in a Ferrari and wearing an Armani suit in comes the guy who was worst in his class in all subjects—including math. After a while we all understood he had become a real success. So naturally, everyone was curious how this could have happened. His reply, 'It wasn't all that difficult—I am a trader—I buy stuff for one dollar and sell it for two dollars and on that single percent I have had a pretty decent life."

BUFFETT   "There are really only three kinds of people in the world: those who can count and those who can't."[1586]

SEEKER   "Good one."

BUFFETT   "Advanced math is of no use in the investment process. But understanding mathematical relationships—the ability to quantify...is generally helpful."

"Something that tells you when things make sense or when they don't sort of helps—when an item in one area relates to something someplace else. But that doesn't require great mathematical ability."[1587]

LIBRARIAN "Yeah, some people could have used that during the Internet mania."

BUFFETT   "When we buy a stock, we always think in terms of buying the whole enterprise because it enables us to think as businessmen rather than stock speculators."

"So let's just take a company that has marvelous prospects, that paying you nothing now where you buy it at a valuation of $500 billion... For example, let's assume that there's only going to be a one-year delay before the business starts paying out to you and you want to get a 10% return. If you paid $500 billion, then $55 billion in cash is the amount that it's going to have to be able to disgorge to you year after year after year. To do that, it has to make perhaps $80 billion, or close to it, pretax. Look around at the universe of businesses in this world and see how many are earning $80 billion pretax—or $70 billion or $60 or $50 or $40 or even $30 billion. You won't find any."[1588]

"Any time you get involved in these things where if you trace out the mathematics of it, you bump into absurdities, then you better change your expectations somewhat. Charlie?"[1589]

MUNGER   "I don't think we've reached a new order of things where the laws of mathematics have been repealed."[1590]

"A wise economist once said, 'If a thing can't go on forever, it will eventually stop' ...and it might even get a lot worse[1591]...All man's desired geometric progressions, if a high rate of growth is chosen, at last come to grief on a finite earth."[1592]

SEEKER   "Similar to what you talked about earlier—the absurd consequences that would follow if what they expect should be true."

LIBRARIAN "Trends that can't continue, will not continue."

BUFFETT "I bought up a farm for $600 an acre that the bank had lent $2,000 an acre against. And the farm didn't know what I'd paid for it or the other guy had paid, or lent on it. And that farm had a productive capacity of probably $60 an acre in terms of what corn soybeans were selling for. To lend $2,000 against it when interest rates were 10% was madness."[1593]

LIBRARIAN "And when you analyze something—don't overweigh easily available numbers or what can be counted and underweigh what cannot. What is less quantifiable may be more important than what can be calculated."

MUNGER "A special version of this "man with a hammer syndrome" is terrible, not only in economics but practically everywhere else, including business. It's really terrible in business. You've got a complex system, and it spews out a lot of wonderful numbers that enable you to measure some factors. But there are other factors that are terribly important, [yet] there's no precise numbering you can put to these factors. You know they're important, but you don't have the numbers. Well, practically everybody (1) overweighs the stuff that can be numbered …and (2) doesn't mix in the hard-to-measure stuff that may be more important."[1594]

LIBRARIAN "As Rene Dubos said, 'Sometimes the more measurable drives out the most important.'"[1595]

SEEKER "But you two don't suffer from that 'blindness.'"

MUNGER "Warren and I always cite Lord Keynes, 'We'd rather be roughly right than precisely wrong'[1596]…In other words, if something is terribly important, we'll guess at it rather than just make our judgment based on what happens to be easily countable."[1597]

BUFFETT "We want our managers to think about what counts, not how it will be counted."[1598]

LIBRARIAN "And when you 'count', don't make anything more precise than necessary. Often a rough approximation is good enough. Take a lesson from engineers—7 times 7 are 49 to an accountant, but to an engineer it's about 50."

"And just because something precise pops out of a computer doesn't automatically imply it is important or accurate."

BUFFETT "We believe the precision they project is a chimera. In fact, such models can lull decision-makers into a false sense of security and thereby increase their chances of making a really huge mistake."[1599]

LIBRARIAN "Common sense is better than computer models."

MUNGER "Common sense is an enormously powerful tool."[1600]

SEEKER "What about spreadsheets—you use them?"

BUFFETT   "If you need to use a computer or calculator to make the calculation, you shouldn't buy it…It should scream at you…we do not sit down with spreadsheets and do all that sort of thing. We just see something that obviously is better than anything else around that we understand — and then we act."[1601]

MUNGER   "Well, I'd go further. I'd say some of the worst business decisions I've ever seen are those that are done with a lot of formal projections and discounts back… And the trouble with that approach is that you get to believing the figures. And it seems that higher mathematics with more false precision should help you, but it doesn't."[1602]

LIBRARIAN   "Your calculation is only as good as your assumptions. Change the assumptions a little bit and Voila!—Suddenly what looked like a bargain turns into a nightmare."

BUFFETT   "False precision is a real problem for American management… [Most] companies'… strategic planning department and acquisition officers have a way of getting to the answers that they want. It's just not that precise."

"The worst mistakes I've ever made in business have been accompanied by pretty charts and graphs.[1603]

MUNGER   "Are there dangers in getting too caught up in the minutiae of using a computer so that you miss the organized common sense? There are huge dangers. There'll always be huge dangers. People calculate too much and think too little."[1604]

LIBRARIAN   "The chess grandmaster Alexander Kotov once described one of the problems with doing complicated calculations and analysis, 'And then it often happens that at the very first move, right at the base of the analytical tree, the player fails to notice an elementary piece of tactics or an obvious threat…such blindness, such a failure to spot what has been right under my nose, has been a common occurrence.'"[1605]

"And personally I believe that the smarter you think you are or the higher IQ you have the more you will be a victim of this. As the German poet Christoph Martin Wieland said in 1768, 'Too much light often blinds gentlemen of this sort. They cannot see the forest for the trees.'"[1606]

"Now, let's summarize some important things."

- If you are an investor think like a businessman and if you're a businessman think like an investor

- Investing is about where to allocate your capital—laying out cash today to get more cash later—how much cash you lay out, how much cash you get back, when you get it back, how sure you are and how it compares to other alternatives

- Invest where you have an edge and find a game that is easy for you

- Look at the downside (how much you can lose) before the upside (how much you can make) and if and how you can protect yourself — if you can't assess the risk — stay away
- Buy cheap productive assets relative to their future prospects and watch out for "appear-cheap-on-the-surface" assets — ask if they are cheap for the right or wrong reason. The cheaper you buy an asset relative what it's worth the better off you are.
- It should be obvious it is a financially fat opportunity — otherwise wait for the fat pitch and when it comes, seize it — A quick back-of-the-envelope calculation is enough
- Things are often cheapest when people are fearful and pessimistic
- First decide if you can understand what an asset's economic future is likely to be (what will the asset look like 5 — 10 years from now?) — If you can reasonably well estimate a future range of earning power and whether the price makes sense in relation to that. If not, stay away
- Stick to productive cash-generating assets you understand — where you can reasonably well assess their economic future and productivity — meaning relatively simple and stable assets that aren't susceptible to very much change and assets whose productivity and prices will improve over time and has been tested for their resilience during turbulent or bad times — something that is going to be worth more in ten years
- And protected with a durable competitive advantage or moat run by able and honest people with great records
- Understand why it has a moat — the key factors and their permanence and its weakest link — and if the economic moat is widening or narrowing

  a) Understand what key criteria customers choose on and if there is something they experience as differentiating between suppliers on these criteria. Why they choose this company and what would make them switch to a competitor (incentive to switch, how difficult is it to switch — money and effort? How easy is it for a competitor to offer what the customer wants?)

  b) Understand whether there are any ways customers in the future will get what the company offer from different sources or any changes in the ways they use it/do it.
  Assuming of course, you are competent enough to a) identify or pick what the dominant or key factors are and b) also evaluate them including their predictability. Watch out so you don't think you need to know X when you really need to know Y — the critical

knowledge that counts in the situation with regards to what you want to achieve (As Mr. Munger says "It's not a competency if you don't know the edge of it."[1607])

- One test of the strength of a moat is essentiality and pricing power
- The best businesses have high returns on capital and pricing power and require little incremental capital to grow
- Follow the cash and remember that cash flow from a business is after capital expenditures
- When looking at the business results, ask: Will it continue? ➔ Why did it happen—What key factors have caused the outcome? ➔ Chances continue? ➔ Are these factors still present? Any changes in conditions or circumstances? ➔ Invert –What forces can change these factors? What is required to make it continue? Likelihood?
- To avoid problem, make sure the management is able and trustworthy
- Forget master plans—be opportunistic, adapt and change when the facts and circumstances change
- When you make a mistake in your original purchase, or the business, its competitive position or management permanently deteriorates, get out
- Add, do what you have an interest in, talent for and an edge in and go where there is no, dumb or very weak competition

SEEKER "I understood this better until you started to explain it. No, just kidding."

LIBRARIAN "As Niels Bohr said, 'Some subjects are so serious that one can only joke about them.'"[1608]

SEEKER "I am never as serious as when I am joking."
"Anything more to add?"

BUFFETT "Be wary of highly leveraged entities or businesses in weak competitive positions."[1609]

LIBRARIAN "And look for good businesses where one or a few key factors are critical. As the German poet Christoph Martin Wieland said in 1774, 'And less is often more.'"[1610]

BUFFETT "Stay with simple propositions…If only one variable is key to a decision, and the variable has a 90% chance of going your way, the chance for a successful outcome is obviously 90%. But if ten independent variables need to break favorably for a successful result, and each has a 90% probability of success, the likelihood of having a winner is only 35%… Since a chain is no stronger than its weakest link, it makes sense to look for—if you'll excuse an oxymoron—mono-linked chains."[1611]

"The truly big investment idea can usually be explained in a short paragraph[1612]…Almost all of the big, great ideas in business are very simple."[1613]

SEEKER   "Anything else?"

BUFFETT   "I want to have it in things that I understand and I think are attractive and I think are going to earn more money five years from now and 10 years from now than they are now."[1614]

"In order to best understand a company, you first have to understand the industry. Only focus on companies and industries you understand. Don't go outside your circle of competence. You need to know what the strengths of the company are in relation to the competition, if they have a good management team, and most importantly, what the moat is."[1615]

SEEKER   "And when I buy stocks?"

BUFFETT   "When Charlie and I buy stocks — which we think of as small portions of businesses –our analysis is very similar to that which we use in buying entire businesses. We first have to decide whether we can sensibly estimate an earnings range for five years out or more. If the answer is yes, we will buy the stock (or business) if it sells at a reasonable price in relation to the bottom boundary of our estimate."

"If, however, we lack the ability to estimate future earnings — which is usually the case — we simply move on to other prospects."[1616]

MUNGER   "Sandy Gottesman, a Berkshire director, runs a large, successful investment firm…When he interviews someone, he asks: 'What do you own and why do you own it?' If you're not interested enough to own something, then he'd tell you to find something else to do."[1617]

BUFFETT   "There is nothing complicated about the way we invest. It is very understandable. I've felt that before people buy a stock, they should take a piece of paper and simply write, 'I'm buying General Motors at 47,' or 'I'm buying US Steel at 83.' They should just write out what their reasoning is, and they should be able to get it all on one side of one piece of paper. In fact, they should be able to get it into a paragraph."[1618]

SEEKER   "You sure believe this 'repetition is the mother of learning.'"

BUFFETT   "So I want a simple business, easy to understand, great economics now, honest and able management, and then I can see about in a general way where they will be ten (10) years from now. If I can't see where they will be ten years from now, I don't want to buy it."[1619]

MUNGER   "The number one idea, is to view a stock as an ownership of the business [and] to judge the staying quality of the business in terms of its competitive advantage. Look for more value in terms of discounted future cash flow than you're paying for. Move only when you have an advantage. It's very basic. You have to understand the odds and have the discipline to bet only when the odds are in your favor[1620]…You're looking for a mispriced gamble. That's what investing is. And you have to know enough to know whether the gamble is mispriced."[1621]

BUFFETT "In the end, what counts in investing is what you pay for a business…and what that business earns in the succeeding decade or two."[1622]

LIBRARIAN "I would like to add one more thing—a backward test. Since we can never figure out what such geniuses as Buffett and Munger would do in a given situation, it is better to ask something that is easier to figure out— 'What would Warren Buffett and Charles Munger NOT do in this situation?'"

SEEKER "Great test—I need to have that stamped on my forehead."

"Can you please give an amateur like me an example of an investment you've done with a low downside and high upside that illustrates how you think? Something that contains predictability, advantage and sustainability—an investment that even someone like me could have done."

BUFFETT "In 1986, I purchased a 400-acre farm…from the FDIC. It cost me $280,000, considerably less than what a failed bank had lent against the farm a few years earlier."[1623]

SEEKER "What did you know about farming?"

BUFFETT "I knew nothing about operating a farm. But I have a son who loves farming, and I learned from him both how many bushels of corn and soybeans the farm would produce and what the operating expenses would be."

"From these estimates, I calculated the normalized return from the farm to then be about 10%. I also thought it was likely that productivity would improve over time and that crop prices would move higher as well. Both expectations proved out."[1624]

SEEKER "See if I got that right—you looked at what you could reasonable expect the farm to produce on average over time, how much it would cost to operate and then you measured that against the price. You paid a price that assuming normal times initially gave you a 10% return. That's good. You didn't look at forecasts like most others would have done. You used the normalized record. But since you believed the farm would over time a) increase its productivity and b) get higher prices for its crop, you concluded that the initial return would grow. Not bad."

"Of course, the reason you could make the estimate on both the normal return and possible growth was that you knew what to focus on—the key factors productivity and crop prices—and partly what you've learned from your son."

BUFFETT   "I needed no unusual knowledge or intelligence to conclude that the investment had no downside and potentially had substantial upside. There would, of course, be the occasional bad crop, and prices would sometimes disappoint. But so what? There would be some unusually good years as well, and I would never be under any pressure to sell the property. Now, 28 years later, the farm has tripled its earnings and is worth five times or more what I paid. I still know nothing about farming and recently made just my second visit to the farm."[1625]

LIBRARIAN   "And had it been a publicly traded farm you could have taken advantage of Mr. Market's mood swings."

BUFFETT   "It should be an enormous advantage for investors in stocks to have those wildly fluctuating valuations placed on their holdings — and for some investors, it is. After all, if a moody fellow with a farm bordering my property yelled out a price every day to me at which he would either buy my farm or sell me his — and those prices varied widely over short periods of time depending on his mental state — how in the world could I be other than benefited by his erratic behavior?"

"If his daily shout-out was ridiculously low, and I had some spare cash, I would buy his farm. If the number he yelled was absurdly high, I could either sell to him or just go on farming."[1626]

SEEKER   "Ok, using the market instead of it using me."

BUFFETT   "The fact that you can get quotes should be an advantage, but people turn it to a disadvantage because they think it's telling them to do something all the time."[1627]

"The market, like the Lord, helps those who help themselves. But, unlike the Lord, the market does not forgive those who know not what they do."[1628]

SEEKER   "Another one — and it sticks better."

BUFFETT   "In 1993, I made another small investment. Larry Silverstein, Salomon's landlord when I was the company's CEO, told me about a New York retail property adjacent to New York University that the Resolution Trust Corp. was selling. Again, a bubble had popped — this one involving commercial real estate — and the RTC had been created to dispose of the assets of failed savings institutions whose optimistic lending practices had fueled the folly."[1629]

SEEKER   "How did you analyze it?"

BUFFETT   "Here, too, the analysis was simple. As had been the case with the farm, the unleveraged current yield from the property was about 10%. But the property had been undermanaged by the RTC, and its income would increase when several vacant stores were leased."

"Even more important, the largest tenant — who occupied around 20% of the project's space — was paying rent of about $5 per foot, whereas other tenants averaged $70. The expiration of this bargain lease in nine years was certain to provide a major boost to earnings. The property's location was also superb: NYU wasn't going anywhere."[1630]

SEEKER   "So you bought it?"

BUFFETT   "I joined a small group, including Larry and my friend Fred Rose, that purchased the parcel. Fred was an experienced, high-grade real estate investor who, with his family, would manage the property. And manage it they did. As old leases expired, earnings tripled. Annual distributions now exceed 35% of our initial equity investment. Moreover, our original mortgage was refinanced in 1996 and again in 1999, moves that allowed several special distributions totaling more than 150% of what we had invested. I've yet to view the property."[1631]

SEEKER   "See, if I got this one right—you paid a price that initially gave you a 10% return. That's good. Here too, you believed this return would grow over time both from leasing vacant areas and rent increases—two key factors to create value in real estate."

BUFFETT   "I don't know that much about real estate or farms…And yet, it was perfectly possible to come to an intelligent decision that you could not lose money in those investments and that you were probably going to make quite a bit of money."

"I thought only of what the properties would produce and cared not at all about their daily valuations. Games are won by players who focus on the playing field—not by those whose eyes are glued to the scoreboard."[1632]

SEEKER   "Ok, from now on I will focus on how the businesses are doing."

BUFFETT   "Focus on the future productivity of the asset you are considering[1633]…Follow Wayne Gretzky's advice: 'Go to where the puck is going to be, not to where it is.'"[1634]

SEEKER   "What the asset produce—seems a key thing."

BUFFETT   "You look to the asset itself to determine your decision to lay out some money now to get some more money back later on. So you look to the apartment house, you look to the stock, you look to the farm in terms of what that will produce. And you don't really care whether there's a quote under it all. You are basically committing some funds now to get more funds later on through the operation of the asset."[1635]

LIBRARIAN "This imply both some predictability and competence—how else can you estimate the future?"

BUFFETT   "The way to look at a business is asking, is this going to keep producing more and more money over time? And if the answer to that is yes, you don't need to ask any more questions."[1636]

"If you don't feel comfortable making a rough estimate of the asset's future earnings, just forget it and move on...you only need to understand the actions you undertake."[1637]

SEEKER   "I wish I had known some of this stuff before."
"One more question—but aren't stocks a very risky asset?"

BUFFETT   "Stocks are riskless if held over a long time frame as you are simply giving up purchasing power now for later. Cash is the risky asset. Risk in stocks is not what the companies will do. Traditional finance teaches that Beta is a measure of risk but volatility isn't risk. Risk is loss of purchasing power. Volatility declines over a long enough timeframe. It is individuals that make investments risky...People think stocks are riskier than bonds, which is not true for a long time horizon."[1638]

"Investors, of course, can, by their own behavior, make stock ownership highly risky. And many do. Active trading, attempts to 'time' market movements, inadequate diversification, the payment of high and unnecessary fees to managers and advisors, and the use of borrowed money can destroy the decent returns that a life-long owner of equities would otherwise enjoy."[1639]

SEEKER   "I better start using my brain then and be careful with leverage."

BUFFETT   "Indeed, borrowed money has no place in the investor's tool kit: Anything can happen anytime in markets. And no advisor, economist, or TV commentator—and definitely not Charlie nor I—can tell you when chaos will occur. Market forecasters will fill your ear but will never fill your wallet."[1640]

SEEKER   "I put wax in my ears."

BUFFETT   "So I think that it comes down to those ideas - although they sound so simple and commonplace that it kind of seems like a waste to go to school and get a PhD in Economics and have it all come back to that. It's a little like spending eight years in divinity school and having somebody tell you that the 10 commandments were all that counted. There is a certain natural tendency to overlook anything that simple and important."[1641]

SEEKER   "You guys have for sure changed my view on investments."

LIBRARIAN "Let's end this session with a little test. Assume you are presented a business for investment. What type of questions will go through your mind in order to value the business? To simplify, we assume its management is able and trustworthy."

"Take your time."

SEEKER   "Can I understand it—figure out its economic future/estimate an earnings range? What are the key factors in this type of business and how predictable are they? Is it an essential business to customers now and in the future? Or is the need likely to go away or can what the business offer be copied or replaced by other sources? Has it earned high returns on tangible capital? Is it going to produce more money over time?"

"Does it have a moat—a sustainable competitive advantage and defense against threats?

"And then of course, even if the economics are great, the investment can still be bad if the price is too high."

Librarian "And what can cause you to decline the opportunity?"

Seeker "I have no idea where the business will be in the future—how it will look like, it isn't essential and can easily be replaced and it involves rapid and constant change where it's extremely hard to know how the winners will be. I have no clue as to what the key factors to look at are. I can't even roughly guess their future average earning power or return on capital."

"Furthermore, I can't judge why customers use this kind of product or why they should buy them from this company rather from someone else. Also their return on capital is lousy."

Librarian "So far so good."

Seeker "I don't see how they are protected from its many competitors. I have no idea what their competitors will be offering in the future or even how they will look like in the future. Neither do I have any idea what differentiates the business from their competitors or how to spot competitive advantage in this type of business."

"And even if I could—I can't judge if their moat will last or not."

Buffett "If you can't recognize the moat, it doesn't mean there isn't one there. It may be you can't recognize it and then you go onto the next one."[1642]

Librarian "There are always more fish in the sea."

Seeker "And what would cause you to turn it down?"

Buffett "Situations where I don't know the competitive situation—what competition do in the field—and where I can't see the future—I don't know what it will look like in terms of who's going to sell what to whom and at what prices and against whom 10 years from now."[1643]

"If you buy businesses for less than what they are worth, you're going to make money. If you know which businesses you can and cannot value, you're going to make money."[1644]

Librarian "And the best time…"

Buffett "The best time to get rich is a crisis. You just need independent thinking, financial preparation, and mental preparation[1645]…If you can detach yourself temperamentally from the crowd—you get very rich. And you won't have to be very bright…It doesn't take brains, it takes temperament."[1646]

MUNGER "But temperament alone won't do it...You have to have the temperament and the right basic idea—and then you have to keep at it with a lot of curiosity for a long, long time."[1647]

SEEKER "Still it is not easy to do."

MUNGER "It's not supposed to be easy. Anyone who finds it easy is stupid."[1648]

LIBRARIAN "Like the rest of the human species, I sometimes violate these criteria and the result has sometimes been good and sometimes bad but net, lousy."

SEEKER "Thanks for your illuminating expose of stupidities."

"Before I leave, is there something more I could use that will help me...some simple tricks or rules of thumbs or something like that?"

–PART FOUR–

ON FILTERS AND RULES

*"To avoid the various foolish opinions to which mankind are prone,
no superhuman genius is required. A few simple rules
will keep you, not from all error, but from silly error."*

- Bertrand Russell[1649]

THE RIGHT FILTERS CONSERVE THOUGHT AND SIMPLIFY LIFE

LIBRARIAN "Didn't we tell you that we like to keep it simple here? The right filters help you prioritize and figure out what makes sense or not."
        "But let's start with…

BUFFETT   "The most elusive of human goals—keeping things simple and remembering what you set out to do."[1650]

NEVER LOSE SIGHT OF WHAT YOU'RE TRYING TO ACHIEVE OR AVOID

MUNGER   "A majority of life's errors are caused by forgetting what one is really trying to do."[1651]

LIBRARIAN "What do you want to achieve or avoid—what outcome do you want to see or not see? To add some ancient Chinese wisdom, 'Unless we change our direction we are likely to end up where we are headed.'"

SEEKER   "You guys for sure have something to say about everything."

LIBRARIAN "…and just like pilots are educated and trained to think, learn to know when it is most important to focus on what you want to achieve or what you want to avoid."

SEEKER   "Pilots do this?"

MUNGER   "Like any good algebraist, he is made to think sometimes in a forward fashion and sometimes in reverse; and so he learns when to concentrate mostly on what he wants to happen and also when to concentrate mostly on avoiding what he does not want to happen."
        "His training time is allocated among subjects so as to minimize damage from his later malfunctions; and so what is most important in his performance gets the most training coverage and is raised to the highest fluency levels."[1652]

SEEKER "The inversion trick again."

LIBRARIAN "And goals should be subject to change since the world, you, threats and opportunities change. And when reality changes, you better change with it."

"Also make sure your goal really is the right goal for what you want to accomplish. Ask, 'assume I have reached my goal—is this what I wanted?' Some people chase a certain goal all their life and when they finally reach it find out that it wasn't what they really wanted."

BUFFETT "There's no use running if you're on the wrong road."[1653]

SEEKER "Good advice."
"You mentioned filters?"

BUFFETT "At Berkshire we have certain filters that have been developed."[1654]

The TUNE OUT "FOLLY" filter

LIBRARIAN "Great thinkers have an instant ability to exclude things—like disqualifying features or nonsense."

SEEKER "Like the chess players did and the efficiency by eliminating what doesn't work."

MUNGER "Part of being a wise person is…to know nonsense when you see it."[1655]

"I never believed there was a talking snake in the Garden of Eden. I had a gift for recognizing twaddle."[1656]

BUFFETT "We are rational…we don't waste a lot of time exploring things that are just nonsense."[1657]

MUNGER "Rationality is a really good idea. It requires that you must avoid the nonsense that is conventional in one's one time."[1658]

"Part of [having uncommon sense], I think, is being able to tune out folly, as distinguished from recognizing wisdom. You've got whole categories of things you just bat away so your brain isn't cluttered with them. That way, you're better able to pick up a few sensible things to do."[1659]

BUFFETT "Yeah, we don't consider many stupid things. I mean, we get rid of 'em fast. In fact, get irritated with us because they'll call us, and when they're in the middle of the first sentence, we'll just tell 'em, 'Forget it.'"

"Just getting rid of the nonsense—just figuring out that if people call you and say, 'I've got this great, wonderful idea', you don't spend 10 minutes once you know in the first sentence that it isn't a great, wonderful idea…Don't be polite and go through the whole process."[1660]

MUNGER "We make a lot of decisions about a lot of things very fast and very easily….And the reason why we're able to do that is that there's such an enormous amount of things that we won't allow ourselves to think about. It's just that simple."[1661]

SEEKER   "Assume I have an investment I want to sell to you."

BUFFETT   "If somebody calls me about an investment in a business or an investment in securities, I usually know in two or three minutes whether I have an interest. I don't waste any time with the ones which I don't have an interest in."[1662]

"I don't fool a lot around with negotiations. If they name a price that makes sense to me, I buy it. If they don't, I was happy the day before, so I will be happy the day after without owning it."[1663]

MUNGER   "We have to deal in things that we are capable of understanding and then once we're over that filter we have to have a business with some intrinsic characteristics that give it a durable competitive advantage. And of course, we would vastly prefer a management in place with a lot of integrity and talent. And finally, no matter how wonderful it is, it's not worth an infinite price so we have to have a price that makes sense and gives a margin of safety considering the natural vicissitudes of life."

"That's a very simple set of ideas and the reason that our ideas have not spread faster is they are too simple."[1664]

LIBRARIAN "Elimination is a great conservator of time and effort. "

BUFFETT   "There's a lot of things going through our mind, and most of the things going through our mind are things that will stop us. Including who we are dealing with…I consider an important question to be: 'Do we really want to be in partnership with this person and count on them to behave well in the future when they no longer own the business?' That stops a fair number of deals."[1665]

MUNGER   "When people make pitches to me, I have one phrase I often use about half way through the first sentence. I say, 'We don't do start-ups.' Well, if you blot out start-ups, there's a whole layer of complexity that goes out of your life. And we've got many other areas of blot-out assistance."[1666]

LIBRARIAN "Alexander Pope's advice is, 'Be not the first by whom the new are tried, nor yet the last to lay the old aside.'"

"What is it you always say on start-ups?"

BUFFETT   "The early bird might get the worm, but the second mouse gets the cheese."[1667]

SEEKER   "My experience of start-ups or investing in new ventures is that they seem to have a never ending demand for new cash—issuing of new shares in absurdum. Anyway, I have got burned too many times to enter that arena again."

LIBRARIAN "Hofstadter's Law is also apt here, 'It always takes longer than you expect, even when you take into account Hofstadter's Law'[1668]…But people always believe they are the exception."

Seeker   "It reminds me of the saying, 'There's many a pessimist who got that way by financing an optimist.'"

"You mentioned rationality — are you always perfectly rational?"

Munger   "It is a mistake to believe that rationality is going to be perfect… We prove that all the time."[1669]

Librarian "As Erasmus said, 'No man is wise at all times, or is without his blind side.'"

Munger   "To expect total rationality either in humans or human institutions, is expecting what's not going to happen."[1670]

Seeker   "Ok, I try to be as rational as possible."

Munger   "I think rationality is a moral duty. That's why I like Confucius. He had the same ideas years ago. I think Berkshire is a template of rationality. And what's really admired at Berkshire is people who sees it the way it really is…That goes beyond a technique for wealth, for me it's a moral principle… If you have an easily removable ignorance and keep it, I think it's dishonorable. It's dishonorable to stay stupider than you have to be. That's my ethos."[1671]

"Rationality…won't save you from a terrible accident or the death of a child, but character and rationality will save you from a lot…It's playing the game all the way through with both character and rationality."[1672]

Seeker   "Apart from this 'folly' filter, any more filters?"

Buffett   "You have to have a basic understanding of what counts and what doesn't."[1673]

Librarian "Part of wisdom is to understand what is predictable and what is unknowable and ignore things that are irrelevant and unknowable."

The IMPORTANT AND KNOWABLE filter

Buffett   "Our job really is to focus on things that we can know that make a difference. If something can't make a difference or if we can't know it, then we write it off."[1674]

Librarian "Just narrow it down to the important and knowable facts. And remember that there is an awful lot of verbal and numerate diarrhea out there that can easily interfere with facts or wisdom."

Buffett   "We try to think about things that are both important and knowable. There are important things that are not knowable…And there are things that are knowable, but not important – and we don't want to clutter up our minds with those."

"We ask ourselves: 'What's important and knowable? And what among those things can we translate into some kind of action that's useful for Berkshire?'"[1675]

The CIRCLE OF COMPETENCE filter

Librarian "One we talked about many times today is staying within your own circle of competence—know what you know and understand and what you have competence in."

Buffett "We have tended to avoid the losers and we have done that by trying to stick in what I call my circle of competence[1676]…What counts for most people in investing is not how much they know, but rather how realistically they define what they don't know."[1677]

Munger "People chronically misappraise the limits of their own knowledge; that's one of the most basic parts of human nature. Knowing the edge of your circle of competence is one of the most difficult things for a human being to do. Knowing what you don't know is much more useful in life and business than being brilliant."[1678]

Buffett "You're either in, out, or it's too hard of a decision to make. The good decisions scream at you[1679]…If you have doubts if something is in your circle of competence, it's not."[1680]

Seeker "These filters of yours seem to be very efficient."

Buffett "We really can say 'no' in 10 seconds or so to 90%+ of all of the things that come along simply because we have these filters."[1681]

Munger "Yeah. We have to have an idea that is (A) a good idea and (B) a good idea that we can understand. It's that simple. So our filters are filters against consequences from our own lack of talent."[1682]

Seeker "Useful stuff, this. Any other simple filter?"

Librarian "Yes, one that ties in with the circle of competence filter."

The TOO TOUGH filter

Munger "If something is too hard, we move on to something else. What could be more simple than that?"[1683]

Buffett "We like easy problems. We don't try to solve tough problems and we don't go around looking for tough problems."[1684]

Munger "There are a lot of things we pass on. We have three baskets: in, out, and too tough. We have to have a special insight, or we'll put it in the 'too tough' basket. All you have to look for is a special area of competency and focus on that."[1685]

Buffett "There are things in life that you don't have to make a decision on that are too hard."[1686]

Munger "What Warren and I have done is to just exclude a lot of things because they're in our 'too tough' pile. If you insist on thinking about things that are practically insoluble and very complicated, I don't think you can be usefully wise."[1687]

LIBRARIAN "I recently talked to someone who didn't follow your 'too tough' prescription but instead wanted to solve his tough business problems with an acquisition."

MUNGER "When you have tough competitors it is easy to think that any change in your business will solve all of your problems. Most of the time it doesn't work out that well."[1688]

BUFFETT "And they will have lawyers, consultants, investment banks and others in who get paid for deals, telling them to do a deal."[1689]

MUNGER "You're...the CEO of the place and you see it's getting tough. Your duty, your acquired self-image is a guy that knows how to fix things. You never have a category in your mind that reads, 'this is too tough for me to fix,' which is a really stupid idea. You can recognize all kinds of things that are too tough to fix."

"But if you don't, then you are a sucker for some narrative like, 'maybe there's some company in your industry that makes something really complicated that other people can't match.' And you say, 'Well, I'll buy that. That solves my problem.' But your friendly investment banker and your friendly management consultant want you to buy it at 30 times' earnings and 12 times' book. Of course, at that price, it won't solve your problems. And you do it anyway. After all, you've got consultants and it gives you hope."[1690]

SEEKER "So his belief didn't make it work?"

MUNGER "A lot of American industry helped by their friendly investment bankers and consultants...want to believe that in this terrible, tough business, there's an easy solution. It just requires listening to the siren song and writing the check. Of course, usually it doesn't work."

"There are all kinds of things you can't buy your way out of. You have to adapt to them."[1691]

LIBRARIAN "Neither does it work merging a lousy business with a good one."

MUNGER "When you mix raisins and turds, you've still got turds."[1692]

LIBRARIAN "And consolidating two lousy businesses doesn't usually work either."

BUFFETT "If you have two lousy businesses and you put 'em together, you've got one big lousy business usually."[1693]

LIBRARIAN "Like the CEO who many years ago said to his directors when they discussed a possible merger between two companies in the European car industry, 'If you have one fist full of shit and the other fist full of shit and merge the hands, you get two fists full of shit and furthermore, it flows over.'"

Seeker   "But aren't there sometimes benefits in combining two companies — so called synergies?"

Librarian   "Don't be seduced by the synergy argument — many are only illusory or unworkable."

Buffett   "In some mergers there truly are major synergies — though often times the acquirer pays too much to obtain them — but at other times the cost and revenue benefits that are projected prove illusory[1694]...You always have these things that investment bankers will tell you produce synergies but most of the time they don't work."[1695]

Munger   "The reason we avoid the word 'synergy' is because people generally claim more synergistic benefits than will come. Yes, it exists, but there are so many false promises. Berkshire is full of synergies — we don't avoid synergies, just claims of synergies."[1696]

Buffett   "As a director of 19 companies over the years, I've never heard 'dis-synergies' mentioned, though I've witnessed plenty of these once deals have closed. Post mortems of acquisitions, in which reality is honestly compared to the original projections, are rare in American boardrooms. They should instead be standard practice."[1697]

Librarian   "Instead, successes are exaggerated and mistakes are hidden."

Munger   "You tend to forget your own mistakes when reputation is threatened by remembering."[1698]

Buffett   "Part of making good decisions in business is recognizing the poor decisions you've made and why they were poor."[1699]

Munger   "At most corporations, if you make an acquisition and it turns out to be a disaster, all the people, paperwork, and presentations that caused the foolish acquisition are quickly forgotten. Nobody wants to be associated with the poor outcome by mentioning it. But at Johnson & Johnson, the rules make everybody revisit old acquisitions, comparing predictions with outcomes. That is a very smart thing to do."[1700]

Buffett   "I think you're a better doctor if you drop by the pathology department occasionally. And I think you're a better manager or investor if you look at each decision that you've made of importance and see which ones worked out and which ones didn't — and figure your batting average. Then, if your batting average gets too bad, you better hand the decision-making over to someone else."[1701]

Seeker   "Reminds me of what Yoda from *Star Wars* said, 'If no mistake have you made, yet losing you are ... a different game you should play.'"[1702]

        "Anyway — the competence and too tough filters are something I really need to pick up."

MUNGER   "You know what you know, and what you don't know, and you work at that concept. You learn what to avoid, and you learn just a few mental habits."[1703]

"There are a lot of things we pass on…We have to have a special insight, or we'll put it in the 'too tough' basket."[1704]

SEEKER   "Tell me one of the mental habits you have."

MUNGER   "One of my habits is that I get the no-brainers off my desk immediately. Otherwise, it gets cluttered. For some people, decisions worry them, and they pile up the desk and get totally dysfunctional. There are a lot of little tricks that simplify life."[1705]

SEEKER   "Any more—say on problem-solving?"

LIBRARIAN "First make sure the problem is a real problem, worth solving and solvable by you. As Edward Tufte said, 'The idea is to find important problems that can be solved.'"[1706]

MUNGER   "I generally try to approach a complex task by first disposing of the easy decisions[1707]…It is usually best to simplify problems by deciding big 'no-brainer' questions first."[1708]

"The other thing we do, if the problem is really hard and important, we rag it. We keep working at it, and come back to it and so forth. You have a lot of time to do that because of all the things you avoid that other people do."[1709]

"If any successes come to me, it came because I insisted on thinking things through…thinking pretty hard about trying to get the right answer and then acting on it."[1710]

LIBRARIAN "Of course, this demands having a prepared mind."

SEEKER   "Yes, I first have to understand what works and not—how else can I find a solution or know what to do."

LIBRARIAN "And never make important decisions when you are tired."

MUNGER   "When we started we didn't know this modern psychological evidence that you shouldn't make decisions when you were tired and how tiring it is to make decisions…I can't remember an important decision Warren has made when he was tired."[1711]

LIBRARIAN "Sometimes it also helps to remove you from the problem and do something else. Let the unconscious mind go to work—distance gives perspective. As the German physicist Helmholtz said on his 70th birthday, 'After investigating a problem in all directions, happy ideas come unexpectedly, without effort, like an inspiration. So far as I am concerned, they have never come to me when my mind was fatigued, or when I was at my working table. . . . They came particularly readily during the slow ascent of wooded hills on a sunny day.'"[1712]

"And to put your unconscious to work, you need to give it time."

SEEKER   "Tell me another filter."

MUNGER   "Opportunity cost is a huge filter in life."[1713]

The OPPORTUNITY COST filter

MUNGER   "Decisions in life are all about opportunity costs[1714]...And wise people think in terms of personal opportunity costs[1715]...in other words, it's your alternatives that matter. That's how we make all of our decisions."[1716]

LIBRARIAN "It is a filter to help you use your resources — time, money, talent, energy, attention — in the best possible way. How to decide, choose or behave."

SEEKER   "I don't get it. How can an opportunity have a cost? And take it slowly — must you always talk this fast?"

LIBRARIAN "Do you always listen this slow? — Sorry, I couldn't help myself."
          "Assume you have two alternatives — A and B — available to you and they both achieve the same purpose and you pick A. The opportunity cost of choosing A is then the possible value you lose, miss or give up by not choosing B. And of course, if A is the best one, there is no value lost."
          "It is the cost of making the wrong choice, decision or action."

MUNGER   "Most people take into account opportunities in important decisions in life — what job to take, what school to go to, etc."[1717]

SEEKER   "I get it — there can be huge costs of making the wrong choice — picking the wrong spouse, job, employee, advisor, investment or behaving like a jerk."

LIBRARIAN "Or not knowing what works and not."
          "So the test is, 'What do I want to achieve? Based on my resources, what opportunities or alternatives are available to me that I can understand? Which one will give me the most value based on what I want to achieve?'"

MUNGER   "In life, if opportunity A is better than B, and you have only one opportunity, you do A."[1718]

LIBRARIAN "Try to figure out your best alternative and remember, as Mr. Munger said, wise people think in terms of personal opportunity costs. That includes considering both constraints and resources. An opportunity is always personal — it has to be available to you..."

MUNGER   "That you can understand is the best opportunity."[1719]

LIBRARIAN "And fit your nature and talents. Do what you're good at and spend your resources on the things that create the most value for you."

SEEKER   "I assume different people have different opportunities."

MUNGER   "You are located in a certain place, you have a certain amount of opportunities, and you find opportunity A that's better than opportunity B, which is the best alternative you know of. You therefore do A instead of

B. Somebody else may have a better bet. But opportunity A may be the best you have, given where you're located and what you know. So you don't have one-size-fits-all solution as you go through life."[1720]

SEEKER   "Mr. Munger, how did you use this filter?"

MUNGER   "I just wanted to do the best I could reasonably do with the talent, time and resources I had available. That's what I was doing then and now."

"Think of how life is simplified if you approach it this way."[1721]

SEEKER   "Same with investments?"

BUFFETT   "We just look to do the most intelligent thing we can with the capital that we have. We measure everything against our alternatives[1722]… Capitalism is about capital allocation. The whole idea is putting resources in the right places. And we've got the ability to look at 70-plus companies, various industries and everything else, and allocate capital wherever it makes the most sense…saying, where can this money be used best?"[1723]

LIBRARIAN "What is the best use of my cash—Do I want to invest my cash into this asset at this price today or is there something else I would rather do with my cash?"

MUNGER   "When you find the one that you regard as the best opportunity— that you can understand is the best opportunity—now you've got one to buy."[1724]

LIBRARIAN "Since both your resources and available opportunities and circumstances change over time, your opportunity cost naturally changes over time. So do what makes most sense under the given circumstances."

BUFFETT   "Obviously, events change from day to day, prices change from day to day, opportunities change from day to day. Every day I come to work, I'm thinking about what makes the most sense for Berkshire."[1725]

MUNGER   "The more attractive things are, the higher the bar is. Berkshire has raised the opportunity cost bar by looking at stocks, bonds, private companies, public companies, etc. We have more opportunities by operating in a wider range."

"The danger is that you have more risk of operating outside of your circle of competence. I don't think we're ever gone outside our circle of competence. We find things across a fairly wide range that we think is within our circle of competency."[1726]

BUFFETT   "At Berkshire we face no institutional restraints when we deploy capital. Charlie and I are limited only by our ability to understand the likely future of a possible acquisition. If we clear that hurdle—and frequently we can't—we are then able to compare any one opportunity against a host of others."

"When I took control of Berkshire in 1965, I didn't exploit this advantage. Berkshire was then only in textiles, where it had in the previous decade lost significant money. The dumbest thing I could have done was to pursue 'opportunities' to improve and expand the existing textile operation—so for years that's exactly what I did. And then, in a final burst of brilliance, I went out and bought another textile company. Aaaaaaargh! Eventually I came to my senses, heading first into insurance and then into other industries."[1727]

LIBRARIAN "Also, some opportunities have a time limit of availability, for example the opportunity to spend time with your kids since they grow up."

SEEKER "How can I use opportunity cost, in let's say marriage?"

MUNGER "Like all other things in life you have to look for your best option and live with it[1728]...You have to marry the best person who you can conveniently find who's also willing to have you. And the person who would have you whom you can't find doesn't do you any good."[1729]

"We have to do what's available[1730]...The rest of life is the same damn way."[1731]

SEEKER "When I marry someone, I expect her to look at my face. That's the price she has to pay. But my looks and my wallet definitely limit the number of available spouses."

MUNGER "If you're an medium-attractive person and somebody wants to marry you, you have a certain opportunity to have that marriage—or you can say, 'Well, I'll try and do better.'"[1732]

"If you've got two suitors who are really eager to have you and one is way the hell better than the other, you do not have to spend much time with the other."[1733]

LIBRARIAN "Carolyn Wells said, 'A fool and his money are soon married'[1734]...A beautiful woman that only marries you for your money is nothing to build a long-term relationship on anyway. You may have some fun for a while but a person who gets married for his or her money marries trouble."

MUNGER "It reminds me of the old quote, where the husband asks, 'Will you still love me if I lost all my money?' And the wife replies: 'I will always love you but I will miss you terribly.'"[1735]

SEEKER "On the other hand, as someone once said, 'Money cannot buy love, but it places one in an excellent bargaining position.'"

LIBRARIAN "Maybe, but as Benjamin Franklin said, 'Where there's marriage without love, there will be love without marriage.'"

SEEKER "I agree. Assume I like something I have but am thinking of changing it, how would you reason then?"

LIBRARIAN "We all have a lot of things we like: our spouse, job, house, car, investments, etc. When you decide whether to change something, measure it against the best of what you already have and that is available to you."

SEEKER   "Take a new investment idea for example."

BUFFETT   "New ideas are continually measured against present ideas."[1736]

MUNGER   "For an ordinary individual, the best thing you already have should be your measuring stick. If the new thing isn't better than what you already know is available, then it hasn't met your threshold. And that screens out 99% of what you see…If the new opportunity is not better, why should you seize it?"[1737]

LIBRARIAN   "This is of course also valid for a marriage—if you already have the best spouse, why should you even 'look' at other woman or man?"

SEEKER   "Yes, why would I—if I had a wife?"

BUFFETT   "We believe that it is almost impossible for us to 'trade up' from our present businesses and managements. Our situation is the opposite of Camelot's Mordred, of whom Guinevere commented, 'The one thing I can say for him is that he is bound to marry well. Everybody is above him.' Marrying well is extremely difficult for Berkshire."[1738]

MUNGER   "Berkshire Hathaway is constantly kicking off ideas in about two seconds flat. We know we've got opportunity X, which is better than the new opportunity. Why do we want to waste two seconds thinking about the new opportunity?[1739]…If I know I have something that yields 8% for sure, and something else came along at 7%, I'd reject it instantly. It's like the mail-order-bride firm offering a bride who has AIDS—I don't need to waste a moment considering it."[1740]

BUFFETT   "Any new company, any new stock I look at, I measure it against the best idea I've got among the present ones."[1741]

MUNGER   "Somebody recently asked me to look at a company in China…I really liked the look of it. But it didn't take me five seconds to reject it, because I could say, 'I know I already have something I like more at current prices—and I can buy more of that if I wish.' Why should I look at something new when I've got something I can do more of that I like better?"[1742]

"Think of the simplification that such consideration of edge of competency and opportunity cost gives to our life."[1743]

SEEKER   "When you look at new investment opportunities, wouldn't it be better to measure them against your best past deal—I mean, a really high threshold?"

BUFFETT   "It is a huge error to try and measure every deal against the best deal you've ever made. Market conditions and opportunity costs are different in every case. We each have to do what is available at any given time. The goal is not to make the greatest deal you've ever made—it's to make the best deal you can make at that time."[1744]

LIBRARIAN "There is a difference in trying to always get the best possible result and trying for the best result possible given the circumstances — circumstances changes what to do."

SEEKER "Going back to the cost of making the wrong decision — give me some more examples."

LIBRARIAN "Assume a company acquires another company for $100 million and it turn out to be a catastrophe — a total loss. They have then suffered three losses, 1) the actual $100 million lost, 2) the opportunity cost loss since they could have done something else — hopefully better — with those dollars, and 3) the loss of focus on the main business — all the time and talent wasted — including the costs of competitive effects."

BUFFETT "I love focused management… And when you lose that focus… it shows…GEICO actually started fooling around in a number of things in the early 1980s. And they paid a price for it — actually a very big price. They paid a direct price in terms of the cost for those things — because they almost all worked out badly. And then they paid an additional price in terms of the loss of focus on the main business."[1745]

LIBRARIAN "The money invested could also have tied the company in other ways. This doesn't include the mental stress they may have experienced during the ride."

"Life is filled with tragic opportunity cost losses for actions that seemed good at the time."

SEEKER "Like the story Mr. Munger told about the guy who managed to conceive an illegitimate child on a train ride."

MUNGER "Chris Davis [Davis Funds] has a wall of shame. He celebrates the things they did that lost them a lot of money. What is also needed is a wall of shame squared for things you didn't do that would have made you rich. Forgetting your mistakes is a terrible mistake if you are trying to improve your cognition. Reality doesn't remind you. Why not celebrate stupidities in both categories?"[1746]

SEEKER "Useful stuff, this. Any other filter?"

LIBRARIAN "Yes — not a real filter but still something very useful — to think about consequences and their consequences."

The "AND THEN WHAT?" filter

BUFFETT "The most important question to ask in economics is 'X happens, and then what?' Actually, it's not such a bad idea to ask it about everything. But you should always ask, 'And then what?'…What else does that mean?"[1747]

SEEKER "And then what — what?"

LIBRARIAN "Every action has consequences."

BUFFETT "Anything you do triggers another corresponding action[1748]... There are always other effects that come out of it."[1749]

LIBRARIAN "Where some may be unwanted—for example, we solve problem A but create problem B. Sometimes worse than the problem we are trying to solve."

BUFFETT "When you start focusing on one variable, you often get some side effects you didn't expect."[1750]

MUNGER "This defect is quite understandable because the consequences have consequences, and the consequences of the consequences have consequences, and so on. It gets very complicated."[1751]

"The problem is grounded deep into the nature of things, in the principle that in a complex system you can never 'do merely one thing.' When one variable is maximized other variables often get minimized in an undesired way."[1752]

LIBRARIAN "And there is always at least one unwanted consequence."

SEEKER "So what should we do?"

BUFFETT "Anytime somebody says 'I'm going to do this', you have to say, 'And then what?' And there is no free lunch, so...you do have aftereffects."[1753]

LIBRARIAN "We have to challenge our actions and think forward as best as we can by asking 'and then what will happen and what will happen after that etc.?' to estimate an action's net consequences and implications over time and whether it will achieve what we want or not. Ask: 'Considering the whole system and over time—all key factors, including constraints, scale effects, human nature, how the world works—what other effects are likely to happen?'"

BUFFETT "Sometimes you can foresee them and sometimes you can't."[1754]

LIBRARIAN "There is always a set of problems attached with any approach— we have to pick our poison. The key is to try to move to a better set of problems one can accept after comparing what appear to be the consequences of each."

"You try to get the best result possible—what on balance is best— considering the prevailing circumstances and constraints."

SEEKER "I get it—I think—But please give me an example of this filter."

MUNGER "When they passed Medicare originally, they had all these actuarial studies that showed the cost would be X. And the cost turned out to be more than 10X."[1755]

SEEKER "Ten times more! What did they miss?"

MUNGER "They did simple extrapolations of past costs. Once they put in place various new incentives, the behavior changed in response to the incentives, and the numbers became quite different from their projection."

"How could a great group of experts make such a silly forecast? Answer: They oversimplified to get easy figures…They chose not to consider effects of effects on effects, and so on."[1756]

LIBRARIAN "They didn't think about the unintended consequences."

MUNGER "They didn't think through the incentive effects of the way they were changing the rules. They created a system wherein they were reimbursing both doctors and hospitals, in effect, on a cost plus percentage of cost basis. The minute they did that, the hospitals and doctors found wonderful ways to talk the patients into buying all kinds of care that got reimbursed…good for the hospital and good for the doctor, but bad for the patient and bad for the taxpayers."[1757]

SEEKER "I assume it caused a lot of unnecessary things."

MUNGER "If the government is going to pay A anything he wants for selling services to B, who doesn't have to pay anything, of course the system is going to create a lot of unnecessary tests, unnecessary costs, unnecessary procedures, unnecessary interventions. All the bills go to the government. As long as the incentives allow that, people will do it and they'll rationalize their behavior."[1758]

SEEKER "The importance of the right incentives again."

MUNGER "This result demonstrates the impossibility of revising a complex system without undesired 'by-product' effects. The first law of ecology and the first law of legislation are one and the same: 'You can never do merely one thing.'"[1759]

LIBRARIAN "Another example is your experience from the textile business."

MUNGER "The business version of the Medicare-type insanity is when you own a textile plant and a guy comes in and says, 'Oh, isn't this wonderful. They invented a new loom. It'll pay for itself in three years at current prices because it adds so much efficiency to the production of textiles.' And you keep buying these looms, and their equivalent, for twenty years, and you keep making four percent on capital; you never go anywhere."[1760]

SEEKER "What do you mean—'never go anywhere'?"

BUFFETT "Over the years, we had the option of making large capital expenditures in the textile operation that would have allowed us to somewhat reduce variable costs. Each proposal to do so looked like an immediate winner. Measured by standard return-on-investment tests, in fact, these proposals usually promised greater economic benefits than would have resulted from comparable expenditures in our highly-profitable candy and newspaper businesses."[1761]

SEEKER "Sounds good—doesn't it?"

BUFFETT "We always had new machinery that held the promise of increasing our profit, but it never did because everyone else bought the

214

same machinery. It was sort of like being in a crowd, and everyone stands on tip-toes—your view doesn't improve, but your legs hurt."[1762]

LIBRARIAN "The problem is that most people only see the immediate—but illusory—benefits of investment in machines. They don't see what else happens—like competitive actions and that all the benefits or the efficiency gains go to the customer."

BUFFETT "Many of our competitors, both domestic and foreign, were stepping up to the same kind of expenditures and, once enough companies did so, their reduced costs became the baseline for reduced prices industry wide."[1763]

MUNGER "It wasn't that technology didn't work, it's that the laws of economics caused the benefit from the new looms to go to the people that bought the textiles, not the guy that owned the textile plant."[1764]

SEEKER "Strange this—what looks like increased productivity results in falling price and lower profits. Not something one learns in business school."

MUNGER "Lots of things increase efficiency without increasing profits."[1765]

BUFFETT "Viewed individually, each company's capital investment decision appeared cost-effective and rational; viewed collectively, the decisions neutralized each other and were irrational (just as happens when each person watching a parade decides he can see a little better if he stands on tiptoes). After each round of investment, all the players had more money in the game and returns remained anemic."[1766]

LIBRARIAN "The 'standing-on-tiptoe-at-a-parade-problem'—you do something you believe is beneficial but shortly thereafter everyone is doing the same thing. Once anybody did it, everyone else had to follow. Didn't you experience that in the department store business?"

BUFFETT "If my competitor had air-conditioning, I had air-conditioning… If they put in an escalator, I had to put in an escalator. All of those were defensive decisions."[1767]

SEEKER "As you said before—retailing is a tough business."

BUFFETT "In a business selling a commodity-type product, it's impossible to be a lot smarter than your dumbest competitor."[1768]

LIBRARIAN "Instead search for companies with moats where you neither lose unit volume or competitive position but instead get the benefits of the increased cost efficiencies."

SEEKER "Can you give me another example?"

LIBRARIAN "You remember when we talked about the workers' compensation system in California?"

SEEKER "Yes, wasn't that about the problem with creating systems where it is easy for people to cheat?"

LIBRARIAN "Once more 'and then what?' or a decisions ripple effects come into play."

MUNGER "It's just the incentive structure that so rewards all this fraud is put in place by these ignorant legislatures, many members of which have been to law school, and they just don't think about what terrible things they're doing to the civilization because they don't take into account the second order effects and the third-order effects in lying and cheating."[1769]

SEEKER "So what should they have done better? Asked 'And then what?"

MUNGER "Think through that effects have effects — and that incentives are always going to have super-effects — because that's a basic law of biological life."[1770]

"Anyway, as the Medicare example showed, all human systems are gamed, for reasons rooted deeply in psychology, and great skill is displayed in the gaming."[1771]

SEEKER "I understand now that having the right incentives is really important."

LIBRARIAN "One example of perverse incentives with bad consequences happened when 19th century paleontologists were in China to find dinosaur bones and they paid peasants for each fragment of dinosaur bones that they found. The result: the peasants dug up the bones and then smashed them into pieces, to maximize their payments."[1772]

SEEKER "Not what the paleontologists aimed for."

LIBRARIAN "Equivalent to what Mark Twain said in his autobiography, 'The best way to increase wolves in America, rabbits in Australia, and snakes in India, is to pay a bounty on their scalps. Then every patriot goes to raising them.'"

"Once more, the truth that rewards determine consequences is confirmed."

BUFFETT "There must be incentives to do the right thing and incentives not to do the wrong thing."[1773]

LIBRARIAN "Gresham's Law is another example of unwanted consequences."

SEEKER "Like you told me earlier where bad loan practices drives out good."

LIBRARIAN "Yes, in fact it can be generalized to any process or system where the bad drives out the good. Gresham is an example of what Garrett Hardin calls a pejoristic system – a system which by its very nature makes matters worse. Another example of this is our overuse and misuse of antimicrobials. What happens is that every antimicrobial selects for its own failure. Antibiotics selects for antibiotic-resistant bacteria just as DDT selected for DDT-resistant mosquitoes."

216

SEEKER "Is this why antibiotic resistance is a huge health care problem? I mean, how does it happen?"

LIBRARIAN "It is just natural selection at work. There are a lot of bacteria around and in any population of bacteria, there are some individuals that through mutations have developed genes causing them to escape elimination. The more non-resistant bacteria that are eliminated, the more opportunities for the resistant to reproduce and spread. Over time, the resistant bugs win the race, meaning the antibiotics become less and less effective."

"This also means that the more we use antibiotics, the faster resistance spreads."

SEEKER "Very useful this 'see the whole picture' and 'things bite back' idea of yours."

LIBRARIAN "Just as we get what we reward for, we get what we select for."

"Even extra care in thinking may have negative consequences."

MUNGER "Most good things have undesired 'side effects', and thinking is no exception. The best defense is that of the best physicists, who systematically criticize themselves to an extreme degree, using a mindset described by Nobel laureate Richard Feynman as follows: 'The first principle is that you must not fool yourself and you're the easiest person to fool.'"[1774]

"The ethos of not fooling yourself is one of the best you could possibly have. It's powerful because it's so rare."[1775]

The "COMPARED TO WHAT?" filter

LIBRARIAN "Another filter that is really the key question behind opportunity cost is, 'Compared to what?' Because what you really do is compare different alternatives or opportunities."

"You can also ask the 'compared to what' question when someone explains 'why' an outcome happened. You have to consider alternative explanations."

SEEKER "Give me an example."

LIBRARIAN "Ok, let's use Cicero writings about the poet and clear thinker Diagoras of Milos. One day a friend of Diagoras tried to convince him that the gods existed — 'You think the gods have no care for man? Why, you can see from all these votive pictures here how many people have escaped the fury of storms at sea by praying to the gods who have brought them safe to harbor.' Diagoras replied, 'Yes, indeed, but where are the pictures of all those who suffered shipwreck and perished in the waves?'"[1776]

"Let's call it the Diagoras trick or considering both positive and negative outcomes."

SEEKER "Give me a more useful example."

LIBRARIAN "Assume someone tells you that 'I have studied successful businesses and have found that their secret to success is visionary leaders.'"

SEEKER   "Makes sense."

LIBRARIAN "But then you have to ask yourself, 'Visionary leaders is great but compared to what?' What about all those businesses that had visionary leaders but ended up at the corporate cemetery? Or what about all those companies that didn't have visionary leaders but were successful?"

     "To understand what qualities cause success, we need to compare business successes with failures. We must include companies that started with the same quality but failed. We need to compare the proportion of supporting cases with not supporting cases. We need the whole sample — both the good and the bad."

SEEKER   "You mean some companies who lack visionary leaders are successful and some are not and the same is true with companies who have visionary leaders?"

LIBRARIAN "Yes, Just because a company lack a visionary leader doesn't give us any insights if it is important or not, unless we know that all or most successful companies have visionary leaders."

BUFFETT   "It is important to study failure as much as you study success."[1777]

LIBRARIAN "Same with the stock market or corporate acquisitions. You see the survivors, the winners; you don't see the losers because you don't look at the corporate cemetery."

MUNGER   "It is assumed by many business school graduates, and by almost all consultants, that a corporation can easily improve its outcome by purchasing unrelated or tenuously related businesses. Our experience, both actual and vicarious, makes us less optimistic about easy solutions through business acquisition. We think undue optimism arises because successful records draw too much attention. Many people then reason as I would if I forecasted good prospects in big-time tennis after observation limited to Ivan Lendl and Steffi Graf, or good prospects in the California lottery after limiting observations to winners."

     "The converse is also true, only more so. Far too little attention is given to the terrible effects on shareholders (or other owners) of the worst examples of corporate acquisitions."[1778]

SEEKER   "Once more, I learn how little I know. Next time someone tells me they have this miracle cure for whatever, I will not only look at the gold medalists but also the ones lying in the cemetery."

LIBRARIAN "Another use of the 'compared to what'-question is for example, when you try to find out why something bad happened."

SEEKER   "You mean another tool except for the Occam or fundamental cause one and the Einstein slash Munger 'counter-corollary' one when dealing with complexity and Lollapaloozas? I almost stumbled over the

218

words there...Please tell me...meanwhile I better take another scope of ice cream."

"Hmm—I see there is none left—so I help myself to one of your See's Candy instead."

LIBRARIAN "Try to find out what is different when things go wrong. What was different—the underlying conditions, some variable, the behavior—when you had the problem compared to what normally happens in similar situations. Or if a problem persist over time, what factor, etc. is consistently different when we have problems? Also, ask 'what normally causes this kind of problem?' It could of course also have been a pure random event."

SEEKER "Great, gives me something to think about the next time my home's electrical system malfunction."

LIBRARIAN "Let's tie three filters together—'opportunity cost', 'compared to what?' and 'and then what?'"

"Do you see what they have in common?"

SEEKER "No, so please tell me."

LIBRARIAN "As I said, the compared to what-question lies behind opportunity cost and to decide what is the best course of action you need to consider available opportunities or alternatives and circumstances considering 'And then what?' or other effects—their higher order effects and implications. And expect there is at least one unwanted consequence."

SEEKER "Some other advice you have?"

CHECKLISTS HELP—Assuming we are competent enough to pick the key factors and evaluate them

MUNGER "Checklist routines...prevent a lot of errors, and not just for pilots. You should not only possess wide-ranging elementary wisdom but also go through mental checklist routines in using it. There is no other procedure that will work as well."[1779]

"How can smart people so often be wrong? They don't do what I'm telling you to do: use a checklist to be sure you get all the main models and use them together in a multimodular way."[1780]

SEEKER "Can you give me a simple checklist for how to learn to be wise?"

MUNGER "I can never make it easy by saying, 'Here are three things.' You have to derive it yourself to ingrain it in your head for the rest of your life."[1781]

SEEKER "I assume you are an avid user of checklists?"

MUNGER "I'm a great believer in solving hard problems by the use of a checklist, because you get all the issues in front of you that way—and otherwise it's too easy to miss something important[1782]...Now if there are two or three items that are very important that aren't on your checklist—well, if you're an airplane pilot, you can crash."[1783]

LIBRARIAN "And don't make the checklist so long and complicated that you don't follow it. Make it as simple and concise as possible."

"But don't put all your trust in checklists which can cause a false sense of security and control just like wearing seat belt makes drivers feel more secure, making them drive faster or more recklessly."

BUFFETT "A checklist is no substitute for thinking."[1784]

SEEKER "I get it—every tool has its limitations."

BUFFETT "Occasionally...the unthinkable happens."[1785]

LIBRARIAN "Often trouble comes from the direction we least expect. As 'The One-Eyed Doe' in Aesop's fable experienced before she died—'Alas, ill-fated creature that I am! I was safe on the land side, whence I looked for danger, but my enemy came from the sea, to which I looked for protection.'"

SEEKER "You are protected in one direction while the real danger comes from another."

LIBRARIAN "Yes, and many times because you learned a little too precisely from your own or others' bad experiences—you prevent 'yesterday's' dangers when reality—conditions, objectives, and enemies—has changed. You prevent something from happening again—until something else happens."

"That is what France experienced when Germany attacked them by entering the thick Ardennes forest—something the French never anticipated since they considered it pretty much impenetrable. Their Maginot Lane made them feel secure but it was a false sense of security."

SEEKER "Now you lost me—again."

LIBRARIAN "The Maginot Line was a chain of defensive concrete fortifications France built along its eastern border between WW1 and 2 and named after the French Minister of defence who proposed the idea. Based on experiences from WW1 it was designed to prevent future invasions from German ground forces. Unfortunately, in WW2, German ground forces instead attacked France through the weakly hold Ardennes forest near Luxemburg and its Luftwaffe flew over the fortifications."

"It is often referred to as the danger of only relying of precise past experiences—preventing a disaster tomorrow with a strategy that worked in the past. The French prepared for a defensive war similar to WW1 and didn't consider that they may face new conditions—new technologies and tactics. WW 2 was a different kind of war. WW1 was more of a trench war while Germany brought more of a mechanized blitzkrieg—tanks, motorized infantry, and air support—to WW2."[1786]

MUNGER "Misanalysing a situation that is not representative of reality."[1787]

SEEKER "Let's see—they prepared themselves for old threats and strengthened past vulnerabilities. It reinforces what you said earlier about the need for learning the right lesson from the past and the importance of adapting to changing situations."

BUFFETT "It's not only generals that prefer to fight the last war. Most business and investment analysis also comes from the rear-view mirror... Future profitability of the industry will be determined by current competitive characteristics, not past ones. Many managers have been slow to recognize this."[1788]

LIBRARIAN "It comes natural to learn from past experiences and especially bad ones and then try to prevent the same from happening again. Just like people assume some past disaster would never exceed its historical maximum and only protect for that."

"Both the French and the Germans learned the right lesson from WW1—that it was mostly a defensive war. But while the French adopted the lesson, the Germans adapted to it. And as any good military strategist know—when you want to surprise an enemy, go where they are not—hit hard where not expected. As Thomas J. 'Stonewall' Jackson said, 'Always mystify, mislead, and surprise the enemy.'"[1789]

SEEKER "Like the Dark Horse you mentioned earlier—where the real danger may come from new competitors that turn up from completely unexpected places."

LIBRARIAN "Or dismissed enemies. As Howard Bloom said, 'Like the Babylonians before them, the Persians were blind to the barbarians and expected trouble only from nations celebrated for military might. They forgot that the real danger often comes from a people everyone has totally dismissed.'"[1790]

"As Ike Skelton writes, 'History teaches that every war is unique. 'Lessons learned' typically focus on what worked—and what did not—in the last conflict. History is replete with examples of militaries staying with successful technology and doctrine from previous conflicts only to suffer disastrous results in the next.'"[1791]

SEEKER "Anything more I need to think about?"

MUNGER "Don't overlook the obvious by drowning in minutiae."[1792]

SEEKER "Anything else—honestly, I'm starting to get pretty full now. And I don't mean of ice cream or See's Candy. In fact, I better have another peanut brittle."

HAVE SOME AVOID-RULES

LIBRARIAN "To help you stay out of trouble have some avoid or what not to do-rules based on what doesn't work so you don't go there."

MUNGER   "When a guy is offering you free money, don't listen to the rest of the sentence. This is the Munger rule[1793]...If it promises high rates of return and has high commissions don't read it."[1794]

BUFFETT   "You need very few good ideas in your lifetime. You have to be willing to have the discipline to say, 'I'm not going to do something I don't understand.'"[1795]

"You have to come to your own conclusions, and you have to do it based on facts that are available. If you don't have enough facts to reach a conclusion, you forget it. You go on to the next one. You have to also have the willingness to walk away from things that other people think are very simple."[1796]

SEEKER   "Is this all now?"

LIBRARIAN "You can of course have some 'what-to-do-rules' like: 'Stay within my circle of competence, go where the competition is low, always have a margin of safety, work only with people I can trust, treat people according to the 'golden rule.'"

"Now it's time to end this session."

SEEKER   "I have really appreciated your time—and I love this simplicity and common sense ethos you have."

MUNGER   "Organized common (or uncommon) sense—very basic knowledge—is an enormously powerful tool."[1797]

LIBRARIAN "As Samuel Taylor Coleridge said, 'Common sense in an uncommon degree is what the world calls wisdom.' Unfortunately as Plutarch said, 'Common sense is very uncommon.'"

MUNGER   "What people mean when they say a man has common sense is uncommon sense...What they mean is a man that can operate over a pretty broad range of human territory without making any big boners. And that is a very important thing to be good at."[1798]

SEEKER   "I assume nothing comes easy."

LIBRARIAN "You're right—both simplicity and common sense is the result of careful preparation—knowing what works and not—and having a clear mind."

SEEKER   "But don't I need to specialize in something?"

MUNGER   "You can be quite competent in your specialized field and also have the common sense over a broad area if you work at it appropriately."

"Let's take the case of Newton. More than half of the powerful creative period in Newton's life was totally wasted on alchemy and theology and in the remaining half he managed to create quite a distinction in his chosen profession. He had power to burn."[1799]

SEEKER   "But I am for sure no Newton."

MUNGER "So, assume you're not Newton. You're just a good guy who is going to be a good mechanical engineer. Don't you think you can get a general competency just as you might be a good engineer and also play golf? There is plenty of time to do it without ruining your specialized competency. All you have to have is the will and the technique and every hour you're delaying doing it…you're just increasing the chances that you remain in the shallows."[1800]

SEEKER "You sure have a lot of new tricks I need to learn."

MUNGER "We don't have any new tricks. We just know the old tricks better."[1801]

"I would argue that what Berkshire has done has mostly been using trivial knowledge…if you absorb the important basic knowledge… and you absorb all the big basic points across a broad range of disciplines, one day you'll walk down the street and you'll find that you're one of the very most competent members of your generation, and that many people who were quicker mentally and worked harder are in your dust."[1802]

BUFFETT "What we do is simple, although it's not necessarily easy. The checklist going through our mind isn't very complicated. Knowing what you don't know is important. Sometimes that's not easy."[1803]

SEEKER "I thank you so very much for taking the time to wise me up. I will continue to learn and practice being wiser."

MUNGER "Berkshire loves education, and it loves people who like to learn."[1804]

LEARNING NEVER STOPS

LIBRARIAN "And learning never stops."

MUNGER "Without lifetime learning you…are not going to do very well. You are not going to get very far in life based on what you already know. You're going to advance in life by what you learn after you leave here."[1805]

SEEKER "Constant and never-ending improvement will be my mantra."

MUNGER "I think the one thing that we did that worked best of all…we were always dissatisfied with what we already knew — we wanted to know more. If Warren and I had stayed frozen in time, [Berkshire] would have been a terrible place. It's only that we kept learning that made it work… and I don't think that'll ever stop."[1806]

BUFFETT "There's so much to learn. Learning what works and what doesn't work, where value resides and where value doesn't reside."[1807]

MUNGER "Had he [Warren] not been learning all this time, our record would be a mere shadow of what it is. And he's actually improved since he passed the age at which most other people retire. Most people don't even try this — it takes practice."[1808]

"And I don't see how you can wise up all the time if you aren't working at it."[1809]

SEEKER   "Do you read every day?"

MUNGER   "Sure."[1810]

BUFFETT   "Actually, I probably spend five or six hours a day on reading. We have no meetings at Berkshire. We have a directors meeting once a year, after the shareholders meeting, at lunch. And at the end, I say 'I'll see you next year.' It's a very economical operation. We don't have a slide projector. We don't have a calculator. We do not have meetings on anything."[1811]

MUNGER   "You'd be amazed at how much Warren reads—and at how much I read."[1812]

"Nothing has served me better in my long life than continuous learning."[1813]

SEEKER   "I better get started."

MUNGER   "Even if you're very well trained and have some natural aptitude, you still need to keep learning."[1814]

SEEKER   "Now you're really making fun of me. Seriously, is there some book that contains some of your wisdom, I should read?"

MUNGER   "Peter Kaufman has tried to do that in a book...*Poor Charlie's Almanack*...that he stitched together out of my old speeches—plus a lot else...I think if you assimilate everything in that simple book, you'll know a lot more than about 95% of your compatriots. And it's not hard to do. So Peter Kaufman has made it easy for you."[1815]

BUFFETT   "It's a sensational book. Anybody that reads it is going to learn a lot about life."[1816]

LIBRARIAN   "Personally, I love the editor Peter Kaufman's summary of Mr. Munger's approach, 'Charlie generally focuses first on what to avoid— that is, on what NOT to do—before he considers the affirmative steps he will take in a given situation...Charlie gains enormous advantage by summarily eliminating the unpromising portions of 'the chess board,' freeing his time and attention for the more productive regions.'"

"'Charlie strives to reduce complex situations to their most basic, unemotional fundamentals. Yet, within this pursuit of rationality and simplicity, he is careful to avoid what he calls 'physics envy,' the common human craving to reduce enormously complex systems...to one-size-fits-all Newtonian formulas.'"[1817]

MUNGER   "If you find you don't like it, you can always give it to a more intelligent friend."[1818]

224

LIBRARIAN "And of course, when it comes to business, managing and investing, nothing beats reading *Warren Buffett's Letters to Berkshire Hathaway Shareholders.*"

SEEKER "But you honestly think that someone like me can wise up?"

MUNGER "I constantly see people rise in life who were not the smartest, sometimes not even the most diligent. But they are learning machines[1819]... They go to bed every night a little wiser than they were that morning. And boy, does that habit help, particularly when you have a long run ahead of you."[1820]

"It helps to have a generalized competency in dealing with words, and numbers and quantities, and concepts. Of course, it helps to practise with that competency. And if you then collect follies the way I do and stay away from the follies, when you're as old as I am, you'll be a rich old man."[1821]

SEEKER "Encouraging and remarkable."

MUNGER "There's nothing remarkable about it. I don't have any wonderful insights that other people don't have. Just slightly more consistently than others, I've avoided idiocy[1822]...All I'm trying to be is be non-idiotic. I find that that's all you have to do to get ahead in life is to be non-idiotic and live a long time."[1823]

BUFFETT "It really is simple — just avoid doing the dumb things. Avoiding the dumb things is the most important."[1824]

MUNGER "So if you just avoid idiocy, have a good character and do it every day — it's amazing how well it works."[1825]

SEEKER "I love this."

MUNGER "What works, what fails? Have that temperament."[1826]

SEEKER "Thanks."

MUNGER "There will be immense worldly rewards...in a more multidisciplinary approach to many problems, common or uncommon. And more fun as well as more accomplishment. The happier mental realm I recommend is one from which no one willingly returns. A return would be like cutting off one's hands."[1827]

LIBRARIAN "Few are willing to prepare and do the work that is needed to make better decisions. Therefore, if you prepare today what few else will do, 'tomorrow' you can accomplish what most others can't. Prepare — learn and understand what works and not — and you will know what to do."

"If you can learn some things to improve your life — why wouldn't you like to learn it?"

SEEKER "Thank you Mr. Buffett, Mr. Munger and Mrs. Librarian for this visit, I will...."

The man woke up from his dream. And the first thing he observed was a sign on his living room wall.

"Cherish some man of high character, and keep him ever before your eyes, living as if he were watching you, and ordering all your actions as if he beheld them."

- Seneca

And the man smiled to himself—and for the first time in many years he felt good about the future.

SOURCE NOTES

1   Meditations, Book IV, 38 (c.161-180 CE)
2   From Flywheel, Shyster & Flywheel, The Marx Brothers' Lost Radio Show
3   Warren Buffett meeting with University of Maryland MBA Students November 15, 2013, Notes by Professor David Kass, www.blogs.rhsmith.umd.edu/davidkass
4   Daily Journal Corporation annual meeting, 2013, Notes by Shane Parrish, Farnam Street
5   Bruce Upbin, Jay-Z, Buffett and Forbes on Success and Giving Back, Forbes, 23.9.2010, http://www.forbes.com/forbes/2010/1011/rich-list-10-omaha-warren-buffett-jay-z-steve-forbes-summit-interview.html
6   Berkshire Hathaway annual meeting, 1994, Notes by author
7   Gillian Zoe Segal, Getting There: A Book of Mentors, New York, Abrams Image, 2015, p.19.
8   Transcript of Warren Buffett's 'Ask Warren' appearance on CNBC's Squawk Box, March 1, 2010, buffettwatch.cnbc.com
9   Transcript from visit in India, NDTV Studios, April 2011, Notes by Shane Parrish, Farnam Street
10   Berkshire Hathaway, Press Conference May 6, 2007, Notes by The Motley Fool
11   "A Conversation With Charlie Munger", Charlie Munger Speaks to University of Michigan Students, September 14, 2010, http://www.law.umich.edu/newsandinfo/amicus/archive/sept2010/1.html and http://rossmedia.bus.umich.edu/rossmedia/Viewer/?peid=4d21 5177cbe44b1e8e94d0dd68f5058f
12   Berkshire Hathaway annual meeting, 1994, Notes by Philip Swigard
13   Daily Journal Corporation annual meeting, 2010, Notes by author
14   Wesco Financial annual meeting, 2008, Outstanding Investor Digest, August 31, 2008, p.43.
15   Berkshire Hathaway annual meeting, 2010, Notes by author
16   Transcript of Warren Buffett's 'Ask Warren' appearance on CNBC's Squawk Box, March 1, 2010, buffettwatch.cnbc.com
17   Dr. House from the episode The Mistake, Air date Nov. 29, 2005, Fox Network
18   Berkshire Hathaway annual meeting, 2003, Outstanding Investor Digest, Year End 2003 Edition, p.43.
19   Gillian Zoe Segal, Getting There: A Book of Mentors, New York, Abrams Image, 2015, p.19.
20   Transcript from visit in India, NDTV Studios, April 2011, Notes by Shane Parrish, Farnam Street
21   Warren Buffett meeting with students from Emory's Goizueta Business School and McCombs School of Business at UT Austin, February 15, 2008, www.undergroundvalue.blogspot.com
22   Peter D. Kaufman, Poor Charlie's Almanack: The Wit and Wisdom of Charles T. Munger, PCA Publication, L.L.C. 2005, 2006, 2008, p.263.
23   Wesco Financial annual meeting, 2002, Notes by author
24   Wesco Financial annual meeting, 2010, Notes by author
25   ABC's Nightline with Ted Koppel, Regarding Last Best Chance, May 18, 2005
26   Wesco Financial annual meeting, 2010, Outstanding Investor Digest, August 9, 2010, p.35.
27   Berkshire Hathaway, Press Conference, April 2001, Notes by The Motley Fool
28   Jean Starobinski, Montaigne in Motion, University of Chicago Press, 1985
29   Wesco Financial annual meeting, 2010, Outstanding Investor Digest, August 9, 2010, p.34.
30   Charles T. Munger, If Standard Oil Is Trying to Be Greedy, it's Doing a Poor Job of It, Los Angeles Times, October 1, 1978
31   Berkshire Hathaway Inc., 2005 Annual Report
32   "An Evening with Warren Buffett", Warren Buffett Q&A with the Oquirrh Club, October 2003, http://www.oquirrhinstitute.org/about-buffett-transcripts.html, seen at http://www.rbcpa.com/WEB_omaha1992.html
33   Wesco Financial annual meeting, 2007, Outstanding Investor Digest, February 29, 2008, pp.48-49.
34   Josh Funk, "Berkshire's No. 2 man helps from the background", Business Week, May 16, 2008

35   Notes from the Meeting Dr. George Athanassakos and Ivey MBA and HBA students had with Mr. Warren Buffett, Omaha February 27, 2015, The Ben Graham Center for Value Investing, Ivey Business School, Western University, www.bengrahaminvesting.ca These notes and others mentioned from this site in this book may in some cases not accurately reflect Mr. Buffett's direct quotes but may instead be paraphrases of Mr. Buffett's words.

36   Berkshire Hathaway annual meeting, 2004, Notes by Whitney Tilson, www.tilsonfunds.com

37   Lecture at the University of Florida School of Business, October 15, 1998, Martin Lee www.intelligentinvestorclub.com/downloads/warren-buffett-mba-talk-at-university-of-florida-transcripts

38   From the BBC sitcom Blackadder, episode Blackadder's Christmas Carol, 1988

39   Berkshire Hathaway Inc., 1990 Annual Report

40   Peter D. Kaufman, Poor Charlie's Almanack, p.134.

41   Berkshire Hathaway annual meeting, 1999, Outstanding Investor Digest, December 10, 1999, p.47.

42   Notes from the Meeting Dr. George Athanassakos and Ivey MBA and HBA students had with Mr. Warren Buffett, Omaha February 27, 2015, The Ben Graham Center for Value Investing

43   Warren Buffett responds to questions from Wharton Students, November 12, 2004, www.tilsonfunds.com

44   Steven Goldberg, "The World According to 'Poor Charlie'", Kiplinger.com, December 2005

45   Berkshire Hathaway Inc., 1982 Annual Report

46   Conversation with Charlie Munger, Pasadena Convention Center, July 1, 2011, Notes by Shane Parrish, Farnam Street

47   Wesco Financial annual meeting, 2007, Outstanding Investor Digest, February 29, 2008, p.49.

48   Ibid.

49   Notes from the Meeting Dr. George Athanassakos and Ivey MBA and HBA students had with Mr. Warren Buffett, Omaha February 27, 2015, The Ben Graham Center for Value Investing

50   Daily Journal Corporation annual meeting, 2015, Notes by Shane Parrish, Farnam Street

51   Berkshire Hathaway annual meeting, 2015, Notes by author

52   Berkshire Hathaway annual meeting, 2013, Notes by Peter Boodell, Boodell & Company Capital Management

53   Wesco Financial annual meeting, 2010, Notes by author

54   Berkshire Hathaway annual meeting, 1997, Outstanding Investor Digest, August 8, 1997, p.6.

55   Wesco Financial annual meeting, 2010, Notes by author

56   Berkshire Hathaway annual meeting, 2010, Notes by author

57   Wesco Financial annual meeting, 2010, Outstanding Investor Digest, August 9, 2010, p.25.

58   Berkshire Hathaway annual meeting, 1998, Notes by author

59   Peter D. Kaufman, Poor Charlie's Almanack, p.219.

60   Berkshire Hathaway annual meeting, 1999, Outstanding Investor Digest, December 10, 1999, p.49.

61   Scott Patterson, "In Year of Investing Dangerously, Buffett looked 'Into the Abyss'", The Wall Street Journal, December 14, 2009

62   Wesco Financial annual meeting, 2007, Outstanding Investor Digest, February 29, 2008, p.46.

63   1994 Lecture of The E. J. Faulkner Lecture Series, A Colloquium with University of Nebraska-Lincoln Students by Warren E. Buffett

64   Ragnar Frisch, Lecture to the memory of Alfred Nobel, June 17, 1970, www.nobelprize.org

65   Daily Journal Corporation annual meeting, 2015, Notes by Shane Parrish, Farnam Street

66   Berkshire Hathaway annual meeting, 2002, Notes by Selena Maranjian, The Motley Fool

67   Berkshire Hathaway annual meeting, 2007, Notes by Whitney Tilson, www.tilsonfunds.com

68   Warren Buffett on Adam Smith's Money Game, Transcript #105, Air Date: May 15, 1998

69   Charles Munger, speech at breakfast meeting of the Philanthropy Round Table, November 10, 2000

70   Investment Practices of Leading Charitable Foundations, Speech at Miramar Sheraton Hotel, Santa Monica, CA, on October 14, 1998 to a meeting of the Foundation Financial Officer Group'

71   The Psychology of Human Misjudgment, Peter D. Kaufman, Poor Charlie's Almanack, p.476.
72   Warren Buffett on Adam Smith's Money Game, Transcript #105, Air Date: May 15, 1998
73   Steven Goldberg, "The World According to 'Poor Charlie'", Kiplinger.com, December 2005
74   Berkshire Hathaway annual meeting, 2013, Notes by Peter Boodell, Boodell & Company Capital Management
75   Berkshire Hathaway, Press Conference, 2010, Notes by The Motley Fool
76   Wesco Financial Inc., 1989 Annual Report
77   Wesco Financial annual meeting, 2003, Outstanding Investor Digest, April 30, 2004, p.63.
78   Ibid.
79   The Need for More Multidisciplinary Skills from Professionals: Educational Implications, Fiftieth Reunion of Harvard Law School Class of 1948, April 24, 1998, Peter D. Kaufman, Poor Charlie's Almanack, p.304.
80   Wesco Financial annual meeting, 2003, Outstanding Investor Digest, April 30, 2004, p.63.
81   The Psychology of Human Misjudgment, Peter D. Kaufman, Poor Charlie's Almanack, p.443.
82   Charlie Munger at Harvard-Westlake School January 19, 2010, www.santangelsreview.com
83   The Psychology of Human Misjudgment, Peter D. Kaufman, Poor Charlie's Almanack, p.444.
84   Berkshire Hathaway Inc., 1985 Annual Report
85   Woody Allen, Without Feathers (Death—a play), Random House, 1975
86   Unofficial transcript of Warren Buffett, Charlie Munger and Bill Gates appearing live with Becky Quick on CNBC's "Squawk Box," Monday, May 5, 2014, buffettwatch.cnbc.com
87   Foreword to the authorized Chinese translation of Poor Charlie's Almanack: The Wit and Wisdom of Charles T. Munger, PCA Publication, L.L.C. 2010 by Peter D. Kaufman
88   The Psychology of Human Misjudgment, Peter D. Kaufman, Poor Charlie's Almanack, pp.444-445.
89   A Conversation with Charlie Munger at Caltech, DuBridge Distinguished Lecture, March 11, 2008, DVD
90   Ibid.
91   "Bad Judgments, Common Causes", Charles Munger speech at the California Institute of Technology, February 17, 1992
92   Berkshire Hathaway annual meeting, 2012, Notes by Peter Boodell, Boodell & Company Capital Management
93   From the Coca-Cola Company annual meeting, 2013, http://www.coca-colacompany.com/investors/annual-meeting-of-shareowners, http://mfile2.akamai.com/9538/wmv/estream.download.akamai.com/9538/cocacola/cocacola_160isl_2013_annual_meeting_of_shareowners.wvx?obj=20130424v1
94   Warren Buffett from a speech at the Emory Business School as reported in, "Track record is everything", Across the Board, October 1991, p.59.
95   Peter D. Kaufman, Poor Charlie's Almanack, p.137.
96   Berkshire Hathaway annual meeting, 2004, Outstanding Investor Digest, December 31, 2004, p.32.
97   Ibid.
98   Warren Buffett from a speech at the Emory Business School as reported in, "Track record is everything", Across the Board, October 1991, p.59.
99   USC Gould School of Law Commencement Address, May 13, 2007, Peter D. Kaufman, Poor Charlie's Almanack, p.429.
100   Practical Thought About Practical Thought? An Informal Talk, July 20, 1996, Peter D. Kaufman, Poor Charlie's Almanack, p.290.
101   USC Gould School of Law Commencement Address, May 13, 2007, Peter D. Kaufman, Poor Charlie's Almanack, p.429.
102   Lecture by Charles T. Munger to the students of Professor William Lazier at Stanford Law School, Outstanding Investor Digest, December 29, 1997, p.24.
103   Wesco Financial annual meeting, 2007, Outstanding Investor Digest, February 29, 2008, p.52.
104   Ibid.

105   Charlie Munger at Harvard-Westlake School January 19, 2010, www.santangelsreview.com
106   Ibid.
107   Berkshire Hathaway annual meeting, 1996, Notes by author
108   Berkshire Hathaway annual meeting, 2005, Outstanding Investor Digest, March 9, 2006, p.62.
109   Berkshire Hathaway annual meeting, 1997, Outstanding Investor Digest, August 8, 1997, p.16.
110   1994 Lecture of The E. J. Faulkner Lecture Series, A Colloquium with University of Nebraska-Lincoln Students by Warren E. Buffett
111   François de La Rochefoucauld, Maxim 199. Reflections; or Sentences and Moral Maxims
112   Berkshire Hathaway annual meeting, 1991, Outstanding Investor Digest, May 24, 1991, p.31.
113   Daily Journal Corporation annual meeting, 2014, Notes by Shane Parrish, Farnam Street
114   Said by Charles T. Munger but source unknown
115   Berkshire Hathaway Inc., 1989 Annual Report
116   Wesco Financial annual meeting, 2008, Notes by author
117   Wesco Financial annual meeting, 2006, Notes by author
118   Berkshire Hathaway annual meeting, 1994, Outstanding Investor Digest, June 23, 1994, p.23.
119   Ibid.
120   Berkshire Hathaway annual meeting, 2000, Outstanding Investor Digest, Year End 2000 Edition, p.63.
121   Ibid.
122   Arthur Schopenhauer, The essays of Arthur Schopenhauer, http://www.gutenberg.org/files/10741/10741-8.txt
123   Berkshire Hathaway annual meeting, 2014, Notes by author
124   Quoted by Diogenes Laertius, iv. 49.
125   Michel de Montaigne, The Complete Essays; translated by M.A. Screech, Penguin Books, Ltd, London, 1987, 1991, 2003
126   Ethan Baron, "Warren Buffett's Unconventional Advice to MBAs", November 27, 2014, reported by The Chinese University of Hong Kong Business School student Sharad Golchha, www.poetsandquants.com/2014/11/27/warren-buffetts-unconventional-advice-to-mbas/
127   Office Hours with Warren Buffett, May 7, 2013, interview with Caroline Ghosn, Levo League, www.levo.com
128   Bianca Mulaney, "Meeting Warren Buffett", Smart Woman Securities meeting in Omaha, harvardindependent.com, April 12, 2014
129   "An Evening with Warren Buffett", Warren Buffett Q&A with the Oquirrh Club, October 2003
130   Warren Buffett speech to University of Georgia students, Terry College of Business, 2001, GuruFocus, http://www.nasdaq.com/article/warren-buffett-speech-to-university-of-georgia-students-part-1-cm238914
131   Warren Buffett meeting with University of Maryland MBA Students November 15, 2013, Notes by Professor David Kass
132   Notes from Buffett meeting with students from Emory and 5 other business schools, February 6, 2009, www.undergroundvalue.blogspot.com
133   Peter D. Kaufman, Poor Charlie's Almanack, p.136.
134   Meeting with Warren Buffett May 23, 2005 — University of Maryland Student Trek to Omaha, Notes by Shai Dardashti
135   Warren Buffett meeting with University of Maryland MBA Students November 15, 2013, Notes by Professor David Kass
136   USC Gould School of Law Commencement Address, May 13, 2007, Peter D. Kaufman, Poor Charlie's Almanack, p.439.
137   "When I Buy a Company, I'm a Journalist", taped interview with Arizona State University Professor Jeff Cunningham, creator and host of Iconic Voices, Walter Cronkite School of Journalism, March 5, 2015, http://iconicvoices.jmc.asu.edu/warren-buffett-on-journalism-to-jpmorgan/
138   Said by Warren E. Buffett but source unknown

139   The Psychology of Human Misjudgment, Talk at the Cambridge Center for Behavioral Studies, April 24, 1995.
140   Liz Claman interviews Warren Buffett, Charlie Munger and Bill Gates, May 5, 2014, Foxbusiness.com
141   Notes from the Meeting Dr. George Athanassakos and Ivey MBA and HBA students had with Mr. Warren Buffett, Omaha January 31, 2014, The Ben Graham Center for Value Investing
142   Berkshire Hathaway annual meeting, 2002, Notes by Selena Maranjian, The Motley Fool
143   Ibid.
144   Charles T. Munger Harvard School Commencement Speech June 13, 1986
145   Ibid.
146   Wesco Financial annual meeting, 2007, Outstanding Investor Digest, February 29, 2008, p.44.
147   Berkshire Hathaway Inc., 1985 Annual Report
148   Peter D. Kaufman, Poor Charlie's Almanack, p.76.
149   Berkshire Hathaway annual meeting, 2012, Notes by Peter Boodell, Boodell & Company Capital Management
150   Berkshire Hathaway annual meeting, 2010, Notes by author
151   Charles T. Munger Harvard School Commencement Speech June 13, 1986
152   Ibid.
153   Berkshire Hathaway annual meeting, 1995, Outstanding Investor Digest, August 10, 1995, p.21.
154   R.W. Hamming, Methods of Mathematics Applied to Calculus, Probability, and Statistics, Prentice Hall, 1985
155   Berkshire Hathaway annual meeting, 2008, Notes by author
156   Wesco Financial annual meeting, 2008, Outstanding Investor Digest, August 31, 2008, p.48.
157   Warren Buffett's Video Tour of Berkshire Hathaway Headquarters, December 1, 2007, CNBC.com
158   Thucydides, History of the Peloponnesian War 1.22 (transl. Rex Warner), Penguin Books
159   A Conversation with Charlie Munger at Caltech, DuBridge Distinguished Lecture, March 11, 2008, DVD
160   Berkshire Hathaway annual meeting, 2004, Notes by Whitney Tilson, www.tilsonfunds.com
161   Speech in House of Commons, May 2, 1935), seen in Robert Rhodes James, ed., Winston S. Churchill: His Complete Speeches, 1897–1963 (1974)
162   Henry A. Kissinger, White House Years, Little, Brown and Company, 1979
163   Peter D. Kaufman, Poor Charlie's Almanack, p.134.
164   Wesco Financial Inc., 1990 Annual Report
165   Wesco Financial annual meeting, 2000, Outstanding Investor Digest, December 18, 2000, p.52.
166   Wesco Financial Inc., 1990 Annual Report
167   The Need for More Multidisciplinary Skills from Professionals: Educational Implications, Fiftieth Reunion of Harvard Law School Class of 1948, April 24, 1998, Peter D. Kaufman, Poor Charlie's Almanack, pp.304-305
168   Academic Economics: Strengths and Faults After Considering Interdisciplinary Needs, Herb Key Undergraduate Lecture, University of California, Santa Barbara, Economics Department, October 3, 2003, Peter D. Kaufman, Poor Charlie's Almanack, pp.382-283.
169   Peter D. Kaufman, Poor Charlie's Almanack, p.134.
170   Wesco Financial annual meeting, 2007, Notes by author
171   Steven Goldberg, "The World According to 'Poor Charlie'", Kiplinger.com, December 2005
172   USC Gould School of Law Commencement Address, May 13, 2007, Peter D. Kaufman, Poor Charlie's Almanack, pp.425-426.
173   Lecture by Charles T. Munger to the students of Professor William Lazier at Stanford Law School, Outstanding Investor Digest, December 29, 1997, p.24.
174   Berkshire Hathaway annual meeting, 1996, Outstanding Investor Digest, August 8, 1996, p.39.
175   Conversations from the Warren Buffett Symposium, Cardozo Law Review (1997), vol. 19. Edited by Lawrence A Cunningham and reissued by Cunningham in 2016.

176   The Need for More Multidisciplinary Skills from Professionals: Educational Implications, Fiftieth Reunion of Harvard Law School Class of 1948, April 24, 1998, Peter D. Kaufman, Poor Charlie's Almanack, p.305

177   A Conversation with Charlie Munger at Caltech, DuBridge Distinguished Lecture, March 11, 2008, DVD

178   Practical Thought About Practical Thought? An Informal Talk, July 20, 1996, Peter D. Kaufman, Poor Charlie's Almanack, p.293.

179   Wesco Financial annual meeting, 2007, Notes by author

180   Practical Thought About Practical Thought? An Informal Talk, July 20, 1996, Peter D. Kaufman, Poor Charlie's Almanack: p.293.

181   Academic Economics: Strengths and Faults After Considering Interdisciplinary Needs, Herb Key Undergraduate Lecture, University of California, Santa Barbara, Economics Department, October 3, 2003, Peter D. Kaufman, Poor Charlie's Almanack, p.382.

182   Practical Thought About Practical Thought? An Informal Talk, July 20, 1996, Peter D. Kaufman, Poor Charlie's Almanack, p.293.

183   "Bad Judgments, Common Causes", Charles Munger speech at the California Institute of Technology, February 17, 1992

184   Peter D. Kaufman, Poor Charlie's Almanack, p.74.

185   A Conversation with Charlie Munger at Caltech, DuBridge Distinguished Lecture, March 11, 2008, DVD

186   Academic Economics: Strengths and Faults After Considering Interdisciplinary Needs, Herb Key Undergraduate Lecture, University of California, Santa Barbara, Economics Department, October 3, 2003, Peter D. Kaufman, Poor Charlie's Almanack, pp.378-379.

187   Dr. House from the episode Occam's Razor, Air date Nov. 30, 2004, Fox Network

188   Wesco Financial annual meeting, 1998, Notes by author

189   Academic Economics: Strengths and Faults After Considering Interdisciplinary Needs, Herb Key Undergraduate Lecture, University of California, Santa Barbara, Economics Department, October 3, 2003, Peter D. Kaufman, Poor Charlie's Almanack, p.379.

190   Wesco Financial annual meeting, 1998, Notes by author

191   A Conversation with Charlie Munger at Caltech, DuBridge Distinguished Lecture, March 11, 2008, DVD

192   Ibid.

193   Ibid.

194   Jim Rasmussen, "Buffett Partner's Impact 'Huge'", Sunday Omaha World-Herald, May 2, 1999

195   Transcript of Warren Buffett's 'Ask Warren' appearance on CNBC's Squawk Box, March 1, 2010, buffettwatch.cnbc.com

196   Said by Warren E. Buffett but source unknown and may not be original with him

197   Berkshire Hathaway annual meeting, 2011, Notes by author

198   Tommy Armour, How to Play Your Best Golf All the Time, Touchstone, 1995

199   Lecture by Charles T. Munger to the students of Professor Guilford Babcock at the University of Southern California School of Business on April 14, 1994, Outstanding Investor Digest, May 5, 1995, p.51.

200   Said by Warren E. Buffett but source unknown and may not be original with him

201   Analects, XV.24

202   Berkshire Hathaway annual meeting, 1994, Outstanding Investor Digest, June 23, 1994, p.24.

203   Berkshire Hathaway Inc., 2011 Annual Report

204   Warren Buffett meeting with students from Emory's Goizueta Business School and McCombs School of Business at UT Austin, February 15, 2008, www.undergroundvalue.blogspot.com

205   Dr. House from the episode TB or Not TB, Air date Nov. 1, 2005, Fox Network

206   Dorothy Sayers, Have his Carcase, 1932

207   The Psychology of Human Misjudgment, Peter D. Kaufman, Poor Charlie's Almanack, p.466.

208   Ibid, p.467.

209   Buffett Partnership Letter, January 18, 1963

210   Buffett Partnership Letter, January 18, 1965

211   Buffett Partnership Letter, January 18, 1963

212   Buffett Partnership Letter, January 18, 1964

213   1994 Lecture of The E. J. Faulkner Lecture Series, A Colloquium with University of Nebraska-Lincoln Students by Warren E. Buffett

214   Warren Buffett speech at Caltech, October 21, 1997, Transcript by Richard Rockwood

215   Berkshire Hathaway annual meeting, 2008, Notes by Peter Boodell, Boodell & Company Capital Management

216   Academic Economics: Strengths and Faults After Considering Interdisciplinary Needs, Herb Key Undergraduate Lecture, University of California, Santa Barbara, Economics Department, October 3, 2003, Peter D. Kaufman, Poor Charlie's Almanack, p.383.

217   Berkshire Hathaway annual meeting, 2015, Notes by author

218   A Conversation with Charlie Munger at Caltech, DuBridge Distinguished Lecture, March 11, 2008, DVD

219   Sententiae, III, De Prudentia: Sententiae monostichae

220   George Santayana, The Life of Reason: The Phases of Human Progress, http://www. gutenberg.org/files/15000/15000-h/15000-h.htm

221   C.H. Spurgeon, The Fourfold Treasure, No. 991, A sermon delivered April 27th, 1871

222   Lecture by Charles T. Munger to the students of Professor William Lazier at Stanford Law School, Outstanding Investor Digest, March 13, 1998, p.50.

223   Practical Thought About Practical Thought? An Informal Talk, July 20, 1996, Peter D. Kaufman, Poor Charlie's Almanack, p.281.

224   Lecture by Charles T. Munger to the students of Professor William Lazier at Stanford Law School, Outstanding Investor Digest, December 29, 1997, p.28.

225   Academic Economics: Strengths and Faults After Considering Interdisciplinary Needs, Herb Key Undergraduate Lecture, University of California, Santa Barbara, Economics Department, October 3, 2003, Peter D. Kaufman, Poor Charlie's Almanack, pp.390-391.

226   Lecture by Charles T. Munger to the students of Professor Guilford Babcock at the University of Southern California School of Business on April 14, 1994, Outstanding Investor Digest, May 5, 1995, p.56.

227   Academic Economics: Strengths and Faults After Considering Interdisciplinary Needs, Herb Key Undergraduate Lecture, University of California, Santa Barbara, Economics Department, October 3, 2003, Peter D. Kaufman, Poor Charlie's Almanack, p.391.

228   The Psychology of Human Misjudgment, Peter D. Kaufman, Poor Charlie's Almanack, p.481.

229   Ibid, p.458.

230   Daily Journal Corporation annual meeting, 2014, Notes by Shane Parrish, Farnam Street

231   Notes from the Meeting Dr. George Athanassakos and Ivey MBA and HBA students had with Mr. Warren Buffett, Omaha March 31, 2008, The Ben Graham Center for Value Investing

232   The Psychology of Human Misjudgment, Peter D. Kaufman, Poor Charlie's Almanack, p.457.

233   www.marykay.com

234   "An Evening with Warren Buffett", Warren Buffett Q&A with the Oquirrh Club, October 2003

235   Wesco Financial annual meeting, 2005, Notes by Whitney Tilson, www.tilsonfunds.com

236   Office Hours with Warren Buffett, May 7, 2013, interview with Caroline Ghosn, Levo League, www.levo.com

237   Wesco Financial annual meeting, 2007, Outstanding Investor Digest, February 29, 2008, pp.45-46.

238   Lecture by Charles T. Munger to the students of Professor William Lazier at Stanford Law School, Outstanding Investor Digest, March 13, 1998, p.50.

239   Lecture by Charles T. Munger to the students of Professor Guilford Babcock at the University of Southern California School of Business on April 14, 1994, Outstanding Investor Digest, May 5, 1995, p.51.

240   Said by Charles T. Munger but source unknown

241   The Psychology of Human Misjudgment, Talk at the Cambridge Center for Behavioral Studies, April 24, 1995

242   "Bad Judgments, Common Causes", Charlie Munger speech at the California Institute of Technology, February 17, 1992

243   The Psychology of Human Misjudgment, Talk at the Cambridge Center for Behavioral Studies, April 24, 1995

244   "Bad Judgments, Common Causes", Charles Munger speech at the California Institute of Technology, February 17, 1992

245   The Psychology of Human Misjudgment, Peter D. Kaufman, Poor Charlie's Almanack, p.482.

246   USC Gould School of Law Commencement Address, May 13, 2007, Peter D. Kaufman, Poor Charlie's Almanack, p.433.

247   Wesco Financial annual meeting, 2004, Notes by Whitney Tilson, www.tilsonfunds.com

248   The Psychology of Human Misjudgment, Talk at the Cambridge Center for Behavioral Studies, April 24, 1995.

249   Berkshire Hathaway annual meeting, 2014, Notes by George Traganidis, www.thepracticalway.com

250   Berkshire Hathaway Inc., 2002 Annual Report

251   Berkshire Hathaway annual meeting, 2005, Notes by Whitney Tilson, www.tilsonfunds.com

252   Unofficial transcript of Warren Buffett, Charlie Munger and Bill Gates appearing live with Becky Quick on CNBC's "Squawk Box," Monday, May 5, 2014, buffettwatch.cnbc.com

253   Ibid.

254   Keynote Breakfast Speech by Charles Munger at Stanford University's Director's College, June 26, 2006, Stanford Law School, Transcript, www.rockcenter.law.stanford.edu

255   "Q&A: Legal Matters with Charles T. Munger", Stanford Lawyer, Spring 2009, Video, http://stanfordlawyer.law.stanford.edu/2009/11/qa-with-charles-t-munger/

256   Wesco Financial annual meeting, 2005, Notes by Whitney Tilson, www.tilsonfunds.com

257   Berkshire Hathaway annual meeting, 2005, Notes by Whitney Tilson, www.tilsonfunds.com

258   Berkshire Hathaway Inc., 2003 Annual Report

259   Wesco Financial annual meeting, 2004, Notes by Whitney Tilson, www.tilsonfunds.com

260   Berkshire Hathaway Inc., An Owner's Manual

261   Berkshire Hathaway Inc., 2003 Annual Report

262   Daily Journal Corporation annual meeting, 2014, Notes by Shane Parrish, Farnam Street

263   Berkshire Hathaway annual meeting, 2009, Outstanding Investor Digest, OID.COM Feature, p.19.

264   Berkshire Hathaway annual meeting, 2005, Outstanding Investor Digest, March 9, 2006, p.56.

265   Berkshire Hathaway Inc., 2003 Annual Report

266   "An Evening with Warren Buffett", Warren Buffett Q&A with the Oquirrh Club, October 2003

267   Berkshire Hathaway Inc., 2014 Annual Report

268   Berkshire Hathaway Inc., 2002 Annual Report

269   Berkshire Hathaway annual meeting, 2005, Notes by Whitney Tilson, www.tilsonfunds.com

270   Berkshire Hathaway Inc., 2002 Annual Report

271   Ibid.

272   Unofficial transcript of Warren Buffett, Charlie Munger and Bill Gates appearing live with Becky Quick on CNBC's "Squawk Box," Monday, May 5, 2014, buffettwatch.cnbc.com

273   Berkshire Hathaway annual meeting, 2005, Outstanding Investor Digest, March 9, 2006, p.55.

274   Unofficial transcript of Warren Buffett, Charlie Munger and Bill Gates appearing live with Becky Quick on CNBC's "Squawk Box," Monday, May 5, 2014, buffettwatch.cnbc.com

275   Berkshire Hathaway Inc., 1988 Annual Report

276   Conversations from the Warren Buffett Symposium, Cardozo Law Review (1997), vol. 19. Edited by Lawrence A. Cunningham and reissued by Cunningham in 2016.

277   Berkshire Hathaway annual meeting, 2005, Notes by Whitney Tilson, www.tilsonfunds.com

278   "An Evening with Warren Buffett", Warren Buffett Q&A with the Oquirrh Club, October 2003

279   The Psychology of Human Misjudgment, Peter D. Kaufman, Poor Charlie's Almanack, p.489.

280   Alice Schroeder, The Snowball: Warren Buffett and the Business of Life, Bloomsbury Publishing, London, 2008, p.671. Also by Bantam Books, a division of Penguin Random House LLC.

281   Wesco Financial annual meeting, 2002, Outstanding Investor Digest, December 31, 2002, p.25.

282   Berkshire Hathaway annual meeting, 2012, Notes by author

283   Unofficial transcript of Warren Buffett, Charlie Munger and Bill Gates appearing live with Becky Quick on CNBC's "Squawk Box," Monday, May 5, 2014, buffettwatch.cnbc.com

284   Wesco Financial annual meeting, 2004, Notes by author

285   The Psychology of Human Misjudgment, Peter D. Kaufman, Poor Charlie's Almanack, p.482.

286   Berkshire Hathaway annual meeting, 2009, Outstanding Investor Digest, OID.COM Feature, p.12.

287   Berkshire Hathaway annual meeting, 2001, Outstanding Investor Digest, Year End 2001 Edition, p.24.

288   Practical Thought About Practical Thought? An Informal Talk, July 20, 1996, Peter D. Kaufman, Poor Charlie's Almanack, p.308.

289   Conversations from the Warren Buffett Symposium, Cardozo Law Review (1997), vol. 19. Edited by Lawrence A. Cunningham and reissued by Cunningham in 2016.

290   Peter D. Kaufman, Poor Charlie's Almanack, p.135.

291   Wesco Financial annual meeting, 1997, Outstanding Investor Digest, August 8, 1997, p.61.

292   Berkshire Hathaway annual meeting, 1997, Notes by author

293   Berkshire Hathaway annual meeting, 2015, Notes by author

294   Academic Economics: Strengths and Faults After Considering Interdisciplinary Needs, Herb Key Undergraduate Lecture, University of California, Santa Barbara, Economics Department, October 3, 2003, Peter D. Kaufman, Poor Charlie's Almanack, p.378.

295   Charles Munger remarks before the UC Santa Barbara Foundation Board of Trustees, Coastlines Online Winter 2015

296   USC Gould School of Law Commencement Address, May 13, 2007, Peter D. Kaufman, Poor Charlie's Almanack, p.426.

297   The Psychology of Human Misjudgment, Peter D. Kaufman, Poor Charlie's Almanack, p.487.

298   Peter D. Kaufman, Poor Charlie's Almanack, p.74.

299   Berkshire Hathaway Inc., 1983 Annual Report

300   Berkshire Hathaway annual meeting, 1995, Notes by author

301   Ibid.

302   A Conversation with Charlie Munger at Caltech, DuBridge Distinguished Lecture, March 11, 2008, DVD

303   Daily Journal Corporation annual meeting, 2014, Notes by Shane Parrish, Farnam Street

304   Berkshire Hathaway annual meeting, 2005, Notes by Whitney Tilson, www.tilsonfunds.com

305   Ibid.

306   Berkshire Hathaway, Press Conference, April 2001, Notes by The Motley Fool

307   USC Gould School of Law Commencement Address, May 13, 2007, Peter D. Kaufman, Poor Charlie's Almanack, p.431.

308   Wesco Financial annual meeting, 2007, Notes by Whitney Tilson, www.tilsonfunds.com

309   USC Gould School of Law Commencement Address, May 13, 2007, Peter D. Kaufman, Poor Charlie's Almanack, p.431.

310   Ibid., p.432.

311   Zig Ziglar, Secrets of Closing the Sale, 1984

312   USC Gould School of Law Commencement Address, May 13, 2007, Peter D. Kaufman, Poor Charlie's Almanack, p.432.

313   Wesco Financial annual meeting, 1988, Outstanding Investor Digest, April 30, 1988, p.21.

314   Daily Journal Corporation annual meeting, 2015, Notes by Shane Parrish, Farnam Street

315   Ibid.

316   The Psychology of Human Misjudgment, Peter D. Kaufman, Poor Charlie's Almanack, p.452.

317   Berkshire Hathaway annual meeting, 1995, Outstanding Investor Digest, August 10, 1995, p. 14.

318   Berkshire Hathaway Inc., 1987 Annual Report

319   Berkshire Hathaway Inc., 1983 Annual Report

320   Lecture at the University of Florida School of Business, October 15, 1998, Martin Lee

321   Warren Buffett's 'Ask Warren' appearance on CNBC's Squawk Box, March 2, 2015, cnbc.com

322   From the movie Monkey Business (1931)

323   Berkshire Hathaway Inc., 2006 Annual Report

324   Berkshire Hathaway Inc., 1983 Annual Report

325   Berkshire Hathaway Inc., 2008 Annual Report
326   Warren Buffett on Adam Smith's Money Game, Transcript #105, Air Date: May 15, 1998
327   Rudyard Kipling, The Gods of the Copybook Headings, 1919, www.kiplingsociety.co.uk/poems_copybook.htm
328   Berkshire Hathaway Inc., 2014 Annual Report
329   Berkshire Hathaway Inc., 2013 Annual Report
330   Wesco Financial annual meeting, 2003, Notes by Whitney Tilson, www.tilsonfunds.com
331   USC Gould School of Law Commencement Address, May 13, 2007, Peter D. Kaufman, Poor Charlie's Almanack, p.432.
332   Berkshire Hathaway Inc., 2009 Annual Report
333   Daniel S. Greenberg, "Don't ask the barber whether you need a haircut", Saturday Review Associates, November 25, 1972
334   The Psychology of Human Misjudgment, Peter D. Kaufman, Poor Charlie's Almanack, p.452.
335   John Train, The Midas Touch, Harper & Row, New York, 1987, p.83.
336   Wesco Financial annual meeting, 2006, Notes by Whitney Tilson, www.tilsonfunds.com
337   Charlie Munger at Harvard-Westlake School January 19, 2010, www.santangelsreview.com
338   Daily Journal Corporation annual meeting, 2014, Notes by Shane Parrish, Farnam Street
339   Berkshire Hathaway annual meeting, 2002, Notes by Whitney Tilson, www.tilsonfunds.com
340   Thomas Fuller, Worthies of England, 1662, http://thames.me.uk/s00690.htm
341   L.J. Davis, "Buffett Takes Stock," The New York Times Magazine, April 1, 1990, p.64.
342   Wesco Financial annual meeting, 2008, Outstanding Investor Digest, August 31, 2008, p.35.
343   U.S. News & World Report, June 20, 1994
344   Berkshire Hathaway Inc., 1984 Annual Report
345   Wesco Financial annual meeting, 2008, Outstanding Investor Digest, August 31, 2008, p.35.
346   Transcript from visit in India, NDTV Studios, April 2011, Notes by Shane Parrish, Farnam Street
347   Agatha Christie, The Lost Mine from Poirot's Early Cases, HarperCollins, 2010
348   Financial Crisis Inquiry Commission Staff Audiotape of Interview with Warren Buffett, May 26, 2010, p.5. www.santangelsreview.com
349   Charlie Rose interview: "I haven't seen as much economic fear in my adult lifetime", October 1, 2008, buffettwatch.com
350   Berkshire Hathaway Inc., 2011 Annual Report
351   Warren Buffett speaking to students from the Kansas University School of Business, May 6, 2005, Notes by Mark Hirschey, The Motley Fool, July 13, 2005
352   Berkshire Hathaway Inc., 2000 Annual Report
353   Financial Crisis Inquiry Commission Staff Audiotape of Interview with Warren Buffett, May 26, 2010, p.3. www.santangelsreview.com
354   Wesco Financial Inc., 1990 Annual Report
355   Blue Chip Stamps, 1982 Annual Report
356   Wesco Financial Inc., 1990 Annual Report
357   Charles Munger interview by CNBC, May 4, 2012, cnbc.com
358   Wesco Financial annual meeting, 1999, Notes by author
359   Berkshire Hathaway annual meeting, 1997, Outstanding Investor Digest, August 8, 1997, p.22.
360   Berkshire Hathaway, Press Conference, May 2006, Notes by The Motley Fool
361   Financial Crisis Inquiry Commission Staff Audiotape of Interview with Warren Buffett, May 26, 2010, p.5. www.santangelsreview.com
362   Ibid., pp.4-5.
363   Ibid., p.5.
364   Berkshire Hathaway Inc., 2010 Annual Report
365   Berkshire Hathaway Inc., 2011 Annual Report
366   "Pretty Good for Government Work", New York Times Op-Ed, November 16, 2010
367   Financial Crisis Inquiry Commission Staff Audiotape of Interview with Warren Buffett, May 26, 2010, p.5. www.santangelsreview.com
368   Berkshire Hathaway Inc., 2008 Annual Report
369   Warren Buffett speaking to students from the Kansas University School of Business, May 6, 2005, Notes by Mark Hirschey, The Motley Fool, July 13, 2005

370   Berkshire Hathaway Inc., 1988 Annual Report
371   "What should the federal government do to avoid a recession?", Hearing before the Joint Economic Committee, Congress of the United States, One Hundred Tenth Congress, second session, January 16, 2008, Volume 4, p. 44.
372   Berkshire Hathaway annual meeting, 2005, Notes by Whitney Tilson, www.tilsonfunds.com
373   Three Lectures by Warren Buffett to Notre Dame Faculty, MBA students and Undergraduate students, Spring 1991, Lightly edited by Whitney Tilson. www.tilsonfunds.com/BuffettNotreDame/pdf
374   Wesco Financial annual meeting, 2008, Outstanding Investor Digest, August 31, 2008, p.34.
375   Wesco Financial annual meeting, 2010, Outstanding Investor Digest, August 9, 2010, p.19.
376   Berkshire Hathaway Inc., 1989 Annual Report
377   Drennan RE, The Algonquin Wits, 1968
378   Charlie Munger at Harvard-Westlake School January 19, 2010, www.santangelsreview.com
379   Berkshire Hathaway Inc., 2005 Annual Report
380   Wesco Financial Inc., 1990 Annual Report
381   Wesco Financial annual meeting, 2010, Outstanding Investor Digest, August 9, 2010, p.25.
382   Wesco Financial annual meeting, 1992, Outstanding Investor Digest, June 22, 1992, p.8.
383   Berkshire Hathaway Inc., 1990 Annual Report
384   Warren Buffett from a speech at the Emory Business School as reported in, "Track record is everything", Across the Board, October 1991, pp.59-60.
385   Berkshire Hathaway Inc., 1989 Annual Report
386   Ibid.
387   Berkshire Hathaway Inc., 1989 Annual Report
388   Berkshire Hathaway Inc., 2012 Annual Report
389   Warren Buffett memo to Berkshire Hathaway Managers, September 27, 2006
390   Warren Buffett memo to Berkshire Hathaway Managers, December 19, 2014
391   Berkshire Hathaway annual meeting, 2009, Notes by author
392   Wesco Financial annual meeting, 2010, Notes by author
393   Wesco Financial annual meeting, 2008, Outstanding Investor Digest, August 31, 2008, p.38.
394   Berkshire Hathaway Inc., 1977 Annual Report
395   Berkshire Hathaway Inc., 1971 Annual Report
396   Charlie Munger at Harvard-Westlake School January 19, 2010, www.santangelsreview.com
397   Berkshire Hathaway annual meeting, 2000, Outstanding Investor Digest, OID.Com, continued from December 18, 2000 & Year End 2000 Editions
398   Wesco Financial annual meeting 2010, Notes by author
399   Daily Journal Corporation annual meeting, 2014, Notes by Shane Parrish, Farnam Street
400   Three Lectures by Warren Buffett to Notre Dame Faculty, MBA students and Undergraduate students, Spring 1991, Lightly edited by Whitney Tilson
401   Berkshire Hathaway annual meeting, 2009, Outstanding Investor Digest, OID.COM Feature, p.26.
402   Notes from the Meeting Dr. George Athanassakos and Ivey MBA and HBA students had with Mr. Warren Buffett, Omaha February 27, 2015, The Ben Graham Center for Value Investing
403   Wesco Financial annual meeting, 2003, Notes by Whitney Tilson, www.tilsonfunds.com
404   Buffett Partnership Letter, January 18, 1965
405   Michael D. Eisner with Aaron Cohen, Working Together: Why Great Partnerships Succeed, New York, Harper Collins Publishers, 2010, p.39.
406   Buffett Partnership Letter, January 24, 1962
407   Ibid.
408   Michel de Montaigne, The Complete Essays; translated by M.A. Screech, Penguin Books, Ltd, London, 1987, 1991, 2003
409   Variant of Josh Billings saying, "It is better not to know so much, than to know so many things that ain't so", http://quoteinvestigator.com/2015/05/30/better-know/#more-11302
410   Berkshire Hathaway annual meeting, 2005, Notes by Whitney Tilson, www.tilsonfunds.com
411   Berkshire Hathaway annual meeting, 1999, Notes by author
412   Gertrude Stein, Reflection on the Atomic Bomb, 1946, [first published in Yale Poetry Review], December 1947
413   Alice Schroeder, The Snowball: Warren Buffett and the Business of Life, Bloomsbury Publishing, London, 2008, p.33. Also by Bantam Books, a division of Penguin Random House LLC.

414   Ibid.

415   Notes from the Meeting Dr. George Athanassakos and Ivey MBA and HBA students had with Mr. Warren Buffett, Omaha February 27, 2015, The Ben Graham Center for Value Investing

416   Nicolas Chamfort: Reflections on Life, Love & Society, Short Books, 2003

417   Janet Lowe, Damn Right: Behind the Scenes with Berkshire Hathaway Billionaire Charlie Munger, John Wiley & Sons, New York, 2000, p.iii.

418   Agatha Christie, After The Funeral, from wikiquote Agatha Christie

419   Alice Schroeder, The Snowball: Warren Buffett and the Business of Life, Bloomsbury Publishing, London, 2008, p.33. Also by Bantam Books, a division of Penguin Random House LLC.

420   "Why saying 'no' will boost your career", March 14, 2014, bbc.com

421   Office Hours with Warren Buffett, May 7, 2013, interview with Caroline Ghosn, Levo League, www.levo.com

422   Said by Charles T. Munger but source unknown

423   Warren Buffett memo to Berkshire Hathaway Managers, December 19, 2014

424   USC Gould School of Law Commencement Address, May 13, 2007, Peter D. Kaufman, Poor Charlie's Almanack, p.431.

425   Berkshire Hathaway annual meeting, 2008, Outstanding Investor Digest, August 31, 2008, p.21.

426   Jim Rasmussen, "Buffett Partner's Impact 'Huge'", Sunday Omaha World-Herald, May 2, 1999

427   Notes from Fiscal Fitness Forum, Omaha, November 10, 1997

428   Berkshire Hathaway Inc., 2010 Annual Report

429   Berkshire Hathaway annual meeting, 2015, Notes by author

430   Wesco Financial annual meeting, 2003, Notes by Whitney Tilson, www.tilsonfunds.com

431   Berkshire Hathaway annual meeting, 2015, Notes by author

432   Aaron Task, "The 'Oracle of Omaha' is Bullish on Financial Education", April 8, 2013, Yahoo Finance

433   Berkshire Hathaway annual meeting, 2015, Notes by author

434   Berkshire Hathaway annual meeting, 2014, Notes by author

435   Ibid.

436   Ibid.

437   Ibid.

438   Conversation with Charlie Munger, Pasadena Convention Center, July 1, 2011, Notes by Shane Parrish, Farnam Street

439   Berkshire Hathaway annual meeting, 1990, Outstanding Investor Digest, May 31 1990, p.23.

440   Rana Foroohar, "Warren Buffett is on a Radical Track", Time Magazine, January 23, 2012

441   Alice Schroeder, The Snowball: Warren Buffett and the Business of Life, Bloomsbury Publishing, London, 2008, p.63. Also by Bantam Books, a division of Penguin Random House LLC

442   Notes from the Meeting Dr. George Athanassakos and Ivey MBA and HBA students had with Mr. Warren Buffett, Omaha February 27, 2015, The Ben Graham Center for Value Investing

443   Alice Schroeder, The Snowball: Warren Buffett and the Business of Life, Bloomsbury Publishing, London, 2008, p.63. Also by Bantam Books, a division of Penguin Random House LLC

444   Rana Foroohar, "Warren Buffett is on a Radical Track", Time Magazine, January 23, 2012

445   Wesco Financial annual meeting, 2007, Notes by author

446   Jim Rasmussen, "Buffett Partner's Impact 'Huge'", Sunday Omaha World-Herald, May 2, 1999

447   Berkshire Hathaway annual meeting 1994, Outstanding Investor Digest, June 23, 1994, p.19.

448   Berkshire Hathaway Inc., 2010 Annual Report

449   1994 Lecture of The E. J. Faulkner Lecture Series, A Colloquium with University of Nebraska-Lincoln Students by Warren E. Buffett

450   Berkshire Hathaway annual meeting, 2009, Notes by author

451   Said by Charles T. Munger but source unknown

452   Berkshire Hathaway annual meeting, 1999, Notes by author

453   Berkshire Hathaway, Inc., 2010 Annual Report

454   Charley Ellis, "Living Legends", CFA Institute Magazine, January/February 2003, Vol. 14, Issue 1.

455   Three Lectures by Warren Buffett to Notre Dame Faculty, MBA students and Undergraduate students, Spring 1991, Lightly edited by Whitney Tilson

456   Warren Buffett, Capital Cities/ABC management conference, 1986, seen in Roger Lowenstein, Buffett: The Making of an American Capitalist, New York: Random House, 1995, New York, p.273.

457   Financial Crisis Inquiry Commission Staff Audiotape of Interview with Warren Buffett, May 26, 2010, p.6. www.santangelsreview.com

458   Wesco Financial annual meeting, 2002, Notes by Whitney Tilson, www.tilsonfunds.com

459   Berkshire Hathaway annual meeting, 2001, Outstanding Investor Digest, December 24, 2001, p.53.

460   Berkshire Hathaway annual meeting, 2005, Notes by Whitney Tilson, www.tilsonfunds.com

461   Peter D. Kaufman, Poor Charlie's Almanack, p.125.

462   Daily Journal Corporation annual meeting, 2011, Notes by author

463   Berkshire Hathaway Inc., 1990 Annual Report

464   "Q&A: Legal Matters with Charles T. Munger", Stanford Lawyer, Spring 2009, http://stanfordlawyer.law.stanford.edu/2009/11/qa-with-charles-t-munger/

465   Lecture at the University of Florida School of Business, October 15, 1998, Martin Lee

466   Berkshire Hathaway annual meeting, 2009, Notes by author

467   Berkshire Hathaway Inc., 1987 Annual Report

468   Berkshire Hathaway annual meeting, 2008, Notes by author

469   Wesco Financial annual meeting, 1991, Outstanding Investor Digest, May 24, 1991, p.5.

470   Berkshire Hathaway Inc., 1987 Annual Report

471   Lecture at the University of Florida School of Business, October 15, 1998, Martin Lee

472   1994 Lecture of The E. J. Faulkner Lecture Series, A Colloquium with University of Nebraska-Lincoln Students by Warren E. Buffett

473   Charles T. Munger Harvard School Commencement Speech June 13, 1986

474   Charles Munger at See's Candy's 75th Anniversary Luncheon, March 1998, seen in Janet Lowe, Damn Right: Behind the Scenes with Berkshire Hathaway Billionaire Charlie Munger, John Wiley & Sons, New York, 2000, p.242.

475   Wesco Financial annual meeting, 2007, Notes by author

476   USC Gould School of Law Commencement Address, May 13, 2007, Peter D. Kaufman, Poor Charlie's Almanack, p.437.

477   Daily Journal Corporation annual meeting, 2013, Notes by Shane Parrish, Farnam Street

478   Peter D. Kaufman, Poor Charlie's Almanack, p.276.

479   Ibid., p.219.

480   Steve Jordon, The Oracle of Omaha: How Warren Buffett and his Hometown shaped each other, Omaha World-Herald Co. 2013, p.10.

481   Conversation with Charlie Munger, Pasadena Convention Center, July 1, 2011, Notes by Shane Parrish, Farnam Street

482   The World of René Dubos: A Collection from His Writings, Henry Holt & Co, 1990

483   Wesco Financial annual meeting, 2002, Notes by author

484   Wesco Financial annual meeting, 2000, Notes by Whitney Tilson, www.tilsonfunds.com

485   Berkshire Hathaway annual meeting, 2008, Outstanding Investor Digest, August 31, 2008, p.8.

486   Berkshire Hathaway Inc., 2002 Annual Report

487   Wesco Financial annual meeting, 2008, Notes by author

488   Berkshire Hathaway annual meeting, 2003, Notes by Whitney Tilson, www.tilsonfunds.com

489   Berkshire Hathaway annual meeting, 2008, Outstanding Investor Digest, August 31, 2008, p.16.

490   Berkshire Hathaway annual meeting, 2012, Notes by author

491   Berkshire Hathaway annual meeting, 2001, Outstanding Investor Digest, December 24, 2001, p.52.

492   Jon Louis Bentley, Programming Pearls, 2000

493   "A Conversation With Charlie Munger", Charlie Munger Speaks to University of Michigan Students, September 14, 2010

494   Berkshire Hathaway annual meeting, 2009, Notes by author

495   Berkshire Hathaway annual meeting, 2012, Notes by author

496   Wesco Financial annual meeting, 2008, Notes by author

497   Berkshire Hathaway Inc., 2009 Annual Report

498   Berkshire Hathaway annual meeting, 2009, Notes by author
499   Wesco Financial annual meeting, 2008, Outstanding Investor Digest, August 31, 2008, p.38.
500   Berkshire Hathaway Inc., 2012 Annual Report
501   Berkshire Hathaway annual meeting, 2014, Notes by author
502   Berkshire Hathaway Inc., 2014 Annual Report
503   Berkshire Hathaway Inc., 2012 Annual Report
504   Berkshire Hathaway Inc., 2014 Annual Report
505   Wesco Financial Inc., 1992 Annual Report
506   Berkshire Hathaway Inc., 1980 Annual Report
507   Berkshire Hathaway Inc., 1987 Annual Report
508   Berkshire Hathaway annual meeting, 2009, Outstanding Investor Digest, OID.COM
Feature, p.15.
509   Berkshire Hathaway Inc., 2010 Annual Report
510   Wesco Financial annual meeting, 2001, Notes by Whitney Tilson, www.tilsonfunds.com
511   Wesco Financial annual meeting, 2008, Notes by Peter Boodell, Boodell & Company
Capital Management
512   Berkshire Hathaway annual meeting, 2003, Notes by Whitney Tilson, www.tilsonfunds.com
513   Wesco Financial annual meeting, 2010, Notes by author
514   Berkshire Hathaway annual meeting, 2003, Notes by Whitney Tilson, www.tilsonfunds.com
515   Berkshire Hathaway annual meeting, 2012, Notes by author
516   Berkshire Hathaway annual meeting, 2005, Notes by Whitney Tilson, www.tilsonfunds.com
517   Wesco Financial annual meeting, 2001, Notes by Whitney Tilson, www.tilsonfunds.com
518   http://www.encyclopedia-titanica.org/disaster-at-last-befalls-capt-smith.html
519   Berkshire Hathaway annual meeting, 2005, Outstanding Investor Digest, March 9, 2006,
p.50.
520   Berkshire Hathaway Inc., 2014 Annual Report
521   Berkshire Hathaway annual meeting, 2004, Notes by Whitney Tilson, www.tilsonfunds.com
522   Berkshire Hathaway annual meeting, 2003, Notes by author
523   Berkshire Hathaway annual meeting, 2004, Notes by Whitney Tilson, www.tilsonfunds.com
524   Based on Nassim Taleb, Antifragile: Things That Gain from Disorder, Random House, 2012
525   Ibid.
526   Downton Abbey, Series 1 (2010), Episode 1
527   Berkshire Hathaway Inc., 2006 Annual Report
528   Wesco Financial annual meeting, 2003, Outstanding Investor Digest, Year End 2003
Edition, p.47.
529   Howard Marks, The Most Important Thing, Uncommon Sense for the Thoughtful Investor,
Columbia Business School Publishing, 2011
530   Transcript of Warren Buffett's 'Ask Warren' appearance on CNBC's Squawk Box, March 1,
2010, buffettwatch.cnbc.com
531   Berkshire Hathaway Inc., 2014 Annual Report
532   Berkshire Hathaway annual meeting, 1993, Outstanding Investor Digest, June 30, 1993,
p.28.
533   Berkshire Hathaway Inc., 2001 Annual Report
534   Berkshire Hathaway annual meeting, 2003, Notes by Whitney Tilson, www.tilsonfunds.com
535   USC Gould School of Law Commencement Address, May 13, 2007, Peter D. Kaufman,
Poor Charlie's Almanack, p.439.
536   Wesco Financial annual meeting, 2007, Notes by Whitney Tilson, www.tilsonfunds.com
537   USC Gould School of Law Commencement Address, May 13, 2007, Peter D. Kaufman,
Poor Charlie's Almanack, p.431.
538   Wesco Financial annual meeting, 2001, Notes by Whitney Tilson, www.tilsonfunds.com
539   USC Gould School of Law Commencement Address, May 13, 2007, Peter D. Kaufman,
Poor Charlie's Almanack, p.431.
540   Daily Journal Corporation annual meeting, 2014, Notes by Shane Parrish, Farnam Street
541   Wesco Financial annual meeting, 2001, Outstanding Investor Digest, OID.COM Edition,
2003, p.20.
542   "Munger on Sokol: 'I'm sad'", CNNMoney Interview, May 3, 2011
543   Berkshire Hathaway annual meeting, 2009, Outstanding Investor Digest, OID.COM
Feature, p.38.

544   Berkshire Hathaway annual meeting, 2008, Notes by Peter Boodell, Boodell & Company Capital Management

545   Wesco Financial annual meeting, 2006, Notes by Whitney Tilson, www.tilsonfunds.com

546   Charles T. Munger Harvard School Commencement Speech June 13, 1986

547   Wesco Financial annual meeting, 2007, Notes by author

548   Charles T. Munger Harvard School Commencement Speech June 13, 1986

549   Gillian Zoe Segal, Getting There: A Book of Mentors, New York, Abrams Image, 2015, p.18.

550   http://quoteinvestigator.com/2014/05/17/angry-speech/

551   Warren Buffett's 'Ask Warren' appearance on CNBC's Squawk Box, March 2, 2015, cnbc.com

552   Berkshire Hathaway annual meeting, 2011, Notes by author

553   Charles T. Munger Harvard School Commencement Speech June 13, 1986

554   Unofficial transcript of Warren Buffett, Charlie Munger and Bill Gates appearing live with Becky Quick on CNBC's "Squawk Box," Monday, May 5, 2014, buffettwatch.cnbc.com

555   USC Gould School of Law Commencement Address, May 13, 2007, Peter D. Kaufman, Poor Charlie's Almanack, p.431.

556   Patricia Sellers, "Warren Buffett and Charlie Munger's best advice", Fortune.com, October 31, 2013

557   Notes from the Meeting Dr. George Athanassakos and Ivey MBA and HBA students had with Mr. Warren Buffett, Omaha March 31, 2008, The Ben Graham Center for Value Investing

558   The Psychology of Human Misjudgment, Talk at the Cambridge Center for Behavioral Studies, April 24, 1995

559   Berkshire Hathaway annual meeting, 2006, Notes by author

560   Wesco Financial annual meeting, 2007, Notes by author

561   Berkshire Hathaway annual meeting, 2008, Notes by Peter Boodell, Boodell & Company Capital Management

562   Daily Journal Corporation annual meeting, 2014, Notes by Shane Parrish, Farnam Street

563   Wesco Financial annual meeting, 2000, Notes by Whitney Tilson, www.tilsonfunds.com

564   Wesco Financial annual meeting, 2000, Outstanding Investor Digest, December 18, 2000, p.60.

565   Practical Thought About Practical Thought? An Informal Talk, July 20, 1996, Peter D. Kaufman, Poor Charlie's Almanack, p.291.

566   Conversation with Charlie Munger, Pasadena Convention Center, July 1, 2011, Notes by Shane Parrish, Farnam Street

567   Charles T. Munger Harvard School Commencement Speech June 13, 1986

568   "Warren Buffett on What's Next in the Payment Industry", Interview by Business Wire CEO Cathy Baron Tamraz, October 17, 2009, Transcript, PYMNTS.com, http://www.pymnts.com/businesswire-feed/transcript-warren-buffett-on-what-s-next-in-the-payments-industry/

569   Charles T. Munger Harvard School Commencement Speech June 13, 1986

570   Berkshire Hathaway annual meeting, 2007, Notes by Whitney Tilson, www.tilsonfunds.com

571   Berkshire Hathaway annual meeting, 2009, Notes by author

572   Wesco Financial annual meeting, 2005, Notes by Whitney Tilson, www.tilsonfunds.com

573   Ibid.

574   Berkshire Hathaway annual meeting, 2011, Notes by author

575   Peter D. Kaufman, Poor Charlie's Almanack, p.79.

576   Berkshire Hathaway annual meeting, 2015, Notes by author

577   Daily Journal Corporation annual meeting, 2014, Notes by Shane Parrish, Farnam Street

578   Roger Lowenstein, Buffett: The Making of an American Capitalist, New York: Random House, 1995, New York, p.111.

579   Berkshire Hathaway annual meeting, 2008, Notes by author

580   "When I Buy a Company, I'm a Journalist", taped interview with Arizona State University Professor Jeff Cunningham, creator and host of Iconic Voices, Walter Cronkite School of Journalism, March 5, 2015

581   Warren Buffett memo to Berkshire Hathaway Managers, Jan. 6, 2005

582   Wesco Financial annual meeting, 2007, Notes by Whitney Tilson, www.tilsonfunds.com

583   Berkshire Hathaway annual meeting, 2015, Notes by author

584   Carol J. Loomis, transcript: Warren Buffett at Fortune MPW, October 17, 2013, http://fortune.com/2013/10/17/transcript-warren-buffett-at-fortune-mpw/

585   Berkshire Hathaway annual meeting, 2015, Notes by author

586   Wesco Financial annual meeting, 2007, Notes by Whitney Tilson, www.tilsonfunds.com
587   Peter D. Kaufman, Poor Charlie's Almanack, p.80.
588   Ibid.
589   Wesco Financial annual meeting, 2007, Notes by author
590   Daily Journal Corporation annual meeting, 2013, Notes by Shane Parrish, Farnam Street
591   Ibid.
592   Ibid.
593   Cynthia H. Milligan, "Warren, A Conversation with Dean Cynthia H. Milligan", Nebraska Business, Fall 2001
594   David Ogilvy, Confessions of an Advertising Man, Southbank Publishing, 2012
595   Daily Journal Corporation annual meeting, 2014, Notes by Shane Parrish, Farnam Street
596   Margie Kelley, "In the Money: Alumni financiers take stock of the market and careers spent trying to beat it," Harvard Law Bulletin, Summer 2001
597   Wesco Financial annual meeting, 2004, Outstanding Investor Digest, December 31, 2004, p.50.
598   Wesco Financial annual meeting, 2005, Notes by Whitney Tilson, www.tilsonfunds.com
599   Berkshire Hathaway annual meeting, 2008, Notes by author
600   Catherine Aird, His Burial Too, Doubleday, 1973
601   Berkshire Hathaway annual meeting, 2008, Notes by Peter Boodell, Boodell & Company Capital Management
602   Conversation with Charlie Munger, Pasadena Convention Center, July 1, 2011, Notes by Shane Parrish, Farnam Street
603   Charlie Munger at Harvard-Westlake School January 19, 2010, www.santangelsreview.com
604   Wesco Financial annual meeting, 2004, Notes by Whitney Tilson, www.tilsonfunds.com
605   Peter D. Kaufman, Poor Charlie's Almanack, p.497.
606   The Psychology of Human Misjudgment, Peter D. Kaufman, Poor Charlie's Almanack, p.481.
607   1994 Lecture of The E. J. Faulkner Lecture Series, A Colloquium with University of Nebraska-Lincoln Students by Warren E. Buffett
608   Alice Schroeder, The Snowball: Warren Buffett and the Business of Life, Bloomsbury Publishing, London, 2008, p.158. Also by Bantam Books, a division of Penguin Random House LLC
609   Berkshire Hathaway annual meeting, 2008, Outstanding Investor Digest, August 31, 2008, p.28.
610   Berkshire Hathaway annual meeting, 2002, Notes by Selena Maranjian, The Motley Fool
611   Berkshire Hathaway annual meeting, 2003, Notes by Whitney Tilson, www.tilsonfunds.com
612   From the movie Radio Days (1987)
613   Bill George, Discover Your True North, John Wiley & Sons, New Jersey, 2015, p. 124.
614   Berkshire Hathaway annual meeting, 2014, Notes by author
615   Counsels And Maxims, Kessinger Publishing, 2010
616   Notes from the Meeting Dr. George Athanassakos and Ivey MBA and HBA students had with Mr. Warren Buffett, Omaha February 27, 2015, The Ben Graham Center for Value Investing
617   Wesco Financial annual meeting, 2003, Notes by Whitney Tilson, www.tilsonfunds.com
618   Wesco Financial annual meeting, 2007, Notes by Whitney Tilson, www.tilsonfunds.com
619   USC Gould School of Law Commencement Address, May 13, 2007, Peter D. Kaufman, Poor Charlie's Almanack, p.422.
620   Notes from the Meeting Dr. George Athanassakos and Ivey MBA and HBA students had with Mr. Warren Buffett, Omaha March 31, 2008, The Ben Graham Center for Value Investing
621   Berkshire Hathaway annual meeting, 2003, Notes by Whitney Tilson, www.tilsonfunds.com
622   Ibid.
623   Kimberley Link-Wills, "Money Can't Buy You Love", Speech at the College of Management Georgia Tech, Techtopics, Spring 2005
624   Notes from the Meeting Dr. George Athanassakos and Ivey MBA and HBA students had with Mr. Warren Buffett, Omaha January 31, 2014, The Ben Graham Center for Value Investing
625   1994 Lecture of The E. J. Faulkner Lecture Series, A Colloquium with University of Nebraska-Lincoln Students by Warren E. Buffett
626   Ibid.
627   Transcript from visit in India, NDTV Studios, April 2011, Notes by Shane Parrish, Farnam Street

628   Berkshire Hathaway annual meeting, 2008, Outstanding Investor Digest, August 31, 2008, p.28.
629   1994 Lecture of The E. J. Faulkner Lecture Series, A Colloquium with University of Nebraska-Lincoln Students by Warren E. Buffett
630   Berkshire Hathaway annual meeting, 2000, Outstanding Investor Digest, Year End 2000 Edition, p.62.
631   Wesco Financial annual meeting, 2007, Notes by Whitney Tilson, www.tilsonfunds.com
632   Ibid.
633   Wesco Financial annual meeting, 2007, Notes by author
634   Wesco Financial annual meeting, 2007, Notes by Whitney Tilson, www.tilsonfunds.com
635   Benjamin Franklin, Rules for Making Oneself a Disagreeable Companion, Printed in The Pennsylvania Gazette, November 15, 1750.
636   Warren Buffett in an interview with Ted Koppel on ABC's Nightline, March 2, 1999
637   Notes from the Meeting Dr. George Athanassakos and Ivey MBA and HBA students had with Mr. Warren Buffett, Omaha March 30, 2012, The Ben Graham Center for Value Investing
638   Berkshire Hathaway annual meeting, 2013, Notes by author
639   Steve Jordon, "Warren Watch: Buffett, 'Dilbert' creator Scott Adams differ on passion", Omaha World-Herald, December 29, 2014
640   Conversation with Charlie Munger, Pasadena Convention Center, July 1, 2011, Notes by Shane Parrish, Farnam Street
641   Wesco Financial annual meeting, 2007, Notes by Whitney Tilson, www.tilsonfunds.com
642   "Buffett & Gates on Success", KCTS/Seattle, May 1998, Transcript p.20.
643   Warren Buffett speech to University of Tennessee students, 2006
644   Lecture at the University of Florida School of Business, October 15, 1998, Martin Lee
645   Notes from the Meeting Dr. George Athanassakos and Ivey MBA and HBA students had with Mr. Warren Buffett, Omaha March 30, 2012, The Ben Graham Center for Value Investing
646   Peter D. Kaufman, Poor Charlie's Almanack, p.219.
647   Transcript from Warren Buffett meeting with Wharton students, February 17, 2006, Notes by Timothy Viles & Aaron Byrd, seen in www.rbcpa.com
648   USC Gould School of Law Commencement Address, May 13, 2007, Peter D. Kaufman, Poor Charlie's Almanack, p.433.
649   Office Hours with Warren Buffett, May 7, 2013, interview with Caroline Ghosn, Levo League, www.levo.com
650   Todd A. Finkle & Paul F. Buller, Gonzaga University, "Wisdom from Warren Buffett", Research in Higher Education Journal, 16, 2012, http://works.bepress.com/todd_finkle/20
651   Wesco Financial annual meeting, 2009, Notes by author
652   Berkshire Hathaway annual meeting, 2015, Notes by author
653   Conversation with Charlie Munger, Pasadena Convention Center, July 1, 2011, Notes by Shane Parrish, Farnam Street
654   Berkshire Hathaway annual meeting, 2014, Notes by author
655   Unofficial transcript of Warren Buffett, Charlie Munger and Bill Gates appearing live with Becky Quick on CNBC's "Squawk Box," Monday, May 5, 2014, buffettwatch.cnbc.com
656   Notes by Professor Scott McDermott from Warren Buffett meeting with Carroll School MBA students and students from five other universities in Omaha, April 12, 2013, https://www.bc.edu/schools/csom/graduate/news/2013/buffett.html
657   Berkshire Hathaway annual meeting, 2014, Notes by author
658   Wesco Financial annual meeting, 2007, Notes by Whitney Tilson, www.tilsonfunds.com
659   Bob Reilly, "The Richest Man in America", USWest, Autumn 1987, p.2.
660   Berkshire Hathaway annual meeting, 2008, Notes by Peter Boodell, Boodell & Company Capital Management
661   Lecture by Charles T. Munger to the students of Professor William Lazier at Stanford Law School, Outstanding Investor Digest, March 13, 1998, p.57.
662   Berkshire Hathaway Inc., 2003 Annual Report
663   A Conversation with Charlie Munger at Caltech, DuBridge Distinguished Lecture, March 11, 2008, DVD
664   1994 Lecture of The E. J. Faulkner Lecture Series, A Colloquium with University of Nebraska-Lincoln Students by Warren E. Buffett
665   Berkshire Hathaway annual meeting, 2013, Notes by author

666   1994 Lecture of The E. J. Faulkner Lecture Series, A Colloquium with University of Nebraska-Lincoln Students by Warren E. Buffett

667   A Conversation with Charlie Munger at Caltech, DuBridge Distinguished Lecture, March 11, 2008, DVD

668   Warren Buffett talk at Georgetown University Sept. 19, 2013, www.georgetown.edu

669   Berkshire Hathaway annual meeting, 2004, Notes by Whitney Tilson, www.tilsonfunds.com

670   Ludwig Wittgenstein, Tractatus Logico-Philosophicus, Ch. 7, Routledge & Kegan Paul Ltd, 1922

671   Laurence J. Peter, Peter's Almanac, William Morrow & Co., 1982 (entry for Sept. 24)

672   Lecture by Charles T. Munger to the students of Professor William Lazier at Stanford Law School, Outstanding Investor Digest, March 13, 1998, p. 58.

673   Daily Journal Corporation annual meeting, 2014, Notes by Shane Parrish, Farnam Street

674   The Psychology of Human Misjudgment, Talk at the Cambridge Center for Behavioral Studies, April 24, 1995.

675   Alice Schroeder, The Snowball: Warren Buffett and the Business of Life, Bloomsbury Publishing, London, 2008, p.25. Also by Bantam Books, a division of Penguin Random House LLC

676   "Buffett & Gates on Success", KCTS/Seattle, May 1998, transcript p.13.

677   USC Gould School of Law Commencement Address, May 13, 2007, Peter D. Kaufman, Poor Charlie's Almanack, p.435.

678   Ibid.

679   Ibid., p.436.

680   John Cleese, "The real reason I had to join the Spectator", The Spectator, March 22, 2009

681   From Roy Rowan, The Intuitive Manager, Little, Brown and Company, 1986

682   USC Gould School of Law Commencement Address, May 13, 2007, Peter D. Kaufman, Poor Charlie's Almanack, p.436.

683   The Psychology of Human Misjudgment, Peter D. Kaufman, Poor Charlie's Almanack, p.490.

684   Berkshire Hathaway annual meeting, 1996, Outstanding Investor Digest, August 8, 1996, p.33.

685   Transcript of Warren Buffett's 'Ask Warren' appearance on CNBC's Squawk Box, March 1, 2010, buffettwatch.cnbc.com

686   Berkshire Hathaway Inc., 1987 Annual Report

687   Charlie Munger at Harvard-Westlake School January 19, 2010, www.santangelsreview.com

688   Warren Buffett, lecture at Stanford Law School, March 23, 1990, Outstanding Investor Digest, April 18, 1990, p.14.

689   Wesco Financial Inc., 1989 Annual Report

690   "Q&A: Legal Matters with Charles T. Munger", Stanford Lawyer, Spring 2009, http://stanfordlawyer.law.stanford.edu/2009/11/qa-with-charles-t-munger/

691   Daily Journal Corporation annual meeting, 2014, Notes by Shane Parrish, Farnam Street

692   Investment Practices of Leading Charitable Foundations, Speech at Miramar Sheraton Hotel, Santa Monica, CA, on October 14, 1998 to a meeting of the Foundation Financial Officer Group'

693   "Q&A: Legal Matters with Charles T. Munger", Stanford Lawyer, Spring 2009

694   Berkshire Hathaway annual meeting, 2014, Notes by author

695   Ibid.

696   Berkshire Hathaway annual meeting, 2001, Notes by Whitney Tilson, www.tilsonfunds.com

697   Berkshire Hathaway Inc., 1982 Annual Report

698   Berkshire Hathaway Inc., 1997 Annual Report

699   Berkshire Hathaway Inc., 2014 Annual Report

700   Berkshire Hathaway annual meeting, 2014, Notes by Peter Boodell, Boodell & Company Capital Management

701   Peter D. Kaufman, Poor Charlie's Almanack, p.91.

702   Ibid., p.219.

703   Unofficial transcript of Warren Buffett, Charlie Munger and Bill Gates appearing live with Becky Quick on CNBC's "Squawk Box," Monday, May 5, 2014, buffettwatch.cnbc.com

704   Warren Buffett meeting with students from Emory's Goizueta Business School and McCombs School of Business at UT Austin, February 15, 2008, www.undergroundvalue.blogspot.com

705   Notes from Buffett meeting with students from Emory and 5 other business schools, February 6, 2009, www.undergroundvalue.blogspot.com

706   Peter D. Kaufman, Poor Charlie's Almanack, p.73.

707   Alice Schroeder, The Snowball: Warren Buffett and the Business of Life, Bloomsbury Publishing, London, 2008, p.388. Also by Bantam Books, a division of Penguin Random House LLC

708   "Buffett & Gates on Success", KCTS/Seattle, May 1998, transcript p.6.

709   Warren Buffett in an interview with Ted Koppel on ABC's Nightline, March 2, 1999

710   Wesco Financial annual meeting 1989, Outstanding Investor Digest, July 26, 1989, p.7.

711   Berkshire Hathaway annual meeting, 1995, Outstanding Investor Digest, August 10, 1995, p.20.

712   Daily Journal Corporation annual meeting, 2015, Notes by Shane Parrish, Farnam Street

713   Office Hours with Warren Buffett, May 7, 2013, interview with Caroline Ghosn, Levo League, www.levo.com

714   Notes from the Meeting Dr. George Athanassakos and Ivey MBA and HBA students had with Mr. Warren Buffett, Omaha February 27, 2015, The Ben Graham Center for Value Investing

715   Callie Worsham, "6 Richest alumni (and two dropouts) — Interview with Charles Munger", The Michigan Daily, February 21, 2007

716   Daily Journal Corporation annual meeting, 2015, Notes by Shane Parrish, Farnam Street

717   Gillian Zoe Segal, Getting There: A Book of Mentors, New York, Abrams Image, 2015, p.16.

718   Wesco Financial annual meeting, 2007, Notes by author

719   Daily Journal Corporation annual meeting, 2014, Notes by Shane Parrish, Farnam Street

720   Wesco Financial annual meeting, 2005, Notes by Whitney Tilson, www.tilsonfunds.com

721   Buffett Partnership Letter, October 9, 1969

722   Mark Calvey, "Friendly investment advice from Warren Buffett's buddy", San Francisco Business Times, October 21, 1996

723   Berkshire Hathaway annual meeting, 2007, Notes by Whitney Tilson, www.tilsonfunds.com

724   Berkshire Hathaway Inc., 1989 Annual Report

725   Students from Tuck School of Business at Dartmouth meet Warren Buffett, 2004, http://www.thinkfn.com/wikibolsa/Visita_a_Warren_Buffett

726   Notes from the Meeting Dr. George Athanassakos and Ivey MBA and HBA students had with Mr. Warren Buffett, Omaha February 27, 2015, The Ben Graham Center for Value Investing

727   1994 Lecture of The E. J. Faulkner Lecture Series, A Colloquium with University of Nebraska-Lincoln Students by Warren E. Buffett

728   Three Lectures by Warren Buffett to Notre Dame Faculty, MBA students and Undergraduate students, Spring 1991, Lightly edited by Whitney Tilson

729   Berkshire Hathaway annual meeting, 1993, Outstanding Investor Digest, June 30, 1993, p.29.

730   William Green, The Great Minds of Investing, München, FinanzBuch Verlag, 2015, p.140, text written by Dr. Gisela Baur, copyright by ACATIS Investment GmbH

731   USC Gould School of Law Commencement Address, May 13, 2007, Peter D. Kaufman, Poor Charlie's Almanack, p.439.

732   Berkshire Hathaway annual meeting, 2009, Outstanding Investor Digest, OID.COM Feature, p.20.

733   Keynote Breakfast Speech by Charles Munger at Stanford University's Director's College, June 26, 2006, Stanford Law School, Transcript, www.rockcenter.law.stanford.edu

734   Warren Buffett, lecture at Stanford Law School, March 23, 1990, Outstanding Investor Digest, April 18, 1990, p.18.

735   From the movie At the Circus (1939)

736   Berkshire Hathaway annual meeting, 2009, Outstanding Investor Digest, OID.COM Feature, p.21

737   Office Hours with Warren Buffett, May 7, 2013, interview with Caroline Ghosn, Levo League, www.levo.com

738   Berkshire Hathaway, An Owner's Manual

739   Berkshire Hathaway annual meeting, 1998, Notes by author

740   Berkshire Hathaway annual meeting, 1996, Outstanding Investor Digest, August 8, 1996, p.37.

741   Three Lectures by Warren Buffett to Notre Dame Faculty, MBA students and Undergraduate students, Spring 1991, Lightly edited by Whitney Tilson

742   1994 Lecture of The E. J. Faulkner Lecture Series, A Colloquium with University of Nebraska-Lincoln Students by Warren E. Buffett

743   Wesco Financial annual meeting, 2010, Notes by author

744   Berkshire Hathaway Inc., 2014 Annual Report

745   Berkshire Hathaway Inc., 2009 Annual Report

746   Berkshire Hathaway annual meeting, 1999, Outstanding Investor Digest, December 31, 1999, p.49.

747   Berkshire Hathaway annual meeting, 2005, Notes by Whitney Tilson, www.tilsonfunds.com

748   Wesco Financial annual meeting, 1999, Outstanding Investor Digest, December 31, 1999, pp.42-43.

749   Berkshire Hathaway annual meeting, 2010, Notes by author

750   Ibid.

751   Astrid Dörner, "Warren Buffett's German To-Do List", Handelsblatt Global Edition no. 123, February 25, 2015

752   Berkshire Hathaway Inc., 1990 Annual Report

753   Steven Goldberg, "The World According to 'Poor Charlie'", Kiplinger.com, December 2005

754   From Tom Murphy's foreword to Berkshire Beyond Buffett by Lawrence Cunningham, Columbia University Press, 2014

755   Berkshire Hathaway Inc., 1998 Annual Report

756   Berkshire Hathaway annual meeting, 2000, Notes by Whitney Tilson, www.tilsonfunds.com

757   Berkshire Hathaway Inc., 1977 Annual Report

758   Berkshire Hathaway annual meeting, 2012, Notes by author

759   Office Hours with Warren Buffett, May 7, 2013, interview with Caroline Ghosn, Levo League, www.levo.com

760   Berkshire Hathaway annual meeting, 2014, Notes by author

761   Berkshire Hathaway annual meeting, 2005, Notes by Whitney Tilson, www.tilsonfunds.com

762   Ibid.

763   Berkshire Hathaway annual meeting, 2005, Notes by author

764   Peter D. Kaufman, Poor Charlie's Almanack, p.80.

765   Berkshire Hathaway Inc., 1979 Annual Report

766   Berkshire Hathaway Inc., 2009 Annual Report

767   Berkshire Hathaway annual meeting, 2014, Notes by author

768   Warren Buffett memo to Berkshire Hathaway Managers, December 19, 2014

769   Charlie Rose interview: "In his own words — Conversation with Charlie Rose", PBS, May 2, 2004

770   Berkshire Hathaway annual meeting, 2015, Notes by author

771   Ibid.

772   Wesco Financial annual meeting, 2002, Notes by Whitney Tilson, www.tilsonfunds.com

773   Berkshire Hathaway annual meeting, 2014, Notes by author

774   Ibid.

775   Berkshire Hathaway Inc., 2010 Annual Report

776   Berkshire Hathaway annual meeting, 2014, Notes by author

777   Berkshire Hathaway Inc., 2008 Annual Report

778   Wesco Financial annual meeting, 2007, Outstanding Investor Digest, February 29, 2008, p.54.

779   Berkshire Hathaway annual meeting, 2014, Notes by author

780   Berkshire Hathaway Inc., 2000 Annual Report

781   Wesco Financial annual meeting, 2001, Wesco Special Report, Outstanding Investor Digest, OID.COM Edition, 2003, p.14.

782   Peter D. Kaufman, Poor Charlie's Almanack, p.417.

783   Berkshire Hathaway annual meeting, 2014, Notes by author

784   Ibid.

785   University of Kansas Business School Students - Q&A with Warren Buffett, December 2, 2005, http://www.rbcpa.com/WEB_20051202.html

786   Michael D. Eisner with Aaron Cohen, Working Together: Why Great Partnerships Succeed, New York, Harper Collins Publishers, 2010, p.33.

787   "Buffett & Gates on Success", KCTS/Seattle, May 1998, transcript p.20.

788   Michael D. Eisner with Aaron Cohen, Working Together: Why Great Partnerships Succeed, New York, Harper Collins Publishers, 2010, p.52.

789   Ibid., p.53.
790   Unofficial transcript of Warren Buffett, Charlie Munger and Bill Gates appearing live with Becky Quick on CNBC's "Squawk Box," Monday, May 5, 2014, buffettwatch.cnbc.com
791   Interview with the physicist Abraham Pais, Oral History Interviews, American Institute of Physics, https://www.aip.org/history-programs/niels-bohr-library/oral-histories/5047
792   From Mohnish Pabrai's December 2014 talk to Sanjay Bakshi's MDI class, www.valueinvestingworld.com
793   Garrett Hardin, Living Within Limits: Ecology, Economics, and Population Taboos, Oxford University Press Inc, New York, 1993
794   Berkshire Hathaway annual meeting, 2014, Notes by author
795   Janet Lowe, Damn Right: Behind the Scenes with Berkshire Hathaway Billionaire Charlie Munger, John Wiley & Sons, New York, 2000, p.75.
796   Warren Buffett responds to questions from Wharton students, November 12, 2004, www.tilsonfunds.com
797   Unofficial transcript of Warren Buffett, Charlie Munger and Bill Gates appearing live with Becky Quick on CNBC's "Squawk Box," Monday, May 5, 2014, buffettwatch.cnbc.com
798   Michael D. Eisner with Aaron Cohen, Working Together: Why Great Partnerships Succeed, New York, Harper Collins Publishers, 2010, p.45.
799   Unofficial transcript of Warren Buffett, Charlie Munger and Bill Gates appearing live with Becky Quick on CNBC's "Squawk Box," Monday, May 5, 2014, buffettwatch.cnbc.com
800   Berkshire Hathaway Inc., 2014 Annual Report
801   Michael D. Eisner with Aaron Cohen, Working Together: Why Great Partnerships Succeed, New York, Harper Collins Publishers, 2010, p.47.
802   Wesco Financial annual meeting, 2008, Outstanding Investor Digest, August 31, 2008, p.48.
803   Michael D. Eisner with Aaron Cohen, Working Together: Why Great Partnerships Succeed, New York, Harper Collins Publishers, 2010, p.47.
804   Ibid., p.48.
805   Ibid., p.47.
806   Graham Bowley, "Closely Watched Buffett Recalculating his Bets," New York Times, Sept. 7, 2009
807   Berkshire Hathaway annual meeting, 1998, Notes by author
808   Daily Journal Corporation annual meeting, 2015, Notes by Shane Parrish, Farnam Street
809   1994 Lecture of The E. J. Faulkner Lecture Series, A Colloquium with University of Nebraska-Lincoln Students by Warren E. Buffett
810   Berkshire Hathaway, Press Conference, May 2005, Notes by valueinvestorinsight.com
811   The Psychology of Human Misjudgment, Talk at the Cambridge Center for Behavioral Studies, April 24, 1995.
812   Daily Journal Corporation annual meeting, 2011, Notes by author
813   The Psychology of Human Misjudgment, Talk at the Cambridge Center for Behavioral Studies, April 24, 1995.
814   The Psychology of Human Misjudgment, Peter D. Kaufman, Poor Charlie's Almanack, p.473.
815   Isaac Asimov, The Gods Themselves, Spectra, 1972
816   Investment Practices of Leading Charitable Foundations, Speech at Miramar Sheraton Hotel, Santa Monica, CA, on October 14, 1998 to a meeting of the Foundation Financial Officer Group'
817   Berkshire Hathaway Inc., 2012 Annual Report
818   Berkshire Hathaway Inc., 2000 Annual Report
819   "A Conversation With Charlie Munger", Charlie Munger Speaks to University of Michigan Students, September 14, 2010
820   Berkshire Hathaway annual meeting, 1997, Outstanding Investor Digest, August 8, 1997, p.21.
821   Berkshire Hathaway Inc., 2014 Annual Report
822   Charles T. Munger testimony, In the Matter of Certain Treasury Notes and Other Government Securities, File No. HO-2513, February 6, 1992
823   Jet Magazine, March 27, 1980, p.30.
824   Berkshire Hathaway Inc., 2005 Annual Report
825   Berkshire Hathaway annual meeting, 2005, Notes by Whitney Tilson, www.tilsonfunds.com
826   Berkshire Hathaway Inc., 1987 Annual Report

827   Berkshire Hathaway annual meeting, 2007, Notes by author
828   "A Conversation With Charlie Munger", Charlie Munger Speaks to University of Michigan Students, September 14, 2010
829   Wesco Financial annual meeting, 2010, Notes by author
830   Wesco Financial annual meeting, 2010, Outstanding Investor Digest, August 9, 2010, p.34.
831   Berkshire Hathaway annual meeting, 2010, Notes by author
832   Norman R. Augustine, "Managing the Crisis You Tried to Prevent", Harvard Business Review, November 1995 Issue, www.//hbr.org/1995/11/managing-the-crisis-you-tried-to-prevent
833   The Psychology of Human Misjudgment, Peter D. Kaufman, Poor Charlie's Almanack, p.471.
834   Ibid., pp.471-472.
835   Berkshire Hathaway Inc., 1995 Annual Report
836   The Psychology of Human Misjudgment, Peter D. Kaufman, Poor Charlie's Almanack, p.472.
837   Jason Zweig, "A Fireside Chat With Charlie Munger," The Wall Street Journal, Sept. 12, 2014
838   From Jim Collins book, Good to Great: Why Some Companies Make the Leap…and Others Don't, Harper Business, New York, 2001 and Churchill quote from Winston Churchill, The Gathering Storm, Mariner Books, 1986
839   Berkshire Hathaway annual meeting, 1995, Notes by author
840   Warren Buffett memo to Berkshire Hathaway Managers, December 19, 2014
841   The Psychology of Human Misjudgment, Peter D. Kaufman, Poor Charlie's Almanack, p.479.
842   Ibid., p.462.
843   Ibid., p.463.
844   "Bad Judgments, Common Causes", Charles Munger speech at the California Institute of Technology, February 17, 1992
845   The Psychology of Human Misjudgment, Talk at the Cambridge Center for Behavioral Studies, April 24, 1995.
846   Berkshire Hathaway Inc., 1986 Annual Report
847   http://www.theguardian.com/books/2008/may/24/booksonhealth.scienceandnature
848   Berkshire Hathaway annual meeting, 2002, Notes by author
849   The Psychology of Human Misjudgment, Peter D. Kaufman, Poor Charlie's Almanack, p.461.
850   Wilson Edward O., Consilience: The Unity of Knowledge, Alfred A. Knopf, New York, 1998
851   Charles Munger interview by CNBC, May 4, 2012, cnbc.com
852   The Entire Memoirs Of Cardinal De Retz, Kessinger Publishing, 2010
853   Berkshire Hathaway Inc., 1983 Annual Report
854   Wesco Financial annual meeting, 2010, Outstanding Investor Digest, August 9, 2010, p.32.
855   Rudyard Kipling, The Man Who Would be King and Other Stories, Dover Publications, 1994
856   The Psychology of Human Misjudgment, Talk at the Cambridge Center for Behavioral Studies, April 24, 1995
857   Berkshire Hathaway Inc., 1989 Annual Report
858   Berkshire Hathaway annual meeting, 2009, Outstanding Investor Digest, OID.COM Feature, p.26.
859   Berkshire Hathaway annual meeting, 1998, Outstanding Investor Digest, September 24, 1998, p.40.
860   Wesco Financial annual meeting, 2006, Notes by Whitney Tilson, www.tilsonfunds.com
861   Warren Buffett, "Warren Buffett is bullish…on women", Fortune Magazine, May 2, 2013
862   The Psychology of Human Misjudgment, Talk at the Cambridge Center for Behavioral Studies, April 24, 1995.
863   Peter D. Kaufman, Poor Charlie's Almanack, p.56.
864   Wesco Financial annual meeting, 2003, Notes by author
865   Said by Charles T. Munger but source unknown
866   Soros on Soros: Staying Ahead of the Curve, Wiley, New York, 1995, p.11.
867   Said by Charles T. Munger but source unknown

868   Wesco Financial annual meeting, 2004, Outstanding Investor Digest, December 31, 2004, p.47.
869   Charles T. Munger Harvard School Commencement Speech June 13, 1986
870   Ibid.
871   Berkshire Hathaway Inc., 2000 Annual Report
872   Berkshire Hathaway annual meeting, 1998, Outstanding Investor Digest, September 24, 1998, p.40.
873   H. L. Mencken's, Minority Report: H. L. Mencken's Notebooks, Knopf, 1956, p. 232.
874   "When I Buy a Company, I'm a Journalist", taped interview with Arizona State University Professor Jeff Cunningham, creator and host of Iconic Voices, Walter Cronkite School of Journalism, March 5, 2015
875   Charles T. Munger Harvard School Commencement Speech June 13, 1986
876   Three Lectures by Warren Buffett to Notre Dame Faculty, MBA students and Undergraduate students, Spring 1991, Lightly edited by Whitney Tilson
877   Based on research by Mitchell D.J., Russo J.E., Pennington N., Back to the Future: Temporal Perspective in the Explanation of Events, Journal of Behavioral Decision Making, Vol. 2, 1989 and Gary Klein, Performing a Project Premortem, Harvard Business Review, September 2007
878   From Doris Kearns Goodwin, Team of Rivals: The Political Genius of Abraham Lincoln, Simon & Schuster 2006
879   The Psychology of Human Misjudgment, Peter D. Kaufman, Poor Charlie's Almanack, p.461.
880   Berkshire Hathaway annual meeting, 2003, Notes by author
881   Berkshire Hathaway annual meeting, 2014, Notes by Peter Boodell, Boodell & Company Capital Management
882   Ibid.
883   Berkshire Hathaway annual meeting, 2000, Outstanding Investor Digest, Year End 2000 Edition, p.60.
884   Berkshire Hathaway annual meeting, 2014, Notes by author
885   Daily Journal Corporation annual meeting, 2013, Notes by author
886   Daily Journal Corporation annual meeting, 2013, Notes by Shane Parrish, Farnam Street
887   "Buffett on Bridge", Warren Buffett Bridge Cup 2013, Buffettcup.com
888   Charles Munger interview by CNBC, May 4, 2012, cnbc.com
889   Wesco Financial annual meeting, 2004, Notes by Whitney Tilson, www.tilsonfunds.com
890   Wesco Financial annual meeting, 2004, Outstanding Investor Digest, December 31, 2004, pp.43-44.
891   As quoted by Teles of Megara, fr. 2., On Self-Sufficiency
892   Conversations from the Warren Buffett Symposium, Cardozo Law Review (1997), vol. 19. Edited by Lawrence A. Cunningham and reissued by Cunningham in 2016.
893   Berkshire Hathaway Inc., 1995 Annual Report
894   Berkshire Hathaway annual meeting, 2001, Notes by Whitney Tilson, www.tilsonfunds.com
895   Berkshire Hathaway Inc., 1984 Annual Report
896   Wesco Financial annual meeting, 2004, Outstanding Investor Digest, December 31, 2004, p.44.
897   Wesco Financial annual meeting, 2004, Notes by Whitney Tilson, www.tilsonfunds.com
898   The Psychology of Human Misjudgment, Peter D. Kaufman, Poor Charlie's Almanack, p.477.
899   Ibid.
900   Practical Thought About Practical Thought? An Informal Talk, July 20, 1996, Peter D. Kaufman, Poor Charlie's Almanack, p.291.
901   The Psychology of Human Misjudgment, Talk at the Cambridge Center for Behavioral Studies, April 24, 1995.
902   The Psychology of Human Misjudgment, Peter D. Kaufman, Poor Charlie's Almanack, p.477.
903   "Bad Judgments, Common Causes", Charles Munger speech at the California Institute of Technology, February 17, 1992
904   The Psychology of Human Misjudgment, Peter D. Kaufman, Poor Charlie's Almanack, p.477.

905   The Psychology of Human Misjudgment, Talk at the Cambridge Center for Behavioral Studies, April 24, 1995.
906   The Psychology of Human Misjudgment, Peter D. Kaufman, Poor Charlie's Almanack, p.478.
907   Eyal Zamir, Loss Aversion: An Overview by Eyal Zamir, January 27, 2014, http://papers.ssrn.com/sol3/papers.cfm?abstract_id=1919642
908   See more on this in Daniel Kahneman & Jonathan Renshon, Hawkish Biases, https://www.princeton.edu/~kahneman/docs/Publications/Hawkish%20Biases.pdf
909   Warren Buffett meeting with University of Maryland MBA Students November 15, 2013, Notes by Professor David Kass, www.blogs.rhsmith.umd.edu/davidkass
910   Berkshire Hathaway annual meeting, 1995, Outstanding Investor Digest, August 10, 1995, p.6.
911   Hersh Shefrin, Beyond Greed and Fear: Understanding Behavioral Finance and the Psychology of Investing, Oxford University Press, 2002
912   Berkshire Hathaway annual meeting, 1995, Notes by author
913   Lecture at the University of Florida School of Business, October 15, 1998, Martin Lee
914   The Psychology of Human Misjudgment, Peter D. Kaufman, Poor Charlie's Almanack, p.479.
915   Janet Lowe, Damn Right: Behind the Scenes with Berkshire Hathaway Billionaire Charlie Munger, John Wiley & Sons, New York, 2000, p.36.
916   Lecture by Charles T. Munger to the students of Professor William Lazier at Stanford Law School, Outstanding Investor Digest, March 13, 1998, p.55.
917   Berkshire Hathaway Inc., 1994 Annual Report
918   "Bad Judgments, Common Causes", Charles Munger speech at the California Institute of Technology, February 17, 1992
919   Ibid.
920   The Psychology of Human Misjudgment, Talk at the Cambridge Center for Behavioral Studies, April 24, 1995.
921   Berkshire Hathaway annual meeting, 2015, Notes by author
922   Berkshire Hathaway annual meeting, 2001, Outstanding Investor Digest, Year End 2001 Edition, p.24.
923   Berkshire Hathaway Inc., 1987 Annual Report
924   Berkshire Hathaway annual meeting, 2012, Notes by author
925   Berkshire Hathaway annual meeting, 2010, Notes by author
926   1994 Lecture of The E. J. Faulkner Lecture Series, A Colloquium with University of Nebraska-Lincoln Students by Warren E. Buffett
927   Berkshire Hathaway annual meeting, 2000, Outstanding Investor Digest, OID.Com, continued from December 18, 2000 & Year End 2000 Editions
928   Peter D. Kaufman, Poor Charlie's Almanack, p.92.
929   Berkshire Hathaway annual meeting, 1993, Outstanding Investor Digest, June 30, 1993, pp.29-30.
930   Said by Charles T. Munger but source unknown
931   "What Buffett learned from Munger", CNN Money Video, November 7, 2013
932   Berkshire Hathaway annual meeting, 1991, Outstanding Investor Digest, May 24, 1991, p.34.
933   From the movie Horse Feathers (1932)
934   The Psychology of Human Misjudgment, Peter D. Kaufman, Poor Charlie's Almanack, p.377.
935   USC Gould School of Law Commencement Address, May 13, 2007, Peter D. Kaufman, Poor Charlie's Almanack, p.432.
936   Berkshire Hathaway annual meeting, 2008, Outstanding Investor Digest, August 31, 2008, p.18.
937   Ibid.
938   The Psychology of Human Misjudgment, Talk at the Cambridge Center for Behavioral Studies, April 24, 1995.
939   The Psychology of Human Misjudgment, Peter D. Kaufman, Poor Charlie's Almanack, pp.490-491.
940   Berkshire Hathaway annual meeting, 2014, Notes by author

941   The Psychology of Human Misjudgment, Peter D. Kaufman, Poor Charlie's Almanack, pp.450-451.
942   The Psychology of Human Misjudgment, Talk at the Cambridge Center for Behavioral Studies, April 24, 1995
943   Janet Lowe, Damn Right: Behind the Scenes with Berkshire Hathaway Billionaire Charlie Munger, John Wiley & Sons, New York, 2000, p.194.
944   USC Gould School of Law Commencement Address, May 13, 2007, Peter D. Kaufman, Poor Charlie's Almanack, p.432.
945   Janet Lowe, Damn Right: Behind the Scenes with Berkshire Hathaway Billionaire Charlie Munger, John Wiley & Sons, New York, 2000, p.194.
946   USC Gould School of Law Commencement Address, May 13, 2007, Peter D. Kaufman, Poor Charlie's Almanack, pp.432-433.
947   The Psychology of Human Misjudgment, Talk at the Cambridge Center for Behavioral Studies, April 24, 1995
948   The Psychology of Human Misjudgment, Peter D. Kaufman, Poor Charlie's Almanack, p.462.
949   Ibid., pp.462-463.
950   Berkshire Hathaway annual meeting, 2009, Notes by J.V. Bruni and Company, http://jvbruni.com/commentary.htm
951   Wesco Financial annual meeting, 2006, Notes by author
952   Wesco Financial annual meeting, 2007, Outstanding Investor Digest, February 29, 2008, p.52.
953   Johann, Wolfgang von Goethe, Die Leiden des jungen Werthers (The Sorrows of Young Werther), May 4, 1774-1787
954   Friedrich Nietzsche, Twilight of the Idols, or, How to Philosophize with a Hammer, 1888
955   Berkshire Hathaway annual meeting, 2014, Notes by Peter Boodell, Boodell & Company Capital Management
956   Unofficial transcript of Warren Buffett, Charlie Munger and Bill Gates appearing live with Becky Quick on CNBC's "Squawk Box," Monday, May 5, 2014, buffettwatch.cnbc.com
957   Berkshire Hathaway annual meeting, 2014, Notes by author
958   Berkshire Hathaway annual meeting, 2014, Notes by George Traganidis, www.thepracticalway.com
959   Berkshire Hathaway annual meeting, 2014, Notes by author
960   John Adams, The Works of John Adams, Second President of the United States, 1851, https://archive.org/details/worksofjohnadams06adam
961   Wesco Financial annual meeting, 2007, Outstanding Investor Digest, February 29, 2008, p.46.
962   Wesco Financial annual meeting, 2008, Notes by author
963   Peter D. Kaufman, Poor Charlie's Almanack, p.276.
964   Wesco Financial annual meeting, 2008, Notes by author
965   The Psychology of Human Misjudgment, Peter D. Kaufman, Poor Charlie's Almanack, p.478.
966   USC Gould School of Law Commencement Address, May 13, 2007, Peter D. Kaufman, Poor Charlie's Almanack, pp.429-430.
967   Wesco Financial annual meeting, 2007, Notes by Whitney Tilson, www.tilsonfunds.com
968   USC Gould School of Law Commencement Address, May 13, 2007, Peter D. Kaufman, Poor Charlie's Almanack, p.430.
969   Peter Medawar, Advice to a Young Scientist, Harpercollins Childrens Books, 1979
970   Lecture by Charles T. Munger to the students of Professor William Lazier at Stanford Law School, Outstanding Investor Digest, March 13, 1998, p.57.
971   Berkshire Hathaway annual meeting, 2012, Notes by author
972   "Interview with Henri Matisse" by Jacques Guenne, L'Art Vivant (15 September 1925), translated by Jack Flam in Matisse on Art (1995)
973   http://www-history.mcs.st-and.ac.uk/Quotations/Von_Neumann.html
974   Bertrand Russell, Mortals and Others (1931-35)
975   Wesco Financial annual meeting, 2002, Outstanding Investor Digest, December 31, 2002, p.36.
976   Peter D. Kaufman, Poor Charlie's Almanack, p.67.

977   Based on research by Fernbach, Rogers, Fox & Sloman, "Political Extremism is Supported by an Illusion of Understanding", Psychological Science OnlineFirst, April 25, 2013, pss.sagepub.com
978   "Warren Buffett Talks Business", Kenan-Flagler, PBSTV program produced by the University of North Carolina, Center for Public Television, Chapel Hill, October 1995 (VHS)
979   Lee Iacocca, Iacocca, Bantam Books, New York, 1984
980   Three Lectures by Warren Buffett to Notre Dame Faculty, MBA students and Undergraduate students, Spring 1991, Lightly edited by Whitney Tilson
981   Wesco Financial annual meeting, 1987, Outstanding Investor Digest, October 7, 1987, p.8.
982   Daniel C. Dennett, Intuition Pumps and other Tools for Thinking, Allen Lane, The Penguin Group, London, 2014
983   Albert Einstein, The Expanded Quotable Einstein, edited by Alice Calaprice, Princeton University Press, 2005 (an explanation of relativity Einstein told to his secretary Helen Dukas)
984   Katherine Graham, Personal History, New York, Vintage, 1998.
985   Said by Warren E. Buffett but source unknown and may not be original with him
986   "Epilog vid Magisterpromotionen i Lund 1820", https://en.wikiquote.org/wiki/Esaias_Tegn%C3%A9r
987   Lin Yutang, The Importance Of Living, Patterson Press, 2008
988   Douglas Hofstadter, I Am a Strange Loop, Basic Books, 2006
989   J.A. Wheeler, "Mercer Street and Other Memories", in Albert Einstein, His Influence on Physics, Philosophy and Politics, ed. P.C. Aichelburg and R.U. Sexl , Braunscheig: Vieweg, 1979
990   "STEVE JOBS: 'THERE'S SANITY RETURNING'" online-only version of a Q&A from Business Week, May 25, 1998
991   The Psychology of Human Misjudgment, Peter D. Kaufman, Poor Charlie's Almanack, pp.481-482.
992   "A Conversation With Charlie Munger", Charlie Munger Speaks to University of Michigan Students, September 14, 2010
993   Warren Buffett, Roundtable Discussion on Financial Disclosure and Auditor Oversight, March 4, 2002, www.sec.gov
994   Peter D. Kaufman, Poor Charlie's Almanack, p.373.
995   Wesco Financial annual meeting, 2001, Outstanding Investor Digest, OID.COM Edition, 2003, p.9.
996   Alice Schroeder, The Snowball: Warren Buffett and the Business of Life, Bloomsbury Publishing, London, 2008, p.778. Also by Bantam Books, a division of Penguin Random House LLC
997   The Psychology of Human Misjudgment, Peter D. Kaufman, Poor Charlie's Almanack, pp.481-482.
998   Wesco Financial annual meeting, 2000, Outstanding Investor Digest, December 18, 2000, p.51.
999   The Psychology of Human Misjudgment, Peter D. Kaufman, Poor Charlie's Almanack, p.482.
1000   Berkshire Hathaway annual meeting, 1999, Outstanding Investor Digest, December 31, 1999, p.52.
1001   Conversation with Charlie Munger, Pasadena Convention Center, July 1, 2011
1002   The Psychology of Human Misjudgment, Peter D. Kaufman, Poor Charlie's Almanack, p.481.
1003   Academic Economics: Strengths and Faults After Considering Interdisciplinary Needs, Herb Key Undergraduate Lecture, University of California, Santa Barbara, Economics Department, October 3, 2003, Peter D. Kaufman, Poor Charlie's Almanack, p.409.
1004   Conversation with Charlie Munger, Pasadena Convention Center, July 1, 2011, Notes by Shane Parrish, Farnam Street
1005   Wesco Financial annual meeting, 2008, Outstanding Investor Digest, August 31, 2008, p.36.
1006   Financial Crisis Inquiry Commission Staff Audiotape of Interview with Warren Buffett, May 26, 2010, p.17. www.santangelsreview.com
1007   Wesco Financial annual meeting, 2007, Notes by Whitney Tilson, www.tilsonfunds.com
1008   Peter D. Kaufman, Poor Charlie's Almanack, pp.276-277.
1009   "A Conversation With Charlie Munger", Charlie Munger Speaks to University of Michigan Students, September 14, 2010
1010   Daily Journal Corporation annual meeting, 2015, Notes by Shane Parrish, Farnam Street
1011   The Psychology of Human Misjudgment, Peter D. Kaufman, Poor Charlie's Almanack, p.450.

1012   USC Gould School of Law Commencement Address, May 13, 2007, Peter D. Kaufman, Poor Charlie's Almanack, p.433.
1013   "A Conversation With Charlie Munger", Charlie Munger Speaks to University of Michigan Students, September 14, 2010
1014   Ibid.
1015   The Psychology of Human Misjudgment, Peter D. Kaufman, Poor Charlie's Almanack, p.450.
1016   Ibid.
1017   Wesco Financial annual meeting, 2001, Notes by author
1018   Warren Buffett's 'Ask Warren' appearance on CNBC's Squawk Box, March 2, 2015, cnbc.com
1019   "Warren Buffett on What's Next in the Payment Industry", Interview by Business Wire CEO Cathy Baron Tamraz, October 17, 2009
1020   Charles Munger advice to Lawrence McDonald, "How to Fix the Problem by the Smartest Guy I've Ever Met", www.lawrencegmcdonald
1021   Wesco Financial Inc., 1990 Annual Report
1022   The Psychology of Human Misjudgment, Peter D. Kaufman, Poor Charlie's Almanack, p.456.
1023   Berkshire Hathaway, Press Conference May 6, 2007, Notes by The Motley Fool
1024   The "Characters" of Jean de La Bruyère, Scribner & Welford, 1885
1025   Wesco Financial annual meeting, 2010, Notes by author
1026   Wesco Financial annual meeting, 2002, Outstanding Investor Digest, December 31, 2002, p.25.
1027   Wesco Financial Inc., 1990 Annual Report
1028   Berkshire Hathaway annual meeting, 1993, Outstanding Investor Digest, June 30, 1993, p.29.
1029   Thomas Sowell, Knowledge and Decisions, Basic Books, 1996
1030   Berkshire Hathaway Inc., 2006 Annual Report
1031   Berkshire Hathaway Inc., 1994 Annual Report
1032   Wesco Financial annual meeting, 2005, Notes by author
1033   Berkshire Hathaway Inc., 1999 Annual Report
1034   Berkshire Hathaway annual meeting, 2004, Notes by Whitney Tilson, www.tilsonfunds.com
1035   Ibid.
1036   Berkshire Hathaway annual meeting, 2007, Notes by Whitney Tilson, www.tilsonfunds.com
1037   Berkshire Hathaway Inc., 2006 Annual Report
1038   The Psychology of Human Misjudgment, Peter D. Kaufman, Poor Charlie's Almanack, p.451.
1039   Financial Crisis Inquiry Commission Staff Audiotape of Interview with Warren Buffett, May 26, 2010, p.20. www.santangelsreview.com
1040   Daily Journal Corporation annual meeting, 2015, Notes by Shane Parrish, Farnam Street
1041   Berkshire Hathaway Inc., 1994 Annual Report
1042   Financial Crisis Inquiry Commission Staff Audiotape of Interview with Warren Buffett, May 26, 2010, p.10. www.santangelsreview.com
1043   2009 Berkshire Hathaway Press Conference, May 3, 2009, Notes by Philip Durell, The Motley Fool & added and edited by Robert Miles
1044   "Warren Buffett on What's Next in the Payment Industry", Interview by Business Wire CEO Cathy Baron Tamraz, October 17, 2009
1045   Financial Crisis Inquiry Commission Staff Audiotape of Interview with Warren Buffett, May 26, 2010, p.16. www.santangelsreview.com
1046   Charlie Munger at Harvard-Westlake School January 19, 2010, www.santangelsreview.com
1047   Berkshire Hathaway annual meeting, 2010, Notes by author
1048   Berkshire Hathaway annual meeting, 1993, Outstanding Investor Digest, June 30, 1993, p.29.
1049   Wesco Financial annual meeting, 1993, Outstanding Investor Digest, June 30, 1993, p.20.
1050   Berkshire Hathaway annual meeting, 2010, Notes by author
1051   Warren Buffett, Roundtable Discussion on Financial Disclosure and Auditor Oversight, March 4, 2002, www.sec.gov
1052   Financial Crisis Inquiry Commission Staff Audiotape of Interview with Warren Buffett, May 26, 2010, p.3. www.santangelsreview.com

1053 "A Conversation With Charlie Munger", Charlie Munger Speaks to University of Michigan Students, September 14, 2010

1054 Berkshire Hathaway, Press Conference, 2010, Notes by The Motley Fool

1055 The Psychology of Human Misjudgment, Peter D. Kaufman, Poor Charlie's Almanack, p.456.

1056 Daily Journal Corporation annual meeting, 2014, Notes by Shane Parrish, Farnam Street

1057 Academic Economics: Strengths and Faults After Considering Interdisciplinary Needs, Herb Key Undergraduate Lecture, University of California, Santa Barbara, Economics Department, October 3, 2003, Peter D. Kaufman, Poor Charlie's Almanack, p.410.

1058 Berkshire Hathaway annual meeting, 2003, Outstanding Investor Digest, Year End 2003 Edition, p.41.

1059 Academic Economics: Strengths and Faults After Considering Interdisciplinary Needs, Herb Key Undergraduate Lecture, University of California, Santa Barbara, Economics Department, October 3, 2003, Peter D. Kaufman, Poor Charlie's Almanack, pp.410-411.

1060 Ibid. p.51.

1061 Wesco Financial annual meeting, 2001, Notes by Whitney Tilson, www.tilsonfunds.com

1062 The Psychology of Human Misjudgment, Peter D. Kaufman, Poor Charlie's Almanack, p.476.

1063 Wesco Financial annual meeting, 2008, Outstanding Investor Digest, August 31, 2008, p.35.

1064 Berkshire Hathaway annual meeting, 2005, Outstanding Investor Digest, March 9, 2006, p.50.

1065 Wesco Financial annual meeting, 1995, Outstanding Investor Digest, August 10, 1995, p.62

1066 Berkshire Hathaway, Press Conference, 2010, Notes by The Motley Fool

1067 Lecture at the University of Florida School of Business, October 15, 1998, Martin Lee

1068 Daily Journal Corporation annual meeting, 2013, Notes by author

1069 Lecture at the University of Florida School of Business, October 15, 1998, Martin Lee

1070 William Osler, Osler's A Way of Life and Other Addresses, with Commentary and Annotations Duke University Press Books; 1 edition, 2001

1071 Charlie Munger at Harvard-Westlake School January 19, 2010, www.santangelsreview.com

1072 Ibid.

1073 Berkshire Hathaway, Press Conference, 2007, Notes by The Motley Fool

1074 Warren Buffett referring to Charles Munger, notes from Buffett meeting with students from Emory and 5 other business schools, February 6, 2009, www.undergroundvalue.blogspot.com

1075 Berkshire Hathaway annual meeting, 2015, Notes by author

1076 Lecture at the University of Florida School of Business, October 15, 1998, Martin Lee

1077 From the BBC sitcom Blackadder, episode Blackadder the Third

1078 Berkshire Hathaway annual meeting, 2005, Notes by Whitney Tilson, www.tilsonfunds.com

1079 Lecture at the University of Florida School of Business, October 15, 1998, Martin Lee

1080 Wesco Financial annual meeting, 2005, Notes by Whitney Tilson, www.tilsonfunds.com

1081 Lecture at the University of Florida School of Business, October 15, 1998, Martin Lee

1082 Berkshire Hathaway annual meeting, 1999, Outstanding Investor Digest, December 31, 1999, p.56.

1083 Wesco Financial annual meeting, 2006, Notes by author

1084 Lecture at the University of Florida School of Business, October 15, 1998, Martin Lee

1085 Berkshire Hathaway Inc., 2014 Annual Report

1086 Transcript of Warren Buffett's 'Ask Warren' appearance on CNBC's Squawk Box, March 1, 2010, buffettwatch.cnbc.com

1087 Berkshire Hathaway annual meeting, 2007, Notes by Whitney Tilson, www.tilsonfunds.com

1088 Berkshire Hathaway Inc., 1996 Annual Report

1089 Warren Buffett meeting with University of Maryland MBA Students November 15, 2013, Notes by Professor David Kass

1090 Transcript of Warren Buffett's 'Ask Warren' appearance on CNBC's Squawk Box, March 1, 2010, buffettwatch.cnbc.com

1091 Berkshire Hathaway annual meeting, 2005, Outstanding Investor Digest, March 9, 2006, p.50.

1092 Report of the PRESIDENTIAL COMMISSION on the Space Shuttle Challenger Accident, Volume 2: Appendix F - Personal Observations on Reliability of Shuttle by R. P. Feynman, http://history.nasa.gov/rogersrep/v2appf.htm

1093 Berkshire Hathaway Inc., 2010 Annual Report

1094   http://quoteinvestigator.com/2013/04/19/brains-beauty/

1095   Notes from Buffett meeting with students from Emory and 5 other business schools, February 6, 2009, www.undergroundvalue.blogspot.com

1096   The Entire Memoirs Of Cardinal De Retz, Kessinger Publishing, 2010

1097   Transcript of Warren Buffett's 'Ask Warren' appearance on CNBC's Squawk Box, March 1, 2010, buffettwatch.cnbc.com

1098   Berkshire Hathaway annual meeting, 2008, Outstanding Investor Digest, August 31, 2008, p.13.

1099   Notes from the Meeting Dr. George Athanassakos and Ivey MBA and HBA students had with Mr. Warren Buffett, Omaha January 31, 2014, The Ben Graham Center for Value Investing

1100   Berkshire Hathaway, Press Conference May 6, 2007, Notes by The Motley Fool

1101   Berkshire Hathaway Inc., 1994 Annual Report

1102   Berkshire Hathaway annual meeting, 2000, Outstanding Investor Digest, OID.Com, continued from December 18, 2000 & Year End 2000 Editions

1103   Adapted from an example in Mahoney David and Restak Richard, The Longevity Strategy: How to Live to 100 using the Brain-Body Connection, John Wiley & Sons, Inc., New York, 1998, p.41.

1104   Wesco Financial annual meeting, 1998, Outstanding Investor Digest, December 29, 1998, p.45.

1105   Kai Ryssdal, "Warren Buffett on Jamie Dimon as Treasury Secretary, the fiscal cliff, and taxes", April 29, 2015, http://www.marketplace.org/topics/business/big-book/warren-buffett-jamie-dimon-treasury-secretary-fiscal-cliff-and-taxes

1106   Berkshire Hathaway annual meeting, 1998, Outstanding Investor Digest, September 24, 1998, p.51.

1107   Wesco Financial annual meeting, 2010, Outstanding Investor Digest, August 9, 2010, p.40.

1108   A Conversation with Charlie Munger at Caltech, DuBridge Distinguished Lecture, March 11, 2008, DVD

1109   Berkshire Hathaway annual meeting, 2005, Outstanding Investor Digest, March 9, 2006, p.34.

1110   Berkshire Hathaway Inc., 1984 Annual Report

1111   Berkshire Hathaway annual meeting, 1998, Outstanding Investor Digest, September 24, 1998, p.51.

1112   Warren Buffett speech to University of Georgia students, Terry College of Business, 2001, GuruFocus, http://www.nasdaq.com/article/warren-buffett-speech-to-university-of-georgia-students-part-1-cm238914

1113   Berkshire Hathaway annual meeting, 1993, Outstanding Investor Digest, June 30, 1993, p.24.

1114   Warren Buffett speech to University of Georgia students, Terry College of Business, 2001, GuruFocus

1115   Berkshire Hathaway annual meeting, 2009, Outstanding Investor Digest, OID.COM Feature, p.25.

1116   Berkshire Hathaway annual meeting, 2000, Notes by author

1117   Berkshire Hathaway annual meeting 1994, Outstanding Investor Digest, June 23, 1994, p.20.

1118   Berkshire Hathaway annual meeting, 2013, Notes by Peter Boodell, Boodell & Company Capital Management

1119   Berkshire Hathaway annual meeting, 2015, Notes by author

1120   Berkshire Hathaway annual meeting, 2013, Notes by Peter Boodell, Boodell & Company Capital Management

1121   Daily Journal Corporation annual meeting, 2015, Notes by Shane Parrish, Farnam Street

1122   Warren Buffett speech to University of Georgia students, Terry College of Business, 2001, GuruFocus

1123   Berkshire Hathaway annual meeting 1994, Outstanding Investor Digest, June 23, 1994, p.26.

1124   Warren Buffett, A tribute to Ben Graham, December 6, 1994, Outstanding Investor Digest, May 5, 1995, p.7.

1125   Transcript of Warren Buffett's 'Ask Warren' appearance on CNBC's Squawk Box, March 4, 2013, buffettwatch.cnbc.com

1126   Berkshire Hathaway Inc., 2011 Annual Report

1127   Berkshire Hathaway Inc., 2008 Annual Report
1128   Three Lectures by Warren Buffett to Notre Dame Faculty, MBA students and Undergraduate students, Spring 1991, Lightly edited by Whitney Tilson
1129   Berkshire Hathaway Inc., 1989 Annual Report
1130   Lecture at the University of Florida School of Business, October 15, 1998, Martin Lee
1131   Berkshire Hathaway Inc., 1987 Annual Report
1132   Berkshire Hathaway Inc., 2012 Annual Report
1133   Janet Lowe, Damn Right: Behind the Scenes with Berkshire Hathaway Billionaire Charlie Munger, John Wiley & Sons, New York, 2000, p.78.
1134   Berkshire Hathaway annual meeting, 2013, Notes by Peter Boodell, Boodell & Company Capital Management
1135   Berkshire Hathaway Inc., 2014 Annual Report
1136   Warren Buffett Talks Philanthropy with Bank of America CEO, September 19, 2013, Georgetown University, www.georgetown.edu
1137   Berkshire Hathaway Inc., 1996 Annual Report
1138   Berkshire Hathaway annual meeting, 2008, Outstanding Investor Digest, August 31, 2008, p.16.
1139   Berkshire Hathaway annual meeting, 1990, Outstanding Investor Digest, May 31 1990, p.25.
1140   Berkshire Hathaway Inc., 2000 Annual Report
1141   Berkshire Hathaway annual meeting, 1990, Outstanding Investor Digest, May 31 1990, p.25.
1142   Berkshire Hathaway annual meeting, 2004, Outstanding Investor Digest, December 31, 2004, p.32.
1143   Berkshire Hathaway annual meeting, 2004, Notes by Whitney Tilson, www.tilsonfunds.com
1144   Ibid.
1145   Berkshire Hathaway annual meeting, 2007, Notes by author
1146   Berkshire Hathaway annual meeting, 2006, Notes by Whitney Tilson, www.tilsonfunds.com
1147   Berkshire Hathaway, Press Conference, 2002, Notes by Selena Maranjian, The Motley Fool
1148   Daily Journal Corporation annual meeting, 2015, Notes by Shane Parrish, Farnam Street
1149   Berkshire Hathaway Inc., 1985, Annual Report
1150   Peter D. Kaufman, Poor Charlie's Almanack, p.61.
1151   Berkshire Hathaway Inc., 1993, Annual Report
1152   Daily Journal Corporation annual meeting, 2014, Notes by Shane Parrish, Farnam Street
1153   Janet Lowe, Damn Right: Behind the Scenes with Berkshire Hathaway Billionaire Charlie Munger, John Wiley & Sons, New York, 2000, p.36.
1154   Wesco Financial Inc., 1996 Annual Report
1155   Wesco Financial annual meeting, 2003, Notes by Whitney Tilson, www.tilsonfunds.com
1156   Berkshire Hathaway annual meeting, 2008, Outstanding Investor Digest, August 31, 2008, p.10.
1157   Three Lectures by Warren Buffett to Notre Dame Faculty, MBA students and Undergraduate students, Spring 1991, Lightly edited by Whitney Tilson
1158   Janet Lowe, Damn Right: Behind the Scenes with Berkshire Hathaway Billionaire Charlie Munger, John Wiley & Sons, New York, 2000, p.118.
1159   Daily Journal Corporation annual meeting, 2014, Notes by Shane Parrish, Farnam Street
1160   Ibid.
1161   Jason Zweig, "Charles Munger: Secrets of Buffett's Success?", The Wall Street Journal, Sept. 12, 2014
1162   Said by Warren E. Buffett but source unknown and may not be original with him
1163   Berkshire Hathaway annual meeting, 1998, Notes by author
1164   Anupreeta Das, "Buffett's Crisis- Lending Haul Reaches $10 Billion", The Wall Street Journal, Oct. 6, 2013
1165   Berkshire Hathaway Inc., 1990 Annual Report
1166   Charles Munger interview by CNBC, May 4, 2012, cnbc.com
1167   Berkshire Hathaway Inc., 2011 Annual Report
1168   Berkshire Hathaway Inc., 2013 Annual Report
1169   Berkshire Hathaway Inc., 1995 Annual Report
1170   Berkshire Hathaway Inc., 2007 Annual Report
1171   Charlie Rose interview: "An Exclusive Conversation with Warren Buffett", May 10, 2007

1172   "Warren Buffett on What's Next in the Payment Industry", Interview by Business Wire CEO Cathy Baron Tamraz, October 17, 2009
1173   Berkshire Hathaway Inc., 2013 Annual Report
1174   Warren Buffett speech to University of Georgia, Terry College of Business students, January 30, 2007, Sham Gad, www.gurufocus.com/news/4434
1175   Daily Journal Corporation annual meeting, 2014, Notes by Shane Parrish, Farnam Street
1176   Jesse Livermore, How to Trade In Stocks , McGraw-Hill Education, 2006
1177   Anthony Bianco, "Homespun Wisdom from the 'Oracle of Omaha'", July 5, 1999, BusinessWeek Online
1178   Warren Buffett meeting students from the University of Pennsylvania's Wharton School April 2008
1179   Berkshire Hathaway Inc., 1986 Annual Report
1180   Ibid.
1181   Berkshire Hathaway Inc., 1988 Annual Report
1182   Berkshire Hathaway Inc., 1990 Annual Report
1183   Wesco Financial annual meeting, 2001, Outstanding Investor Digest, OID.COM Edition, 2003, p.6.
1184   Berkshire Hathaway Inc., 2000 Annual Report
1185   Berkshire Hathaway Inc., 2014 Annual Report
1186   Daily Journal Corporation annual meeting, 2013, Notes by Shane Parrish, Farnam Street
1187   Berkshire Hathaway annual meeting, 2003, Outstanding Investor Digest, Year End 2003 Edition, p.43.
1188   Peter D. Kaufman, Poor Charlie's Almanack, p.73.
1189   Berkshire Hathaway Inc., 1993 Annual Report
1190   Berkshire Hathaway Inc., 1992 Annual Report
1191   Wesco Financial Inc., 1992 Annual Report
1192   Benjamin Graham, The Intelligent Investor: A Book of Practical Counsel, Harper & Row Publishers, 1986
1193   Berkshire Hathaway annual meeting, 2015, Notes by author
1194   Notes from the Meeting Dr. George Athanassakos and Ivey MBA and HBA students had with Mr. Warren Buffett, Omaha January 31, 2014, The Ben Graham Center for Value Investing
1195   Berkshire Hathaway Inc., 2014 Annual Report
1196   The Superinvestors of Graham-and-Doddsville, Hermes, The Columbia Business School Magazine, 1984.
1197   Wesco Financial annual meeting, 2008, Outstanding Investor Digest, August 31, 2008, p.46.
1198   Daily Journal Corporation annual meeting, 2013, Notes by Shane Parrish, Farnam Street
1199   The Psychology of Human Misjudgment, Peter D. Kaufman, Poor Charlie's Almanack, pp.479-480.
1200   Daily Journal Corporation annual meeting, 2013, Notes by Shane Parrish, Farnam Street
1201   Daily Journal Corporation annual meeting, 2014, Notes by Shane Parrish, Farnam Street
1202   Daily Journal Corporation annual meeting, 2013, Notes by Shane Parrish, Farnam Street
1203   Ibid.
1204   The Ground Rules from Buffett Partnership Letter, January 18, 1963
1205   Berkshire Hathaway Inc., 1983 Annual Report
1206   Berkshire Hathaway annual meeting, 2004, Outstanding Investor Digest, December 31, 2004, p.33.
1207   Transcript of Warren Buffett's 'Ask Warren' appearance on CNBC's Squawk Box, March 4, 2013, buffettwatch.cnbc.com
1208   Berkshire Hathaway Inc., 1992 Annual Report
1209   Berkshire Hathaway annual meeting, 2000, Outstanding Investor Digest, December 18, 2000, pp.39-40.
1210   Berkshire Hathaway annual meeting, 1998, Outstanding Investor Digest, September 24, 1998, p.36.
1211   Berkshire Hathaway annual meeting, 1995, Answer to author question
1212   Transcript from visit in India, NDTV Studios, April 2011, Notes by Shane Parrish, Farnam Street
1213   Berkshire Hathaway annual meeting, 1997, Outstanding Investor Digest, August 8, 1997, p.14.
1214   Berkshire Hathaway Inc., 2014 Annual Report

1215   Berkshire Hathaway annual meeting, 1998, Outstanding Investor Digest, September 24, 1998, p.36.
1216   Berkshire Hathaway Inc., 1992 Annual Report
1217   Lecture at the University of Florida School of Business, October 15, 1998, Martin Lee
1218   Warren Buffett speech to University of Georgia students, Terry College of Business, 2001, GuruFocus
1219   1994 Lecture of The E. J. Faulkner Lecture Series, A Colloquium with University of Nebraska-Lincoln Students by Warren E. Buffett
1220   Berkshire Hathaway Inc., 1996 Annual Report
1221   Berkshire Hathaway Inc., 1987 Annual Report
1222   Berkshire Hathaway Inc., 1996 Annual Report
1223   Berkshire Hathaway annual meeting, 2006, Notes by Whitney Tilson, www.tilsonfunds.com
1224   Berkshire Hathaway annual meeting, 2009, Outstanding Investor Digest, OID.COM Feature, p.26.
1225   "Buffett & Gates on Success", KCTS/Seattle, May 1998, Transcript p.14.
1226   Courier Express v. Evening News, testimony of Buffett, pp. 44-45, seen in Roger Lowenstein, Buffett: The Making of an American Capitalist, New York: Random House, 1995, New York, p.211.
1227   Berkshire Hathaway annual meeting, 2008, Outstanding Investor Digest, August 31, 2008, p.23.
1228   Investment Practices of Leading Charitable Foundations, Speech at Miramar Sheraton Hotel, Santa Monica, CA, on October 14, 1998 to a meeting of the Foundation Financial Officer Group'
1229   Warren Buffett in an interview with Ted Koppel on ABC's Nightline, March 2, 1999
1230   Jim Rasmussen, "Buffett Talks Strategy with Students," Omaha World-Herald, January 2, 1994
1231   Berkshire Hathaway annual meeting, 1997, Outstanding Investor Digest, August 8, 1997, p.16.
1232   Berkshire Hathaway Inc., 1995 Annual Report
1233   Berkshire Hathaway Inc., 2007 Annual Report
1234   Three Lectures by Warren Buffett to Notre Dame Faculty, MBA students and Undergraduate students, Spring 1991, Lightly edited by Whitney Tilson
1235   Warren Buffett meeting with University of Maryland MBA Students November 15, 2013, Notes by Professor David Kass
1236   "Investing in Equity Markets", Transcript of a seminar held at Columbia University Business School, March 13, 1985, seen in The Midas Touch by John Train, Harper & Row, New York, 1987, p.20.
1237   Berkshire Hathaway Inc., 2007 Annual Report
1238   Berkshire Hathaway annual meeting, 1995, Outstanding Investor Digest, August 10, 1995, p.13.
1239   Berkshire Hathaway annual meeting, 2013, Notes by author
1240   Berkshire Hathaway annual meeting, 2000, Notes by Whitney Tilson, www.tilsonfunds.com
1241   Transcript from Warren Buffett meeting with Wharton students, February 17, 2006, Notes by Timothy Viles & Aaron Byrd, seen in www.rbcpa.com
1242   Berkshire Hathaway annual meeting, 1995, Outstanding Investor Digest, August 10, 1995, p.13.
1243   Lecture at the University of Florida School of Business, October 15, 1998, Martin Lee
1244   Addison Wiggin & Kate Incontrera, I.O.U.S.A.: One Nation. Under Stress. In Debt., New Jersey, John Wiley & Sons, 2008
1245   Berkshire Hathaway annual meeting, 2004, Outstanding Investor Digest, December 31, 2004, p.38.
1246   Adam Lashinsky , "'Banking is a very good business unless you do dumb things,' says Wells Fargo's largest shareholder", Fortune Magazine, April 24, 2009
1247   Berkshire Hathaway annual meeting, 2009, Notes by author
1248   Berkshire Hathaway annual meeting, 2009, Outstanding Investor Digest, OID.COM Feature, p.7.
1249   Transcript of Warren Buffett's 'Ask Warren' appearance on CNBC's Squawk Box, March 1, 2010, buffettwatch.cnbc.com
1250   Warren Buffett Letter to George D. Young, National Indemnity Company, July 22, 1975

1251   Lecture at the University of Florida School of Business, October 15, 1998, Martin Lee
1252   Berkshire Hathaway annual meeting, 2004, Outstanding Investor Digest, December 31, 2004, p.38.
1253   Berkshire Hathaway Inc., 2013 Annual Report
1254   Lecture at the University of Florida School of Business, October 15, 1998, Martin Lee
1255   Berkshire Hathaway annual meeting, 2009, Outstanding Investor Digest, OID.COM Feature, p.30.
1256   Berkshire Hathaway Inc., 2014 Annual Report
1257   Berkshire Hathaway Inc., 2008 Annual Report
1258   Berkshire Hathaway Inc., 1990 Annual Report
1259   Berkshire Hathaway Inc., 1996 Annual Report
1260   Berkshire Hathaway annual meeting, 2000, Outstanding Investor Digest, OID.Com, continued from December 18, 2000 & Year End 2000 Editions
1261   Ibid.
1262   Berkshire Hathaway Inc., 1983 Annual Report
1263   "Warren Buffett on What's Next in the Payment Industry", Interview by Business Wire CEO Cathy Baron Tamraz, October 17, 2009
1264   Berkshire Hathaway inc., 2006 Annual Report
1265   Michael Bergdahl, What I learned from Sam Walton: How to compete and thrive in a Wal-Mart world, Wiley, 2004
1266   Berkshire Hathaway annual meeting, 2015, Notes by author
1267   Wesco Financial annual meeting, 2005, Notes by Whitney Tilson, www.tilsonfunds.com
1268   Daily Journal Corporation annual Meeting 2010, Notes by author
1269   Berkshire Hathaway inc., 2005 Annual Report
1270   Daily Journal Corporation annual meeting, 2015, Notes by Shane Parrish, Farnam Street
1271   Financial Crisis Inquiry Commission Staff Audiotape of Interview with Warren Buffett, May 26, 2010, p.1. www.santangelsreview.com
1272   On letterhead of the Philadelphia Inquirer to Mr. Eugene Miller, New York, www.historyforsale.com
1273   Three Lectures by Warren Buffett to Notre Dame Faculty, MBA students and Undergraduate students, Spring 1991, Lightly edited by Whitney Tilson
1274   Berkshire Hathaway annual meeting, 2009, Outstanding Investor Digest, OID.COM Feature, p.33.
1275   Berkshire Hathaway Inc., 1990 Annual Report
1276   Berkshire Hathaway Inc., 2006 Annual Report
1277   Daily Journal Corporation annual meeting, 2013, Notes by Shane Parrish, Farnam Street
1278   Berkshire Hathaway Inc., 2012 Annual Report
1279   Berkshire Hathaway Inc., 2014 Annual Report
1280   Berkshire Hathaway Inc., 2009 Annual Report
1281   Notes from the Meeting Dr. George Athanassakos and Ivey MBA and HBA students had with Mr. Warren Buffett, Omaha February 27, 2015, The Ben Graham Center for Value Investing
1282   Wesco Financial annual meeting, 2008, Outstanding Investor Digest, August 31, 2008, p.43.
1283   Berkshire Hathaway Inc., 2014 Annual Report
1284   Berkshire Hathaway annual meeting, 2000, Outstanding Investor Digest, December 18, 2000, p.42.
1285   Berkshire Hathaway annual meeting, 2005, Outstanding Investor Digest, March 9, 2006, p.60.
1286   Berkshire Hathaway Inc., 1991 Annual Report
1287   Three Lectures by Warren Buffett to Notre Dame Faculty, MBA students and Undergraduate students, Spring 1991, Lightly edited by Whitney Tilson
1288   Ibid.
1289   Notes from the Meeting Dr. George Athanassakos and Ivey MBA and HBA students had with Mr. Warren Buffett, Omaha March 30, 2012, The Ben Graham Center for Value Investing
1290   Transcript from visit in India, NDTV Studios, April 2011, Notes by Shane Parrish, Farnam Street
1291   Lecture at the University of Florida School of Business, October 15, 1998, Martin Lee
1292   Berkshire Hathaway Inc., 2005 Annual Report
1293   Berkshire Hathaway annual meeting, 2004, Notes by Whitney Tilson, www.tilsonfunds.com

1294   Transcript from visit in India, NDTV Studios, April 2011, Notes by Shane Parrish, Farnam Street

1295   Wesco Financial annual meeting, 2008, Outstanding Investor Digest, August 31, 2008, p.40.

1296   The Superinvestors of Graham-and-Doddsville, Hermes, The Columbia Business School Magazine, 1984.

1297   Berkshire Hathaway Inc., 1994 Annual Report

1298   Berkshire Hathaway annual meeting, 1999, How to Pick Stocks like Warren Buffett, Timothy Vick, McGraw Hill, 2001

1299   Berkshire Hathaway annual meeting, 2013, Notes by Peter Boodell, Boodell & Company Capital Management

1300   Carol J. Loomis, "Mr. Buffett on the Stock Market", Fortune Magazine, November 22, 1999, a Warren Buffett speech converted to an article by Carol J. Loomis

1301   Warren Buffett, lecture at Stanford Law School, March 23, 1990, Outstanding Investor Digest, April 18, 1990, p.14.

1302   Warren Buffett speech to University of Georgia students, Terry College of Business, 2001, GuruFocus

1303   Ibid.

1304   Berkshire Hathaway Inc., 2009 Annual Report

1305   Ibid.

1306   Carol J. Loomis, "Mr. Buffett on the Stock Market", Fortune Magazine, November 22, 1999, a Warren Buffett speech converted to an article by Carol J. Loomis

1307   Warren Buffett from a speech at the Emory Business School as reported in, "Track record is everything", Across the Board, October 1991, p.63

1308   Berkshire Hathaway annual meeting, 1996, Notes by author

1309   "An Evening with Warren Buffett", Warren Buffett Q&A with the Oquirrh Club, October 2003

1310   Notes from the Meeting Dr. George Athanassakos and Ivey MBA and HBA students had with Mr. Warren Buffett, Omaha March 31, 2008, The Ben Graham Center for Value Investing

1311   Lecture at the University of Florida School of Business, October 15, 1998, Martin Lee

1312   Berkshire Hathaway annual meeting, 2012, Notes by author

1313   Berkshire Hathaway annual meeting, 2014, Notes by author

1314   Berkshire Hathaway annual meeting, 2013, Notes by author

1315   Warren Buffett speech to University of Georgia students, Terry College of Business, 2001, GuruFocus

1316   Berkshire Hathaway annual meeting, 1990, Outstanding Investor Digest, May 31 1990, p.25.

1317   Berkshire Hathaway annual meeting, 2014, Notes by author

1318   Berkshire Hathaway annual meeting, 1993, Outstanding Investor Digest, June 30, 1993, p.34.

1319   Berkshire Hathaway Inc., 1991 Annual Report

1320   Berkshire Hathaway annual meeting, 2009, Outstanding Investor Digest, OID.COM Feature, p.22.

1321   "Investing in Equity Markets", Transcript of a seminar held at Columbia University Business School, March 13, 1985, seen in The Midas Touch by John Train, Harper & Row, New York, 1987, pp.19-20.

1322   Berkshire Hathaway Inc., 1991 Annual Report

1323   Berkshire Hathaway Inc., 2007 Annual Report

1324   Berkshire Hathaway Inc., 1980 Annual Report

1325   Berkshire Hathaway Inc., 1989 Annual Report

1326   Berkshire Hathaway annual meeting, 2015, Notes by author

1327   Berkshire Hathaway Inc., 1989 Annual Report

1328   Berkshire Hathaway Inc., 2014 Annual Report

1329   Berkshire Hathaway Inc., 1989 Annual Report

1330   Berkshire Hathaway Inc., 2004 Annual Report

1331   Berkshire Hathaway annual meeting, 1997, Outstanding Investor Digest, August 8, 1997, p.5.

1332   An Evening with Warren Buffett", Warren Buffett Q&A with the Oquirrh Club, October 2003

1333   Warren Buffett meeting with University of Maryland MBA Students November 15, 2013, Notes by Professor David Kass
1334   Lecture at the University of Florida School of Business, October 15, 1998, Martin Lee
1335   Berkshire Hathaway annual meeting, 1997, Outstanding Investor Digest, August 8, 1997, p.5.
1336   Warren Buffett meeting with University of Maryland MBA Students November 15, 2013, Notes by Professor David Kass
1337   Lecture at the University of Florida School of Business, October 15, 1998, Martin Lee
1338   Berkshire Hathaway annual meeting, 1996, Outstanding Investor Digest, August 8, 1996 p.30.
1339   Berkshire Hathaway annual meeting, 2000, Outstanding Investor Digest, December 18, 2000, p.43.
1340   Wesco Financial annual meeting, 1996, Outstanding Investor Digest, August 8, 1996, p.62.
1341   Berkshire Hathaway Inc., 2009 Annual Report
1342   Berkshire Hathaway, Press Conference May 6, 2007, Notes by The Motley Fool
1343   Berkshire Hathaway annual meeting, 1994, Outstanding Investor Digest, June 23, 1994, p.27.
1344   Berkshire Hathaway annual meeting, 1998, Outstanding Investor Digest, September 24, 1998, p.36.
1345   Berkshire Hathaway Inc., 2007 Annual Report
1346   Ibid.
1347   Berkshire Hathaway Inc., 2009 Annual Report
1348   Berkshire Hathaway annual meeting, 2009, Outstanding Investor Digest, OID.COM Feature, p.14.
1349   Berkshire Hathaway annual meeting, 1998, Outstanding Investor Digest, September 24, 1998, p.38.
1350   Berkshire Hathaway annual meeting, 2013, Notes by author
1351   Berkshire Hathaway Inc., 2007 Annual Report
1352   Warren Buffett speech to University of Georgia, Terry College of Business students, January 30, 2007, Sham Gad, www.gurufocus.com/news/4434
1353   Berkshire Hathaway Inc., 1990 Annual Report
1354   Lecture at the University of Florida School of Business, October 15, 1998, Martin Lee
1355   Berkshire Hathaway Inc., 2007 Annual Report
1356   Berkshire Hathaway Inc., 1987 Annual Report
1357   Daily Journal Corporation annual meeting, 2015, Notes by Shane Parrish, Farnam Street
1358   Berkshire Hathaway Inc., 2000 Annual Report
1359   Wesco Financial annual meeting, 1994, Outstanding Investor Digest, June 23, 1994, p.12.
1360   Berkshire Hathaway Inc., 1980 Annual Report
1361   Warren Buffett quoted in Andy Kilpatrick, Of Permanent Value, 2004
1362   Berkshire Hathaway annual meeting, 1998, Outstanding Investor Digest, September 24, 1998, pp.36-37.
1363   Berkshire Hathaway Inc., 1993 Annual Report
1364   Berkshire Hathaway, Press Conference May 6, 2007, Notes by The Motley Fool
1365   Wesco Financial annual meeting, 1994, Outstanding Investor Digest, June 23, 1994, p.12.
1366   Daily Journal Corporation annual meeting, 2015, Notes by Shane Parrish, Farnam Street
1367   Students from Tuck School of Business at Dartmouth meet Warren Buffett, 2004, http://www.thinkfn.com/wikibolsa/Visita_a_Warren_Buffett
1368   Berkshire Hathaway Inc., 2007 Annual Report
1369   Daily Journal Corporation annual meeting, 2015, Notes by Shane Parrish, Farnam Street
1370   Daily Journal Corporation annual meeting, 2014, Notes by Shane Parrish, Farnam Street
1371   Berkshire Hathaway annual meeting, 2000, Notes by Whitney Tilson, www.tilsonfunds.com
1372   Berkshire Hathaway annual meeting, 2002, Notes by Whitney Tilson, www.tilsonfunds.com
1373   Lecture at the University of Florida School of Business, October 15, 1998, Martin Lee
1374   Berkshire Hathaway, Press Conference, 2000, Notes by The Motley Fool
1375   Lecture at the University of Florida School of Business, October 15, 1998, Martin Lee
1376   Wesco Financial annual meeting, 1999, Outstanding Investor Digest, December 31, 1999, p.32.
1377   Notes from the Meeting Dr. George Athanassakos and Ivey MBA and HBA students had with Mr. Warren Buffett, Omaha February 27, 2015, The Ben Graham Center for Value Investing

1378   Transcript from Warren Buffett meeting with Wharton students, February 17, 2006, Notes by Timothy Viles & Aaron Byrd, seen in www.rbcpa.com
1379   Berkshire Hathaway Inc., 2011 Annual Report
1380   Berkshire Hathaway annual meeting, 2014, Notes by author
1381   Berkshire Hathaway Inc., 2011 Annual Report
1382   Wesco Financial annual meeting, 2002, Outstanding Investor Digest, December 31, 2002, p.31.
1383   Berkshire Hathaway Inc., 2002 Annual Report
1384   Unofficial transcript of Warren Buffett, Charlie Munger and Bill Gates appearing live with Becky Quick on CNBC's "Squawk Box," Monday, May 5, 2014, buffettwatch.cnbc.com
1385   Ibid.
1386   Ibid.
1387   Ibid.
1388   Charles T. Munger testimony, In the Matter of Blue Chip Stamps, Berkshire Hathaway Inc., HQ-784, March 20, 1975, p.187.
1389   Berkshire Hathaway Inc., 1989 Annual Report
1390   Daily Journal Corporation annual meeting, 2013, Notes by Shane Parrish, Farnam Street
1391   Berkshire Hathaway annual meeting, 2012, Notes by author
1392   Ibid.
1393   Berkshire Hathaway annual meeting, 1999, Notes by author
1394   Daily Journal Corporation annual meeting, 2013, Notes by Shane Parrish, Farnam Street
1395   Berkshire Hathaway annual meeting, 1999, Outstanding Investor Digest, December 10, 1999, p.57
1396   Berkshire Hathaway Inc., 2008 Annual Report
1397   Berkshire Hathaway annual meeting, 2009, Outstanding Investor Digest, OID.COM Feature, p.7.
1398   Berkshire Hathaway Inc., 2008 Annual Report
1399   Daily Journal Corporation, annual meeting, 2013, Notes by author
1400   Berkshire Hathaway annual meeting, 2007, Notes by Whitney Tilson, www.tilsonfunds.com
1401   Wesco Financial annual meeting, 2003, Notes by Whitney Tilson, www.tilsonfunds.com
1402   Berkshire Hathaway annual meeting, 2015, Notes by author
1403   Berkshire Hathaway annual meeting, 2012, Notes by author
1404   Berkshire Hathaway Inc., 2014 Annual Report
1405   Daily Journal Corporation, annual meeting, 2013, Notes by author
1406   Berkshire Hathaway annual meeting, 1999, Outstanding Investor Digest, December 31, 1999, p.45.
1407   Berkshire Hathaway Inc., 2007 Annual Report
1408   Peter D. Kaufman, Poor Charlie's Almanack, p.104.
1409   Berkshire Hathaway annual meeting, 2015, Notes by author
1410   Ibid.
1411   Berkshire Hathaway Inc., 2010 Annual Report
1412   Berkshire Hathaway annual meeting, 1998, Outstanding Investor Digest, September 24, 1998, p.50.
1413   Notes by Daniel Sweet of Warren Buffett's responses to questions from Notre Dame and Stanford MBA students, October 9, 2007, http://danielsweet.com/dan-sweet/2009/01/
1414   Berkshire Hathaway annual meeting, 1998, Outstanding Investor Digest, September 24, 1998, p.50.
1415   Berkshire Hathaway annual meeting, 1997, Outstanding Investor Digest, August 8, 1997, p.13.
1416   Berkshire Hathaway annual meeting, 2008, Notes by Peter Boodell, Boodell & Company Capital Management
1417   Berkshire Hathaway annual meeting, 1998, Outstanding Investor Digest, September 24, 1998, p.50.
1418   Berkshire Hathaway annual meeting, 2014, Notes by author
1419   "Billionaire Investor Warren Buffett Speaks with CNBC's ' Squawk Box'", October 16, 2013, CNBC.com
1420   Berkshire Hathaway Inc., 2014 Annual Report
1421   Berkshire Hathaway Inc., 2012 Annual Report
1422   Berkshire Hathaway Inc., 2011 Annual Report

1423   Jack D. Schwager, The New Market Wizards: Conversations with America's Top Traders, HarperBusiness, 1994
1424   Berkshire Hathaway Inc., 1990 Annual Report
1425   Berkshire Hathaway Inc., 2000 Annual Report
1426   Berkshire Hathaway annual meeting, 2001, Outstanding Investor Digest, Year End 2001 Edition, p.44.
1427   Wesco Financial annual meeting, 1999, Outstanding Investor Digest, December 31, 1999, p.41.
1428   Transcript from Warren Buffett meeting with Wharton students, February 17, 2006, Notes by Timothy Viles & Aaron Byrd, seen in www.rbcpa.com
1429   Patricia Sellers, "Warren Buffett and Charlie Munger's best advice", Fortune Magazine, November 18, 2013
1430   Berkshire Hathaway annual meeting, 2010, Notes by author
1431   "Buffett & Gates on Success", KCTS/Seattle, May 1998, Transcript p.7.
1432   Transcript from visit in India, NDTV Studios, April 2011, Notes by Shane Parrish, Farnam Street
1433   Peter D. Kaufman, Poor Charlie's Almanack, p.70.
1434   Wesco Financial annual meeting, 2001, Notes by Whitney Tilson, www.tilsonfunds.com
1435   Wesco Financial Inc., 1990 Annual Report
1436   Berkshire Hathaway Inc., 1997 Annual Report
1437   Buffett Partnership Letter, July 8, 1964
1438   Berkshire Hathaway Inc., 1997 Annual Report
1439   Wesco Financial annual meeting, 2004, Notes by Whitney Tilson, www.tilsonfunds.com
1440   The Psychology of Human Misjudgment, Peter D. Kaufman, Poor Charlie's Almanack, p.470.
1441   Ibid.
1442   Berkshire Hathaway annual meeting, 1995, Answer to author question
1443   Berkshire Hathaway annual meeting, 2000, Outstanding Investor Digest, Year End 2000 Edition, p.54.
1444   Berkshire Hathaway annual meeting 1994, Outstanding Investor Digest, June 23, 1994, p.27.
1445   Berkshire Hathaway Inc., 2008 Annual Report
1446   Berkshire Hathaway Inc., 1982 Annual Report
1447   Berkshire Hathaway Inc., 2003 Annual Report
1448   Berkshire Hathaway Inc., 1995 Annual Report
1449   Berkshire Hathaway annual meeting, 1995, Notes by author
1450   Berkshire Hathaway Inc., 1995 Annual Report
1451   Academic Economics: Strengths and Faults After Considering Interdisciplinary Needs, Herb Key Undergraduate Lecture, University of California, Santa Barbara, Economics Department, October 3, 2003, Peter D. Kaufman, Poor Charlie's Almanack, p.403.
1452   Berkshire Hathaway Inc., 1989 Annual Report
1453   Berkshire Hathaway annual meeting, 2003, Notes by Whitney Tilson, www.tilsonfunds.com
1454   Berkshire Hathaway Inc., 2009 Annual Report
1455   Berkshire Hathaway annual meeting, 1994, Outstanding Investor Digest, June 23, 1994, pp.23-24.
1456   Berkshire Hathaway Inc., 1988 Annual Report
1457   1994 Lecture of The E. J. Faulkner Lecture Series, A Colloquium with University of Nebraska-Lincoln Students by Warren E. Buffett
1458   Carol J. Loomis, "Warren Buffett on the Stock Market", Fortune Magazine, December 10, 2001, a Warren Buffett speech converted to an article by Carol J. Loomis
1459   Berkshire Hathaway annual meeting, 2007, Notes by Whitney Tilson, www.tilsonfunds.com
1460   Warren Buffett from a speech at the Emory Business School as reported in, "Track record is everything", Across the Board, October 1991, p.62.
1461   Wesco Financial annual meeting, 1998, Outstanding Investor Digest, December 29, 1998, p.47.
1462   Berkshire Hathaway annual meeting, 1998, Outstanding Investor Digest, September 24, 1998, p.40.
1463   Berkshire Hathaway annual meeting, 2014, Notes by author

1464   The Psychology of Human Misjudgment, Talk at the Cambridge Center for Behavioral Studies, April 24, 1995.
1465   The Psychology of Human Misjudgment, Peter D. Kaufman, Poor Charlie's Almanack, p.484.
1466   Wesco Financial Inc., 1988 Annual Report (roughly recalled iron prediction of a Victorian prime minister)
1467   Niccolò Machiavelli, The Prince, Dover Publications, 2000
1468   Berkshire Hathaway annual meeting, 2009, Outstanding Investor Digest, OID.COM Feature, p.32
1469   Berkshire Hathaway Inc., 2014 Annual Report
1470   Notes from the Meeting Dr. George Athanassakos and Ivey MBA and HBA students had with Mr. Warren Buffett, Omaha February 27, 2015, The Ben Graham Center for Value Investing
1471   From the Coca-Cola Company annual meeting, 2013, http://www.coca-colacompany.com/investors/annual-meeting-of-shareowners, http://mfile2.akamai.com/9538/wmv/estream.download.akamai.com/9538/cocacola/cocacola_160isl_2013_annual_meeting_of_shareowners.wvx?obj=20130424v1
1472   Alexander Kotov, Think Like a Grandmaster Paperback, B.T. Batsford, 1976
1473   Daily Journal Corporation annual meeting, 2015, Notes by Shane Parrish, Farnam Street
1474   Daily Journal Corporation annual meeting, 2011, Notes by author
1475   Berkshire Hathaway annual meeting, 2015, Notes by author
1476   Berkshire Hathaway Inc., 2004 Annual Report
1477   Daily Journal Corporation annual meeting, 2015, Notes by Shane Parrish, Farnam Street
1478   Berkshire Hathaway annual meeting, 2015, Notes by author
1479   Berkshire Hathaway Inc., 1978 Annual Report
1480   Warren Buffett memo to Berkshire Hathaway Managers, September 26, 2001
1481   1994 Lecture of The E. J. Faulkner Lecture Series, A Colloquium with University of Nebraska-Lincoln Students by Warren E. Buffett
1482   Kenneth Turan, "CROSSROADS: Looking at 1996 and beyond with influential figures in the worlds of art and entertainment", Los Angeles Times, December 31, 1996
1483   The Psychology of Human Misjudgment, Peter D. Kaufman, Poor Charlie's Almanack, p.471.
1484   Berkshire Hathaway annual meeting, 2008, Outstanding Investor Digest, August 31, 2008, p.19.
1485   Berkshire Hathaway annual meeting, 2013, Notes by Peter Boodell, Boodell & Company Capital Management
1486   Berkshire Hathaway Inc., 2006 Annual Report
1487   Berkshire Hathaway Inc., 2014 Annual Report
1488   Andrew Carnegie, The Autobiography of Andrew Carnegie, Penguin Publishing Group, London, 2006
1489   Wesco Financial annual meeting, 2001, Notes by Whitney Tilson, www.tilsonfunds.com
1490   Daily Journal Corporation annual meeting, 2014, Notes by Shane Parrish, Farnam Street
1491   Berkshire Hathaway, Press Conference, May 2006, Notes by The Motley Fool
1492   Joseph A. Schumpeter, Capitalism, Socialism and Democracy , Chapter VII: The Process of Creative Destruction, 3rd Edition 1950, Harper Torchbooks, New York, 1962
1493   Berkshire Hathaway annual meeting, 2000, Outstanding Investor Digest, Year End 2000 Edition, p.51.
1494   Berkshire Hathaway Inc., 2014 Annual Report
1495   Wesco Financial annual meeting, 1989, Outstanding Investor Digest, July 26, 1989, p.9.
1496   Berkshire Hathaway Inc., 1986 Annual Report
1497   Wesco Financial annual meeting, 2010, Notes by author
1498   Berkshire Hathaway Inc., 1990 Annual Report
1499   Daily Journal Corporation annual meeting, 2011, Notes by author
1500   Berkshire Hathaway Inc., 1985 Annual Report
1501   Wesco Financial annual meeting 1989, Outstanding Investor Digest, July 26, 1989, p.9.
1502   From the song The Gambler
1503   Berkshire Hathaway Inc., 1994 Annual Report
1504   Berkshire Hathaway annual meeting, 2009, Outstanding Investor Digest, OID.COM Feature, p.27

1505   Notes from Buffett meeting with students from Emory and 5 other business schools, February 6, 2009, www.undergroundvalue.blogspot.com
1506   Berkshire Hathaway annual meeting, 2005, Outstanding Investor Digest, March 9, 2006, p.62.
1507   Berkshire Hathaway Inc., 1989 Annual Report
1508   Berkshire Hathaway Inc., 2014 Annual Report
1509   Berkshire Hathaway annual meeting 1994, Outstanding Investor Digest, June 23, 1994, p.24.
1510   Berkshire Hathaway annual meeting, 1995, Outstanding Investor Digest, August 10, 1995, p.14.
1511   Said by Charles T. Munger but source unknown
1512   Berkshire Hathaway annual meeting, 2015, Notes by author
1513   Charles Munger, speech at breakfast meeting of the Philanthropy Round Table, November 10, 2000
1514   Berkshire Hathaway Inc., 1982 Annual Report
1515   Berkshire Hathaway annual meeting, 2005, Notes by Whitney Tilson, www.tilsonfunds.com
1516   Berkshire Hathaway annual meeting, 2008, Notes by Peter Boodell, Boodell & Company Capital Management
1517   Wesco Financial annual meeting, 2006, Notes by Whitney Tilson, www.tilsonfunds.com
1518   Berkshire Hathaway annual meeting, 1991, Outstanding Investor Digest, May 24, 1991, p.33.
1519   Berkshire Hathaway annual meeting, 2006, Notes by Whitney Tilson, www.tilsonfunds.com
1520   Berkshire Hathaway annual meeting, 2005, Notes by Whitney Tilson, www.tilsonfunds.com
1521   Berkshire Hathaway annual meeting, 2008, Outstanding Investor Digest, August 31, 2008, p.17.
1522   Berkshire Hathaway annual meeting, 2012, Notes by Peter Boodell, Boodell & Company Capital Management
1523   Berkshire Hathaway Inc., 2002 Annual Report
1524   Ibid.
1525   "Buffett & Gates on Success", KCTS/Seattle, May 1998, Transcript p.20.
1526   Berkshire Hathaway annual meeting, 2003, Notes by Whitney Tilson, www.tilsonfunds.com
1527   Wesco Financial annual meeting, 2003, Notes by Whitney Tilson, www.tilsonfunds.com
1528   Daily Journal Corporation annual meeting, 2010, Notes by author
1529   Berkshire Hathaway annual meeting, 2011, Notes by author
1530   USC Gould School of Law Commencement Address, May 13, 2007, Peter D. Kaufman, Poor Charlie's Almanack, p.436.
1531   Berkshire Hathaway annual meeting, 2013, Notes by Peter Boodell, Boodell & Company Capital Management
1532   Warren Buffett speech at Caltech, October 21, 1997, Transcript by Richard Rockwood
1533   Warren Buffett Talks Philanthropy with Bank of America CEO, September 19, 2013, Georgetown University, www.georgetown.edu
1534   Warren Buffett speech to University of Georgia, Terry College of Business students, January 30, 2007, Sham Gad, www.gurufocus.com/news/4434
1535   Berkshire Hathaway annual meeting, 2005, Notes by Whitney Tilson, www.tilsonfunds.com
1536   Berkshire Hathaway annual meeting, 2015, Notes by author
1537   Berkshire Hathaway annual meeting, 2003, Outstanding Investor Digest, Year End 2003 Edition, p.44.
1538   Berkshire Hathaway Inc., 1990 Annual Report
1539   Berkshire Hathaway annual meeting, 1998, Notes by author
1540   Berkshire Hathaway annual meeting, 2014, Notes by Peter Boodell, Boodell & Company Capital Management
1541   Berkshire Hathaway annual meeting, 2014, Notes by author
1542   Wesco Financial annual meeting, 2010, Outstanding Investor Digest, August 9, 2010, p.35.
1543   Daily Journal Corporation annual meeting, 2015, Notes by Shane Parrish, Farnam Street
1544   Wesco Financial annual meeting, 2008, Notes by author
1545   Conversation with Charlie Munger, Pasadena Convention Center, July 1, 2011, Notes by Shane Parrish, Farnam Street
1546   Addison Wiggin & Kate Incontrera, I.O.U.S.A.: One Nation. Under Stress. In Debt., New Jersey, John Wiley & Sons, 2008

1547   Notes from Warren Buffett meeting with MBA students from Wharton, October 10, 2003, www.tilsonfunds.com

1548   Berkshire Hathaway annual meeting, 1998, Outstanding Investor Digest, September 24, 1998, p.45.

1549   Wesco Financial annual meeting, 2010, Outstanding Investor Digest, August 9, 2010, p.36.

1550   Warren Buffett letter on pensions to Katherine Graham, Washington Post, October 14, 1975

1551   Wesco Financial annual meeting, 2010, Outstanding Investor Digest, August 9, 2010, p.23.

1552   Berkshire Hathaway annual meeting, 2014, Notes by author

1553   Berkshire Hathaway Inc., 1977 Annual Report

1554   Office Hours with Warren Buffett, May 7, 2013, interview with Caroline Ghosn, Levo League, www.levo.com

1555   Ibid.

1556   Patricia Sellers, "Warren Buffett and Charlie Munger's best advice", Fortune Magazine, November 18, 2013

1557   "What Buffett learned from Munger", CNN Money Video, November 7, 2013

1558   Berkshire Hathaway Inc., 1977 Annual Report

1559   Berkshire Hathaway annual meeting, 2010, Notes by Peter Boodell, Boodell & Company Capital Management

1560   Berkshire Hathaway Inc., 2013 Annual Report

1561   Charles Munger, speech at breakfast meeting of the Philanthropy Round Table, November 10, 2000

1562   Academic Economics: Strengths and Faults After Considering Interdisciplinary Needs, Herb Key Undergraduate Lecture, University of California, Santa Barbara, Economics Department, October 3, 2003, Peter D. Kaufman, Poor Charlie's Almanack, p.388.

1563   "An Evening with Warren Buffett", Warren Buffett Q&A with the Oquirrh Club, October 2003

1564   Said by Warren E. Buffett but source unknown and may not be original with him

1565   Berkshire Hathaway annual meeting, 2015, Notes by author

1566   Academic Economics: Strengths and Faults After Considering Interdisciplinary Needs, Herb Key Undergraduate Lecture, University of California, Santa Barbara, Economics Department, October 3, 2003, Peter D. Kaufman, Poor Charlie's Almanack, p.388.

1567   Berkshire Hathaway annual meeting, 1994, Outstanding Investor Digest, June 23, 1994, p.20.

1568   Berkshire Hathaway Inc., 2013 Annual Report

1569   Astrid Dörner, "Warren Buffett's German To-Do List", Handelsblatt Global Edition no. 123, February 25, 2015

1570   Berkshire Hathaway Inc., 1981 Annual Report

1571   Academic Economics: Strengths and Faults After Considering Interdisciplinary Needs, Herb Key Undergraduate Lecture, University of California, Santa Barbara, Economics Department, October 3, 2003, Peter D. Kaufman, Poor Charlie's Almanack, p.388.

1572   Berkshire Hathaway annual meeting, 2015, Notes by author

1573   Berkshire Hathaway annual meeting, 2000, Notes by author

1574   Peter D. Kaufman, Poor Charlie's Almanack, p.108.

1575   Berkshire Hathaway annual meeting, 2013, Notes by author

1576   "A Conversation With Charlie Munger", Charlie Munger Speaks to University of Michigan Students, September 14, 2010

1577   Unofficial transcript of Warren Buffett, Charlie Munger and Bill Gates appearing live with Becky Quick on CNBC's "Squawk Box," Monday, May 5, 2014, buffettwatch.cnbc.com

1578   Berkshire Hathaway Inc., 2010 Annual Report

1579   Berkshire Hathaway Inc., 2008 Annual Report

1580   From Josiah Hotchkiss Gilbert, Dictionary of Burning Words of Brilliant Writers, 1895

1581   Berkshire Hathaway annual meeting, 2009, Outstanding Investor Digest, OID.COM Feature, p.25.

1582   Said by Charles T. Munger but source unknown

1583   Berkshire Hathaway annual meeting, 2013, Notes by author

1584   A Conversation with Charlie Munger at Caltech, DuBridge Distinguished Lecture, March 11, 2008, DVD

1585   Daily Journal Corporation annual meeting, 2011, Notes by author

1586   Berkshire Hathaway Inc., 1998 Annual Report
1587   Berkshire Hathaway annual meeting, 1995, Outstanding Investor Digest, August 10, 1995, p.10.
1588   Berkshire Hathaway annual meeting, 2000, Outstanding Investor Digest, December 18, 2000, pp.34-35.
1589   Berkshire Hathaway annual meeting, 1999, Outstanding Investor Digest, December 10, 1999, p.52.
1590   Berkshire Hathaway annual meeting, 1997, Notes by author
1591   Wesco Financial annual meeting, 2003, Notes by Whitney Tilson, www.tilsonfunds.com
1592   The Great Financial Scandal of 2003: An Account by Charles T Munger, Summer 2000, Peter D. Kaufman, Poor Charlie's Almanack, p.366.
1593   Financial Crisis Inquiry Commission Staff Audiotape of Interview with Warren Buffett, May 26, 2010, pp.5-6. www.santangelsreview.com
1594   Academic Economics: Strengths and Faults After Considering Interdisciplinary Needs, Herb Key Undergraduate Lecture, University of California, Santa Barbara, Economics Department, October 3, 2003, Peter D. Kaufman, Poor Charlie's Almanack, p.383.
1595   The Pharos of Alpha Omega Alpha-Honor Medical Society, Volume 44, Alpha Omega Alpha Honor Medical Society, 1981
1596   A Conversation with Charlie Munger at Caltech, DuBridge Distinguished Lecture, March 11, 2008, DVD
1597   Wesco Financial annual meeting, 1990, Outstanding Investor Digest, June 28, 1990, pp.20-21.
1598   Berkshire Hathaway Inc., 1998 Annual Report
1599   Berkshire Hathaway Inc., 1996 Annual Report
1600   Wesco Financial annual meeting, 2002, Notes by author
1601   Berkshire Hathaway annual meeting, 2009, Outstanding Investor Digest, OID.COM Feature, p.25.
1602   Ibid.
1603   Berkshire Hathaway annual meeting, 1987, Outstanding Investor Digest, October 7, 1987, p.12.
1604   Wesco Financial annual meeting, 2002, Outstanding Investor Digest, December 31, 2002, p.38.
1605   Alexander Kotov, Think Like a Grandmaster Paperback, B.T. Batsford, 1976
1606   Musarion oder die Philosophie der Grazien, 1768
1607   "Q&A: Legal Matters with Charles T. Munger", Stanford Lawyer, Spring 2009
1608   Quoted in The Genius of Science: A Portrait Gallery by Abraham Pais, Oxford University Press, 2000
1609   "Buy American. I Am.", New York Times Op-Ed, October 16, 2008
1610   "Neujahrswunsch", in Der Teutsche Merkur, 1774, translation from The Quote…Unquote Newsletter, October 1997
1611   Berkshire Hathaway Inc., 2004 Annual Report
1612   Berkshire Hathaway Inc., 1994 Annual Report
1613   1994 Lecture of The E. J. Faulkner Lecture Series, A Colloquium with University of Nebraska-Lincoln Students by Warren E. Buffett
1614   Transcript of Warren Buffett's 'Ask Warren' appearance on CNBC's Squawk Box, March 1, 2010, buffettwatch.cnbc.com
1615   Notes from the Meeting Dr. George Athanassakos and Ivey MBA and HBA students had with Mr. Warren Buffett, Omaha February 27, 2015, The Ben Graham Center for Value Investing
1616   Berkshire Hathaway Inc., 2013 Annual Report
1617   Berkshire Hathaway annual meeting, 2007, Notes by Whitney Tilson, www.tilsonfunds.com
1618   1994 Lecture of The E. J. Faulkner Lecture Series, A Colloquium with University of Nebraska-Lincoln Students by Warren E. Buffett
1619   Lecture at the University of Florida School of Business, October 15, 1998, Martin Lee
1620   Margie Kelley, "In the Money: Alumni financiers take stock of the market and careers spent trying to beat it," Harvard Law Bulletin, Summer 2001
1621   Berkshire Hathaway annual meeting, 1993, Outstanding Investor Digest, June 30, 1993, p.25.
1622   Berkshire Hathaway Inc., 2009 Annual Report
1623   Berkshire Hathaway Inc., 2013 Annual Report
1624   Ibid.

1625   Ibid.

1626   Ibid.

1627   Transcript of Warren Buffett's 'Ask Warren' appearance on CNBC's Squawk Box, March 4, 2013, buffettwatch.cnbc.com

1628   Berkshire Hathaway Inc., 1982 Annual Report

1629   Berkshire Hathaway Inc., 2013 Annual Report

1630   Ibid.

1631   Ibid.

1632   Ibid.

1633   Ibid.

1634   Berkshire Hathaway Inc., 1994 Annual Report

1635   Financial Crisis Inquiry Commission Staff Audiotape of Interview with Warren Buffett, May 26, 2010, p.5. www.santangelsreview.com

1636   Lecture at the University of Florida School of Business, October 15, 1998, Martin Lee

1637   Berkshire Hathaway Inc., 2013 Annual Report

1638   Notes from the Meeting Dr. George Athanassakos and Ivey MBA and HBA students had with Mr. Warren Buffett, Omaha February 27, 2015, The Ben Graham Center for Value Investing

1639   Berkshire Hathaway Inc., 2014 Annual Report

1640   Ibid.

1641   Warren Buffett, "A Tribute to Ben Graham", December 6, 1994, New York Society of Financial Analysts, seen in The View from Burgundy, June 1995

1642   Transcript from visit in India, NDTV Studios, April 2011, Notes by Shane Parrish, Farnam Street

1643   Said by Warren E. Buffett but source unknown

1644   Berkshire Hathaway annual meeting, 2012, Notes by author

1645   Q&A with Warren Buffett, November 19, 2009, Notes by Rice University student John S. Reuwer, 2010, http://business.rice.edu/uploadedFiles/Newsroom/Press_Releases/2009/BuffettNotes.pdf?n=2732

1646   Warren Buffett speech to University of Georgia students, Terry College of Business, 2001, GuruFocus

1647   Berkshire Hathaway annual meeting, 2004, Outstanding Investor Digest, December 31, 2004, p.31.

1648   Charles Munger remark to Howard Marks, "Dare to be Great II", Memo to Oaktree clients, April, 2014

1649   Bertrand Russell, The Basic Writings of Bertrand Russell: 1903-1959, (ed. L. Denonn & R. Egner), Simon & Schuster, 1961

1650   Berkshire Hathaway Inc., 1982 Annual Report

1651   Buffett Partnership Letter, January 18, 1965 (Buffett referring to a "West Coast philosopher")

1652   The Need for More Multidisciplinary Skills from Professionals: Educational Implications, Fiftieth Reunion of Harvard Law School Class of 1948, April 24, 1998, Peter D. Kaufman, Poor Charlie's Almanack, p.307.

1653   Berkshire Hathaway Inc., 1992 Annual Report

1654   Notes from the Meeting Dr. George Athanassakos and Ivey MBA and HBA students had with Mr. Warren Buffett, Omaha February 27, 2015, The Ben Graham Center for Value Investing

1655   Wesco Financial annual meeting, 2006, Notes by author

1656   Daily Journal Corporation annual meeting, 2015, Notes by Shane Parrish, Farnam Street

1657   Unofficial transcript of Warren Buffett, Charlie Munger and Bill Gates appearing live with Becky Quick on CNBC's "Squawk Box," Monday, May 5, 2014, buffettwatch.cnbc.com

1658   Wesco Financial annual meeting, 2006, Notes by author

1659   Berkshire Hathaway annual meeting, 2004, Outstanding Investor Digest, December 31, 2004, p.32.

1660   Ibid.

1661   Berkshire Hathaway annual meeting, 2008, Outstanding Investor Digest, August 31, 2008, p.15.

1662   "When I Buy a Company, I'm a Journalist", taped interview with Arizona State University Professor Jeff Cunningham, creator and host of Iconic Voices, Walter Cronkite School of Journalism, March 5, 2015

1663   Lecture at the University of Florida School of Business, October 15, 1998, Martin Lee

1664   Boom and Bust is Normal, Charles Munger interview with Evan Davis, BBC, October 26, 2009, http://news.bbc.co.uk/2/hi/business/8326369.stm
1665   Berkshire Hathaway annual meeting, 2015, Notes by author
1666   Berkshire Hathaway annual meeting, 2008, Outstanding Investor Digest, August 31, 2008, p.15.
1667   Said by Warren E. Buffett but source unknown and may not be original with him
1668   Douglas Hofstadter, Gödel, Escher, Bach: An Eternal Golden Braid, Basic Books, 1999
1669   Berkshire Hathaway annual meeting, 2011, Notes by author
1670   Daily Journal Corporation annual meeting, 2014, Notes by author
1671   Berkshire Hathaway annual meeting, 2015, Notes by author
1672   Wesco Financial annual meeting, 2004, Notes by Whitney Tilson, www.tilsonfunds.com
1673   Berkshire Hathaway, Press Conference, May 2005, Notes by valueinvestorinsight.com
1674   Berkshire Hathaway annual meeting, 1997, Outstanding Investor Digest, August 8, 1997, p.23.
1675   Berkshire Hathaway annual meeting, 1998, Outstanding Investor Digest, September 24, 1998, p.56.
1676   Warren Buffett speech at Caltech, October 21, 1997, Transcript by Richard Rockwood
1677   Berkshire Hathaway Inc., 1992 Annual Report
1678   Jason Zweig, "Charles Munger: Secrets of Buffett's Success?", The Wall Street Journal, Sept. 12, 2014
1679   Lessons from Warren Buffett to a Group of MBA students, University of Iowa, www.biz.uiowa.edu/tippiemba/lessons-from-warren-buffett-to-a-group-of-mba-students/
1680   Berkshire Hathaway annual meeting, 2002, Notes by Selena Maranjian, The Motley Fool
1681   Berkshire Hathaway annual meeting, 1998, Outstanding Investor Digest, September 24, 1998, p.48.
1682   Ibid.
1683   Berkshire Hathaway annual meeting, 2006, Notes by author
1684   Berkshire Hathaway annual meeting, 2007, Notes by author
1685   Peter D. Kaufman, Poor Charlie's Almanack, p.107.
1686   Berkshire Hathaway annual meeting, 2005, Outstanding Investor Digest, March 9, 2006, p.41.
1687   Wesco Financial annual meeting, 2008, Outstanding Investor Digest, August 31, 2008, p.45.
1688   Berkshire Hathaway annual meeting, 2010, Notes by Peter Boodell, Boodell & Company Capital Management
1689   Ibid.
1690   Daily Journal Corporation annual meeting, 2013, Notes by Shane Parrish, Farnam Street
1691   Ibid.
1692   Peter D. Kaufman, Poor Charlie's Almanack, p.141.
1693   Berkshire Hathaway annual meeting, 1999, Outstanding Investor Digest, December 31, 1999, p.46.
1694   Berkshire Hathaway Inc., 1997 Annual Report
1695   Berkshire Hathaway annual meeting, 2015, Notes by author
1696   Peter D. Kaufman, Poor Charlie's Almanack, p.93.
1697   Berkshire Hathaway Inc., 2014 Annual Report
1698   Wesco Financial annual meeting, 1998, Notes by author
1699   Bruce Upbin, Jay-Z, Buffett and Forbes on Success and Giving Back, Forbes, 23.9.2010
1700   The Psychology of Human Misjudgment, Peter D. Kaufman, Poor Charlie's Almanack, p.474.
1701   Berkshire Hathaway annual meeting, 1999, Outstanding Investor Digest, December 31, 1999, p.60.
1702   Matthew Stover, Shatterpoint (Star Wars: Clone Wars), LucasBooks, 2004
1703   Daily Journal Corporation annual meeting, 2014, Notes by Shane Parrish, Farnam Street
1704   Wesco Financial annual meeting, 2002, Notes by author
1705   Daily Journal Corporation annual meeting, 2014, Notes by Shane Parrish, Farnam Street
1706   http://www.edwardtufte.com/bboard/q-and-a-fetch-msg?msg_id=0002bA
1707   Berkshire Hathaway annual meeting, 2006, Notes by author
1708   Practical Thought About Practical Thought? An Informal Talk, July 20, 1996, Peter D. Kaufman, Poor Charlie's Almanack, p.279.
1709   Daily Journal Corporation annual meeting, 2014, Notes by Shane Parrish, Farnam Street

1710   Daily Journal Corporation annual meeting, 2015, Notes by Shane Parrish, Farnam Street
1711   Berkshire Hathaway annual meeting, 2013, Notes by author
1712   Graham Wallas, The art of thought, Harcourt, Brace and Company, New York, 1926
1713   Berkshire Hathaway annual meeting, 1997, Notes by author
1714   Berkshire Hathaway annual meeting, 2011, Notes by author
1715   Wesco Financial annual meeting, 1998, Notes by author
1716   Peter D. Kaufman, Poor Charlie's Almanack, p.107.
1717   Wesco Financial annual meeting, 2003, Outstanding Investor Digest, Year End 2003 Edition, p.46.
1718   Wesco Financial annual meeting, 2007, Notes by Whitney Tilson, www.tilsonfunds.com
1719   Berkshire Hathaway annual meeting, 1997, Outstanding Investor Digest, August 8, 1997, p.18.
1720   Wesco Financial annual meeting, 2007, Outstanding Investor Digest, February 29, 2008, p.55.
1721   Wesco Financial annual meeting, 2007, Notes by Whitney Tilson, www.tilsonfunds.com
1722   Peter D. Kaufman, Poor Charlie's Almanack, p.107.
1723   Unofficial transcript of Warren Buffett, Charlie Munger and Bill Gates appearing live with Becky Quick on CNBC's "Squawk Box," Monday, May 5, 2014, buffettwatch.cnbc.com
1724   Berkshire Hathaway annual meeting, 1997, Outstanding Investor Digest, August 8, 1997, p.18.
1725   Steve Jordon, ", "Berkshire's Stock Portfolio passed $100 billion Milestone in 2013, and a long-term outlook paved the way", Omaha World-Herald, May 3, 2014
1726   Wesco Financial annual meeting, 2003, Notes by Whitney Tilson, www.tilsonfunds.com
1727   Berkshire Hathaway Inc., 2010, Annual Report
1728   Berkshire Hathaway annual meeting, 2015, Notes by author
1729   Wesco Financial annual meeting, 1998, Outstanding Investor Digest, December 29, 1998, p.49.
1730   Conversation with Charlie Munger, Pasadena Convention Center, July 1, 2011, Notes by Shane Parrish, Farnam Street
1731   Charlie Munger at Harvard-Westlake School January 19, 2010, www.santangelsreview.com
1732   Wesco Financial annual meeting, 2003, Outstanding Investor Digest, Year End 2003 Edition, p.46.
1733   Berkshire Hathaway annual meeting, 1997, Outstanding Investor Digest, August 8, 1997, p.16.
1734   Carolyn Wells from Love's Laws in The Hampton Magazine, Volume 21, Issue 4, 1908
1735   Berkshire Hathaway annual meeting, 2010, Notes by author
1736   Buffett Partnership Letter, January 25, 1967
1737   Berkshire Hathaway annual meeting, 1995, Outstanding Investor Digest, August 10, 1995, p.10.
1738   Berkshire Hathaway Inc., 1997 Annual Report
1739   Charlie Munger at Harvard-Westlake School January 19, 2010, www.santangelsreview.com
1740   Berkshire Hathaway annual meeting, 2007, Notes by Whitney Tilson, www.tilsonfunds.com
1741   Buffett to CNBC: I'm 'Salivating' For 'Big Acquisition', October 24, 2012, CNBC.com
1742   Wesco Financial annual meeting, 2010, Outstanding Investor Digest, August 9, 2010, p.27.
1743   Wesco Financial annual meeting, 2007, Outstanding Investor Digest, February 29, 2008, p.61.
1744   Berkshire Hathaway annual meeting, 2011, Notes by author
1745   Berkshire Hathaway annual meeting, 1996, Outstanding Investor Digest, August 8, 1996, pp.24-25.
1746   Wesco Financial annual meeting, 2006, Notes by author
1747   Berkshire Hathaway annual meeting, 1997, Outstanding Investor Digest, August 8 1997, p. 23
1748   Addison Wiggin & Kate Incontrera, I.O.U.S.A.: One Nation. Under Stress. In Debt., New Jersey, John Wiley & Sons, 2008
1749   Notes from the Meeting Dr. George Athanassakos and Ivey MBA and HBA students had with Mr. Warren Buffett, Omaha March 31, 2008, The Ben Graham Center for Value Investing

1750   Berkshire Hathaway annual meeting, 1992, Outstanding Investor Digest, June 22, 1992, p.42.
1751   Academic Economics: Strengths and Faults After Considering Interdisciplinary Needs, Herb Key Undergraduate Lecture, University of California, Santa Barbara, Economics Department, October 3, 2003, Peter D. Kaufman, Poor Charlie's Almanack, p.402.
1752   Wesco Financial Inc., 1988 Annual Report
1753   Transcript of Susie Gharib's interview with Warren Buffett, PBS' NIGHTLY BUSINESS REPORT, January 22, 2009
1754   Notes from the Meeting Dr. George Athanassakos and Ivey MBA and HBA students had with Mr. Warren Buffett, Omaha March 31, 2008, The Ben Graham Center for Value Investing
1755   Wesco Financial annual meeting, 2001, Outstanding Investor Digest, OID.COM Edition, 2003, p.10.
1756   Academic Economics: Strengths and Faults After Considering Interdisciplinary Needs, Herb Key Undergraduate Lecture, University of California, Santa Barbara, Economics Department, October 3, 2003, Peter D. Kaufman, Poor Charlie's Almanack, pp.402-403.
1757   Wesco Financial annual meeting, 2001, Outstanding Investor Digest, OID.COM Edition, 2003, p.10.
1758   Daily Journal Corporation annual meeting, 2015, Notes by Shane Parrish, Farnam Street
1759   Wesco Financial Inc., 1989 Annual Report
1760   Academic Economics: Strengths and Faults After Considering Interdisciplinary Needs, Herb Key Undergraduate Lecture, University of California, Santa Barbara, Economics Department, October 3, 2003, Peter D. Kaufman, Poor Charlie's Almanack, p.403.
1761   Berkshire Hathaway Inc., 1985 Annual Report
1762   Berkshire Hathaway annual meeting, 2004, Notes by Whitney Tilson, www.tilsonfunds.com
1763   Berkshire Hathaway Inc., 1985 Annual Report
1764   Academic Economics: Strengths and Faults After Considering Interdisciplinary Needs, Herb Key Undergraduate Lecture, University of California, Santa Barbara, Economics Department, October 3, 2003, Peter D. Kaufman, Poor Charlie's Almanack, p.403.
1765   Berkshire Hathaway annual meeting, 2000, Notes by Whitney Tilson, www.tilsonfunds.com
1766   Berkshire Hathaway Inc., 1985 Annual Report
1767   "Warren Buffett Talks Business", Kenan-Flagler, PBSTV program produced by the University of North Carolina, Center for Public Television, Chapel Hill, October 1995 (VHS)
1768   Berkshire Hathaway Inc., 1990 Annual Report
1769   Academic Economics: Strengths and Faults After Considering Interdisciplinary Needs, Herb Key Undergraduate Lecture, University of California, Santa Barbara, Economics Department, October 3, 2003, Peter D. Kaufman, Poor Charlie's Almanack, pp.404-405.
1770   Wesco Financial annual meeting, 2001, Outstanding Investor Digest, OID.COM Edition, 2003, p.10.
1771   Academic Economics: Strengths and Faults After Considering Interdisciplinary Needs, Herb Key Undergraduate Lecture, University of California, Santa Barbara, Economics Department, October 3, 2003, Peter D. Kaufman, Poor Charlie's Almanack, p.404.
1772   From Bill Brysons book, A Short History of Nearly Everything, Broadway Books, 2003
1773   Berkshire Hathaway annual meeting, 1999, Notes by author
1774   Investment Practices of Leading Charitable Foundations, Speech at Miramar Sheraton Hotel, Santa Monica, CA, on October 14, 1998 to a meeting of the Foundation Financial Officer Group
1775   Wesco Financial annual meeting, 2002, Notes by author
1776   Marcus Tullius Cicero, On the Nature of the Gods, www.oll.libertyfund.org/titles/539
1777   Said by Warren E. Buffett but source unknown and may not be original with him
1778   Wesco Financial Inc., 1989 Annual Report
1779   USC Gould School of Law Commencement Address, May 13, 2007, Peter D. Kaufman, Poor Charlie's Almanack, p.434.
1780   Peter D. Kaufman, Poor Charlie's Almanack, p.320.
1781   Ibid., p.72.
1782   Wesco Financial annual meeting, 2007, Outstanding Investor Digest, February 29, 2008, p.52.
1783   Wesco Financial annual meeting, 2002, Outstanding Investor Digest, December 31, 2002, p.26.
1784   Berkshire Hathaway annual meeting, 2004, Notes by Whitney Tilson, www.tilsonfunds.com

1785   Berkshire Hathaway Inc., 1992 Annual Report
1786   See more in Groupthink and France's defeat in the 1940 campaign by David Ahlstrom & Linda C. Wang, Journal of Management History, Vol. 15 No. 2, 2009, pp. 159-177
1787   Charles T. Munger, from author files but source unknown
1788   Berkshire Hathaway Inc., 1982 Annual Report
1789   Battles and Leaders of the Civil War edited by Robert Underwood Clarence C. Buel, Vol. II, Castle Books
1790   Howard Bloom, The Lucifer Principle: A Scientific Expedition into the Forces of History, The Atlantic Monthly Press, New York, 1995
1791   Ike Skelton, Whispers of Warriors: The Importance of History to the Military Professional, Naval War College Review, No 3, Summer 2000
1792   Peter D. Kaufman, Poor Charlie's Almanack, p.76.
1793   Wesco Financial annual meeting, 2010, Outstanding Investor Digest, August 9, 2010, p.24.
1794   Wesco Financial annual meeting, 2009, Notes by Peter Boodell, Boodell & Company Capital Management
1795   Three Lectures by Warren Buffett to Notre Dame Faculty, MBA students and Undergraduate students, Spring 1991, Lightly edited by Whitney Tilson
1796   Transcript from visit in India, NDTV Studios, April 2011, Notes by Shane Parrish, Farnam Street
1797   Peter D. Kaufman, Poor Charlie's Almanack, p.134.
1798   A Conversation with Charlie Munger at Caltech, DuBridge Distinguished Lecture, March 11, 2008, DVD
1799   Ibid.
1800   Ibid.
1801   William Green, The Great Minds of Investing, München, FinanzBuch Verlag, 2015, p.140, text written by Dr. Gisela Baur, copyright by ACATIS Investment GmbH
1802   Conversations from the Warren Buffett Symposium, Cardozo Law Review (1997), vol. 19. Edited by Lawrence A. Cunningham and reissued by Cunningham in 2016.
1803   Berkshire Hathaway annual meeting, 1998, Outstanding Investor Digest, September 24, 1998, p.36.
1804   Wesco Financial annual meeting, 1999, Notes by author
1805   USC Gould School of Law Commencement Address, May 13, 2007, Peter D. Kaufman, Poor Charlie's Almanack, p.423.
1806   Berkshire Hathaway annual meeting, 2015, Notes by author
1807   Warren Buffett meeting with University of Maryland MBA Students November 15, 2013, Notes by Professor David Kass
1808   Berkshire Hathaway annual meeting, 2007, Notes by Whitney Tilson, www.tilsonfunds.com
1809   Unofficial transcript of Warren Buffett, Charlie Munger and Bill Gates appearing live with Becky Quick on CNBC's "Squawk Box," Monday, May 5, 2014, buffettwatch.cnbc.com
1810   Ibid.
1811   Three Lectures by Warren Buffett to Notre Dame Faculty, MBA students and Undergraduate students, Spring 1991, Lightly edited by Whitney Tilson
1812   Peter D. Kaufman, Poor Charlie's Almanack, p.139.
1813   USC Gould School of Law Commencement Address, May 13, 2007, Peter D. Kaufman, Poor Charlie's Almanack, p.424.
1814   Berkshire Hathaway annual meeting, 1997, Outstanding Investor Digest, August 8, 1997, p.6.
1815   Berkshire Hathaway annual meeting, 2005, Outstanding Investor Digest, March 9, 2006, p.61.
1816   Ibid.
1817   Peter D. Kaufman, Poor Charlie's Almanack, p.63.
1818   Wesco Financial annual meeting, 2005, Notes by author
1819   USC Gould School of Law Commencement Address, May 13, 2007, Peter D. Kaufman, Poor Charlie's Almanack, pp.423-424
1820   Ibid.
1821   A Conversation with Charlie Munger at Caltech, DuBridge Distinguished Lecture, March 11, 2008, DVD
1822   Daily Journal Corporation annual meeting, 2015, Notes by Shane Parrish, Farnam Street
1823   Ibid.

1824   Berkshire Hathaway annual meeting, 2010, Notes by author
1825   Berkshire Hathaway annual meeting, 2015, Notes by author
1826   Berkshire Hathaway annual meeting, 2010, Notes by author
1827   The Need for More Multidisciplinary Skills from Professionals: Educational Implications,
Fiftieth Reunion of Harvard Law School Class of 1948, April 24, 1998, Peter D. Kaufman, Poor
Charlie's Almanack, p.318.

- BIBLIOGRAPHY -

Across the Board, Warren Buffett from a speech at the Emory Business School as reported in, "Track record is everything", October 1991

American Institute of Physics,Interview with the physicist Abraham Pais, Oral History Interviews, American Institute of Physics, https://www.aip.org/history-programs/niels-bohr-library/oral-histories/5047

Armour Tommy, How to Play Your Best Golf All the Time, Touchstone, 1995

Asimov Isaac, The Gods Themselves, Spectra, 1972

Augustine Norman R., "Managing the Crisis You Tried to Prevent", Harvard Business Review, November 1995 Issue, www.//hbr.org/1995/11/managing-the-crisis-you-tried-to-prevent

Baron Ethan, "Warren Buffett's Unconventional Advice to MBAs", November 27, 2014, reported by The Chinese University of Hong Kong Business School student Sharad Golchha, www.poetsandquants.com/2014/11/27/warren-buffetts-unconventional-advice-to-mbas/

BBC, "Boom and Bust is Normal", Charles Munger interview with Evan Davis, BBC, October 26, 2009, http://news.bbc.co.uk/2/hi/business/8326369.stm

BBC.com, "Why saying 'no' will boost your career", March 14, 2014, bbc.com

Bergdahl Michael, What I learned from Sam Walton: How to compete and thrive in a Wal-Mart world, Wiley, 2004

Bianco Anthony, "Homespun Wisdom from the 'Oracle of Omaha'", July 5, 1999, BusinessWeek Online

Bloom Howard, The Lucifer Principle: A Scientific Expedition into the Forces of History, The Atlantic Monthly Press, New York, 1995

Blue Chip Stamps, 1982 Annual Report

Boodell Peter, Notes from Berkshire Hathaway annual meeting, 2008, 2010, 2012, 2013, 2014 and Wesco Financial annual meeting, 2008, 2009

Bowley Graham, "Closely Watched Buffett Recalculating his Bets," New York Times, Sept. 7, 2009

Brysons Bill, A Short History of Nearly Everything, Broadway Books, 2003

Buffettcup.com, "Buffett on Bridge", Warren Buffett Bridge Cup 2013

Buffett Warren E.
    Buffett Partnership Letter, 1962, 1964, 1965, 1967, 1969
    Warren Buffett's Letters to Berkshire Hathaway Shareholders, 1971–2014
    An Owner's Manual
    Berkshire Hathaway Code of Business Conduct and Ethics
    Letter to George D. Young, National Indemnity Company, July 22, 1975
    Letter on pensions to Katherine Graham, Washington Post, October 14, 1975
    1994 Lecture of The E. J. Faulkner Lecture Series, A Colloquium with University of Nebraska-Lincoln Students
    Memo to Berkshire Hathaway Managers, September 26, 2001, Jan. 6, 2005, September 27, 2006, December 19, 2014
    "Buy American. I Am.", New York Times Op-Ed, October 16, 2008
    "Pretty Good for Government Work", New York Times Op-Ed, November 16, 2010

Caltech, A Conversation with Charlie Munger at Caltech, DuBridge Distinguished Lecture, March 11, 2008, DVD

Calvey Mark, "Friendly investment advice from Warren Buffett's buddy", San Francisco Business Times, October 21, 1996

Cardinal De Retz, The Entire Memoirs Of Cardinal De Retz, Kessinger Publishing, 2010

Carnegie Andrew, The Autobiography of Andrew Carnegie, Penguin Publishing Group, London, 2006

Charlie Rose interview: "In his own words – Conversation with Charlie Rose", PBS, May 2, 2004; "An Exclusive Conversation with Warren Buffett", May 10, 2007; "I haven't seen as much economic fear in my adult lifetime", October 1, 2008

Churchill Winston, The Gathering Storm, Mariner Books, 1986

Cicero Marcus Tullius, On the Nature of the Gods, www.oll.libertyfund.org/titles/539

Claman Liz, interview with Warren Buffett, Charlie Munger and Bill Gates, May 5, 2014, Foxbusiness.com

Claremon Ben, Notes from Wesco Financial annual meeting, 2010, www.
   inoculatedinvestor,blogspot.com
Cleese John, "The real reason I had to join the Spectator", The Spectator, March 22, 2009
CNBC.com
   Transcript of Warren Buffett's 'Ask Warren' appearance on CNBC's Squawk Box, March 1,
   2010, March 4, 2013, March 2, 2015, buffettwatch.cnbc.com
   Charles Munger interview by CNBC, May 4, 2012, cnbc.com
   Buffett to CNBC: I'm 'Salivating' For 'Big Acquisition', October 24, 2012, CNBC.com
   Unofficial transcript of Warren Buffett, Charlie Munger and Bill Gates appearing live with
   Becky Quick on CNBC's "Squawk Box," Monday, May 5, 2014, buffettwatch.cnbc.com
CNN
   "Munger on Sokol: 'I'm sad'", CNNMoney Interview, May 3, 2011
   "What Buffett learned from Munger", CNN Money Video, November 7, 2013
Coastline Online, Charles Munger remarks before the UC Santa Barbara Foundation Board of
   Trustees, Coastlines Online Winter 2015
Cola-Cola Company, the Coca-Cola Company annual meeting, 2013, http://www.coca-
   colacompany.com/investors/annual-meeting-of-shareowners, http://mfile2.akamai.
   com/9538/wmv/estream.download.akamai.com/9538/cocacola/cocacola_160isl_2013_
   annual_meeting_of_shareowners.wvx?obj=20130424v1
Collins Jim, Good to Great: Why Some Companies Make the Leap...and Others Don't, Harper
   Business, New York, 2001
Cunningham Jeff, "When I Buy a Company, I'm a Journalist", taped interview with Arizona
   State University Professor Jeff Cunningham, creator and host of Iconic Voices, Walter Cronkite
   School of Journalism, March 5, 2015, http://iconicvoices.jmc.asu.edu/warren-buffett-on-
   journalism-to-jpmorgan/
Cunningham Lawrence A., Berkshire Beyond Buffett, Columbia University Press, 2014
Cunningham Lawrence A., Conversations from the Warren Buffett Symposium, Cardozo Law
   Review (1997), vol. 19. Edited by Lawrence A. Cunningham and reissued by Cunningham in
   2016.
Dardashti Shai, Notes from meeting with Warren Buffett May 23, 2005 – University of Maryland
   Student Trek to Omaha
Das Anupreeta, "Buffett's Crisis- Lending Haul Reaches $10 Billion", The Wall Street Journal, Oct.
   6, 2013
Davis L.J., "Buffett Takes Stock," The New York Times Magazine, April 1, 1990
Dennett Daniel C., Intuition Pumps and other Tools for Thinking, Allen Lane, The Penguin
   Group, London, 2014
Dijkstra Edsger W., On the nature of Computing Science, Transcript , www.cs.utexas.edu/users/
   EWD/transcriptions/EWD08xx/EWD896.html
Dornbusch Rudiger, "What should the federal government do to avoid a recession?", Hearing
   before the Joint Economic Committee, Congress of the United States, One Hundred Tenth
   Congress, second session, January 16, 2008, Volume 4
Dörner Astrid, "Warren Buffett's German To-Do List", Handelsblatt Global Edition no. 123,
   February 25, 2015
Drennan RE, The Algonquin Wits, 1968
Durell Philip & Miles Robert, Notes from 2009 Berkshire Hathaway Press Conference, May 3,
   2009, Notes by Philip Durell, The Motley Fool & added and edited by Robert Miles
Einstein Albert, Autobiographical Notes, Open Court; Centennial edition, 1999
Einstein Albert, The Expanded Quotable Einstein, edited by Alice Calaprice, Princeton University
   Press, 2005
Eisner Michael D. with Cohen Aaron, Working Together: Why Great Partnerships Succeed, New
   York, Harper Collins Publishers, 2010
Ellis Charley, "Living Legends", CFA Institute Magazine, January/February 2003, Vol. 14, Issue 1.
Fernbach, Rogers, Fox & Sloman, "Political Extremism is Supported by an Illusion of
   Understanding", Psychological Science OnlineFirst, April 25, 2013, pss.sagepub.com
Feynman R.P., Report of the PRESIDENTIAL COMMISSION on the Space Shuttle Challenger
   Accident, Volume 2: Appendix F - Personal Observations on Reliability of Shuttle http://
   history.nasa.gov/rogersrep/v2appf.htm
Finkle Todd A. & Buller Paul F., Gonzaga University, "Wisdom from Warren Buffett", Research
   in Higher Education Journal, 16, 2012, http://works.bepress.com/todd_finkle/20

Fiscal Fitness Forum, Notes from Fiscal Fitness Forum, Omaha, November 10, 1997
Fortune Magazine
  Carol J. Loomis, "Mr. Buffett on the Stock Market", Fortune Magazine, November 22, 1999
  Carol J. Loomis, "Warren Buffett on the Stock Market", Fortune Magazine, December 10, 2001
  Adam Lashinsky, "'Banking is a very good business unless you do dumb things,' says Wells
  Fargo's largest shareholder",
  Fortune Magazine, April 24, 2009
  "Warren Buffett is bullish...on women", Fortune Magazine, May 2, 2013
  Carol J. Loomis, transcript: Warren Buffett at Fortune MPW, October 17, 2013,
  http://fortune.com/2013/10/17/transcript-warren-buffett-at-fortune-mpw/
  Patricia Sellers, "Warren Buffett and Charlie Munger's best advice", Fortune.com, October 31,
  2013
  Patricia Sellers, "Warren Buffett and Charlie Munger's best advice", Fortune Magazine,
  November 18, 2013
Frisch Ragnar, Lecture to the memory of Alfred Nobel, June 17, 1970, www.nobelprize.org
Funk Josh, "Berkshire's No. 2 man helps from the background", Business Week, May 16, 2008
Gad Sham, Warren Buffett speech to University of Georgia, Terry College of Business students,
  January 30, 2007, www.gurufocus.com/news/4434
George Bill, Discover Your True North, John Wiley & Sons, New Jersey, 2015
Georgetown University, Warren Buffett Talks Philanthropy with Bank of America CEO,
  September 19, 2013, Georgetown University, www.georgetown.edu
Goldberg Steven, "The World According to 'Poor Charlie'", Kiplinger.com, December 2005
Goodwin Doris Kearns, Team of Rivals: The Political Genius of Abraham Lincoln, Simon &
  Schuster 2006
Graham Benjamin, The Intelligent Investor: A Book of Practical Counsel, Harper & Row
  Publishers, 1986
Graham Katherine, Personal History, New York, Vintage, 1998.
Greenberg Daniel S., "Don't ask the barber whether you need a haircut", Saturday Review
  Associates, November25, 1972
GuruFocus, Warren Buffett speech to University of Georgia students, Terry College of Business,
  2001, GuruFocus, http://www.nasdaq.com/article/warren-buffett-speech-to-university-of-
  georgia-students-part-1-cm238914
Hamming R.W., Methods of Mathematics Applied to Calculus, Probability, and Statistics,
  Prentice Hall, 1985
Hardin Garrett, Living Within Limits: Ecology, Economics, and Population Taboos, Oxford
  University Press Inc, New York, 1993
Hermes, The Superinvestors of Graham-and-Doddsville, Hermes, The Columbia Business School
  Magazine, 1984.
Hofstadter Douglas, Gödel, Escher, Bach: An Eternal Golden Braid, Basic Books, 1999
Hofstadter Douglas, I Am a Strange Loop, Basic Books, 2006
Hotchkiss Gilbert Josiah, Dictionary of Burning Words of Brilliant Writers, 1895
Iacocca Lee, Iacocca, Bantam Books, New York, 1984
Jennings, Eugene Emerson, Executive Success: Stresses, Problems, and Adjustment, Meredith
  Publishing Company, 1967
Jet Magazine, March 27, 1980, page 30
J.V. Bruni and Company, Notes from Berkshire Hathaway annual meeting, 2009, http://jvbruni.
  com/commentary.htm
Kahneman Daniel & Renshon Jonathan, Hawkish Biases, www.princeton.edu
Kass David, Warren Buffett meeting with University of Maryland MBA Students November 15,
  2013, www.blogs.rhsmith.umd.edu/davidkass
Kaufman Peter D., Poor Charlie's Almanack: The Wit and Wisdom of Charles T. Munger, PCA
  Publication, L.L.C. 2005, 2006, 2008
KCTS, Transcript from "Buffett & Gates on Success", KCTS/Seattle, May 1998
Kelley Margie, "In the Money: Alumni financiers take stock of the market and careers spent
  trying to beat it," Harvard Law Bulletin, Summer 2001
Kilpatrick Andy, Of Permanent Value: The Story of Warren Buffett, AKPE, 2004
Kipling Rudyard, The Gods of the Copybook Headings, 1919, www.kiplingsociety.co.uk/poems_
  copybook.htm
Kipling Rudyard, The Man Who Would be King and Other Stories, Dover Publications, 1994

Kissinger Henry A., White House Years, Little, Brown and Company, 1979

Koppel Ted, An interview with Warren Buffett on ABC's Nightline, March 2, 1999

Kotov, Alexander, Think Like a Grandmaster Paperback, B.T. Batsford, 1976

Le Dang, notes from Buffett meeting with students from Emory and 5 other business schools, February 6, 2009, www.undergroundvalue.blogspot.com

Le Dang, notes from Warren Buffett meeting with students from Emory's Goizueta Business School and Mc McCombs School of Business at UT Austin, February 15, 2008 www.undergroundvalue.blogspot.com

Lee Martin, Lecture at the University of Florida School of Business, October 15, 1998, www.intelligentinvestorclub.com/downloads/warren-buffett-mba-talk-at-university-of-florida-transcripts

Levo League, Office Hours with Warren Buffett, May 7, 2013, interview with Caroline Ghosn, Levo League, www.levo.com

Link-Wills Kimberley, "Money Can't Buy You Love", Speech at the College of Management Georgia Tech, Techtopics, Spring 2005

Livermore Livermore, How to Trade In Stocks , McGraw-Hill Education, 2006

Lowe Janet, Damn Right: Behind the Scenes with Berkshire Hathaway Billionaire Charlie Munger, John Wiley & Sons, New York, 2000

Lowenstein Roger, Buffett: The Making of an American Capitalist, New York: Random House, 1995, New York

Mahoney David and Restak Richard, The Longevity Strategy: How to Live to 100 using the Brain-Body Connection, John Wiley & Sons, Inc., New York, 1998

Marks Howard, Charles Munger remark to Howard Marks, "Dare to be Great II", Memo to Oaktree clients, April, 2014

Marks Howard, The Most Important Thing, Uncommon Sense for the Thoughtful Investor, Columbia Business School Publishing, 2011

Mc Donald Lawrence, Charles Munger advice to Lawrence McDonald, "How to Fix the Problem by the Smartest Guy I've Ever Met", www.lawrencegmcdonald

Mencken H. L., Minority Report: H. L. Mencken's Notebooks, Knopf, 1956

Michigan University, "A Conversation With Charlie Munger", Charlie Munger Speaks to University of Michigan Students, September 14, 2010, http://www.law.umich.edu/newsandinfo/amicus/archive/sept2010/1.html and http://rossmedia.bus.umich.edu/rossmedia/Viewer/?peid=4d215177cbe44b1e8e94d0dd68f5058f

Milligan Cynthia H., "Warren, A Conversation with Dean Cynthia H. Milligan", Nebraska Business, Fall 2001

Mitchell D.J., Russo J.E., Pennington N., Back to the Future: Temporal Perspective in the Explanation of Events, Journal of Behavioral Decision Making, Vol. 2, 1989 and Gary Klein, Performing a Project Premortem, Harvard Business Review, September 2007

Montaigne Michel de, The Complete Essays; translated by M.A. Screech, Penguin Books, Ltd, London, 1987, 1991, 2003

Mulaney Bianca, "Meeting Warren Buffett", Smart Woman Securities meeting in Omaha, harvardindependent.com, April 12, 2014

Munger Charles T.

  Harvard School Commencement Speech June 13, 1986

  Charles T. Munger testimony, In the Matter of Blue Chip Stamps, Berkshire Hathaway Inc., HQ-784, March 20, 1975

  Charles T. Munger testimony, In the Matter of Certain Treasury Notes and Other Government Securities, File No. HO-2513, February 6, 1992

  Bad Judgments, Common Causes, Charles Munger speech at the California Institute of Technology, February 17, 1992

  Wesco Financial Inc., Annual Report 1988, 1989, 1990, 1996

  The Psychology of Human Misjudgment, Talk at the Cambridge Center for Behavioral Studies, April 24, 1995

  Speech at breakfast meeting of the Philanthropy Round Table, November 10, 2000

Murphy Tom, interview with Harvard Business School, www.hbs.edu/entrepreneurs/pdf/tommurphy.pdf

Musarion oder die Philosophie der Grazien, 1768

Ogilvy David, Confessions of an Advertising Man, Southbank Publishing, 2012

Omaha World-Herald

Jim Rasmussen, "Buffett Talks Strategy with Students," Omaha World-Herald, January 2, 1994

Jim Rasmussen, "Buffett Partner's Impact 'Huge'", Sunday Omaha World-Herald, May 2, 1999

Steve Jordon, "The Oracle of Omaha: How Warren Buffett and his Hometown shaped each other", Omaha World-Herald Co. 2013

Steve Jordon, "Berkshire's Stock Portfolio passed $100 billion Milestone in 2013, and a long-term outlook paved the way", Omaha World-Herald, May 3, 2014

Steve Jordon, "Warren Watch: Buffett, 'Dilbert' creator Scott Adams differ on passion", Omaha World-Herald, December 29, 2014

Oquirrhinstitute, "An Evening with Warren Buffett", Warren Buffett Q&A with the Oquirrh Club, October 2003, http://www.oquirrhinstitute.org/about-buffett-transcripts.html, seen at http://www.rbcpa.com/WEB_omaha1992.

Outstanding Investor Digest 1986 – 2010, www.oid.com

Pais Abraham, The Genius of Science: A Portrait Gallery, Oxford University Press, 2000

Parrish Shane, Farnam Street Media

  Notes from Conversation with Charlie Munger, Pasadena Convention Center, July 1, 2011

  Notes from Daily Journal Corporation annual meeting, 2013, 2014, 2015

  Transcript from visit in India, NDTV Studios, April 2011

Patterson Scott, "In Year of Investing Dangerously, Buffett looked 'Into the Abyss'", The Wall Street Journal, December 14, 2009

PBSTV, "Warren Buffett Talks Business", Kenan-Flagler, PBSTV program produced by the University of North Carolina, Center for Public Television, Chapel Hill, October 1995 (VHS)

Peter J. Laurence Peter's Almanac, William Morrow & Co., 1982

PYMNTS.com, "Warren Buffett on What's Next in the Payment Industry", Interview by Business Wire CEO Cathy Baron Tamraz, October 17, 2009, Transcript, PYMNTS.com, http://www.pymnts.com/businesswire-feed/transcript-warren-buffett-on-what-s-next-in-the-payments-industry/

Rock Center, Keynote Breakfast Speech by Charles Munger at Stanford University's Director's College, June 26, 2006, Stanford Law School, Transcript, www.rockcenter.law.stanford.edu

Rockwood Richard, transcript from Warren Buffett speech at Caltech, October 21, 1997

Rowan Roy, The Intuitive Manager, Little, Brown and Company, 1986

Russell Bertrand, A New Social Analysis, 1938

Russell Bertrand, A New Social Analysis, Allen & Unwin,1938.

Russell Bertrand, Mortals and Others (1931-35)

Kai Ryssdal, "Warren Buffett on Jamie Dimon as Treasury Secretary, the fiscal cliff, and taxes", April 29, 2015, http://www.marketplace.org/topics/business/big-book/warren-buffett-jamie-dimon-treasury-secretary-fiscal-cliff-and-taxes

Santangels Review

  Charlie Munger at Harvard-Westlake School January 19, 2010, www.santangelsreview.com

  Financial Crisis Inquiry Commission Staff Audiotape of Interview with Warren Buffett, May 26, 2010, www.santangelsreview.com

Santayana George, The Life of Reason: The Phases of Human Progress, http://www.gutenberg.org/files/15000/15000-h/15000-h.htm

Schopenhauer Arthur, The essays of Arthur Schopenhauer, http://www.gutenberg.org/files/10741/10741-8.tx

Schopenhauer Arthur, Counsels And Maxims, Kessinger Publishing, 2010

Schroeder Alice, The Snowball: Warren Buffett and the Business of Life, Bloomsbury Publishing, London, 2008

Schumpeter Joseph A., Capitalism, Socialism and Democracy , (Chapter VII: The Process of Creative Destruction, 3rd Edition 1950, Harper Torchbooks, New York, 1962.

Schwager Jack D., The New Market Wizards: Conversations with America's Top Traders, HarperBusiness, 1994

Segal, Gillian Zoe, Getting There: A Book of Mentors, New York, Abrams Image, 2015

Shefrin Hersh, Beyond Greed and Fear: Understanding Behavioral Finance and the Psychology of Investing, Oxford University Press, 2002

Smith Adam, Warren Buffett on Adam Smith's Money Game, Transcript #105, Air Date: May 15, 1998

Soros George, Soros on Soros: Staying Ahead of the Curve, Wiley, New York

Sowell, Thomas, Knowledge and Decisions, Basic Books, 1996

Stanford Lawyer, "Q&A: Legal Matters with Charles T. Munger", Stanford Lawyer, Spring 2009, http://stanfordlawyer.law.stanford.edu/2009/11/qa-with-charles-t-munger/

Starobinski Jean, Montaigne in Motion, University of Chicago Press, 1985

Stein Gertrude, Reflection on the Atomic Bomb, 1946, [first published in Yale Poetry Review], December 1947

Stover Matthew, Shatterpoint (Star Wars: Clone Wars), LucasBooks, 2004

Strauss Gary, "Buffett's a Buddy to Targeted Firms", USA Today, August 9, 1989.

Sweet Daniel, notes of Warren Buffett's responses to questions from Notre Dame and Stanford MBA students, October

Taleb Nassim, Antifragile: Things That Gain from Disorder, Random House, 2012

Ben Graham Center for Value Investing, Notes from the Meeting Dr. George Athanassakos and Ivey MBA and HBA students had with Mr. Warren Buffett, Omaha March 31, 2008, March 30, 2012, January 31, 2014, February 27, 2015 Ben Graham Center for Value Investing, Ivey Business School, Western University, www.bengrahaminvesting.ca

The Motley Fool
Notes from Berkshire Hathaway, Press Conference 2000, 2001, 2002, 2006, 2007, 2010
Notes from Berkshire Hathaway annual meeting, 2002
Warren Buffett speaking to students from the Kansas University School of Business, May 6, 2005, Notes by Mark Hirschey, The Motley Fool, July 13, 2005

Tilson Whitney
Three Lectures by Warren Buffett to Notre Dame Faculty, MBA students and Undergraduate students, Spring 1991, Lightly edited by Whitney Tilson,www.tilsonfunds.com/ BuffettNotreDame/pdf
Notes from Warren Buffett meeting with MBA students from Wharton, October 10, 2003, www.tilsonfunds.com
Notes from Berkshire Hathaway annual meeting, 2000 - 2007, www.tilsonfunds.com
Warren Buffett responds to questions from Wharton students, November 12, 2004, www.tilsonfunds.com
Notes from Berkshire Hathaway, Press Conference, May 2005, valueinvestorinsight.com
Notes from Wesco Financial annual meeting, 2000 - 2007, www.tilsonfunds.com

Traganidis George, Notes from Berkshire Hathaway annual meeting, 2014, George Traganidis, www.thepracticalway.com

Train John, The Midas Touch, Harper & Row, New York, 1987

Students from Tuck School of Business at Dartmouth meet Warren Buffett, 2004, http://www.thinkfn.com/wikibolsa/Visita_a_Warren_Buffett

Turan Kenneth, "CROSSROADS: Looking at 1996 and beyond with influential figures in the worlds of art and entertainment", Los Angeles Times, December 31, 1996

University of Iowa, Lessons from Warren Buffett to a Group of MBA students, University of Iowa, www.biz.uiowa.edu/tippiemba/lessons-from-warren-buffett-to-a-group-of-mba-students/

Upbin Bruce, Bruce Upbin, Jay-Z, Buffett and Forbes on Success and Giving Back, Forbes, 23.9.2010, http://www.forbes.com/forbes/2010/1011/rich-list-10-omaha-warren-buffett-jay-z-steve-forbes-summit-interview.html

Wallas Graham, The art of thought, Harcourt, Brace and Company, New York, 1926

Value investing world, From Mohnish Pabrai's December 2014 talk to Sanjay Bakshi's MDI, class, www.valueinvestingworld.com

Vick Timothy, How to Pick Stocks like Warren Buffett, McGraw Hill, 2001

Viles Timothy & Byrd Aaron, Transcript from Warren Buffett meeting with Wharton students, February 17, 2006, seen in www.rbcpa.com

Wheeler J.A., "Mercer Street and Other Memories", in Albert Einstein, His Influence on Physics, Philosophy and Politics, ed. P.C. Aichelburg and R.U. Sexl , Braunscheig: Vieweg, 1979

Whitehead Alfred North, The Aims of Education and Other Essays, Free Press, 1967

Wiggin Addison & Incontrera Kate, I.O.U.S.A.: One Nation. Under Stress. In Debt., New Jersey, John Wiley & Sons, 2008

Wilson Edward O., Consilience: The Unity of Knowledge, Alfred A. Knopf, New York, 1998

Worsham Callie, "6 Richest alumni (and two dropouts) – Interview with Charles Munger", The Michigan Daily, February 21, 2007

Yahoo Finance, Aaron Task, "The 'Oracle of Omaha' is Bullish on Financial Education", April 8, 2013

Yutang Lin, The Importance Of Living, Patterson Press, 2008

Ziglar Zig, Secrets of Closing the Sale, 1984

Zweig Jason, "Charles Munger: Secrets of Buffett's Success?", The Wall Street Journal, Sept. 12, 2014

Zweig, Jason, "A Fireside Chat With Charlie Munger," The Wall Street Journal, Sept. 12, 2014